New Firm Creation in the United States

For other titles published in this series, go to
http://www.springer.com/series/6149

International Studies in Entrepreneurship

Series Editors

Zoltan J. Acs
George Mason University, Fairfax, VA, USA

David B. Audretsch
Indiana University, Bloomington, IN, USA

Paul D. Reynolds • Richard T. Curtin
Editors

New Firm Creation in the United States

Initial Explorations with the PSED II Data Set

Foreword by Robert Litan
Vice President for Research and Policy
The Kauffman Foundation

Editors
Paul D. Reynolds
George Mason University
Fairfax, VA
USA
pauldavidsonreynolds@gmail.com

Richard T. Curtin
University of Michigan
Ann Arbor, MI
USA
curtin@umich.edu

ISBN 978-0-387-09522-6   e-ISBN 978-0-387-09523-3
DOI 10.1007/978-0-387-09523-3
Springer Dordrecht Heidelberg London New York

Library of Congress Control Number: 2009928016

© Springer Science+Business Media, LLC 2009
All rights reserved. This work may not be translated or copied in whole or in part without the written permission of the publisher (Springer Science+Business Media, LLC, 233 Spring Street, New York, NY 10013, USA), except for brief excerpts in connection with reviews or scholarly analysis. Use in connection with any form of information storage and retrieval, electronic adaptation, computer software, or by similar or dissimilar methodology now known or hereafter developed is forbidden. The use in this publication of trade names, trademarks, service marks, and similar terms, even if they are not identified as such, is not to be taken as an expression of opinion as to whether or not they are subject to proprietary rights.

Printed on acid-free paper

Springer is part of Springer Science + Business Media (www.springer.com)

Foreword by Sponsor

Ewing Marion Kauffman considered entrepreneurship to be one of the most important features in the U.S. economy. A core mission of the foundation he established was the expansion of knowledge about the entrepreneurial process. In supporting this objective, the Ewing Marion Kauffman Foundation has been a major sponsor of the Panel Study of Entrepreneurial Dynamics (PSED) research program. This research project undertook the task of expanding our knowledge of the earliest stage of the entrepreneurial process. The focus is on understanding the circumstances that cause people to attempt to start a new business and which factors facilitate and which represent barriers to successfully implementing a new firm. The project is interdisciplinary in its coverage of potential factors so it can evaluate the independent contribution from a broad array of hypotheses developed from economics, sociology, psychology, management sciences, and the burgeoning field of entrepreneurial studies. Importantly, the research has been based on a representative sample of all U.S. households so that the results can be generalized to the nation as a whole. These features have made this research pathbreaking.

The PSED has focused on the germination of the initial idea for a new business and the steps taken to develop a new venture; it does not emphasize the early years in the life of a new operating business and its survival into adolescence. Although the discontinuation rates are highest in the gestation phase, a vibrant entrepreneurial sector is more likely to flourish if no needless barriers are erected to prevent a steady flow of new business ideas taking form as nascent enterprises. Indeed, the global competitive advantage of the United States depends on an unending source of new ventures of all kinds. Gaining a better understanding of the creation of new businesses is critical to insuring that entrepreneurial activity remains a powerful engine of economic growth and prosperity.

The PSED research program has been a successful example of entrepreneurship. The design and financial support for the initial PSED project was provided by a consortium of 34 research units involving over 120 scholars. Following the successful start of this project, the Kauffman Foundation provided funds for the continuation of the initial panel interviews as well as funding the second panel projects. Many of the initial members of the consortium remain as project advisors to the second project.

The importance of this research has been recognized in the research community. First, there has been widespread use of the data sets for scholarly analysis, with hundreds of students and established scholars using the data for dissertations, scholarly articles, books, conference presentations, and the like. The PSED data sets and research protocols have become part of the scholarly culture of the entrepreneurial research community. Second, the research protocols have been the basis for implementing longitudinal studies of business creation in other countries, including Australia, Canada, China, Latvia, Netherlands, Norway, and Sweden. While all of these projects have followed the same basic procedure, a number have harmonized major design features as well as interview schedules with the PSED projects.

The Kauffman Foundation supports a wide range of research and scholarly initiatives designed to advance the understanding of the entrepreneurial process. Few have been more successful and significant than the PSED research program. It is clear from the preliminary assessments represented in this volume that the PSED data will provide substantial opportunities for entrepreneurial scholars for many years.

Robert Litan
Vice President for Research and Policy
The Kauffman Foundation

Preface

This research program began in 1993. The idea of developing representative samples of those active in the business creation process, now called nascent entrepreneurs, developed from the success of using regional characteristics to predict variations in new firm birth rates in six countries.[1] The initial purpose was to determine those external factors that encouraged individuals to initiate the business creation process and become, as they are now called, nascent entrepreneurs. The research procedures, mainly the critical aspects of the screening procedures, were developed with the Survey Research Laboratory at the University of Wisconsin in Madison to complete the Wisconsin Entrepreneurial Climate Study.[2] Support for an initial test with a national sample was provided by the Institute for Social Research at the University of Michigan. Richard Curtin became involved with the incorporation of the screening module as part of the Survey of Consumers in October and November in 1993.[3]

The success of these efforts in providing a detailed description of the entrepreneurial process based on representative samples led to substantial interest among entrepreneurial scholars. A founding team of Nancy Carter, William Gartner, and Paul Reynolds was able to organize the Entrepreneurial Research Consortium (ERC), a collaborative network of 34 research units that shared the financial cost and sweat equity required to implement the first national project, PSED I. The effort was guided by an elected executive committee;[4] by 2002 there were 118 individuals involved,[5] and additional funding was provided by two NSF grants, one to expand the sample of women and the other to expand the sample of minorities.[6] Funding for the transfer of the data sets to the University of Michigan's Institute for Social Research and the third and fourth waves of the PSED I data collection, under the supervision of Richard Curtin, was provided by the Ewing Marion Kauffman Foundation.

A number of panel studies using the same protocol were implemented in other countries; the initial results suggested that harmonized screening procedures could provide useful national comparisons. This led to the adoption of the PSED screening procedures as the core component of the Global Entrepreneurship Monitor (GEM) research protocol, designed to provide cross-national comparisons of participation in business creation. During the first 6 years of the annual GEM national surveys, an enhanced version of the screening procedure that was more efficient and effective at locating nascent entrepreneurs was developed.[7] It was the basis for the PSED II screening procedure.

The second project, PSED II, was initiated in 2005 with substantial funding from the Ewing Marion Kauffman Foundation and supplemental support from the Office of Advocacy of the U.S. Small Business Administration. With Richard Curtin and Paul Reynolds serving as co-principal investigators, the design was developed with substantial input from a 16-person advisory committee, many with substantial experience with the PSED I data set.[8] Support for the fourth wave of data collection, the 36-month follow-up, was provided by the National Science Foundation.[9] A harmonized project has been implemented in Australia with Per Davidsson as the coordinating principal investigator; and a detailed comparison of the initial Australian and U.S. results is provided in Chapter 13.

There has been substantial use of the data from the PSED I project, including nine other books and monographs, 13 dissertations and theses, over 70 peer-review journal publications, eight book chapters and over five dozen conference proceedings. This does not include the hundreds of reports and multitude of scholarly writings based on the GEM data. An overview of the substantive findings, prepared in 2006 and based on panel studies in various countries, makes clear the value of the PSED paradigm for providing new and unique information about the entrepreneurial process.[10]

Because of the complexity and level of detail in the PSED II interview schedule, it takes some time after the interviews are completed before the fully documented, consolidated data set is ready for analysis. A preliminary assessment of the PSED II data was prepared as soon as the majority of the Wave B (first 12-month follow-up) data was available.[11] This review emphasized the most general features of the nascent entrepreneurs and the business creation process. This volume is designed to allow those familiar with the project and the interview schedules—the advisory committee—to pursue specific specialized topics with more depth. These analyses are preliminary in two senses. First, some may be modified as data from additional follow-ups, the third and fourth waves of data collection, become available. This is of particular relevance to any analysis related to the outcome of the start-up process, when nascent enterprises become new businesses or are deactivated. Second, the chapter teams may elect to refine and enhance their analyses for submission to peer-review academic journals. They have been encouraged to do so as long as they acknowledge initial publication in this volume.

Given that all data sets and documentation from the PSED I and II projects are available at no charge on a public website (www.psed.isr.umich.edu) it is hoped that these preliminary results will encourage others to pursue further analyses. There is much work to be done to fully understand the entrepreneurial process—a complex and important phenomenon.

Richard T. Curtin
Ann Arbor, Michigan

Paul D. Reynolds
Steamboat Springs, Colorado

Notes

1. Reynolds, P. D., Storey, D. J., & Westhead, P. (1994). Cross-national comparisons of the variation in new firm formation rates. *Regional Studies, 28*(4), 443–456.
2. Palit, C., & Reynolds, P. D. (1993). A network sampling procedure for estimating the prevalence of nascent entrepreneurs. In *Proceedings of the International Conference on Establishment Surveys* (pp. 667–661), Alexandria, Virginia: American Statistical Association. Reynolds, P. D., & White, S. (1993). *Wisconsin's entrepreneurial climate study*. Milwaukee, WI: Marquette University, Center for the Study of Entrepreneurship. Submitted to the Wisconsin Housing and Economic Development Authority, June.
3. Curtin, R. (1982). Indicators of consumer behavior: The University of Michigan surveys of consumers. *Public Opinion Quarterly, 46*, 340–362.
4. Candida Brush, Nancy M. Carter, William B. Gartner, Patricia Greene, Paul Reynolds, Kelly G. Shaver, and Mary Williams.
5. More details on the history of the project and a listing of the participating scholars are provided in Gartner, W. B., Shaver, K. G., Carter, N. M., & Reynolds, P. D. (Eds). (2004). *Handbook of entrepreneurial dynamics: The process of business creation* (pp. xiv–xx). Thousand Oaks, CA: Sage.
6. NSF Grant SBR-9809841 to Nancy Carter, Principal Investigator, for the oversample of women. NSF Grant SBR 9905255 to Patricia Green, Principal Investigator, for the oversample of minorities.
7. Reynolds, P., Bosma, N., Autio, E., Hunt, S., De Bono, N., Servais, I., Lopez-Garcia, P., and Chin, N. (2005). Global entrepreneurship monitor: data collection design and implementation: 1998-2003. *Small Business Economics, 24*, 205–231.
8. Howard Aldrich, Diane Burton, Nancy Carter, Per Davidsson, William Gartner, John Haltiwanger, Benson Honig, James Johnson, Philip Kim, Charles Matthews, Michael Meeks, Simon Parker, Martin Reuf, Claudia Bird Schoonhoven, Scott Shane, Kelly Shaver, and Per Stromberg.
9. NSF Grant SES 0818366 to Richard T. Curtin for Panel Study of Entrepreneurial Dynamics: 36 Month Follow-up.
10. Davidsson, P. (2006). Nascent entrepreneurship: Empirical studies and developments. *Foundations and Trends in Entrepreneurship, 2*(1).
11. Reynolds, P. D., & Curtin, R. T. (2008). Business creation in the United States: Panel Study of Entrepreneurial Dynamics II initial assessment. *Foundations and Trends in Entrepreneurship, 4*(3), 155–307.

Contents

1 Introduction 1
   Paul D. Reynolds and Richard T. Curtin

Part I Nascent Entrepreneurs

2 **Social Motives in the PSED II**............................. 19
   Amy E. Davis and Kelly G. Shaver

3 **Contextual Motivation and Growth Aspirations Among Nascent Entrepreneurs**... 35
   Diana M. Hechavarria, Mark T. Schenkel,
   and Charles H. Matthews

4 **Family Background and Influence on Nascent Entrepreneurs**...... 51
   Charles H. Matthews, Mark T. Schenkel,
   and Diana M. Hechavarria

Part II Start-Up Teams

5 **Owner Contributions and Equity** 71
   Amy E. Davis, Kyle C. Longest, Phillip H. Kim,
   and Howard E. Aldrich

6 **Business Owner Demography, Human Capital, and Social Networks** 95
   Martin Ruef, Bart Bonikowski, and Howard E. Aldrich

7 **Owner Founders, Nonowner Founders and Helpers** 115
   M. Diane Burton, Phillip C. Anderson,
   and Howard E. Aldrich

Part III The Start-Up Process

8 Institutional Isomorphism, Business Planning, and Business Plan Revision: The Differential Impact on Teams Versus Solo Entrepreneurs 137
Benson Honig, Jianwen (Jon) Liao, and William B. Gartner

9 The Role of Human and Social Capital and Technology in Nascent Ventures 157
Mark T. Schenkel, Diana M. Hechavarria, and Charles H. Matthews

10 Financing the Emerging Firm: Comparisons Between PSED I and PSED II 185
William B. Gartner, Casey J. Frid, John C. Alexander, and Nancy M. Carter

Part IV Emergence of a New Firm

11 Reconceiving the Gestation Window: The Consequences of Competing Definitions of Firm Conception and Birth. 219
Claudia B. Schoonhoven, M. Diane Burton, and Paul D. Reynolds

12 Start-Up Activities and New Firm Characteristics 239
Tatiana S. Manolova, Candida G. Brush, and Linda F. Edelman

Part V Cross-Study Comparisons

13 PSED II and the Comprehensive Australian Study of Entrepreneurial Emergence [CAUSEE] 263
Per Davidsson and Paul D. Reynolds

14 PSED II and the Kauffman Firm Survey 279
Alicia Robb and Paul D. Reynolds

15 Future Opportunities 303
Paul D. Reynolds and Richard T. Curtin

Appendix A: Panel Study of Entrepreneurial Dynamics II: Research Design. 307

About the Contributors 325

Index 335

List of Illustrations

Tables

Table 1.1	Overview of project design: PSED I and II	6
Table 1.2	Overview of PSED II: phone interview schedule modules	8
Table 2.1	PSED II items for three social motive variables	22
Table 2.2	PSED II items for career reasons	22
Table 2.3	PSED II principal component analysis three-factor solution for career reasons (weighted)	29
Table 2.4	PSED II scales by dataset (weighted, nascents only)	31
Table 3.1	Contextual motivation and growth aspiration items frequencies	40
Table 3.2	Frequencies for context-aspiration typology	41
Table 3.3	Outcome status by context-aspiration typology	46
Table 4.1	Wording for family background items	54
Table 4.2	Business creation type by start-up team ownership structure	55
Table 4.3	Descriptive statistics for family financial support variables (before being registered as a legal entity)	56
Table 4.4	Descriptive statistics for family history and legacy variables	58
Table 4.5	Means for family legacy variables by family background and gender	58
Table 4.6	Means for family legacy variables by family business work experience and gender	60
Table 4.7	Nascent entrepreneur worked in parents business and start-up team ownership	61
Table 5.1	Questionnaire items for assessing start-up team contributions and equity	76
Table 5.2	Median quotients of hours contributed to startup activities between team members in PSED II	79
Table 5.3	Constructed measures of start-up team contributions and equity: PSED I, II	80
Table 5.4	Team contribution variables only available in PSED II	82

Table 5.5	Weighted correlations between contributions provided and full-time devotion to startup	86
Table 5.6	Weighted percentages for contributions and full-time devotion to startup	87
Table 5.7	Weighted descriptive statistics for contributions and full-time devotion to start-up	87
Table 5.8	Weighted cross-tabulations between contributions and 12-month outcomes for PSED II	88
Table 5.9	Controls to consider for nonteam analysis	90
Table 6.1	Selected PSED II interview items for business owners, Sections G, H, and J (Wave A)	99
Table 6.2	Descriptive statistics for individual owners: Panel Study of Entrepreneurial Dynamics, I (1998–2000) and II (2005–2006)	101
Table 6.3	Descriptive statistics for teams of owners: Panel Study of Entrepreneurial Dynamics, I (1998–2000) and II (2005–2006)	103
Table 6.4	Changes in owner team statistics based on sample attrition: Panel Study of Entrepreneurial Dynamics II, Waves A (2005–2006) and B (2006–2007)	106
Table 6.5	Owners who joined or left teams between waves: Panel Study of Entrepreneurial Dynamics II (2005), Waves A and B	108
Table 6.6	Median time required to recruit all owners (from date of initial owner involvement): Panel Study of Entrepreneurial Dynamics II (2005–2006), Wave A	110
Table 7.1	PSED II questionnaire items for named individuals associated with the new venture	118
Table 7.2	Descriptive statistics for owners, key nonowners and helpers	120
Table 7.3	Gender and ethnic homophily when either key nonowners or helpers are included with owners	123
Table 7.4	Tabulation of key nonowners and helpers by gender and owner team type	124
Table 7.5	Comparing PSED I helpers with PSED II key non-owners and helpers	125
Table 7.6	Comparing alternative definitions of founding teams	127
Table 7.7	Nascent venture outcomes for 961 Wave B (12-month) respondents: logistic regression analysis reporting odds ratios and standard errors	130
Table 8.1	Descriptive statistics and correlation matrix	144
Table 8.2	*T*-tests: business planning and business plan modification	145

List of Illustrations xv

Table 8.3	Solo versus team startups: institutional forces and the likelihood of business planning	146
Table 8.4	Solo versus team startups: institutional forces and the formality of business planning	148
Table 8.5	Solo versus team startups: institutional forces and business plan modification	149
Table 9.1	Descriptive statistics for items reflecting human and social capital	170
Table 9.2	MANOVA results predicting outcome by human capital knowledge variables	175
Table 9.3	MANOVA results predicting outcome by knowledge social capital variables among owners	176
Table 9.4	MANOVA results predicting outcome by structural, relational, and cognitive social capital variables	177
Table 10.1	PSED I questions used for personal, unmonitored, and monitored sources	192
Table 10.2	PSED II questions used for personal, unmonitored, and monitored sources	193
Table 10.3	Use of personal and external funding by PSED I or PSED II (weighted)	196
Table 10.4	Independent samples t-tests for differences in mean dollar amount acquired between PSED I and PSED II (log-transformed, weighted)	198
Table 10.5	PSED I correlations of nascent firm/entrepreneur characteristics by expected funding source (as a proportion of total financing, weighted)	200
Table 10.6	PSED I correlations of nascent firm/entrepreneur characteristics by acquired funding source (as a proportion of total financing, weighted)	202
Table 10.7	PSED II correlations of nascent firm/entrepreneur characteristics by acquired funding source (as a proportion of total financing, weighted)	204
Table 10.8	PSED I finance items: first phone interview (Waves 1 and 2)	209
Table 10.9	PSED I investment items: first phone interview (Wave 1)	210
Table 10.10	PSED I investment items: first follow-up interview (Wave 2)	211
Table 10.11	PSED II Section E start-up finances: item overview	211
Table 10.12	PSED II Section Q start-up investments before legal registration: item overview	213
Table 10.13	PSED II Section R start-up investments after legal registration: item overview	214

Table 11.1	Start-up activities: item numbers, content, first wave prevalence	224
Table 11.2	Associations between alternative approaches to new firm birth	228
Table 11.3	Effect of alternative conceptions of firm birth on gestation duration	230
Table 12.1	Descriptive statistics: PSED I	249
Table 12.2	Descriptive statistics: PSED II	250
Table 12.3	Cox regression estimates on likelihood of nascent venture disbanding: joint effects of property categories	252
Table 12.4	Cox regression estimates on likelihood of nascent venture disbanding: effect of property completeness	254
Table 13.1	PSED II and CAUSEE: major operational features	266
Table 13.2	Entrepreneurial activity prevalence, GEM: U.S. and AU: 2000–2006	269
Table 13.3	Personal characteristics, background: U.S. vs. Australia	270
Table 13.4	Family background, motivation: U.S. vs. Australia	271
Table 13.5	Start-up teams: U.S. vs. Australia	272
Table 13.6	Nascent enterprises: U.S. vs. Australia	273
Table 13.7	Nascent enterprise sectors, customer orientations: U.S. vs. Australia	274
Table 14.1	PSED and KFS case comparisons	281
Table 14.2	Major features: PSED II and KFS	282
Table 14.3	Identification of firm registration events	285
Table 14.4	Prevalence of registration listings during start-up	288
Table 14.5	PSED II case allocations during 1st quarter, fourth year of start-up	289
Table 14.6	KFS case classifications	290
Table 14.7	Respondent characteristics by start-up stage: PSED II, KFS (1/2)	292
Table 14.8	Respondent characteristics by start-up stage: PSED II, KFS (2/2)	293
Table 14.9	Venture characteristics by start-up stage: PSED II, KFS [1/3]	294
Table 14.10	Venture characteristics by start-up stage: PSED II, KFS (2/3)	295
Table 14.11	Venture characteristics by start-up stage: PSED II, KFS (3/3)	296
Table 14.12	Venture industry sector: PSED II compared to KFS	297
Table 14.13	Venture industry sector by start-up stage: PSED II, KFS	297

List of Illustrations   xvii

Table 14.14	Cohort comparison overview: PSED II, KFS............	299
Table 15.1	Cumulative status of PSED II start-up efforts by survey wave: actual and projected............	304
Table A.1	Determination of eligibility in screening interview.......	309
Table A.2	Detailed interviews: success, effort, understanding, and interest.....................................	312
Table A.3	Average missing data rates for selected Wave A questions	315
Table A.4	Observed and imputed post-stratification variables for screening interview............................	320
Table A.5	Distributions for CPS, unweighted, and weighted screener survey....................................	321
Table A.6	Comparison of unweighted and weighted distributions for samples of respondents eligible for detailed interviews	323

Figures

Fig. 1.1	Business life course, context, and transitions..............	4
Fig. 3.1	Intrinsic motivation dimensions by context-aspiration typology........................	42
Fig. 3.2	Personal motivation dimensions by sex and contextual motivation	44
Fig. 3.3	Intrinsic motivation dimensions by race, context-aspiration typology........................	45
Fig. 4.1	Five-year projected sales growth: four categories	63
Fig. 4.2	Five-year projected job growth: four categories	64
Fig. 4.3	Total hours per month per team since conception: six categories	64
Fig. 4.4	Total funds per month per team since conception: six categories	65
Fig. 13.1	Nascent entrepreneur screening prevalence rates: United States, AU by gender........................	268
Fig. 14.1	PSED nascent enterprises transitions, time since conception..............................	287
Fig. 14.2	Number of timing of registration events during the start-up process	288
Fig. 14.3	PSED II: case allocation into start-up categories over time..................................	289

Chapter 1
Introduction

Paul D. Reynolds and Richard T. Curtin

The strength of the U.S. economy is rooted in a vast and changing sea of businesses. The United States has slightly more than 6 million businesses with employees and another 16 million who are self-employed (U.S. Small Business Administration, 2007, Table 1.2). They produce the vast majority of goods and services and provided almost 140 million jobs in 2006 (U.S. Census Bureau, 2008, Table 602). Rather than a stable pool of business firms, the most salient feature of the business population is the constant inflow of new firms. Each year over 600,000 new employer firms emerge and millions of individuals become self-employed for the first time. While this continuous renewal involves a substantial number of business deaths, the speed and scope of the renewal process itself appears to be associated with overall economic growth (Acs & Armington, 2004; Davis, Haltiwanger, & Jarmin, 2008).

The birth of new firms can be considered to be the major outcome of the entrepreneurial process. It is now widely recognized that new firms are a major source of job creation, offsetting those jobs lost from firm closures as well as contractions among existing firms. New firms are a major source of technical and market innovations, play a critical role in the emergence of new industries or market sectors, and contribute to improved labor productivity in existing sectors. Importantly, regions that have higher rates of churning, firm births as well as deaths, have higher rates of economic growth. Moreover, not only do new firms provide a range of economic benefits, entrepreneurship is considered an important career option by many. Over 12 million people in the United States are involved in business creation at any given time.

The importance of businesses to the U.S. economy has led to a range of efforts to develop a systematic understanding of business dynamics. The focus on the business life course includes topics ranging from firm creation to firm termination as well as changes in the structure of firms. A systematic assessment of those efforts found 26 data sets that could provide an understanding of U.S.

P.D. Reynolds (✉)
George Mason University, Fairfax, VA, USA
e-mail: pauldavidsonreynolds@gmail.com

business dynamics (Haltiwanger, Lynch, & Mackie, 2007, p. 68). Only one research program, however, could provide information on a representative sample of business firms in the early stages of the business creation process, beginning with the first efforts to implement a new firm. This was the Panel Study of Entrepreneurial Dynamics (PSED). This research program is a unique national resource not available, with a few exceptions, in other countries.

Two longitudinal panels of business creation make up the PSED research program. This book represents the first broad analysis of the data developed as part of the second project, PSED II. The following is an introduction to the conceptual structure underlying the research program and the PSED research paradigm. The analyses prepared by the research teams for the following chapters, however, are designed as stand-alone contributions to understanding business creation.

1.1 Entrepreneurship and New Firm Creation

Although new firm creation is closely associated with entrepreneurship, few concepts reflect more scope and ambiguity than "entrepreneurship." The origin of the French word "entrepreneur" was meant to describe an individual "who unites all means of production and who finds in the value of the products ... the reestablishment of the entire capital he employs, and the value of the wages, the interest, and rent which he pays, as well as profits belonging to himself" (Say, 1816). In other words, the entrepreneur establishes a business venture. Early English writers did not know whether to use the term "undertaker" or "adventurer" to translate the word entrepreneur. The entrepreneurial concept reflects the idea of opportunity recognition and success as a coordinator and administrator but does not necessarily imply creating something new or innovative. It does imply that the entrepreneur bears some risk or uncertainty (Cantillon, 1730; Knight, 1921).

This ambiguity has led some scholars to emphasize specific aspects of the entrepreneurial process as the most beneficial. For example, the idea that entrepreneurship was a positive contribution to economic adaptation and change was conveyed by the idea of "creative destruction" (Schumpeter, 1934). It was suggested that the creation of new productive activities lead to the beneficial replacement of existing firms, displacing them by firms that provided new goods and services or using new procedures to provide established commodities more efficiently. Some now consider "innovative entrepreneurship" as the only form worthy of serious attention (Baumol, Litan, & Schramm, 2007); others have suggested that only those few new firms receiving venture capital support, about 200 each year, make significant contributions (Shane, 2008, p. 162). The challenge of identifying the level of the required "innovation" or the required impact on markets, however, has not been resolved conceptually or operationally.

Others have focused on "opportunity recognition," or how markets are identified for goods and services (Kirzner, 1979; Penrose, 1959). Some have even suggested that opportunity recognition should be the central feature of entrepreneurial research (Shane & Venkataranam, 2001). Opportunities, however, are difficult to define in the absence of an organized effort to take advantage of them. After the fact, it is possible to define a new venture that grows quickly as having exploited a "major opportunity," leading to a tendency to reserve the label "entrepreneurial" for only those new businesses that rapidly expand. Nevertheless, a focus on recognizing and exploiting opportunities allows the concept of entrepreneurship to be applied to any active participant in any market (Pozen, 2008), such as managers in existing firms, now referred to as "intrapreneurs," or even administrators or officials in government organizations or not-for-profit ones, often referred to as "social entrepreneurs."

Not only have entrepreneurs played a special role in the creation of new firms, but many scholars have also viewed them as having special personality characteristics. Since entrepreneurs may seem very focused and driven, compared to normal wage and salary employees, the idea that entrepreneurs would have unique dispositions or personalities has received substantial attention (Kets de Vries, 1985). Perhaps most widely known have been the propositions that they have a need for achievement (McClelland, 1961) or a preference for risk (Knight, 1921). Despite the substantial research effort to characterize an "entrepreneurial personality" few stable empirical relationships have been established (Gartner, 1988). The situational demands of creating new organizations may cause individuals to be focused and driven, perhaps even compulsive for a time, but not all focused and driven individuals will create new businesses. Finally, entrepreneurship is viewed by scholars as a social phenomenon since engaging in the creation of a new firm is generally done in a network of social relationships (Aldrich, 2005; Reynolds, 1991; Thornton, 1999). In this sense entrepreneurship is much more than an individual career choice.

Associated with each of these conceptions of entrepreneurship is the idea that some type of new business venture is created, whether it involves part-time self-employment or a substantial organization involving hundreds. The focus of this research program on the creation of new ventures avoids endless discussions of what entrepreneurship "really" is and focuses on how individuals attempt to translate an idea for a new firm into an ongoing business.

1.2 PSED Conceptual Model

The major objectives of this research program are to (1) provide a comprehensive, objective description of the business creation process and (2) assemble data that can facilitate theory development and hypothesis testing regarding the major processes affecting new firm creation. Central to this research design are the actions of the individual entrepreneur. It is the entrepreneur who organizes and mediates the impacts of many factors that affect the emergence of a new firm. The creation of new firms is not the direct result of macro-economic conditions, the availability of government programs, the entrepreneurial climate, the presence of friendly financial institutions, supportive family and friends, or speeches by politicians. While the impacts of all these contextual factors are important, they are assumed to be mediated by the direct actions taken by individuals.

People create new firms. The PSED research program is a study of who they are and what they do to implement a new business.

The research requires precise operational definitions of the major features of this phenomenon, including measures that capture the critical transition points. This conceptualization reflects a general view of the firm creation process, shown in Fig. 1.1. This approach assumes that individuals pass through the first transition when they first take some action to create a new firm. These actions may have been taken on their own behalf or as part of their job at an existing firm. Thus, nascent entrepreneurs are drawn from the adult population as independent nascent entrepreneurs and from existing businesses as "nascent intrapreneurs."

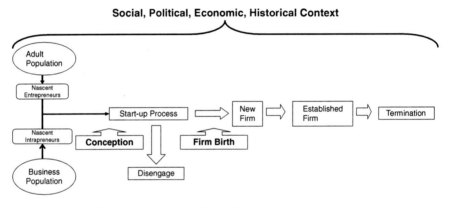

Fig. 1.1 Business life course, context, and transitions

There are two potential outcomes of the start-up process: new firm creation or disengagement. A new firm is defined as a profitable business venture affecting the prices and quantities of goods traded in the market. Following a firm's birth, these entities pass through a period of being a young firm, becoming an established firm, and, as their economic usefulness declines, terminating operations. The identification of the conditions that ensure the survival of profitable firms is outside the scope of the PSED research design.

The alternative transition for nascent entrepreneurs is disengagement from the start-up process. Disengagement is relatively straightforward, as it is represented by individuals who have elected not to continue working on the creation of this new firm. Determining what facilitates and prevents the successful establishment of new firms is a central focus of the PSED research design.

Given that the final transitions often take longer than a few years, the 12 months covered by the first two PSED II interviews mean that only a small proportion of nascent enterprises would have reached a resolution, with most remaining in the start-up process. As the time period covered by the PSED increases, the data will provide a more complete view of the ultimate resolution. Nonetheless, even after 4 or 5 years the number still in the start-up process may not be reduced to zero in the short time covered by the follow-ups.

The entire firm creation process is considered to occur in a distinctive social, political, economic, and historical context.

A new firm, in the PSED paradigm, is one that has begun to report initial profits, operationally defined as positive monthly cash flow for 6 of the past 12 months in PSED II.[1] Rather than profitability, much analysis in economics and elsewhere focuses on market participation. Markets are exchanges between buyers and sellers and a new participant, either as a buyer or as a seller, is of considerable interest. A new participant may affect the quantity or price of transactions. Whether or not the new participant is financially solvent is irrelevant. This leads to defining a new business as any activity that is a participant in a market, whether or not it is profitable. A number of well-known businesses were active for long periods of time before they became profitable, such as the Internet retail firm, Amazon.com, or the newspaper, *USA Today*. Nascent enterprises that are active participants in markets as buyers of goods and services can be identified in the data set, but the conceptual and operational criteria for a new firm birth is related to initial profitability.

1.3 PSED Research Protocol

The U.S. PSED research program consists of two longitudinal projects. PSED I was based on a representative sample of nascent entrepreneurs identified in 1998–2000 and contacted again three times over the following 4 years. PSED II is based on a representative sample of nascent entrepreneurs identified in late 2005 and early 2006 with follow-ups at 12, 24, and 36 months.[2] Although there is a 6-year lag between the screenings to select the nascent entrepreneur cohorts in these two projects, the research procedures, summarized in Table 1.1, are very similar.

The research protocol consisted of three phases. The first was the identification of a representative sample of those actively involved in the new firm creation process, the nascent entrepreneurs. The second phase was the initial detailed interview with the nascent entrepreneurs. The final stage consisted of the annual follow-up interviews. As can be seen in Table 1.1, the outcome resolution data are available for 695 of 830, or 83.7%, of the PSED I nascent cohort and 1,058 of 1,214, or 87.1%, of the PSED II nascent cohort. Details of the operational results of the PSED II research are provided in appendix A.

To identify potential nascent entrepreneurs, a screening module was added to nationally representative omnibus telephone surveys. All respondents were

Table 1.1 Overview of project design: PSED I and II

	PSED I	PSED II
Dates of initial screening, detailed interview 1	July 1998–Jan 2000	Oct 2005–Jan 2006
Time lag to interview 2	14 Months	12 months
Time lag to interview 3	27 Months	24 months
Time lag to interview 4	40 Months	36 months
Size of screening sample: nascent entrepreneurs only	62,612	31,845
Interview 1 sample	830	1,214
Interview 2 sample	501	972
Interview 3 sample	511	746
Interview 4 sample	533	526
Outcome resolution information	695	1,058
Screening interview length	2 minutes	2 minutes
Detailed interview 1, phone	60 minutes	60 minutes
Detailed interview 1, mail	12 pages	None
Detailed interview 2, phone	60 minutes	26 minutes
Detailed interview 2, mail	8 pages	None
Detailed interview 3, phone	60 minutes	25 minutes
Detailed interview 3, mail	8 pages	None
Detailed interview 4, phone	60 minutes	25 minutes
Detailed interview 4, mail	8 pages	None
Phone interview payments	$25	$25
Mail questionnaire payments	*$25*	*Not applicable*

asked a series of questions about their current activities. Two were used in the PSED I screenings:

1. Are you, alone or with others, currently trying to start a new business, including any form of self-employment?
2. Are you, alone or with others, now trying to start a new business for your employer? An effort that is part of your job assignment?

Three were employed in the PSED II screenings:

1. Are you, alone or with others, currently trying to start a new business, including any self-employment or selling any goods or services to others?
2. Are you, alone or with others, currently trying to start a new business or new venture for your employer, an effort that is part of your normal work?
3. Are you, alone or with others, currently the owner of a business you help manage, including self-employment or selling any goods or services to others?

The first two items were similar for both projects. The major difference is the addition of the third item in the PSED II screening. Experience with the Global Entrepreneurship Monitor (GEM) data collection indicated that a number of individuals who considered themselves to be running a business but had not yet achieved a positive monthly cash flow should be considered nascent

1 Introduction

entrepreneurs (Reynolds et al., 2005). Those answering yes to one or more of the screening items indicated that they considered themselves involved in the firm creation process.

Once potential nascent entrepreneurs were identified they were asked additional questions to determine if they met three criteria: (1) they performed some start-up activity in the past 12 months, (2) they expected to own all or part of the new firm, and (3) the initiative had not progressed to the point where it would be considered an operating business. Details about the responses to these items and the attrition between the screening and completion of detailed interviews are provided in appendix A.

About 87% of those identified in the screening as active nascent entrepreneurs agreed to participate in the study.[3] For both projects the initial screening was completed by a commercial survey firm (Market Facts for PSED I; Opinion Research Corporation for PSED II), and the detailed data were collected by survey operations located in academic institutions (the University of Wisconsin Survey Research Laboratory for the initial and first follow-ups for PSED I; the University of Michigan Institute for Social Research for the second and third follow-ups for PSED I and all detailed interviews for PSED II).

The modules provided to the respondents in the PSED II project are summarized in Table 1.2.[4] The first column represents the material in the brief screening procedure. The second column contains the materials for the first detailed interview (Wave A) and the last two columns the follow-up interviews. The second and subsequent follow-up interviews (Wave C and beyond) are adjusted slightly to provide for additional information about a nascent enterprise that has become a new firm.

The questionnaire used in the screening phase provides a small amount of socio-demographic data on all individuals involved in the national population; this is useful for assessing some factors affecting the decision to enter the start-up process.

The first detailed interview, presented in the Wave A column in Table 1.2, includes information on the nature of the business, start-up activities implemented on behalf of the new firm, incorporation into business registries, the nature of the start-up team and helping networks, sources and amounts of financial support, evaluations of the immediate context, competitive strategy and growth expectations, along with details of the motivations, perspectives, self-descriptions, background, and family context of the responding nascent entrepreneur.

The third phase involved the follow-up phone interviews. For PSED II careful scheduling has allowed the initial contact for the first follow-up to occur 52 weeks following completion of the initial detailed interview, the second follow-up 104 weeks, and so forth. The topics of the interview are listed in the Wave B column in Table 1.2 and vary depending on the status of the initiative at the time of the follow-up. Those nascent entrepreneurs who reported that they have disengaged from the initiative were asked additional questions about the reasons for their decision to quit. Those who had started a new firm or were still

Table 1.2 Overview of PSED II: phone interview schedule modules

Topic modules	Screening	Wave A	Wave B[1,2]	Wave C[1,2]
Screening questions	All			
Assessment of criteria for nascent entrepreneur	All			
Socio-demographic	All			
A.1: Why involved, business opportunity (open ended)		All		
A.2: Confirm same business activity			All	All
A.3: Determine status: new firm, quit, continue			All	All
B: Type of business, location		All	NF, SU	NF, SU
C: Legal form		All	All	All
D: Start-up activities		All	All	All
E.1: Start-up finances, entry into firm registries[3]		All	All	All
E.2: Confirm quit, exit interview			Quits	Quits
F: Orientations toward competition		All	NF	NF
G: Owners, key non-owners, & helpers inventory		All	NF, SU	NF, SU
H: Owner demographics		All	NF, SU	NF, SU
J: Relationships among owners		All	NF, SU	NF, SU
K: Juristic (legal entity) owners		All	NF, SU	NF, SU
M: Key non-owner demographics		All	NF, SU	NF, SU
N: Helper demographics		All	NF, SU	NF, SU
P: Community resources, support for new firms		All	NF	NF
Q: Informal start-up financial support		All	NF, SU	NF, SU
R: Legal entity start-up investments, debts, net worth		All	NF, SU	NF, SU
S: Competitive strategy and target markets		All	NF	NF
T: Growth expectations		All	NF	NF
U.1: Respondent's motivation		All		
U.2: Employment structure[3]			NF	NF
V.1: Expense structure: summary[3]			NF	
V.2: Expense structure: detailed[3]				NF
X: Respondent's career background		All	SU	SU
Y: Respondent's self-descriptions		All		
Z: Respondent & household socio-demographics		All	NF, SU	NF, SU

[1] After wave A, modules are provided to All respondents, only those that Quit, or those with a new firm (NF), or still active in the start-up process (SU).
[2] After initial interview, modules are repeated to capture changes or new information about the activity or details on the current status.
[3] Based on Kauffman Firm Survey interview schedule (Mathematica Policy Research, 2007).

in the start-up phase were provided the opportunity to update their case files with reports of new activity or changes in the start-up team or financial structure. Most of the modules relating to enduring features of the responding nascent entrepreneur (self-descriptions, family background, etc.) covered in the first interview were not repeated.

After the first follow-up those who reported that they were managing a new firm for a full year were provided with some additional modules in Wave C. These covered the nature of the cost structure that could be used to estimate labor productivity. These modules, as well as those relating to the organizational structure of the firm, were designed to facilitate comparison with similar modules in the Kauffman-sponsored panel study of new businesses (Haltiwanger et al., 2007, pp. 138–139; Mathematica Policy Research, 2007).

The initial screening was completed with 31 sample replications, each with about 1,000 respondents. The initial case weights to adjust the sample to match the most recent Current Population Surveys demographics were computed for each replication. These case weights were recomputed using the entire screening sample with the Current Population Survey demographics for March 2005. This dramatically reduced the range of case weights and, in turn, reduced the variation among variables associated with the weighting procedure. The details of this adjustment are provided in appendix A.

While the respondents devoted a substantial amount of time to completing the interviews, very few, 1% in PSED I and 2% in PSED II, reported less interest in the start-up by virtue of participation. Most—61% in both cohorts—reported that their interest in the start-up increased upon completion of the initial interview; the remainder, 37–38%, indicated no change in their commitment to the start-up initiative.[5] This strong interest is one reason for the high cooperation reflected in item response rates and completion of the follow-up interviews, as described in appendix A.

The PSED sample was designed to provide a representative sample of individuals involved in business creation. With one caveat, it may be considered a representative sample of nascent enterprises or firms-in-gestation. Any nascent enterprise implemented by more than one nascent entrepreneur is more likely to be included in the cohort. As a result, if the sample is considered to represent nascent enterprises, it should be recognized as including an over-representation of team efforts (Davidsson, 2004). While recognizing this issue, it is assumed that the practical effect is negligible for most analyses. No adjustment for a potential over-sample of team initiatives has been implemented.

1.3.1 Worldwide Replication

The PSED I research design has been the model for similar projects completed or underway in Argentina, Canada, Greece, The Netherlands, Norway, Sweden, and the United Kingdom.[6] The PSED I screening procedure was the basis for the procedures adopted for the cross-national assessment of entrepreneurial activity in the Global Entrepreneurship Monitor (GEM) research program (Reynolds et al., 2005; Reynolds, Bygrave, Autio, Cox, & Hay, 2004).[7] It has been implemented in over 50 countries using a wide range of languages. Experience with the GEM program led to an improved screening procedure in the

PSED II project, which resulted in a higher proportion of respondents who were found to qualify as nascent entrepreneurs. Comparisons of the prevalence rates completed 6 years apart, 1999 and 2005, required adjustments to compensate for differences in the procedures (Reynolds, forthcoming); once such adjustments were implemented, there was little difference in the nascent entrepreneur prevalence rates in the two periods (Reynolds & Curtin, 2008).

One major component of the Comprehensive Australian Study of Entrepreneurial Emergence (CAUSEE) was the location and tracking of Australian nascent entrepreneurs. As much as possible, the procedures and interview schedules were designed to emulate the PSED II procedures; the Queensland University of Technology is the host research institution (www.causee.qut.edu.au). The Latvian Panel Study of Entrepreneurial Dynamics (L-PSED) has been implemented, using as much of the U.S. PSED II interview schedule as possible; this project is being conducted through the Baltic International Centre for Economic Policy Studies in Riga, Latvia (www.biceps.org/en/projects). A panel study for the People's Republic of China was funded in 2008; the Chinese University of Hong Kong and Nankai University will be implementing the project, based on the PSED procedures, in 2009.

1.3.2 Overview of the Contents

This volume is designed to take advantage of the diverse expertise represented by the PSED II advisory committee. Many of these scholars have been involved in the PSED I project and have considerable knowledge about many aspects of the entrepreneurial process and this research program. They have taken the lead, incorporating colleagues and research assistants into chapter teams, in providing the first analyses of the PSED II data. These teams have exercised great latitude in the selection of topics, specific issues to pursue, and implementation of analyses techniques. These assessments have been organized into five groups. The first four relates to the business creation process; the last relates to cross-project comparisons.

The distinctive characteristics of *nascent entrepreneurs* are the focus of the first set of chapters. A substantial amount of effort has focused on the unique personal features or personalities of entrepreneurs. A number of individual differences measures were included in both the PSED I and II interview schedules. Chapter 2 by Davis and Shaver compares the items included to measure entrepreneurial intensity, social skills, expectancy, and career reasons in the two projects. International analysis of the entrepreneurial process has indicated major differences associated with the contextual motivation for pursuing business creation; while most U.S. nascents are responding to opportunities, a substantial minority are responding to the necessity to pursue some labor force activity. These differences in contextual motivation are combined with the anticipated firm growth to create a "context-aspiration" typology for the

PSED II cohort in Chapter 3, by Hechavarria, Schenkel, and Matthews. They find systematic impacts on both intrinsic motivations—the desire for status, wealth, respect, or autonomy—as well as the outcome of the ventures as reported in the first follow-up. Variation in the level of family support and involvement within the PSED II cohort is the focus of Chapter 4, by Matthews, Schenkel, and Hechavarria. A large proportion of new ventures are implemented by individuals related by marriage or kinship, and families are found to consistently provide support for nascent entrepreneurs.

About half of all start-ups are launched by teams and most initiatives involve help from those in the entrepreneur's social networks. Three chapters in the second section focus on different aspects of the *start-up teams*. Chapter 5, by Davis, Longest, Kim, and Aldrich, focuses on the financial and other contributions provided to the start-up effort by the various team members; patterns found in PSED II are compared with those present in PSED I. Chapter 6, by Ruef, Bonikowski, and Aldrich, focuses on the ownership teams, social networks, and the human capital contributions to the nascent enterprises. About half of the nascent entrepreneurs report that they have received substantial support from their social networks, those persons who have provided active assistance to the nascent enterprise. Chapter 7, by Burton, Anderson, and Aldrich, focuses on the nature and extent of assistance provided by the non-owning founders, and how this is related to the outcome reported in the first follow-up interview. A number of new ventures are started by teams that include non-owning founders, individuals who accept responsibility for a critical feature of firm creation, but who do not expect to own part of the new firm.

The third section reflects a focus on what happens during the *start-up process*. The analysis in Chapter 8, by Honig, Liao, and Gartner, explores the differences in approaches taken by solo nascent entrepreneurs compared with teams of nascent entrepreneurs. They consider the factors that may be associated with a more serious approach to business planning. The role of human and social capital among all nascent enterprises as well as those with a technological focus is treated in Chapter 9, by Schenkel, Hechavarria, and Matthews. Following an extensive review of the suitability of the PSED II indicators for measuring different aspects of capital, they explore the impact on the outcomes reported in the first follow-up interview and identify those that have a statistically significant influence. Few topics receive as much attention as financial support for new firms; Chapter 10, by Gartner, Frid, Alexander, and Carter, provides a detailed analysis of the expected financial support reported in PSED I as well as the actual financial support reported in PSED I and II. The assessment makes use of a new conceptual distinction, monitored versus unmonitored financial support, to complement the traditional distinction between debt and equity. The analysis emphasizes those factors associated with variations in the structure of financial support as well as the impact on the outcome reported in the first follow-up interview.

Given the widespread attention to business creation, one might expect more consensus on the definition of a new business. Such is not the case and the fourth section explores alternative perspectives on the *emergence of new firms*. Chapter 11, by Schoonhoven, Burton, and Reynolds, focuses on the impact of alternative definitions on selected characteristics of the start-up process. A quite different perspective regarding the definition of a "firm birth" is taken from those concerned with markets, implementation of task-oriented social systems, changes in labor market behavior, and the creation of a profitable business venture. Operational definitions associated with these three conceptual orientations are associated with different descriptions of the start-up process. The critical features of an operating business are the focus of Chapter 12, by Manolova, Brush, and Edelman. They develop indices from the PSED data sets to represent four facets of a business organization and consider the extent to which the nascent enterprises have developed these features.

Cross-study comparisons are represented by two chapters in the fifth section. Chapter 13, by Davidsson and Reynolds, provides an initial comparison of the nascent cohorts from PSED II and the Comprehensive Australian Study of Entrepreneurial Emergence (CAUSEE). Many of the procedures, particularly the screening interview, for CAUSEE were designed to match the PSED II procedures as closely as possible. This comparison focuses on the data from the first detailed nascent entrepreneur interview. While the two cohorts are similar in many aspects, there is some indication that either the Australian nascents are better prepared and more committed to their nascent enterprises or that the procedures used in the United States are capturing a larger proportion of nascents who are in the earlier stages of the business creation process.

The Kauffman Firm Survey (KFS) was implemented in 2004, with support from the Ewing Marion Kauffman Foundation, with the selection of 4,928 new listings in the Dun & Bradstreet Dun's Market Identifier files, with annual follow-ups to track their survival and growth trajectories. As this project was designed to track firms following the birth event, it provides information on a major stage of the firm's life course. While some interview schedule modules were harmonized for the two projects, they utilized different sampling strategies. Chapter 14, by Robb and Reynolds, compares the two projects with a focus on two issues. Recognizing that the PSED cases represent earlier stages of the business creation process, an effort was made to determine which PSED cases would meet the criteria for inclusion in the KFS cohort. The second emphasis is a comparison of the nature of the individuals and enterprises in the two projects, focusing on those cases that would be incorporated in both data sets. As might be expected, there are many similarities but also a number of differences.

1.4 Final Comment

There is great diversity among these analyses, as each chapter team pursued those topics and issues they considered most important—or interesting. A variety of analytical techniques have been employed and there is some variation in the cases selected from the PSED II cohort as most appropriate for the analysis. The primary rationale for the development of the PSED I and PSED II data sets was to facilitate the broadest possible range of analyses. The following chapters suggest that the objective was achieved. Yet, there are a wide range of topics and issues that have not been pursued; some are discussed in the final chapter.

Notes

1. For three or more months in PSED I.
2. The 24-month follow-up data for the PSED II cohort was available in late fall 2008; the 36-month follow-ups were initiated in the fall of 2008 and the data should be available in the fall of 2009.
3. It should be noted that the low yield of nascent entrepreneurs in PSED I—830 following screening of over 60,000 individuals—reflected a procedure designed to increase the number of women and minorities in the nascent entrepreneur cohort. A large number of white male active nascent entrepreneurs were identified in the screening but not included in the cohort in order to focus available resources on women and minorities. If resources had allowed the inclusion of all active nascent entrepreneurs identified in the PSED I screening, this cohort would have been three times larger.
4. Many of these modules are based on the same modules used in the PSED I interview schedules. Detailed discussions of the rationale and background are found in Gartner, Shaver, Carter, and Reynolds (2004).
5. These estimates are based on the weighted sample.
6. Reports on other countries include Argentina (De Rearte, Lanari, & Atucha, 1998), Canada (Diochon, Menzies, & Gasse, 2005, 2007), the Netherlands (Van Gelderen, 2000), Norway (Alsos & Kolvereid, 1998), and Sweden (Delmar & Davidsson, 2000).
7. Considerable detail about the procedures is available (Reynolds et al., 2005) as well as multiple examples of the resulting cross-national comparisons (Reynolds et al., 2004).

References

Acs, Z. J., & Armington, C. (2004). Employment growth and entrepreneurial activity in cities. *Regional Studies, 38*(9), 911–927.

Aldrich, H. E. (2005). Entrepreneurship. In N. J. Smelser & R. Swedberg (Eds.), *Handbook of economic sociology* (pp. 451–477). Princeton, NJ: Princeton University Press.

Alsos, G. A., & Kolvereid, L. (1998). The business gestation process of novice, serial and parallel business founders. *Entrepreneurship Theory and Practice, 22*(4),101–114.

Baumol, W. J. (2005). Small firms: Why market-driven innovation can't get along without them. In U.S. Small Business Administration, *The small business economy: A report to the president* (pp. 183–206). Washington, DC: U.S. Government Printing Office.

Baumol, W. J., Litan, R. E., & Schramm, C. J. (2007). *Good capitalism, bad capitalism, and the economics of growth and prosperity*. New Haven: Yale University Press.

Cantillon, R. (1730). *Essai sur la nature du commerce in general [Essay on the nature of trade in general]*. Henry Higgs (translator and editor). London: Frank Cass and Company, Ltd.

Davidsson, P. (2004). *Researching entrepreneurship*. New York: Springer.

Davidsson, P. (2006). Nascent entrepreneurship: Empirical studies and developments. *Foundations and Trends in Entrepreneurship, 2*(1), 1–76.

Davis, S. J., Haltiwanger, J., & Jarmin, R. (2008). *Turmoil and growth: Young businesses, economic churning, and productivity gains.* Kansas City, MO: Ewing Marion Kauffman Foundation.

Delmar, F., & Davidsson, P. (2000). Where do they come from? Prevalence and characteristics of nascent entrepreneurs. *Entrepreneurship & Regional Development, 12,* 1–23.

De Rearte, A. G., Lanari, E., & Atucha, P. A. A. J. (1998). *El proceso de creaction de empresas: Abordaje methodologico y primeros resultados de unstudio regional.* Argentina: Universidad Nactional de Mar del Plata.

Diochon, M., Menzies, T. V., & Gasse, Y. (2005). Exploring the relationship between start-up activities and new venture emergence: A longitudinal study of Canadian nascent entrepreneurs. *International Journal of Management and Enterprise Development, 2*(3), 408–426.

Diochon, M., Menzies, T. V., & Gasse, Y. (2007). From becoming to being: Measuring firm creation. *Journal of Enterprising Culture, 15*(1), 21–42.

Gartner, W. B. (1988). "What is an entrepreneur" is the wrong question. *American Journal of Small Business, 12*(4), 11–31.

Gartner, W. B., Shaver, K. G., Carter, N. M., & Reynolds, P. D. (Eds). (2004). *Handbook of entrepreneurial dynamics: The process of business creation.* Thousand Oaks, CA: Sage.

Haltiwanger, J., Lynch, L. M., & Mackie, C. (Eds). (2007). *Understanding business dynamics: An integrated data system for America's future.* Washington, DC: National Academies Press.

Kets de Vries, M. F. R. (1985). The dark side of entrepreneurship. *Harvard Business Review, 64*(6), 60–167.

Kirzner, I. M. (1979). *Perception, opportunity, and profit: Studies in the theory of entrepreneurship.* Chicago: University of Chicago Press.

Knight, F. H. (1921). *Risk, uncertainty, and profit.* New York: A. M. Kelly (1964 reprint).

Mathematica Policy Research. (2007). *Building and sustaining innovative companies: The Kauffman firm survey.* www.mathematica-mpr.com/surveys/kauffmanfirm.asp.

McClelland, D. C. (1961). *The achieving society.* NY: Van Norstrand.

Penrose, E. T. (1959). *The theory of the growth of the firm.* Oxford, UK: Blackwell.

Pozen, D. E. (2008). We are all entrepreneurs now. *Wake Forest Law Review, 43,* 283–340.

Reynolds, P. D. (1991). Sociology and entrepreneurship: Concept and contributions. *Entrepreneurship Theory and Practice, 16*(2), 47–70.

Reynolds, P. D. (2000). National panel study of U.S. business start-ups: Background and methodology. In J. A. Katz (Ed.), *Advances in entrepreneurship, firm emergence and growth, Vol. 4* (pp.153–228). Stamford, CT: JAI Press.

Reynolds, P. D. (2007). New firm creation in the U.S.: A PSED I overview. *Foundations and Trends in Entrepreneurship, 3*(1), 1–149.

Reynolds, P. D. (forthcoming). Screening item effects in estimating the prevalence of nascent entrepreneurs. *Small Business Economics.*

Reynolds, P., Bosma, N., Autio, E., Hunt, S., De Bono, N., Servais, I., et al. (2005). Global entrepreneurship monitor: Data collection design and implementation: 1998–2003. *Small Business Economics, 24,* 205–231.

Reynolds, P. D., Bygrave, W. D., Autio, E., Cox, L. W., & Hay, M. (2004). *Global entrepreneurship monitor: 2003 summary report.* Babson Park, MA: Babson College.

Reynolds, P. D., & Curtin, R. T. (2008). Business creation in the United States: Panel Study of Entrepreneurial Dynamics II first wave results. *Foundations and Trends in Entrepreneurship, 4*(3), 155–307.

Say, J.-B. (1816). *A treatise on political economy.* New York: A. M. Kelley (1964 reprint).

Schumpeter, J. A. (1934). *The theory of economic development.* Cambridge, MA: Harvard University Press.

Shane, S. A. (2008). *The illusions of entrepreneurship.* New Haven, CT: Yale University Press.

Shane, S., & Venkataranam, V. S. (2001). The promise of entrepreneurship as a field of research. *Academy of Management Review, 25*(1), 217–226.

Thornton, P. H. (1999). The sociology of entrepreneurship. *Annual Review of Sociology, 25*, 19–46.

U.S. Census. (2008). *The 2008 statistical abstract of the U.S.* www.census.gov/compendia/statab. Accessed 17 July 2008.

U.S. Small Business Administration. (2007). *The small business economy: A report to the president*. Washington, DC: U.S. Government Printing Office.

Van Gelderen, M. W. (2000). Enterprising behavior or ordinary people. *European Journal of Work and Organizational Psychology, 9*, 81–88.

Part I
Nascent Entrepreneurs

Chapter 2
Social Motives in the PSED II

Amy E. Davis and Kelly G. Shaver

2.1 Introduction

The extent to which those creating new firms have unique individual features or personal profiles has been a major focus of those studying the entrepreneurial process. Scholarly writing on personal factors includes everything from journal special issues focusing on entrepreneurial cognition (Mitchell et al., 2002) to entire books on the *Psychology of Entrepreneurship* (Baum, Frese, & Baron, 2006). Measures of individual differences have been an important component of the interview schedules used in the PSED research program. For example, the *Handbook of Entrepreneurial Dynamics*, describing the background of the modules included in the PSED I interview, contains 38 chapters and 3 appendices (Gartner, Shaver, Carter, & Reynolds, 2004). Of these chapters, 11 deal specifically with personal characteristics and arguably another 7 deal with the background experienced by, or beliefs held by, individual entrepreneurs.

This chapter provides a review of four of the individual difference measures in the PSED II: entrepreneurial intensity, social skills, expectancy, and career reasons. We begin by noting the differences in the data between PSED I and PSED II that apply to all four sections that follow. Then, for each social motive, we present descriptive statistics for the measures. We conclude by discussing potential research applications of the social motive measures.

2.1.1 Numbers of Nascent Entrepreneurs

The total number of respondents, nascent entrepreneurs, and comparison group in the PSED I was 1,261. For the social and psychological measures this number is normally reduced to 1,216 by eliminating people who were in the

---

A.E. Davis (✉)
College of Charleston, 5 Liberty Street, Charleston, SC 29401, USA
e-mail: davisae@cofc.edu

data set although they failed to meet some of the exclusion criteria or who—though members of the comparison group—were actually starting businesses.[1]

For the PSED II, the number of cases that must be eliminated in order to meet all of the presumed selection criteria is much smaller. PSED II begins with a total pool of 1,214 individuals. There is only one selection criterion that is not completely satisfied in the data set—the requirement that each enterprise be owned at least 50% by *persons* rather than by institutions (including persons who are representing institutions).

In the PSED II interview there are detailed questions about up to five potential owners of the business to be established. Respondents were first asked whether they would be the sole owner, whether the owners would be the self and spouse, or whether the owners would be the self and "others." We simply assume that if the answer to this question (item AG1) is either "self" or "self and spouse," no business institutions will be among the owners of the enterprise. Within the "self and others" category, we analyzed the responses to questions about whether an additional owner represented an institution (items AG5_2–AG5_5). If the answer to any of these items indicated that the potential owner represented an institution, we added the percentages together for the responses that indicated institutional representation. This procedure identified eight cases for which there was institutional representation that totaled more than 50% of the business being created. In what follows, we have dropped those eight cases, reducing the PSED II total sample to 1,206 respondents. This group includes 1,183 fully autonomous nascent entrepreneurs (no additional owners represent institutions) and 23 partially autonomous (some additional owners represent institutions, but their total ownership percentage does not exceed 50%). The comparable numbers for the social motive variables in the PSED I are 480 fully autonomous and 73 partially autonomous, for a total of 553 nascent entrepreneurs.[2] Thus, excluding the PSED I comparison group, a combined PSED I/PSED II data set will have 1,759 individuals who answered at least some (but not always all) of the social motive items.

2.1.2 Differences Between the PSED I and PSED II

The capacity to compare a representative sample of nascent entrepreneurs with typical individuals was provided by including a comparison group in the PSED I research design. This facilitated the use of social psychological indicators to distinguish those who were starting businesses from those who were not. A lack of resources precluded inclusion of a comparison group in the PSED II protocol. Even so, social psychological measures can be used to distinguish among different sorts of entrepreneurs based on factors including demographic characteristics, human capital, or industry segment. They can also be used to predict outcomes in the subsequent waves of data. But researchers seeking to make comparisons between nascent entrepreneurs and nonentrepreneurs will need to merge data of the PSED I and the PSED II. Because of differences in procedure and the interview schedules, such merging must be done with care.

One of the difficulties with individual difference measures is that by traditional principles of psychometrics, "multi-item scales" consisting of only a few items are typically regarded with skepticism. More items generally lead to more reliable constructs. Consequently, in an attempt to minimize the concern, the four social motives described in the present chapter were developed on the basis of theory discussed in the relevant sections of the PSED I *Handbook* (Liao & Welsch, 2004, chap. 17; Baron, 2004, chap. 21; Gatewood, 2004, chap. 13; Carter, Gartner, & Shaver, 2004, chap. 12).

Even then, there were not sufficient resources for the PSED I to include all of the items originally suggested for every identified concept. In PSED I the social motive variables were assessed in the mail questionnaire, in a form that facilitated quick responding. In PSED II, however, a lack of resources precluded a self-administered mail-back questionnaire, and phone interview time was at an even greater premium than in PSED I. The result is that in PSED II, none of the four motives described in this chapter had its full complement of PSED I items. Entrepreneurial intensity went from four items to two; social skills went from seven to four; expectancy went from six items to five, and career reasons went from 18 to 14. Thus, these four social motive variables were represented by 25 items, compared to the 35 included in the PSED I self-completed questionnaire. The specific items are shown in Tables 2.1 and 2.2, with weighted means and standard deviations.

When different methods are used to obtain information, there is always the potential for a "method effect." It is possible that responses obtained from a self-completed mail questionnaire may differ from those provided during a phone interview, even if the item content and response scales are the same.

Although approximately 67% of the PSED I nascent entrepreneurs completed the mail questionnaire, there is some evidence that this was not a random subset of those completing the phone interview. For example, statistical analysis shows that PSED I respondents who completed the phone interview in both Wave 1 and Wave 2 but not the mail questionnaire were more likely to discontinue their start-up activities than respondents who completed the Wave 1 and Wave 2 phone interviews *and* the mail questionnaire. Therefore, not only did the mail questionnaire generate a lower number of cases (553) than the PSED I phone interview (830), but it also represented a different set of outcomes than that found among the phone interview cohort.

There are also differences in the response scales used in PSED I and II for some items. For PSED I, the items for Entrepreneurial Intensity were scored as 5-point bipolar scales. In order of appearance from left to right on the page, the descriptive labels for the numerical values were "completely untrue," "mostly untrue," "it depends," "mostly true," and "completely true." Thus the scales became more positive from left to right. For PSED II, the response scales were also 5-point bipolar measures, but this time the labels from left to right were "strongly agree," "agree," "neither," "disagree," and "strongly disagree." Thus the descriptors for the scale midpoint were different from one data set to the next, and were there any position biases, they would have operated in the

Table 2.1 PSED II items for three social motive variables

	Mean	SD	PSED I item no.	PSED II item no.
Entrepreneurial intensity (N = 1203.86, alpha = 0.69)				
There is no limit as to how long I would give maximum effort to establish this new business	4.16	0.98	QL1e	AY9
My personal philosophy is to "do whatever it takes" to establish my own business	4.09	0.97	QL1f	AY10
Social skills (N = 1201.43; alpha = 0.36)				
I can talk to almost anybody about almost anything (reversed)	4.10	1.06	QL1y	AY3
I consider myself a loner	3.49	1.30	QL1u	AY1
I rarely show my feelings	3.33	1.20	QL1s	AY11
Whatever emotion I feel on the inside tends to show on the outside (reversed)	2.89	1.30	QL1v	AY2
Expectancy (N = 1204.28; alpha = 0.70)				
I am confident I can put in the effort needed to start this new business	4.56	0.57	QK1f	AY8
Overall, my skills and abilities will help me start this new business	4.48	0.63	QK1d	AY6
My past experience will be very valuable in starting this new business	4.35	0.86	QK1e	AY7
If I start this new business, it will help me achieve other important goals in my life	4.28	0.79	QK1c	AY5
Starting this new business is much more desirable than other career opportunities I have	4.12	0.94	QK1b	AY4

Table 2.2 PSED II items for career reasons

	Mean	SD	PSED I item no.	PSED II item no.
Career reasons (N = 1197.28, alpha = 0.86)				
To have considerable freedom to adapt your own approach to work	3.95	1.08	QG1f	AW5
To give yourself, your spouse, and your children financial security	3.85	1.25	QG1g	AW6
To have greater flexibility for your personal and family life	3.83	1.22	QG1b	AW2
To earn a larger personal income	3.68	1.17	QG1k	AW9
To fulfill a personal vision	3.65	1.21	QG1o	AW13
To have a chance to build great wealth or a very high income	3.07	1.42	QG1n	AW12
To build a business your children can inherit	2.71	1.56	QG1j	AW8
To achieve something and get recognition for it	2.68	1.40	QG1l	AW10
To develop an idea for a product	2.34	1.45	QG1m	AW11
To have the power to greatly influence an organization	2.26	1.42	QG1q	AW14
To follow the example of a person you admire	2.26	1.42	QG1i	AW7
To achieve a higher position in society	2.12	1.32	QG1a	AW1
To be respected by your friends	1.94	1.25	QG1e	AW4
To continue a family tradition	1.80	1.33	QG1d	AW3

opposite ways across data sets. Moreover, in PSED II, respondents were allowed to give responses of "not relevant," and "don't know," as well as the five descriptors provided for the scale. There were only a few "don't know" responses, but researchers who use the combined data sets should be careful to reverse the Entrepreneurial Intensity items from PSED I to PSED II.

As noted above, only four of the seven Social Skills items from PSED I made it into PSED II. Responses on these four items were measured using the same 5-point bipolar scales used for Entrepreneurial Intensity. Thus, in PSED I, the Social Skills variables had response alternatives that went from "completely untrue" to "completely true," whereas in PSED II the response alternatives went from "strongly agree" to "strongly disagree." Again, researchers seeking to combine the social skills measures across PSED I and PSED II will have to reverse-score one or the other. The Social Skills items have additional difficulties that will be addressed in that section of the present chapter.

The five Expectancy items included in PSED II were scored using 5-point bipolar scales. Again, the response alternatives presented ranged from "strongly agree" to "strongly disagree," whereas in PSED I the response alternatives had ranged from "completely untrue" to "completely true." Consequently, researchers desiring to combine the expectancy measures from one data set to the other will need to reverse-score one of the two measures.

On the other hand, the Career Reasons items have the same wording in both data sets, were scored in the same direction, and had the same response alternatives in both PSED I and PSED II. Respondents in both studies were asked to describe the extent to which each reason applied to them. Responses were measured in both cases by the same 5-point unipolar scale, with response alternatives "to no extent," "to a little extent," "to some extent," "to a great extent," and "to a very great extent." Thus, the Career Reasons items can simply be aggregated across data sets with no need to change the scoring. Of course, researchers should probably keep in mind that the Career Reasons 5-point scale is unipolar, whereas the 5-point scales for the other three social motives included in this chapter are bipolar in nature.

2.2 Social Motives

2.2.1 Entrepreneurial Intensity

One often hears of entrepreneurs who would rather work 80 hours per week on their own businesses than 40 hours per week for someone else. For example, researchers have found that respondents willing to sacrifice for business creation were more likely to report intentions of becoming entrepreneurs (Kolvereid & Isaksen, 2006). Moreover, whether it is called "passion," or "commitment," this level of internal drive is a major asset in overcoming the inevitable challenges to be surmounted in business creation. In the PSED I, such commitment was addressed as "entrepreneurial intensity" (Liao & Welsch, 2004). Although the original entrepreneurial intensity (EI) scale included 12 items (see Gundry & Welsch, 2001), the PSED I was able to include only 4 of these 12. However, the four items selected showed reasonable reliability and validity, and each one showed significant differences between the nascent entrepreneurs and the comparison group included in PSED I.[3] According to Liao and Welsch (2004) the mean differences across groups ranged from a low of 0.12 for "Owning my own business is more important than spending more time with my family" to a high of 0.78 for "I would rather own my own business than earn a higher salary employed by someone else."

The first item included in PSED II was "There is no limit as to how long I would give maximum effort to establish this new business" (PSED II item AY9; PSED I nascent/comparison group mean difference = 0.54). The second entrepreneurial intensity item was "My personal philosophy is to 'do whatever it takes' to establish my own business" (PSED II item AY10; PSED I mean difference between nascents and comparison group = 0.86). The mean scores and standard deviations for these two items in PSED II are shown in the top panel of Table 2.1. The Cronbach alpha for this two-item scale was 0.71. Most respondents either agree or strongly agree that they will extend maximum effort and sacrifice for the sake of establishing new businesses.

2.2.2 Social Skills

Nascent entrepreneurs rely in part on their social skills to establish and maintain relationships they will need for converting their venture opportunities into established businesses. Relationships provide information, referrals, resources, and support (Ibarra, 1992; Ibarra, 1993). These useful outcomes of relationships are often referred to as *social capital* (Baron, 2004; Lin, 2000; Nahapiet & Ghoshal, 1998). Often, social capital is measured by the existence of ties between a focal person (such as an entrepreneur) and particular others as well as the strength of those ties (Beggs, Haines, & Hurlbert 1996; Hurlbert, Haines, & Beggs, 2000; Marsden & Campbell, 1984). However, measures of differences in entrepreneurs' social networks do not illuminate why some entrepreneurs have more favorable social networks than others.

Social skills (also referred to as social competence, Baron & Markman, 2003) will encourage key individuals—employees, customers, investors, suppliers, vendors, or lenders—to enter exchanges with entrepreneurs. Two studies have found that emotional intelligence and impression management, intentionally presenting desired emotions to others, had important effects on the willingness of employees to behave entrepreneurially (Brundin, Patzelt, & Shepherd, 2008; Zampetakis, Beldekos, & Moustakis, 2009). Social skills that might be expected to have particular importance to entrepreneurs include social adaptability and expressiveness. Social adaptability is the ability to be comfortable in a variety of different social situations and to relate effectively to individuals from different backgrounds (Baron, 2004). Independent contractors in the cosmetics industry with high levels of social adaptability had higher incomes over three years than those with lower levels of social adaptability (Baron & Markman, 2003). Moreover, Baron and Markman found that expressiveness was positively associated with revenues from sales in the analysis of entrepreneurs in high-technology industries.

Other social skills examined in previous studies include impression management, social perception, and persuasion (Baron, 2004). Impression management refers to actions aimed at generating favorable responses from others and includes creating a favorable impression in the minds of others through "flattery, agreeing with the target persons, doing small favors for them, or expressing attitudes and preferences that are currently in vogue" (Baron, 2004, pp. 224–225). Entrepreneurs want to convey confidence and competence to others and may use impression management to do so. Social perception is the ability to "accurately perceive the emotions, traits, motives, and intentions of others" (Baron, 2004, p. 228). These are processes of impression formation, attribution, and the judgment of underlying intentions (for details of the processes of judgment of intention, see Gilbert & Jones, 1986; Jones & Davis, 1965; Shaver, 1975; Shaver, 1985). Persuasion can be especially useful to entrepreneurs, as can the knowledge of which persuasive technique might be most appropriate in the setting (see Cialdini, 1993; Petty & Cacioppo, 1984, 1986).

As important to entrepreneurial success as social skills might be, their representation in PSED II is smaller than their representation was in PSED I. Only four of the seven Social Skills items included in PSED I were present in PSED II, and the rationale for which items were included is not entirely clear. Principles for selection might have included the items with the highest intercorrelations in PSED I, or the lowest standard deviations, or the highest mean scores. None of these principles was apparently utilized. As it happens, it would have been difficult to use "highest intercorrelation" as the criterion for inclusion, as only three of the seven PSED I Social Skills variables showed significantly positive correlations, the highest of which was 0.53 (Baron, 2004). These three were "I rarely show my feelings" (included in PSED II as item AY11), "I consider myself a loner" (included in PSED II as item AY1), and "I am often concerned about what others think of me" (not included in PSED II).

Another inclusion criterion might have been to select the items with the lowest standard deviations. In Baron's (2004) *Handbook* chapter for PSED I, the four Social Skills items with the lowest standard deviations were "I am a good judge of other people" (a relatively high mean score of 3.91 and a standard deviation of 0.70), "I usually know what is appropriate in any situation" (the highest mean score 4.16 and a standard deviation of 0.77), "Whatever emotion I feel on the inside tends to show on the outside" (the lowest mean score at 2.31 with a standard deviation of 0.89), and "I can talk to almost anybody about almost anything" (mean score of 3.90 and standard deviation of 1.27). Only the last two of these were included in PSED II, as items AY2 and AY3, respectively.

Finally, the PSED I items with the highest mean scores might have been chosen for inclusion in PSED II. These were "... know what is appropriate...," "... good judge of other people...," "... can talk to almost anybody... (AY3)," and "... rarely show feelings... (AY11)." But clearly two of the high mean score items were omitted.

One might expect that an outgoing and passionate entrepreneur should be able to "talk to almost anybody about almost anything" (in PSED II as AY3). Stated in the positive, this sounds quite reasonable. Respondents strongly agreeing to the statement would be asserting that they not only have social ease in a variety of situations (social adaptability) but are willing to discuss and share on a variety of topics (expressiveness).[4] On the other hand, strong *disagreement* with the item as stated could logically originate from one of three categories of people. The first would consist of individuals who feel comfortable relating to anyone as long as the topics of discussion are within a very narrow range.[5] The second would consist of individuals who feel comfortable talking about anything at all, but with a narrow range of conversation partners. Finally, there would be the individuals who feel uncomfortable even when the topics of discussion are quite limited.

This nuance should be kept in mind when using the item as a predictor variable, especially if the ability to talk to almost any*body* has a different effect on entrepreneurial outcomes than the ability to talk about almost any*thing*. Fortunately, the vast majority of respondents agreed with the statement. Recall that the response alternatives for this section of PSED II were opposite those for PSED I. So to make this item consistent with PSED I and have higher numbers represent *more* social skill we reverse-scored it. Because it was supposed to represent an expressive component of emotional intelligence (a good thing for Social Skills) we also reverse-scored "Whatever emotion I feel on the inside tends to show on the outside" (item AY2). On the other hand, the two remaining items—"I consider myself a loner" and "I rarely show my feelings" both represent less in the way of social skill, so strong *disagreement* should be a positive thing for Social Skill.

In PSED I the correlations among Social Skills items were relatively low (three significant relationships among the 21 possible comparisons). For that reason, as well as to check on the validity of our impressions regarding what should be reverse-scored, we believed it important to test the intercorrelations among the four items included in PSED II. Five of the six possible correlations were positive, and four of these were significantly positive. The only exception to this pattern was a negative correlation ($r = -0.05$, n.s.) between "Whatever emotion I feel on the inside..." and "I consider myself a loner." Means and standard deviations for the Social Skills items included in PSED II are shown in the second panel of Table 2.1. Unfortunately, the Cronbach alpha for this set of items was unacceptably low at 0.36. Therefore, researchers should carefully consider the theoretical and conceptual justifications for the inclusion of Social Skills items and determine which indicators should be used and whether they should be combined as a scale with such a low alpha or kept as separate indicators of different social skills.

2.2.3 Expectancy

Expectancy theory (Vroom, 1964) is addressed in Chapter 13 of the *Handbook of Entrepreneurial Dynamics* (Gatewood, 2004). Expectancy theory is an important motivation theory in the organizational behavior literature and is composed of valence, instrumentality, and expectancy. Valence is the value individuals place on particular outcomes. Employees and entrepreneurs differ on the rewards they value, as evidenced by the Career Reasons section below. First-level outcomes are those which have intrinsic value, such as the satisfaction generated from creating new products. Second-level outcomes lead to other desirable outcomes, the way that earning a high salary enables an individual to achieve a desired lifestyle. Instrumentality is the belief that performance will result in outcomes. Instrumentality is the relationship between a work outcome and desired rewards, sometimes referred to as the relationship between first and second order outcomes (Gatewood, 2004).

Expectancy is the level of confidence individuals have that their work effort will result in high performance. For entrepreneurship, the outcomes of a business may be determined by situational (exogenous factors) such as access to capital or demand potential for the business's product or service, as well as the activities (endogenous factors) of the entrepreneur (Gatewood, 2004). In other words, whether entrepreneurs believe that their business will generate high financial returns depends on their assessment of economic conditions and other external factors. But the belief also depends on their confidence that work will result in desired performance (Gatewood, 2004; Gatewood, Shaver, Powers, & Gartner, 2002; Van Auken, 1999). In the case of entrepreneurship, people with high expectancies involving both sorts of factors believe that their entrepreneurial activities will result in operational businesses.

Many researchers have focused on the related concept of self-efficacy (Bandura, 1986) and have found that high levels of self-efficacy influenced sales growth, satisfaction, perceptions of entrepreneurial opportunities, and moral awareness (Bryant, in press; Krueger, Reilly, & Carsrud, 2000; Mitchell & Shepherd, in press). Townsend, Busenitz, and Arthurs (in press) used data from the PSED I and found that expectancy increased the odds of respondents establishing operational businesses in between the initial interview and the 12-month follow-up.

In the development of PSED I, eight items were identified that represented all of the various links included in the valence–instrumentality–expectancy system. Two of these had to be dropped for lack of space, leaving six items that tested expectancy. Five of the six are present in PSED II. The item dropped from PSED I to PSED II was "If I work hard, I can successfully start a business." Townsend et al. (in press) called this measure outcome expectancy.

As with the other items in this section (AY), the PSED II items for Expectancy need to be reversed in order that (a) scoring will be in the same direction as in PSED I, and (b) higher numbers represent *higher* expectancies for success. The means and standard deviations for the five expectancy variables are shown in the third panel of Table 2.1. All of these items were significantly positively correlated with one another, with the correlations ranging from a high of 0.50 ("past experience" with "skills and abilities") to a low of 0.20 ("past experience" with "achieving other goals"). If all items are combined into a single scale, the Cronbach alpha = 0.70. Thus, although the five Expectancy items show a minimally acceptable level of reliability as a single scale, there is enough internal variation that many researchers may believe it more important to consider the various theoretically-derived pieces as separate entities.

2.2.4 Career Reasons

Individuals may have a variety of goals for starting businesses. These goals are called Career Reasons and are addressed in Chapter 12 of the *Handbook of Entrepreneurial Dynamics* (Carter et al., 2004). This list of reasons was initially developed by Scheinberg and Macmillan (1988), subsequently modified by Shane, Kolvereid, and Westhead (1991), and modified again by Birley and Westhead (1994). The factor analyses performed in these studies typically identified five categories of reasons why an individual might seek to create a business. These were innovation (a desire to create something new), independence (controlling one's own destiny), external validation (need for approval and recognition), roles (following admired individuals or family traditions), and financial success. Because of variations in personal goals found in other research on gender differences, Carter et al. (2004) elected to add a sixth category—self-realization (through challenging the self or leading others).

A factor analysis of the 18 Career Reasons included in the PSED I, using a minimum eigenvalue criterion to terminate the analysis, did not distribute the items in ways similar to those found in prior research. But when the analysis was directed to produce a six-factor solution, the items were indeed distributed much as they had been in earlier studies. The six factors accounted for a total of 68% of the variance, with three of the factors—self-realization, financial success, and recognition—achieving Cronbach alpha levels of 0.70 or above, and the other three achieving alpha levels of 0.60 or above. A comparison of the results for nascent entrepreneurs versus the comparison group showed no differences between the two groups on financial success, innovation, self-realization or independence, but did find differences on roles and recognition. Interestingly, on these two latter comparisons, the scores for the nascent entrepreneurs were lower than those for the members of the comparison group (Carter, Gartner, Shaver, & Gatewood, 2003).

Whereas the PSED I had 18 items representing Career Reasons, the PSED II dropped this number to 14. Once again, the precise reasons for the exclusions are not entirely clear. Of the four items excluded from PSED II, three were originally in the self-realization factor, thus leaving self-realization as a single item. This outcome is difficult to understand in light of the fact that all four PSED I items dealing with financial security were carried over as is to the PSED II. Moreover, the other item excluded from the PSED I was from the innovation factor, which to begin with had only two items, so this factor also became a single item. Given that two of the six factors in the PSED I are reduced to single items in PSED II, it is likely not to be useful to continue to set a solution for six factors. Consequently, researchers interested in these Career Reasons variables—and especially in combining them across data sets—should probably use a minimum eigenvalue criterion as the way to end further iterations within a principal component analysis. In addition, researchers may wish to exclude from their principal component analysis the single measure of innovation and the single measure of self-realization. Mean scores and standard deviations for the 14 Career Reasons items are presented in Table 2.2.

We conducted a principal component factor analysis of the 14 weighted PSED II Reasons items, using a minimum eigenvalue criterion for ending iterations, and subjected the result to a varimax rotation. This procedure produced the three-factor solution shown in Table 2.3.

This solution accounted for 54.93% of the variance and the rotation converged in seven iterations. Items are listed in Table 2.3 in descending order of loading within factors. Items with primary loadings > 0.40 and

Table 2.3 PSED II principal component analysis three-factor solution for career reasons (weighted)

		Factor I	Factor II	Factor III	
Weighted N:	PSED II item no.	1199.47	1205.30	1206.00	PSED I item no.
Cronbach alpha:		$\alpha = 0.81$	$\alpha = 0.75$	$\alpha = 0.62$	
% variance accounted for:		35.11	12.62	7.20	
Item content					
Respected by my friends	AW4	**0.70**	0.11	0.07	QG1e
Achieve, get recognition	AW10	**0.68**	0.32	−0.08	QG1(ell)
Power influence an organization	AW14	**0.67**	0.31	0.01	QG1q
Follow person admired	AW7	**0.65**	0.09	0.24	QG1i
Develop an idea for a product	AW11	**0.65**	0.02	−0.01	QG1m
Continue a family tradition	AW3	**0.62**	−0.15	0.37	QG1d
Higher position for myself	AW1	0.57	0.41	0.03	QG1a
Fulfill personal vision	AW13	**0.56**	0.13	0.11	QG1o
Build business which kid can inherit	AW8	0.48	0.35	0.26	QG1j
Earn large personal income	AW9	0.10	**0.81**	0.22	QG1k
Build great wealth, high income	AW12	0.31	**0.78**	0.11	QG1n
Give family financial security	AW6	0.07	0.64	0.50	QG1g
Greater flexibility in personal life	AW2	−0.01	0.26	**0.80**	QG1b
Considerable freedom to adapt	AW5	0.17	0.14	**0.71**	QG1f

Note: 54.93%, 3 components, 7 iterations, minimum eigenvalue criterion, varimax rotation.

cross-loadings < 0.40 were retained. Applying this decision rule eliminated two items. The first item eliminated was AW1, "gain higher position;" this was dropped from the first factor. The second item eliminated was AW6, "give family financial security;" this was dropped from the second factor obtained. Inspection of the remaining items suggest that Factor I captured (mostly) non-financial reasons for engaging in entrepreneurial behavior, so we shall refer to it as Personal Reasons. The two items remaining in Factor II both deal with financial issues, so we chose to call it Financial Reasons. Finally, the two items in Factor III deal with freedom to adapt, and because they are identical to one of the PSED I factors, we will use the designation Independence.

The items remaining in each factor were subjected to reliability analysis and the results are shown near the top of each Factor column in Table 2.3. Personal Reasons produced an overall mean of the items of 2.45 with an average item variance of 1.92, and a Cronbach alpha of 0.81. Financial Reasons produced an overall mean of the items of 3.37 with an average item variance of 1.69 and a Cronbach alpha of 0.75. Finally, Independence produced an overall mean of items that was equal to 3.89 with an average item variance of 1.34 and a Cronbach alpha = 0.62. The last of these reliability estimates is on the low side, but the first two are acceptable. Stepping back from the details, it appears as though the PSED II respondents care first about the goal of maintaining Independence in one's life by establishing a business, followed by a desire for Financial Success and the various Personal Reasons for establishing a business. The PSED II Personal Reasons encompass elements of what in Chapter 13 of the *Handbook* was referred to as Recognition, Roles, Innovation, and Self-Realization (Carter et al., 2004). The PSED II Financial Reasons factor includes three of the four Financial Success items from PSED I and the PSED II Independence factor overlaps completely the PSED I Independence factor.

2.2.5 Data Set Comparisons

Because the number of social motive items present in PSED II was significantly reduced from the number of such items in PSED I, it may be useful to provide some cross-data set comparisons of the four social motives described in this chapter. By way of summary, we have treated each of the four social motives as if it were a scale all by itself, ignoring for the moment the likely possibility that some researchers will elect to split some of these "scales" into subsets of items. The results of the comparisons are shown in Table 2.4.

To make it very clear that we have combined all items in a subsection for these comparisons, we have indicated the number of items in each subsection and have provided means and variances for each of the four collections of variables. For Entrepreneurial Intensity, the Cronbach alpha within PSED I was 0.73, whereas the Cronbach alpha within PSED II was 0.69. For the four items in Social Skills, the alpha within PSED I was 0.36, the same value that was

Table 2.4 PSED II scales by dataset (weighted, nascents only)

Scale (items in PSED II)	N	Alpha	Mean	SD
Entrepreneurial intensity (2)				
PSED I	546.60	0.73	7.59	1.80
PSED II	1203.86	0.69	8.25	2.90
Social skills (4)				
PSED I	536.92	0.36	13.31	6.89
PSED II	1201.43	0.36	13.81	8.12
Expectancy (5)				
PSED I	543.68	0.76	21.10	9.24
PSED II	1204.28	0.70	21.78	6.64
Career reasons (14)				
PSED I	526.52	0.83	41.00	99.66
PSED II	1197.28	0.86	40.12	119.74

obtained in PSED II. This level is low enough in both data sets that it is probably a mistake to treat these four items as an internally coherent scale. For the five items in Expectancy, the alpha within PSED I was 0.76, whereas the alpha for these items in PSED II was 0.70. Finally, for the 14 items in Career Reasons, the alpha for PSED I was 0.83, and the alpha for PSED II was 0.86. Thus three of the four social motive variables have a level of internal consistency sufficient to warrant analysis as unitary scales (unless there are compelling theoretical reasons to break one or another such "scale" into smaller component parts).

2.2.6 Future Research

Combining data from PSED I and II presents both challenges and opportunities. Many researchers have used the social motive items in PSED I to produce important research findings (for examples, see Cassar, 2006; Townsend et al., in press). Their work should be extended and replicated, using data from the PSED II. The PSED II has more entrepreneurs and a sample that is more representative than the PSED I sample due to attrition between the screener and the phone interview and the phone interview and the mail questionnaire. These respondents will add more statistical power and allow for the exploration of historical changes between the two data sets. As a tradeoff, the PSED II has fewer indicators of entrepreneurial intensity, social skills, expectancy, and career reasons. We recommend that researchers electing to combine data sets not only make the data transformations discussed above, but conduct their analyses of PSED I data with the inclusion and exclusion of variables unavailable in PSED II to demonstrate how differences affect construct or measurement validity.

The social motive indicators have numerous potential research applications. Researchers can examine how the four together or some subset influence a variety of characteristics including the industries entrepreneurs choose, strategies, team formation, and growth intentions. Social motive factors may also be used to predict the outcomes of nascent entrepreneurs' start-ups in the follow-up interviews. Davis and Shaver plan to use social motive factors to distinguish nascent entrepreneurs who have initiated actions toward starting a business for several years prior to the questionnaire from those who began their pursuit of entrepreneurship only a few months prior to the interview. Using both the PSED I and PSED II, we will first distinguish nascent entrepreneurs and the comparison group. Then we will compare the social motive characteristics of entrepreneurs in the PSED I and PSED II who had engaged in activities toward creating the business they are currently pursuing for more than 10 years from those doing so from 1–9 years and then for those for less than 1 year. Then, we will examine the subsequent wave outcomes of respondents' ventures: established, still active, or discontinued. Ideally, our analysis will be predictive with regard to which entrepreneurs who have just begun their pursuit of entrepreneurship will become the entrepreneurs who spin their wheels for 10 or more years and which quickly convert to operational businesses.

Notes

1. This sample is Row G in Table C5 in Appendix C of the *Handbook* (Reynolds & Curtin, 2004). For a detailed description of the respondent selection process that leads to this number of cases, see Shaver, Carter, Gartner, and Reynolds (2001). The reduction can be accomplished by using the SPSS syntax file kscleans06.sps, available through www.cofc.edu/~shaverk/.
2. Once nascent entrepreneurs on teams in which institutions will own greater than 50% of the new company have been eliminated, there are 817 nascent entrepreneur respondents of the phone interview. Only 553 of them answered the mail questionnaire where the social motive indicators are located.
3. For entrepreneurial intensity and the other social motive items, the "stem" was different between the nascent entrepreneur, for whom questions about establishing "my business" made sense as is, and the Comparison Group, who necessarily had to be asked these questions in an "as if" fashion.
4. The willingness to talk to anyone about anything could also reflect low impression management if entrepreneurs are willing to talk to anyone about negative topics and feelings without regard to how such discussions could adversely affect their businesses.
5. These individuals, for example, may have high impression management and be unwilling to discuss topics or feelings that would reflect unfavorably on them.

References

Bandura, A. (1986). *Social foundations of thought and action: A social cognitive theory.* Englewood Cliffs, NJ: Prentice-Hall.

Baron, R. A. (2004). Social skills. In W. B. Gartner, K. G. Shaver, N. M. Carter, & P. D. Reynolds (Eds.), *Handbook of entrepreneurial dynamics: The process of business creation* (pp. 220–234). Thousand Oaks, CA: Sage.

Baron, R. A., & Markman, G. D. (2003). Beyond social capital: The role of entrepreneurs' social competence in their financial success. *Journal of Business Venturing, 18*, 41–60.

Baum, J. R., Frese, M., & Baron, R. A. (Eds.). (2006). *The psychology of entrepreneurship.* Mahwah, NJ: Psychology Press.

Beggs, J. J., Haines, V. A., & Hurlbert, J. S. (1996). Situational contingencies surrounding the receipt of informal support. *Social Forces, 75*(1), 201–222.

Birley, S., & Westhead, P. (1994). A taxonomy of business start-up reasons and their impact on firm growth and size. *Journal of Business Venturing, 9,* 7–31.

Brundin, E., Patzelt, H., & Shepherd, D. A. (2008). Managers' emotional displays and employees' willingness to act entrepreneurially. *Journal of Business Venturing, 23,* 221–243.

Bryant, P. (in press). Self-regulation and moral awareness among entrepreneurs. *Journal of Business Venturing.*

Carter, N. M., Gartner, W. B., & Shaver, K. G. (2004). Career reasons. In W. B. Gartner, K. G. Shaver, N. M. Carter, & P. D. Reynolds (Eds.), *Handbook of entrepreneurial dynamics: The process of business creation* (pp. 142–152). Thousand Oaks, CA: Sage.

Carter, N. M., Gartner, W. B., Shaver, K. G., & Gatewood, E. J. (2003). The career reasons of nascent entrepreneurs. *Journal of Business Venturing, 18,* 13–39.

Cassar, G. (2006). Entrepreneur opportunity costs and intended venture growth. *Journal of Business Venturing, 21,* 610–632.

Cialdini, R. B. (1993). *Influence: The psychology of persuasion.* New York: Morrow.

Gartner, W. B., Shaver, K. G., Carter, N. M., & Reynolds, P. D. (Eds.). (2004). *Handbook of entrepreneurial dynamics: The process of business creation.* Thousand Oaks, CA: Sage.

Gatewood, E. J. (2004). Entrepreneurial expectancies. In W. B. Gartner, K. G. Shaver, N. M. Carter, & P. D. Reynolds (Eds.), *Handbook of entrepreneurial dynamics: The process of business creation* (pp. 153–162). Thousand Oaks, CA: Sage.

Gatewood, E. J., Shaver, K. G., Powers, J. B., & Gartner, W. B. (2002). Entrepreneurial expectancy, task effort, and performance. *Entrepreneurship Theory and Practice, 27,* 187–206.

Gilbert, D. T., & Jones, E. E. (1986). Exemplification: The self-presentation of moral character. *Journal of Personality, 54,* 593–615.

Gundry, L., & Welsch, H. (2001). The ambitious entrepreneur: High growth strategies of women based enterprises. *Journal of Business Venturing, 16,* 453–470.

Hurlbert, J. S., Haines, V. A., & Beggs, J. J. (2000). Core networks and tie activation: What kinds of routine networks allocate resources in nonroutine situations. *American Sociological Review, 65,* 598–618.

Ibarra, H. (1992). Homophily and differential returns: Sex differences in network structure and access in an advertising firm. *Administrative Science Quarterly, 37,* 422–447.

Ibarra, H. (1993). Personal networks of women and minorities in management: A conceptual framework. *Academy of Management Review, 18,* 56–87.

Jones, E. E., & Davis, K. E. (1965). From acts to dispositions: The attribution process in person perception. In L. Berkowitz (Ed.), *Advances in experimental social psychology* (Vol. 2, pp. 216–266). New York: Academic Press.

Kolvereid, L., & Isaksen, E. (2006). New business start-up and subsequent entry into self-employment. *Journal of Business Venturing, 21,* 866–885.

Krueger, N. F., Reilly, M. D., & Carsrud, A. L. (2000). Competing models of entrepreneurial intentions. *Journal of Business Venturing, 15,* 411–432.

Liao, J., & Welsch, H. (2004). Entrepreneurial intensity. In W. B. Gartner, K. G. Shaver, N. M. Carter, & P. D. Reynolds (Eds.), *Handbook of entrepreneurial dynamics: The process of business creation* (pp. 186–195). Thousand Oaks, CA: Sage.

Lin, N. (2000). Inequality in social capital. *Contemporary Sociology, 29,* 785–795.

Marsden, P. V., & Campbell, K. E. (1984). Measuring tie strength. *Social Forces, 63,* 482–501.

Mitchell, R. K., Busenitz, L., Lant, T. M., McDougall, P. P., Morse, E. A., & Smith, J. B. (2002). Toward a theory of entrepreneurial cognition: Rethinking the people side of entrepreneurship research. *Entrepreneurship Theory and Practice, 27,* 93–104.

Mitchell, J. R., & Shepherd, D. A. (in press). To thine own self be true: Images of self, images of opportunity, and entrepreneurial action. *Journal of Business Venturing.*

Nahapiet, J., & Ghoshal, S. (1998). Social capital, intellectual capital, and the organizational advantage. *Academy of Management Review, 23*(2), 242–266.

Petty, R. E., & Cacioppo, J. T. (1984). The effects of involvement on responses to argument quantity and quality: Central and peripheral routes to persuasion. *Journal of Personality and Social Psychology, 46,* 69–81.

Petty, R. E., & Cacioppo, J. T. (1986). *Communication and persuasion: Central and peripheral routes to attitude change,* New York: Springer-Verlag.

Reynolds, P. D., & Curtin, R. T. (2004). Appendix C: Examples of analysis: Work file preparation, comparisons, and adjustment of weights. In W. B. Gartner, K. G. Shaver, N. M. Carter, & P. D. Reynolds (Eds.), *Handbook of entrepreneurial dynamics: The process of business creation* (pp. 495–540). Thousand Oaks, CA: Sage.

Scheinberg, S., & Macmillan, I. C. (1988). An 11-country study of motivations to start a business. In B. A. Kirchoff, W. A. Long, W. E. McMullan, K. H. Vesper, & W. E. Wetzel, Jr. (Eds.), *Frontiers of entrepreneurship research* (pp. 669–687). Wellesley, MA: Babson College.

Shane, S., Kolvereid, L., & Westhead, P. (1991). An exploratory examination of the reasons leading to new firm formation across country and gender. *Journal of Business Venturing, 6,* 431–446.

Shaver, K. G. (1985). *The attribution of blame: Causality, responsibility, and blameworthiness.* New York: Springer-Verlag.

Shaver, K. G. (1975). *An introduction to attribution processes.* Cambridge, MA: Winthrop.

Shaver, K. G., Carter, N. M., Gartner, W. B., & Reynolds, P. D. (2001). Who is a nascent entrepreneur? Decision rules for identifying and selecting entrepreneurs in the Panel Study of Entrepreneurial Dynamics (PSED). In W. D. Bygrave, E. Autio, C. G. Brush, P. Davidsson, P. G. Greene, P. D. Reynolds, & H. J. Sapienza (Eds.), *Frontiers of entrepreneurship research* (p. 122). Babson Park, MA: Babson College.

Townsend, D. M., Busenitz, L. W., & Arthurs, J. D. (in press). To start or not to start: Outcome and ability expectations in the decision to start a new venture. *Journal of Business Venturing.*

Van Auken, H. E. (1999). Obstacles to business launch. *Journal of Developmental Entrepreneurship, 4,* 175–187.

Vroom, V. H. (1964). *Work and motivation.* New York: Wiley.

Zampetakis, L. A., Beldekos, P., & Moustakis, V. S. (2009). "Day-to-day" entrepreneurship within organizations: The role of trait emotional intelligence and perceived organizational support. *European Management Journal, 27,* 165–175.

Chapter 3
Contextual Motivation and Growth Aspirations Among Nascent Entrepreneurs

Diana M. Hechavarria, Mark T. Schenkel, and Charles H. Matthews

3.1 Introduction

"The concept of the nascent entrepreneur captures the flavor of the chaotic and disorderly founding process" (Acs & Audretsch, 2003, p. 3). A *nascent entrepreneur* is defined as someone who initiates activities that are intended to culminate in a viable new firm (Reynolds, 1994; Davidsson, 2004; 2005). Yet, what motivates people to start a new business remains poorly understood (Shane, Locke, & Collins, 2003). Existing research indicates that there are micro-level and macro-level factors that influence the nascent entrepreneurial process. This chapter focuses on the latter, specifically exploring the macro–micro linkages in relation to context. Consequently, this assessment contributes to the understanding of entrepreneurial phenomena by specifically identifying contextual dimensions in which to differentiate types of nascent start-ups, which in turn, will lead to more precise interpretations of why individuals enter the firm creation process.

The goal of the Panel Study of Entrepreneurial Dynamics I & II (PSED) is to identify how new firms come into existence through the study of nascent entrepreneurship. Two emphases have emerged from the project in order to understand the process of entrepreneurship. One centers around personal characteristics of individuals who pursue the new venture (Shaver & Scott, 1991) and the other is centered on the actual behavior initiated to establish a new firm (Gartner, 1998; Gartner, Shaver, Carter, & Reynolds). These factors focus on micro-level issues related to new firm creation. However, the firm birthing process occurs in a unique and specific environment (Reynolds, 2004). The multi-dimensional nature of entrepreneurship as a construct requires scholars to investigate not only the factors that have immediate impact on the start-up process along with those individuals who are directly involved, but also the contextual environment in which the entrepreneur operates.

D.M. Hechavarria (✉)
University of Cincinnati, Lindner Hall 511, Cincinnati, OH 45221-0020
e-mail: hechavda@email.uc.edu

Low and MacMillan (1988) suggested that research into entrepreneurial behavior should consider contextual issues and identify the processes that explain rather than merely describe the entrepreneurial phenomenon. Furthermore, Learned (1992) proposed that the environment affects the situation, which in turn stimulates an entrepreneur's intentionality as well as the eventual decision to start a venture. Because the challenges of founding new organizations vary by context, different types of enterprises are likely to require different types of entrepreneurs (Thornton, 1999; Ucbasaran, Westhead, & Wright, 2001). Unless context is taken into account, the links between the actions of individuals in founding new organizations and the founding rate are likely to remain elusive (Low & Abrahamson, 1997). Hence, to develop a greater understanding of the entrepreneurial phenomena, it is imperative to distinguish among the varied scope of motivation that a nascent entrepreneur perceives based on context-specific issues (Naffziger, Hornsby, & Kuratko, 1994). Thus, contextual motivation is a judgment perception about the environment in which the individual operates. Developing our understanding of how contextual motivation directs entrepreneurial behavior will lead to a more definitive interpretation of this social and economic phenomenon, and ultimately lead to a more concrete language by which to explain the functions of the entrepreneurial process.

3.2 Contextual Motivation and Growth Aspirations

There is an increased awareness of the need for a greater understanding of the actions and strategies selected by different types of entrepreneurs who enter the start-up process (Rosa, 1998). Scholars should not assume that nascent entrepreneurs are a homogenous group. On the contrary, Reynolds (1997) has identified that cohorts of nascent entrepreneurs are in fact very heterogeneous. Therefore, it is imperative that generalizations from representative samples categorize entrepreneurs with similar objectives together in order produce more reliable inferences about antecedents and consequences of the start-up process. In sum, the nascent entrepreneurs' perception of the distinctive environment in which he/she attempts to create a new firm is foundational to developing a framework for understanding the different environmental backgrounds for entry into the entrepreneurial process.

Contextual forces play a strong role in dictating human action. Thus, the objective of this chapter is to introduce readers to a typology that incorporates contextual motivation and growth aspirations by which to conceptualize how environmental circumstances can influence entrepreneurial endeavors. Specifically, this assessment integrates the constructs of perceived environment and desired growth strategy to understand the social–economic context in which the nascent entrepreneur operates. Thus, the *context-aspiration typology* is the product of perceived environment and strategy.

Contextual motivation is the influence of social, economic, and political environments that shape individual behaviors, and thus impacts the likelihood of new firm founding among nascent entrepreneurs. Recent empirical and conceptual evidence, suggests that it is the entrepreneur's perception of the environment which plays a key role in the firm's chances of success (Bruno & Tyebjee, 1982; Gnyawali & Fogel, 1994; Delmar & Davidsson, 2000). Moreover, the interaction of these perceptions with his/her growth strategy may have an impact on the transition to new firm status. Collectively, this evidence suggests that entrepreneurial activity is not uniformly influenced by the same motives in all instances.

Nascent entrepreneurship can be classified as either opportunity- or necessity-driven. *Opportunity entrepreneurship* represents the voluntary nature of participation in the start-up process and *necessity entrepreneurship* reflects the individual's perception that actions aimed at new firm creation presented the best option available for employment (Acs, 2006). Studies have shown that rates of both opportunity and necessity entrepreneurship are conceptually distinct, and should be studied independently to better understand fluctuations in nascent rates (Bhola, Verheul, Thurik, & Grilo, 2006; Hechavarria & Reynolds, 2008).

New ventures can also be classified as small business ventures and entrepreneurial business ventures depending on the growth expectations of the founders. *Small business ventures* are those organizations which aim at remaining small. On the other hand, *entrepreneurial business ventures* are those organizations which identify at high growth, and high capitalization as a strategic objective. Research has shown that these motivations are key in directing the actions an entrepreneur takes in the course of the business life cycle (Churchill & Lewis, 1983; Carland, Hoy, Boulton, & Carland, 1984; Matthews & Scott, 1995).

Consequently, a proposed typology of context and growth aspirations will be developed in the latter sections of this chapter that incorporates the constructs of environmental motivation and nascent firm growth strategy. The following discourse presents a more descriptive overview of the perceived environmental motivation (opportunity/necessity) and desired growth strategy (entrepreneurial/small business) constructs within the PSED II sample and how they can be utilized to differentiate types of nascent ventures.

3.3 Opportunity and Necessity Entrepreneurship

One objective of PSED II was to understand how external factors influence entrance into the start-up process. Specifically, the PSED II inquired if the action was voluntary, reflecting a desire to pursue a new business opportunity, or a reaction to the absence of suitable work options, reflecting a necessity to participate in the economy (Reynolds & Curtin, 2008). The item, "Are you involved in this new business to take advantage of a business opportunity or because you had no better choices for work?" has been widely used in international surveys of nascent entrepreneurs as an objective measure of contextual influence. Although, the PSED I does not have results from this construct, data from the publicly archived Global Entrepreneurship Monitor dataset and the United States Entrepreneurial Assessment: 2004 can be utilized to compare the proportion of engagement levels among nascent entrepreneurs in the United States and internationally (Reynolds, 2007; Reynolds & Hechavarria, 2007).

Data from the Global Entrepreneurship Monitor confirms that countries with higher rates of opportunity entrepreneurship experienced reduced national emphasis on manufacturing, less intrusive government regulation, more availability of informal investors, and a significant level of respect for entrepreneurial activity. Conversely, necessity entrepreneurship rates were higher for countries where there was low economic development, the economy depended on international trade, there was an absence of an extensive social welfare system, and women were less empowered in the economy (Reynolds, Camp, Bygrave, Autio, & Hay, 2001). Data from the Global Entrepreneurship Monitor illustrates that the mechanisms that drive necessity entrepreneurship are different from those that drive opportunity entrepreneurship. They represent different kinds of people and environmental features, but both play vital roles in economic prosperity.

In the PSED II, most active nascent entrepreneurs can be considered volunteers pursuing business opportunities. Only about one in seven are driven into start-ups because of a lack of other options. Furthermore, there is no significant difference between rates of engagement among males and females. Moreover, applying a first-order Markov chain[1] to the PSED II data for waves A and B, we can estimate probabilities of a change in perception of environmental factors for wave C. Respectively, an estimated 83% will self-classify as opportunity driven, 11% as necessity driven, 6% as a combination, and 1% as other. The goodness of fit of the Markov model may be evaluated by comparing predictions with observed results or by comparing transition matrices based on successive pairs of waves.

Despite the conceptually distinct differences for undertaking action, necessity and opportunity motivated entrepreneurs are equally likely to succeed, although they establish somewhat different kinds of businesses. In general, opportunity-motivated entrepreneurs expect their ventures to produce more high-growth firms and provide more new jobs. On the other hand, necessity-based entrepreneurs generally found smaller businesses. Thus, inferences are generally made that opportunity-motivated entrepreneurs would require larger capital investments than necessity-based entrepreneurs (Hechavarria & Reynolds, 2008; Reynolds et al., 2001). But, this inference is likely misguided, without taking into account future growth expectations for the nascent venture.

3.4 Small Business and Entrepreneurial Business Ventures

Although there is some degree of overlap between entrepreneurial firms and small business firms, they can be considered conceptually distinct entities with respect to strategic focus (Carland et al., 1984). Entrepreneurial ventures key on growth as a critical component of their strategy. Although small business ventures may grow, they seek to reach an optimal manageable size that is sustained over the business' life-course. Moreover, it can be inferred that the methods pursued for growth will affect the nascent venture's likelihood of founding. For example, the findings of Solymossy and Hisrich (2000) suggest that growing firms may succeed regardless of their perception of the environment.

The item, "I want this new business to be as large as possible, or I want a size I can manage myself or with a few key employees," has been used to categorize nascents based on growth goals for PSED I and PSED II (Gartner et al. 2004). Small business ventures have low to moderate growth aspirations and entrepreneurial business ventures, also known as "gazelles," have high and rapid growth aspirations. Although small business and entrepreneurial business ventures may be similar in scope of activity, their key differentiator is the expected scalability of the venture.

Among nascent entrepreneurs in the PSED II, about one in five will aspire to be a large-growth entrepreneurial business venture. Moreover, if we compare growth aspirations by gender, a statistically significant difference is found; women are less likely to emphasize maximization of growth.

Many individuals buy into the illusion that the majority of new firms aspire to be high-growth entrepreneurial business ventures. On the contrary, many new firms in the early stages of the firm's life cycle aspire for just the opposite in their growth strategy, a size that is manageable by the founders (Human & Matthews, 2004). This argument is bolstered by employing a first-order Markov model to waves A & B of PSED II to predict possible changes in growth aspirations for successive waves. It is predicted that a third wave would identify that 13% of nascents would classify as entrepreneurial business ventures, and 87% as small business ventures. Again, the goodness of fit of the Markov model may be evaluated by comparing predictions with observed results or by comparing transition matrices based on successive pairs of waves.

Entrepreneurial business ventures will likely enact different strategies and actions than small business ventures due to their growth goals, when they try to establish a new firm. Matthews and Scott (1995) have found support that there are differences between entrepreneurial and small business ventures. For example, entrepreneurial firms are more likely to engage in more sophisticated planning than small firms overall (Matthews & Scott). This is likely, in part, a result of the higher complexity a founder faces if he/she wishes to rapidly grow a business and may lead to selecting more aggressive and risky behaviors that require higher levels of planning. But solely investigating a nascent entrepreneur's desired growth strategy without an assessment of the external context in which he/she perceives such strategy will paint an incomplete picture of the entrepreneurial process and its outcomes.

3.5 Context-Aspiration Typology and Nascent Entrepreneurship

Aldrich and Martinez (2001) cite the importance of the roles both strategy and environment play in shaping the fate of entrepreneurial efforts. Classifying nascent ventures along these dimensions has the potential to yield useful insights toward understanding why some firms get up and running, some quit the entrepreneurial process, and yet others persist in efforts to establish a new firm based on context-specific dimensions. Moreover, it offers the potential to help understand how contextual factors differ with respect to motivating individuals who are in the gestation phase of the firm's life cycle. Therefore, the context-aspiration typology aims at distinguishing nascent ventures along the lines of environment (opportunity vs. necessity) and growth strategy (entrepreneurial vs. small business) in order to make meaningful inferences about how these factors influence produce variation in entrepreneurial forms.

The PSED II provides two variables for waves A & B to decipher the motivational context in which the entrepreneur operates. Variables AT1 and BT1 deal specifically with the growth aspirations of the firm. Moreover, AT6 and BT6 deal specifically with the perceived environment. Table 3.1 presents the questionnaire items and possible responses with frequencies from the PSED II dataset.[2]

Table 3.1 Contextual motivation and growth aspiration items frequencies

Wave A		Wave B		
AT1	Percent	BT1	Percent	Which of the following two statements best describes your preference for the future size of this new business: I want this new business to be as large as possible, or I want a size I can manage myself or with a few key employees?
240	19.8	96	7.9	Want it to be as large as possible
966	79.6	517	42.6	Want a size to manage myself with key employees
6	0.5	0	0	Don't know
2	0.2	0	0	No answer
		601	50.5	System missing
1,214	100	1,214	101	Total
AT6	Percent	BT6	Percent	Are you involved in this new business to take advantage of a business opportunity or because you have no better options for work?
972	80.1	484	39.9	Take advantage of a business opportunity
155	12.8	66	5.4	No better choice for work
51	4.2	31	2.6	Combination of both (if volunteered)
4	0.3	4	0.3	Have job but seek better employment (if volunteered)
31	2.6	23	1.9	Don't know
1	0.1	5	0.4	No answer
		601	49.5	System missing
1214	100.1	1214	100	Total

Four classifications arise from this typology. Necessity-entrepreneurial business ventures are nascents who have no better options for work and aspire to establish a high-growth firm. Opportunity-entrepreneurial business ventures are nascents who also aspire for high-growth firms, but in contrast see an opportunity within the market. Conversely, opportunity-small business

3 Contextual Motivation and Growth Aspirations

ventures see an opportunity, but want to establish a firm that is manageable by the founder(s). Finally, a necessity-small business venture is also a firm that wishes to be small and manageable, but is pushed into the entrepreneurial process due to a lack of better work options.

In the PSED II, about 2% of nascent ventures consider themselves as necessity-entrepreneurial business ventures; 17% as opportunity-business ventures; about 63% as opportunity-small business ventures; and 11% as necessity-small business ventures.[3] The PSED II displays that the majority of nascent ventures consider themselves as opportunity-small business ventures, contradicting the myth that opportunity entrepreneurships by and large are scalable high-growth ventures (see Table 3.2).[4]

Table 3.2 Frequencies for context-aspiration typology

Category	Frequency	Percent
Necessity-entrepreneurial business ventures	19	1.6
Opportunity-entrepreneurial business ventures	207	17.1
Opportunity-small business ventures	759	62.5
Necessity-small business ventures	135	11.1
Total	1,120	92.3
System	94	7.7
	1,214	100.0

It is a common assumption that necessity entrepreneurship is synonymous with small business ventures. A descriptive analysis of the PSED II reveals that about 2% of the sample classifies themselves as necessity-entrepreneurial business ventures. Although this is not a substantial majority of the PSED II sample, it provides preliminary evidence to reconsider certain assumptions previously held about necessity entrepreneurship.

Moreover, this typology can be applied to understand why certain types of entrepreneurs maybe more likely to engage in a specific sequence of actions over a given time frame (Reynolds et al., 2004; Reynolds, 2006). Particularly, since what an individual does has been found to be the most significant factor influencing the transition from nascency to new firm status, more thorough investigations of behaviors in start-up sequence applying this typology will produce more reliable deductions about the entrepreneurial process.

Although contextual motivation and desired growth strategy are extremely influential in facilitating entry into the start-up process, intrinsic motivation is crucial in directing actions taken to culminate into a new venture as well. Within the PSED II, a well-developed set of 14 items were used to determine the intrinsic motivational emphasis of the nascent entrepreneurs using a five-level response scale regarding the importance of the items, ranging from "no extent" to "a very great extent" (Reynolds & Curtin, 2008). These items can be classified into four indices to measure the nascent entrepreneur's level of autonomy, wealth, status, and respect (Reynolds & Curtin).[5] Autonomy reflects the freedom to adapt work activities and family life. Wealth reflects the importance of financial security, larger personal income, and greater wealth. Status reflects the need for higher recognition and status, fulfilling a personal vision, the creation of new business ideas, and the ability to influence an organization. Respect reflects the importance of respect from friends, establishing a business for one's own children, following family tradition and the example of admired persons. Comparing respondents' individual orientations across the four categories of contextual motivation facilitates the identification of differences on how nascent entrepreneurs are drawn into the firm creation process.

The results of the mean rate for the four dimensions of individual motivation orientation for autonomy, wealth, status, and respect are illustrated in Fig. 3.1. Preliminary analysis utilizing t-tests identifies a few differences among these categories. There is no significant difference between opportunity-small business venture, opportunity-entrepreneurial business ventures, necessity-small business ventures, and necessity-entrepreneurial business ventures in regard to the level of autonomy. Therefore, regardless of the form of contextual motivation a nascent is classified by, all individuals in the PSED II sample are internally motivated by relatively high levels of autonomy

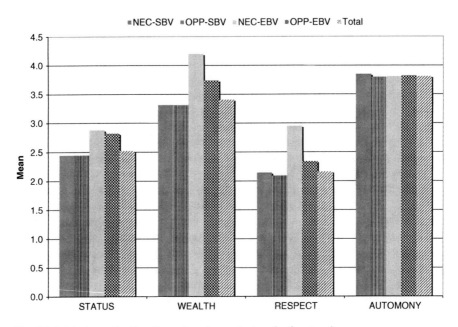

Fig. 3.1 Intrinsic motivation dimensions by context-aspiration typology

The dimension of respect shows a significant difference between necessity-entrepreneurial business ventures and necessity-small business ventures, opportunity-small business ventures as well as opportunity-entrepreneurial business ventures. Additionally, necessity-small business ventures, opportunity-small and entrepreneurial business ventures have similar levels of respect. It appears that necessity-entrepreneurial business ventures are internally motivated by higher levels of respect than their counterparts.

For necessity- and opportunity-entrepreneurial business ventures there is a significant difference to necessity- and opportunity-small business ventures in regard to status. Thus, it seems that entrepreneurial business ventures are motivated more by status than small business ventures, regardless of whether they are being pulled in by an opportunity or pushed out by lack of better work options to start a new business. Similarly, opportunity- and necessity-entrepreneurial business ventures show a significant difference to opportunity- and necessity-small business ventures in regard to wealth as an internal motivator. Again, we see a similar difference between entrepreneurial business ventures and small business ventures when considering wealth as an internal motivator. In particular, necessity-entrepreneurial business ventures are more highly motivated by wealth creation.

Furthermore, examining the context-aspiration categories by demographic variables in the PSED II we can make further inferences about the structures of these groups, and conclude that they are not homogenous. In general, men are twice as likely as women to attempt to start a business. The distribution of sex among these four groups in the PSED II shows that men are about three times as likely as women to pursue a necessity-entrepreneurial business venture and necessity-small business venture. Furthermore, men are about twice as likely as women to pursue an opportunity-entrepreneurial business venture. The least difference is found among opportunity-small business ventures, where men are about one and a half times more likely than women to pursue this initiative. That data provides evidence to support that men are more likely to undertake entrepreneurial initiatives, with the most pronounced difference being for necessity-entrepreneurial business ventures.

Analysis of the context-aspiration typology by gender in regard to personal orientations toward entrepreneurship shows that autonomy and wealth lead as major influences for both sexes regardless of the contextual form (see Fig. 3.2). Among necessity-entrepreneurial business ventures both men and women are motivated mostly by wealth, but women demonstrate a higher average on this measure than men. Among opportunity-entrepreneurial business ventures men are motivated equally by autonomy and wealth, whereas women are motivated slightly more by autonomy than by wealth. Among opportunity-small business ventures, it is again autonomy as the primary force within both sexes that is influential, with wealth coming a close second among men. Finally, for necessity-small business ventures it is again autonomy with a significantly more influential impact both for men and among the dimensions of intrinsic motivations toward entrepreneurship. It seems that status and respect have a minimal affect among all context-aspirational forms for both genders.

Ethnic class has been identified as a factor which influences environmental perception and firm growth strategy (Harvey, 2005; Light & Rosenstein, 1995; Reynolds & White, 1997). Thus, in order to further understand the propensity to engage in the entrepreneurial process, comparisons will be made between

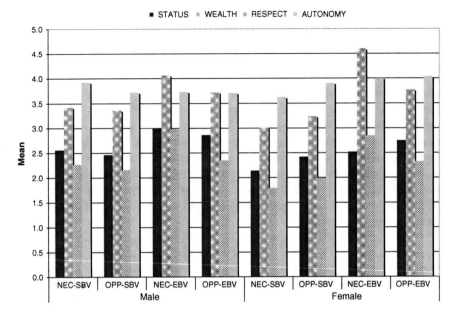

Fig. 3.2 Personal motivation dimensions by sex and contextual motivation

Whites, Blacks, and Hispanics to identify differences among the categories of contextual motivation and growth aspirations.[6] Whites and minorities are equally likely to attempt to establish a necessity-entrepreneurial business venture. In contrast, Whites are twice as likely as all minorities to pursue opportunity-entrepreneurial business ventures. Similarly, Whites are about two and a half times more likely to initiate activity to realize a necessity-small business venture. Finally, among opportunity-small business ventures, Whites are about three times as likely to pursue this activity as minorities.

If the context-aspiration typology is further examined by ethnic class, we find more distinct differences between the dimensions of intrinsic motivations (see Fig. 3.3). Among necessity-entrepreneurial business ventures, all classes are motivated highly by wealth creation, with Hispanics scoring highest on this measure. Among opportunity-entrepreneurial business ventures, Hispanics are more highly motivated by autonomy, and Whites and Blacks are equally motivated by wealth creation and autonomy. Among opportunity-small business ventures, Whites are highly motivated by autonomy, Blacks and Hispanics are highly motivated by autonomy and then wealth creation. Finally, for necessity-small business ventures, Whites, Blacks, and Hispanics, are motivated most by autonomy and then wealth creation.

In summary, men pursue three out of four necessity-entrepreneurial business ventures. Overall, nascent men are highly motivated by wealth creation, followed, respectively, by autonomy, respect, and status. Women who engage under this context express a greater emphasis on wealth creation than their

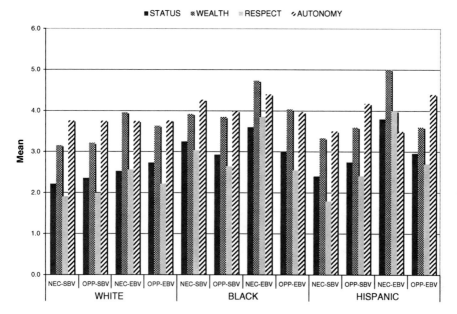

Fig. 3.3 Intrinsic motivation dimensions by race, context-aspiration typology

male counterparts. Additionally, among minorities there is a greater emphasis on wealth creation than Whites. Men are also three out of four necessity-small business ventures. Men rate autonomy, wealth, status, and respect correspondingly to their female counterparts. The data additionally illustrates higher mean scores for men than for women for these intrinsic motivations within this category of context-aspiration typology. Moreover, it appears that Blacks under this motivational context value autonomy more than Whites and Hispanics.

Similar patterns are found in the intrinsic motivations of opportunity-small and entrepreneurial business ventures when compared overall (see Fig. 3.1), but there are differences demographically. Two out of three opportunity-entrepreneurial business ventures are initiated by men, and demonstrate an emphasis on wealth creation and autonomy, with autonomy more highly emphasized among Hispanics. Men initiate slightly more than one in two opportunity-small business ventures, yet women rated autonomy more highly than men within this category as a valued orientation. Also, minorities in general rate autonomy on average more highly than Whites within this category.

Finally, an examination of the context-aspiration typology for the first follow-up of PSED II shows the distribution of outcomes for the four types of nascent ventures. The majority of all start-up forms are continuing efforts toward establishing a new firm. Moreover, after completing a chi-square test, we find that the form of start-up and outcome for the first follow-up are independent constructs ($p = 0.49$). Data from subsequent waves may reveal

Table 3.3 Outcome status by context-aspiration typology

Typology category		Outcome after fist follow-up			Total
		New firm	Start-up continues	Quit	
Necessity-entrepreneurial business ventures	Count	3	8	4	15
	% within category	20.0	53.3	26.7	100.0
Opportunity-entrepreneurial business ventures	Count	18	113	31	162
	% within category	11.1	69.8	19.1	100.0
Opportunity-small business ventures	Count	87	380	146	613
	% within category	14.2	62.0	23.8	100.0
Necessity-small business ventures	Count	10	64	26	100
	% within category	10.0	64.0	26.0	100.0
Total	Count	118	565	207	890
	% within total	13.3	63.5	23.3	100.0

different relationships among the context-aspiration categories and outcome status (Table 3.3).

3.6 Conclusion

Entrepreneurship is also a major career option for millions of Americans (Reynolds & Curtin, 2008). Yet, little is understood about how individuals enter the firm creation process. Studying individual traits of entrepreneurs fails to provide information on the environmental context within which entrepreneurs interpret and make sense of their actions (Kalantaridis, 2004). People are motivated to start businesses by many factors, both at the individual level and at the macro-level. This chapter has elaborated on how contextual motivation and growth aspiration attract different forms of entrepreneurs, who are influenced by different intrinsic orientations at varying degrees.

As Van De Ven (1993) argued, "the study of entrepreneurship is deficient if it focuses exclusively on the characteristics and behaviors of individual entrepreneurs, on the one hand, and if it treats the social, economic, and political factors influencing entrepreneurship as external demographic statistics, on the other hand" (p. 211). The PSED II affords scholars a unique opportunity to bridge this gap. Future waves of PSED II data can be analyzed using the context-aspiration typology, a measure of the perceived conditions in which the nascent entrepreneur functions and his/her desired growth strategy, to understand how factors vary in significance upon the specific aspect of the new venture development process the typology intends to address.

In sum, this chapter has facilitated the creation of a common language in which to understand different environmental and strategic forces under which nascent entrepreneurs operate and in turn, possibly impact the likelihood of new firm founding. This is one proposed typology to understand the entrepreneurial process from the macro-level, but other opportunities exist. Context can be conceptualized in many forms. The notion of context can include individual contexts (e.g., psychological traits, background characteristics, cognitive schemas), spatial contexts (countries, states, regions, communities), temporal contexts (history), organizational contexts (U-form, M-form, network form), and social/cultural/economic contexts (ethnic groups, social classes, economic sectors, cultural logics) (Thornton, 1999). This chapter has elaborated on nascent environmental motivation and nascent organizational strategic context as a means to understand the gestation phase of the entrepreneurial process. Future research can integrate any of the discussed contexts to develop even richer understandings of how individuals enter the firm creation process.

Notes

1. A stochastic process with a finite number of states in which the probability of occurrence of a future state is conditional only upon the current state; past states are inconsequential.
2. Variable AT5 and BT5 can also be utilized to infer growth aspirations. This variable provides a quantitative count of expected jobs within the prospective new venture within five years.
3. Seven percent of PSED II cases classified themselves as a combination of both opportunity and necessity entrepreneurship and were excluded from calculations related to they contextual motivation typology.
4. Individuals interested in applying the contextual motivation typology should pool data from the United States Entrepreneurial Assessment 2004, (ICPSR study 4688), which was developed based on PSED I, in order to generate more reliable inferences.
5. Factor analysis was used to identify the items suitable for four indices. All Chronbach alpha levels were greater than 0.65.
6. To facilitate analysis for the class of minorities, Blacks and Hispanics were grouped together in the class of minorities to minimize degree of differences in calculations.

References

Acs, Z. J., & Audretsch, D. B. (2003). *Handbook of entrepreneurship research: An interdisciplinary survey and introduction.* Norwell, MA: Kluwer.
Acs, Z. J. (2006). How is entrepreneurship good for economic growth? *Innovations, 1*(1), 97–107.
Aldrich, H. E., & Martinez, M. A. (2001). Many are called, but few are chosen: An evolutionary perspective for the study of entrepreneurship. *Entrepreneurship Theory & Practice, 25*(4), 41.
Bruno, A. V., & Tyebjee, T. T. (1982). The environment for entrepreneurship. In C. A. Kent, D. L. Sexton, & K. H. Vesper (Eds.), *Encyclopedia of entrepreneurship* (pp. 288–306). Englewood Cliffs, NJ: Prentice-Hall.
Bhola, R., Verheul, I., Thurik, A. R., & Grilo, I. (2006). *Explaining engagement levels of necessity and opportunity entrepreneurs.* EIM Report Series. Retrieved January 10, 2007, from http://hdl.handle.net/1765/9705

Carland, J. W., Hoy, F., Boulton, W. R., & Carland, J. A. C. (1984). Differentiating entrepreneurs from small business owners: A conceptualization. *Academy of Management Review, 9*(2), 354–359.

Churchill, N. C., & Lewis, V. L. (1983). The five stages of small business growth. *Harvard Business Review, 61*(3), 30.

Davidsson, P. (2004). *Researching entrepreneurship.* New York: Springer.

Davidsson, P. (2005). *Nascent entrepreneurship: Empirical studies and developments.* Hanover, MA: Now Publishers.

Delmar, F., & Davidsson, P. (2000). Where do they come from? Prevalence and characteristics of nascent entrepreneurs. *Entrepreneurship & Regional Development, 12*(1), 1–23.

Gartner, W. B. (1988). "Who is an entrepreneur?" is the wrong question. *American Journal of Small Business, 12*(4), 11–32.

Gartner, W. B., Shaver, K. G., Carter, N. M., & Reynolds, P. D. (Eds.). (2004). *Handbook of entrepreneurial dynamics: The process of business creation.* Thousand Oaks, CA: Sage.

Gnyawali, D. R., & Fogel, D. S. (1994). Environments for entrepreneurship development: Key dimensions and research implications. *Entrepreneurship Theory & Practice, 18*(4), 43–62.

Harvey, A. M. (2005). Becoming entrepreneurs: Intersections of race, class, and gender at the black beauty salon.*Gender & Society, 19*(6), 789–808.

Hechavarria, D., & Reynolds, P. D. (2008, August). *Cultural norms and business start-ups: The impact of national values on necessity and opportunity entrepreneurs.* Paper presented at the Academy of Management, Anaheim, CA.

Human, S. E., & Matthews, C. H. (2004). Future expectations for the new business. In W. B. Gartner, K. G. Shaver, N. M. Carter, & P. D. Reynolds (Eds.), *Handbook of entrepreneurial dynamics: The process of business creation* (pp. 386–399). Thousand Oaks, CA: Sage.

Kalantaridis, C. (2004). *Understanding the entrepreneur: An institutionalist perspective.* Burlington, VT: Ashgate Publishing Limited.

Learned, K. E. (1992). What happened before the organization? A model of organization formation. *Entrepreneurship Theory & Practice, 17*(1), 39–48.

Light, I., & Rosenstein, C. (1995). *Race, ethnicity, and entrepreneurship in urban America.* New York: Aldine De Gruyter.

Low, M. B., & Abrahamson, E. (1997). Movements, bandwagons, and clones: Industry evolution and the entrepreneurial process. *Journal of Business Venturing, 12*(6), 435.

Low, M. B., & MacMillan, I. C. (1988). Entrepreneurship: Past research and future challenges. *Journal of Management, 14*(2), 139–161.

Matthews, C. H., & Scott, S. G. (1995). Uncertainty and planning in small and entrepreneurial firms: An empirical assessment. *Journal of Small Business Management, 33*(4), 34–52.

Naffziger, D. W., Hornsby, J. S., & Kuratko, D. F. (1994). A proposed research model of entrepreneurial motivation. *Entrepreneurship Theory & Practice, 18*(3), 29–42.

Reynolds, P. D. (1994). Autonomous firm dynamics and economic growth in the United States, 1986–1990. *Regional Studies, 28*(4), 429.

Reynolds, P. D. (2004). Overview: The entrepreneurial context and environment. In W. B. Gartner, K. G. Shaver, N. M. Carter, & P. D. Reynolds (Eds.), *Handbook of entrepreneurial dynamics: The process of business creation* (pp. 403–411). Thousand Oaks, CA: Sage.

Reynolds, P. D. (1997). Who starts new firms?—Preliminary explorations of firms-in-gestation. *Small Business Economics, 9*(5), 449.

Reynolds, P. D. (2006). United States entrepreneurial assessment, 2004 (ICPSR04688-v1) [Computer file]. Miami, FL: Paul Reynolds, Florida International University [producer]. Ann Arbor, MI: Inter-university Consortium for Political and Social Research [distributor], 2007-06-27.

Reynolds, P. D. (2007). *Entrepreneurship in the United States: The future is now.* New York: Springer.

Reynolds, P. D., Camp, S. M., Bygrave, W. D., Autio, E., & Hay, M. (2001). *Global entrepreneurship monitor executive report.* Executive Report, Babson College/Ewing Marion Kauffman Foundation, London Business School.

Reynolds, P. D., Carter, N. M., Gartner, W. B., & Greene, P. G. (2004). The prevalence of nascent entrepreneurs in the United States: Evidence from the panel study of entrepreneurial dynamics. *Small Business Economics, 23*(4), 263–284.

Reynolds, P. D., & Curtin, R. (2008). Business creation in the United States: Panel study of entrepreneurial dynamics II initial assessment. *Foundations and Trends in Entrepreneurship, 4*(3), 155.

Reynolds, P. D., & Hechavarria, D. (2007). Global entrepreneurship monitor (GEM) adult population survey data set, 1998–2003 (ICPSR20320-v1) [Computer file]. Miami, FL: Florida International University, Entrepreneurial Research Institute [producer], Ann Arbor, MI: Inter-university Consortium for Political and Social Research [distributor], 2007-10-30.

Reynolds, P. D., & White, S. (1997). *The entrepreneurial process: Economic growth, men, women, and minorities.* Westport, CT: Quorum.

Rosa, P. (1998). Entrepreneurial processes of business cluster formation and growth by "habitual" entrepreneurs. *Entrepreneurship Theory and Practice, 22*(4), 43.

Shane, S., Locke, E. A., & Collins, C. J. (2003). Entrepreneurial motivation. *Human Resource Management Review, 13*(2), 257–279.

Shaver, K. G., & Scott, L. R. (1991). Person, process, choice: The psychology of new venture creation. *Entrepreneurship Theory & Practice, 16*(2), 23–45.

Solymossy, E., & Hisrich, R. D. (2000). Entrepreneurial dimensions: The relationship of individual, venture, and environmental factors to success. *Entrepreneurship Theory & Practice, 24*(4), 79.

Thornton, P. H. (1999). The sociology of entrepreneurship. *The Annual Review of Sociology, 25*, 19–46.

Ucbasaran, D., Westhead, P., & Wright, M. (2001). The focus of entrepreneurial research: Contextual and process issues. *Entrepreneurship Theory & Practice, 25*(4), 57.

Van De Ven, H. (1993). The development of an infrastructure for entrepreneurship. *Journal of Business Venturing, 8*(3), 211–230.

Chapter 4
Family Background and Influence on Nascent Entrepreneurs

Charles H. Matthews, Mark T. Schenkel, and Diana M. Hechavarria

4.1 Introduction

While extant research suggests that entrepreneurial behavior stems from multiple causes ranging from nature to nurture (White, Thornhill, & Hampson, 2007), there is consistent anecdotal and empirical evidence that one's family business background continues to play a role. It seems somewhat counterintuitive that while family-owned and privately held ventures are the dominant business forms in the United States and much of the world, there remains a paucity of research surrounding them. Estimates consistently suggest that over 80% of all businesses in the United States are closely held family businesses, employ over 60% of the U.S. workforce, and contribute to over 60% of the nation's gross domestic product (GDP) (Astrachan & Shanker, 2003). Family-owned businesses are the dominant business types in Australia, Brazil, Canada, Chile, Finland, Germany, Italy, Sweden, and the United Kingdom (Family Firm Institute, 2005).

The lack of focused research is even more prominent when examining the intersection of nascent entrepreneurial ventures and closely held ventures. About one-third of all start-ups are based on people related by marriage or kinship (Ruef, Aldrich, & Carter, 2003). This figure illustrates how prominent a role the family plays in American society as an institution. Indeed, Muntean (2008) in examining the dearth in family enterprise research calls for a better understanding of how family relationships influence behavior in these firms. She specifically notes that, "The greater challenge, perhaps, lies in breaking through cultural biases and entrenched paradigms across disciplines that notoriously underestimate the role of the family in economic enterprise and organizational behavior more generally" (p. 19). Similarly, Aldrich and Cliff (2003) have suggested the need for more research focusing on how family systems affect the new venture creation, decision, and resource mobilization process.

C.H. Matthews (✉)
College of Business, Department of Management, University of Cincinnati, 501 Carl H. Linder Hall, Cincinnati, OH 45221-0165, USA
e-mail: charles.matthews@uc.edu

We concur with these authors and propose that a better understanding of the role of family background, especially in economic enterprise, can be gained by examining the role of family background and all its intricacies in the nascent entrepreneurial process. Accordingly, the purpose of this chapter is to explore family background variables in the Panel Study of Entrepreneurial Dynamics II (PSED II) as a framework for further exploring issues associated with the new venture creation efforts. The first of these comparisons focuses on the level of consciousness with respect to the importance of family life, tradition, and role models reflected in the decision to become an entrepreneur. We then consider the degree to which family is utilized or relied upon as a primary source of funding in the early stages of the new venture creation process, exploring in particular, the extent to which attention is turned toward attracting sources of funding external to family. Third, the extent to which "family"-based motivations and venture structure influences future sales expectations, job growth expectations, and the intensity of investment in terms of both dollars and hours is explored. Finally, potential differences between men and women with respect to family legacy variables by family background and family business work experience are also explored.

4.2 Literature Review of Family Background Measures

While entrepreneurship and family business research streams have tended to develop along two distinctive paths, considerable value exists in examining the intersection of these closely related economic phenomena. For example, Rogoff and Heck (2003) suggest the two paths share three common foci: (1) in each, business is the dominant system (even over the family system); (2) each emphasizes traditional business dimensions; and (3) each focuses on the temporal business stages and transitions between the start-up, growth, maturity, and exit phases. These authors go on to suggest an operational definition of an entrepreneur as one simply evolving toward a "business owner" (p. 560). Given the strong propensity of nascent enterprise and small business ventures to be family-owned and operated and the widespread emphasis on business performance, such an operational definition may facilitate a better understanding of the role family background plays in the development of nascent enterprise and small business ventures.

Overall, the small, entrepreneurial, and family business literatures provide support for theoretical perspectives focusing on the direct relationship between the presence of family/entrepreneurial role models (Brockhaus & Horwitz, 1986; Dyer, 1992; Dyer & Handler, 1994; Scott & Twomey, 1988; Shapero & Sokol, 1982); the business-ownership perception and role models as indirect influencers on career preferences or expectations (Katz, 1992; Krueger, 1993; Matthews & Moser, 1995, 1996); and the family embeddedness of most entrepreneurial activities (Aldrich & Cliff, 2003). These studies collectively suggest that positive impressions of and encouragement from family and social groups may indirectly influence entrepreneurial behaviors through their direct influence on attitudes toward those behaviors (Matthews & Human, 2004). Family members often represent strong ties that provide emotional support for nascent entrepreneurs, yet sometimes they are not in the position to supply the start-up capital that is necessary during the launch phases.

When it comes to understanding the acquisition of microfinance at the nascent venture level, there is evidence that suggests strong relational ties with family members do not necessarily translate into financial support for the prospective venture (Aldrich & Ruef, 2006). Nationally representative data, as well as qualitative research, show that with the exception of spouses, only founders from a handful of ethnic minority groups could count on much financial support from family members (Aldrich, Elam, & Reese, 1996). Therefore, it is of interest to further investigate the sources of start-up capital within a family business at the gestation phase of the firm's life cycle.

4.3 PSED II Variables on Family Background

The involvement of family members or relatives in a start-up is of considerable interest for issues related to policy as well as for understanding the dynamics of business creation (Reynolds & Curtin, 2008). Ten items in the PSED II directly assess the family background influence variables across three dimensions. Five items examine the aspect of family role models; two items assess family financial support (across two time-periods); and three items look at family life and legacy. Table 4.1 lists the wording for these variables.

In addition to the items listed in this table, there are other items which may have both a direct and indirect impact on the role family background plays in nascent entrepreneurial activity. For example, in addition to the family financial support item listed above, the PSED II contains items regarding financing sources from credit cards, financial institutions, and second mortgages.

In addition to financing, a number of items examine the nascent entrepreneur's motivation to achieve a higher position in society, be respected by friends, have considerable freedom to adapt his/her own approach to work, give self, spouse, and children financial security, follow the example of a person he/she admired, earn a larger personal income, achieve something and get recognition for it, develop an idea for a product, have a chance to build great wealth or a very high income, fulfill a personal vision, and have the power to greatly influence an organization. These additional financing and motivation items are discussed elsewhere in this volume and their full assessment is beyond the scope of this chapter. However, future research may want to more fully consider how they may act directly or indirectly or in combination with the family background variables.

Table 4.1 Wording for family background items

Item number	Family history and role model items
AZ6	Was your mother born in the U.S.?
AZ7	Was your father born in the U.S.?
AZ8	Did your parents ever work for themselves or run their own businesses, alone or together?
AZ9	Did you ever work full time or part time for your parents' business?
AP11	Many of your relatives have started new businesses.
Item number	**Family financial support**
AQ5 Wave "A"	What is the dollar amount provided that came from personal loans received by (you/[NAME]) from (your/their) family members and relatives (before the business was registered as a [C1])?
BQ5 Wave "B"	What is the total dollar amount provided that came from personal loans received by (you/[NAME]) from family members or relatives, (including the [$AQ5] you reported last year, before the new business was registered as a [AC1/C1])?
Item number	**Family life and legacy**
	Please indicate the extent to which the following were important to you for establishing this new business.
AW2	To have greater flexibility for your personal and family life.
AW3	To continue a family tradition.
AW8	To build a business your children can inherit.

4.4 Preliminary Analysis of Family Background Variables

Within the PSED II only about 5% of the sample cited that some aspect of familial circumstances motivated their entrepreneurial undertaking, when they were asked, "Why do you want to start this new business?" (item numbers AA2a and AA2b) along with "What are the one or two main opportunities that prompted you to start this new business?" (AA5a and AA5b). Yet, about 28% of nascent enterprises within PSED II are pursued by spousal pair teams and family teams who control at least 50% of the firm. This finding is interesting because it suggests that while self-report motivation stemming from familial ties is lower than would be expected, entrepreneurs may consciously underestimate the role of familial influences. Thus, future research might more fully consider to what extent entrepreneurs are actually aware of the degree and nature of familial role model influences on motivating nascent entrepreneurial interest, as well as on projected outcomes such as expected sales and employee growth, and expectations for success. Longitudinally, it would be of interest as to how much of a relationship, in turn, familial background ultimately bears with actual outcomes and measures of performance over time.

Table 4.2 depicts the type of venture pursued by ownership category. Of the total sample indicating their business type ($n = 1,211$), it appears that independent start-ups are the majority of business type choice by all ownership categories. Looking more closely at type of ventures, independent start-up is the

4 Family Background and Influence on Nascent Entrepreneurs   55

Table 4.2 Business creation type by start-up team ownership structure

	Sole proprietorship	Spousal pair	Family team	Nonfamily team	All
Number of cases	660	267	94	190	1,211
Independent start-up (%)	84.1	80.1	81.9	80.0	82.4
Purchase or takeover (%)	2.1	4.5	2.1	4.7	3.1
Franchise (%)	2.6	3.0	4.3	4.7	3.1
Multi-level marketing (%)	5.5	6.0	1.1	1.1	4.5
Existing business sponsored (%)	5.8	6.4	10.6	9.5	6.9
Total (%)	100.0	100.0	100.0	100.0	100.0

dominant form with 82.4%, followed by existing/sponsored business at 6.9%, multi-level marketing at 4.5%, franchise at 3.1%, and purchase/takeover at 3.1%. Furthermore, looking more closely at the business creation type and start-up team ownership structure, a similar pattern emerges with the exception of family teams (i.e., where family membership is greater than half of the total ownership) and nonfamily teams. Sole proprietors report 84.1% independent start-up, 2.1% purchase/takeover, 2.6% franchise, 5.5% multi-level marketing, and 5.8% existing/sponsored business. Spousal pairs report 80.1% independent start-up, 4.5% purchase/takeover, 3.0% franchise, 6.0% multi-level marketing, and 6.4% existing/sponsored business.

Family teams where family membership is greater than one half of the total ownership report 81.9% independent start-up, 2.1% purchase/takeover, 4.3% franchise, 1.1% multi-level marketing, and 10.6% existing/sponsored business. Nonfamily teams report 80.0% independent start-up, 4.7% purchase/takeover, 4.7% franchise, 1.1% multi-level marketing, and 9.5% existing/sponsored business. While independent start-up is clearly the dominant form within each start-up team ownership structure, the need for future research examining the differences within the other categories is indicated. For example, after independent start-up, why are the family teams where family membership is greater than one half of the total ownership structure more inclined toward existing business and less inclined toward multi-level marketing, franchise, or purchase/take-over than spousal pair?

Data for family microfinancing provide information about support provided in the early stages of the business creation process. The average, total amount of funds, and proportion of total funds provided from seven sources prior to the first detailed interview are presented in Table 4.3. For this preliminary analysis, the sample is not weighted. The average of all the means for funds loaned by family to all start-ups is $3,577. Of all informal funding sources (i.e., personal, family, friends, credit cards, personal bank loans, asset-backed funds, and others), about 8% (including outliers)[1] and about 30% (excluding outliers) are contributed by family members to the nascent start-up before the nascent venture is registered as a legal entity. Overall, as seen in Table 4.3 the traditional

Table 4.3 Descriptive statistics for family financial support variables (before being registered as a legal entity)

Start-up team ownership	Personal funds	Family funds	Friends funds	Credit cards	Personal bank loans	Asset-backed loans	Other	Total money by Wave A
Average amounts								
Sole proprietorship	$18,586	$3,694	$1,974	$698	$8,602	$7,696	$473	$40,655
Spousal pair	$15,923	$1,397	$415	$736	$6,245	$689	$0	$24,536
Family team	$34,168	$4,905	$199	$893	$20,728	$5,721	$5	$65,146
Nonfamily team	$31,674	$5,596	$2,824	$2,478	$4,511	$12,512	$3,474	$60,996
All nascent enterprises	$21,287	$3,577	$1,622	$995	$8,405	$6,741	$799	$42,197
Total for sample								
Sole proprietorship	$11,783,290	$2,397,294	$1,286,812	$457,397	$5,600,200	$5,040,905	$307,000	$26,872,898
Spousal pair	$4,076,208	$365,950	$109,050	$194,250	$1,648,600	$182,000	$0	$6,575,733
Family team	$3,143,450	$456,170	$18,515	$83,975	$1,948,454	$537,780	$500	$6,188,844
Nonfamily team	$5,796,367	$1,029,735	$519,627	$455,950	$830,100	$2,314,700	$642,725	$11,589,204
All nascent enterprises	$24,799,315	$4,249,149	$1,934,004	$1,191,572	$10,027,354	$8,075,385	$950,225	$51,226,679
Percent of total								
Sole proprietorship	43.8%	8.9%	4.8%	1.7%	20.8%	18.8%	1.1%	100.0%
Spousal pair	62.0%	5.6%	1.7%	3.0%	25.1%	2.8%	0.0%	100.0%
Family team	50.8%	7.4%	0.3%	1.4%	31.5%	8.7%	0.0%	100.0%
Nonfamily team	50.0%	8.9%	4.5%	3.9%	7.2%	20.0%	5.5%	100.0%
All nascent enterprises	48.4%	8.3%	3.8%	2.3%	19.6%	15.8%	1.9%	100.0%

friends, family, and founders, including credit cards, account for 63% of the funding sources for this sample, with personal funds accounting for 48.4%.

Furthermore, the data highlight considerable variance in the amount of funding received by the nascent venture from family members (Table 4.3). For this sample, the sum of all funds contributed by family to start-ups is about $4.2 million dollars. However, when asked about the largest investment a family member made some nascent ventures reported receiving as much as $1.4 million in start-up loans from family, while others as little as $12. Of the total 1,214 nascent ventures, 1,016 (83.7%) reported receiving no funding from family sources, while 172 (14.2%) reported receiving family funding (26 nascent ventures did not reply). In sum, these data appear to confirm the findings of earlier work (Aldrich & Ruef, 2006) suggesting that microfinancing contributions received from family members during the earliest stages of new venture creation are modest (i.e., about 14.2%) and strong relational ties with family members do not *necessarily* translate into financial support.

With regard to the total dollar amounts, when asked, "What is the dollar amount provided that came from personal loans received by (you/[NAME]) from (your/their) family members and relatives before the business was registered?" the amount loaned reported is $4.25 million. When asked, "What is the dollar amount of the debts that are in personal loans from spouses, family members, or other kin of the start-up team of the new business after it was registered?" the amount reported is $69,000. This difference is amplified in part by one venture receiving a $1.4 million loan before the firm was registered. Even without this outlier, however, the amount of funding from family members prior to firm registration is noteworthy.

This raises an interesting possibility. Specifically, it may be that the longer the nascent venture matures while it gestates, the more likely it gains legitimacy in the eyes of stakeholders beyond the entrepreneur's family. As a result, this finding may suggest that nascent entrepreneurs quickly turn their attention toward securing more formal or nonfamily funding sources to replace family funding fairly early on in the stages of the new venture creation process. From Table 4.3,[2] we see that approximately 37% of the total funds for start-up come from personal bank loans, asset-backed funds, and others.

Exploring the differences among type of start-up in Table 4.3 further illustrates the dynamic role of family microfinancing. Nonfamily teams and family teams controlling greater than 50% ownership received the largest amount on average from family financing, followed by sole proprietors and spousal pair teams. Yet, sole proprietors had the largest amount in total contributed to their start-ups (about $2 million from family sources).[3] These findings lend additional support to the notion that nascent entrepreneurs turn their attention toward securing more formal or nonfamily funding sources to augment family funding in the early stages of the new venture creation process.

Additionally, analysis of variables related to personal orientation toward entrepreneurship and family history/role models is included in Tables 4.4 and 4.5. Overall, 52% of nascent entrepreneurs had parents who owned a business.

Table 4.4 Descriptive statistics for family history and legacy variables

Name	Label	N	Min	Max	Mean	Std Dev.
AP11	Many relatives started new businesses	1,209	1	5	3.14	1.163
AW2	Greater flexibility in life	1,214	1	5	3.71	1.269
AW3	Continue family tradition	1,214	1	5	1.73	1.276
AW8	Build business which kids can inherit	1,214	1	5	2.53	1.527
	Five-point scale: 1 = No extent, 5 = A great extent.					
AZ6	Father born in U.S.	1,033	0	1	0.90	0.297
AZ7	Mother born in U.S.	1,037	0	1	0.90	0.295
AZ8	Parents ran own business	1,038	0	1	0.53	0.500
	Dichotomous: 0 = No, 1 = Yes.					
AZ9	Ever worked for parent's business	542	0	2	0.88	0.871
	0 = No, 1 = Full-time, 2 = Part-time					

Table 4.5 Means for family legacy variables by family background and gender[1]

	Many relatives started new businesses	Greater flexibility in life	To continue family tradition	Build business which kids can inherit
Variable name	AP11	AW2	AW3	AW8
Parents ran own business[2]				
Men	2.94	3.62*	1.83	2.68***
Women	2.92	3.82*	1.74	2.29***
Total[3]	2.93***	3.70	1.80*	2.53
Parents did not have a business[2]				
Men	3.35	3.63**	1.72*	2.62*
Women	3.40	3.88**	1.55*	2.40*
Total[3]	3.37***	3.72	1.66*	2.54
All parents[2]				
Men	3.14	3.63***	1.78*	2.65***
Women	3.14	3.85***	1.65*	2.34***
Total	3.14	3.71	1.73	2.53

[1]*t*-tests were analyzed between gender.
[2]*t*-tests are conducted between gender in regard to motivation by family background.
[3]*t*-test is conducted between individuals who had parents that ran a business, and those who did not in regard to motivation.
*$p<.10$ **$p<.05$ ***$p<.005$.
All responses on a five-point scale: 1 = To no extent; 5 = To a very great extent.

Also, among nascent entrepreneurs whose parents owned a business, 55% worked in some capacity for their parents venture. Overall, half of the active nascents had parents involved in self-employment or as a business owner; from one-quarter to one-third worked for their parents business (Reynolds & Curtin, 2008). Additionally, when asked about the community in which the nascent entrepreneur now lives, 38% agree or strongly agree that many of their relatives have started new businesses. Finally, the majority of the sample is comprised of individuals who were born in the United States. Only about 9% of the sample had a parent who was not born in the United States.

From a motivational standpoint, nascent entrepreneurs rate greater flexibility in life through the autonomy gained by starting a new venture as a key factor. It also appears that building a business that can be inherited by their children is moderately rated as a personal motivation. By contrast, continuing a family tradition is reported as not as highly motivating to nascents in the entrepreneurial process as one may have assumed, despite the plethora of anecdotal observations suggesting the contrary. This may have implications for applied family business research addressing succession planning. For example, at what point does building a business that the children can inherit become more important than going into business to achieve greater flexibility in life. Also, is there a difference between building a business that children can inherit versus building a business in which the succeeding generation can take over or succeed the prior generation?

Moreover, means comparison tests among males and females reveal some slight differences in these personal orientation dimensions that reflect aspects of family context. For instance, when considering only those whose parents ran their own business, men and women differed significantly in their motivations for greater flexibility in life and building a business which their kids can inherit, but not in continuing the family tradition. By contrast, when considering cases where parents did not have a business, as well as when considering such differences across all parents in general, significant differences were observed across men and women for all three motivations. Furthermore, on average, men rate building a business which children can inherit higher than women. By comparison, on average, women rate greater flexibility in life more highly than men. Both groups score similarly when rating the kinship participation in starting a new business. It is not altogether surprising that women, more so than men, seek flexibility in life, especially given women's continuing dual roles in business and family rearing. Also, with regard to many relatives who started a business, men and woman did not differ significantly.

Also, as can be seen in Table 4.5, for those with a family background in business, men and women both report a stronger desire to continue a family tradition than those not reporting a family background. However, when asked the extent to which greater flexibility for your personal and family life is important to you for establishing this new business, men and women without a family background responded it was more so than for those with a family background. This may suggest that having a family background may lead to a relatively more constrained attitude toward entrepreneurism as a career path than previously considered.

Overall, for respondents who worked full time for their parents, men and women did not differ significantly on any of the four dimensions. For respondents who worked part-time for their parents, men and women differed significantly only when it came to having greater flexibility in life. For those respondents who did not work for their parents, men and women differed significantly for both "many relatives started a new business" and "build a business kids can inherit". On the other hand, working part-time for a parent's business appears to suggest that "greater flexibility in life" is important as a root factor for establishing this new business as reflected in Table 4.6. In contrast, in the case of not working for a parent's business, it appears that a core motivation for building this business is so that the founder's kids can inherit it someday. Furthermore, on average, men with full time experience working for their parent's business give higher ratings to "building a business that provides an opportunity to continue the family tradition and the potential for children to inherit it" when compared with men with only part-time or no experience working for their parents. By comparison, women having part-time experience working for their parents give a higher preference for "greater flexibility in life" than men.

Table 4.6 Means for family legacy variables by family business work experience and gender[1]

	Many relatives started new businesses	Greater flexibility in life	To continue family tradition	Build business which kids can inherit
Variable name	AP11	AW2	AW3	AW8
Worked full time for parents[2]				
Men	2.77	3.82	2.02	2.83
Women	2.56	3.97	1.94	2.44
Total[3]	2.72***	3.85	2.00**	2.73**
Worked part time for parents[2]				
Men	2.74	3.44**	1.84	2.73
Women	2.93	3.94**	1.79	2.47
Total[3]	2.81***	3.62	1.82**	2.64**
Did not work for parents[2]				
Men	3.23*	3.64	1.68	2.53**
Women	3.00*	3.72	1.67	2.16**
Total	3.12	3.68	1.68	2.35
All respondents[2]				
Men	2.94	3.62***	1.83*	2.68***
Women	2.92	3.82***	1.74*	2.29***
Total[3]	2.93***	3.70	1.80***	2.53**

[1] t-tests were analyzed between genders
[2] t-tests were conducted between genders in regard to motivation by family background
[3] t-test was conducted between individuals who had parents that ran a business, and those who did not in regard to motivation.
*$p<.10$ **$p<.05$ ***$p<.005$
All responses on a five-point scale: 1 = To no extent; 5 = To a very great extent.

4.5 Family Teams, Family Background and New Firm Status

Within the entire PSED II sample ($n = 1211$), a little over half, 54%, are sole proprietorship start-ups; 22% are comprised of spousal pair teams; about 8% are comprised of family teams where family membership is greater than one half of the total ownership; and about 16% are nonfamily start-up teams.

Among the nascent start-up ventures, about 55% indicated that they worked either part- or full-time in their parent's business, while 45% indicated not working in the family business. Examining the start-up team ownership structure, of the sole proprietors, about 32% worked part-time while 21% worked full-time; of the spousal pairs, 33% worked part-time and 23% reported they worked full-time; about 37% of the family teams where family membership is greater than one half of the total ownership reported working part-time for their parents business, and about 32% reported working full-time; and for nonfamily teams, 30% reported working part-time and 22% full-time in their parent's business. These findings are summarized in Table 4.7.

Table 4.7 Nascent entrepreneur worked in parents business and start-up team ownership

	Sole proprietorship	Spousal pair	Family team >50%	Nonfamily team	All
Count	337	146	57	90	630
Yes, full time	71 (21%)	34 (23%)	18 (32%)	20 (22%)	143 (23%)
Yes, part time	107 (32%)	48 (33%)	21 (36%)	27 (30%)	203 (32%)
No	159 (47%)	64 (44%)	18 (32%)	43 (48%)	284 (45%)
Total (%)	100.00	100.00	100.00	100.00	100.00

Of the ventures that reached new firm status by the first follow-up interview ($n = 129$), 13% were sole proprietorships, 14% were spousal pair teams, 16% were family teams where family membership is greater than one half of the total ownership, and 14% were nonfamily teams. Of the ventures that were classified as the start-up continues ($n = 614$), 64% were sole proprietorships, 64% were spousal pair teams, 57% were family teams where family membership is greater than one half of the total ownership, and 62% were nonfamily teams. Of the quitters ($n = 229$), 23% were sole proprietorships, 23% were spousal pair teams, 28% were family teams where family membership is greater than one half of the total ownership, and 25% were nonfamily teams. Thus, it appears that the organization team structure has a modest impact on outcome status by the first follow-up. Subsequent analysis is needed to further identify if time and start-up team structure are factors that influence outcome status with subsequent waves of data.

Furthermore, it appears that reports of new firms by the first 12-month follow-up (Wave B) are lower among the PSED II cohort than among PSED I. For example, by the first follow-up, 33% of the PSED II respondents for whom data is available reported reaching new firm status. Conversely, among the PSED II cohort, only 13% of respondents (for whom data is available) reported reaching new firm status. Again, comparing the proportion of individuals reaching new firm status by start-up team structure, the data provides evidence that overall, reports of new firm status among team structure categories are lower in PSED II than in PSED I. For example, in PSED I, about 28% of sole proprietors, 39% of spouse teams, 41% family teams (>50% ownership), 33% of nonfamily teams reported reaching new firm status at the 12- month follow-up interview. This preliminary analysis suggests that it is of interest to further investigate if the report rates for outcome status continue to vary from both samples with subsequent waves of data.

4.6 Expected Sales and Job Growth of Family and Spousal Pair Team Ventures

Overall, when it came to projected sales growth (none, low, medium, extreme) over a 5-year period, nonfamily teams were the most aggressive with 65.4% projecting medium or extreme growth over the 5-year period. Family teams greater than half were the next most aggressive with 64.6% projecting medium or extreme growth. Sole proprietors were not far behind with 60.2% projecting medium or extreme growth. Spousal teams were the most conservative with 55.7% projecting medium or extreme sales growth over the 5 years.

Similarly, when it came to projected job growth over a 5-year period, nonfamily teams were the most aggressive of the four groups, with 50% projecting medium or extreme growth, followed by spousal pairs with 45.9%, sole proprietors with 41.4%, and family teams greater than half with 36.6%. Interestingly, when looking at the low end, family teams greater than half were the most conservative with 63.4% projecting no or low growth, followed by sole proprietors with 58.7%, spousal pairs with 54.4%, and nonfamily teams with 50%. Overall, the data suggest that for this sample, respondents were more comfortable with projecting more aggressive sales growth (60.3% medium or extreme sales growth) than job growth (43.3% medium or extreme job growth).

This reinforces the need to pursue further research in this area, especially around types of venture and aggressive/conservative approaches to projecting job growth. From a policy perspective, these data suggest that over the first 5 years, projected aggressive sales growth is contemplated without much job growth, at least for categories other than nonfamily teams. While these ventures project wealth creation, especially for nonfamily teams, job creation does not appear to be aggressively pursued. Future research in this regard is needed to more fully inform public policy debate on job creation across the small, entrepreneurial, and family business sectors. Also, while not specifically addressed in this chapter, additional research on the role of nascent technology ventures, especially small family-owned start-ups, and their role in job creation is needed.

4.7 Family Teams Investment in Dollars and Hours

Furthermore, by measuring the hours and monetary investments invested by teams per month since conception, inferences can be made regarding the intensity of the effort among family and spousal teams while organizing such investments. Looking across six categories of total hours contributed (0–10, 11–30, 31–75, 76–150, 151–300, and >301 hours), some interesting patterns emerge.

In regard to the total hours per month, about 23% of sole proprietors, 17.1% of spousal pairs, 11.6% of family teams, and 8.8% of nonfamily teams dedicated less than 10 hours per month. Conversely, 19% of nonfamily teams, 17.4% of family teams, 11.6% of spousal teams, and 7% of sole proprietors spent from 301 hours to maximum hours per month working on the start-up (Fig. 4.3). The median overall for all ownership categories is 50 hours per month. Median hours per month for nonfamily teams is 124 hours, family teams greater than half, 69 hours, spousal pairs, 54 hours, and sole proprietors, 39 hours. Comparatively, among all those who reached new firm status in PSED II by Wave "B," the median hours invested per month is 81 ($n = 99$, firms with 6 months positive cash flow).

When examining total funds committedper month, 20.4% of nonfamily teams, 17.4% of family teams, 12.6% of spousal pairs, and 9.3% of sole proprietors invested funds ranging from $4,001 to maximum toward the

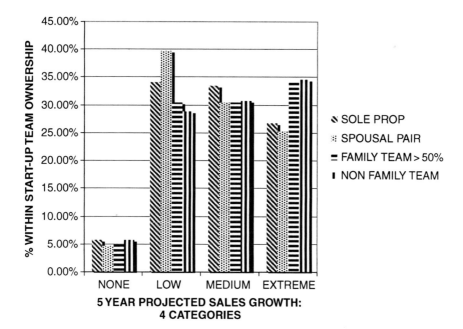

Fig. 4.1 Five-year projected sales growth: four categories

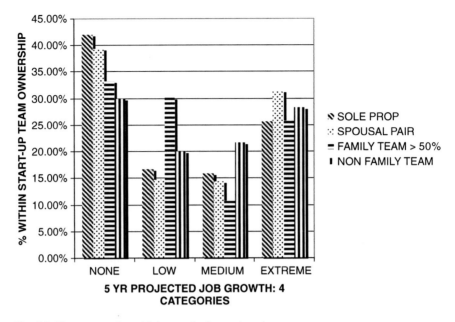

Fig. 4.2 Five-year projected job growth: four categories

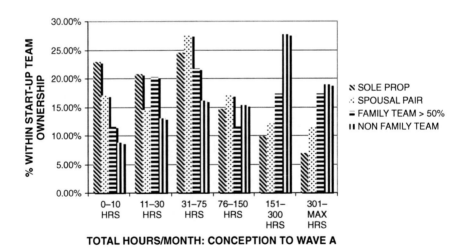

Fig. 4.3 Total hours per month per team since conception: six categories

nascent enterprise. Similarly, 24.8% of nonfamily teams, 20.3% of family teams, 20.1% of spousal pairs, and 17.4% of sole proprietors invested funds up to $30 toward the nascent enterprise (Fig. 4.4). The median funds invested per month by family teams is $553, followed by nonfamily teams at $519, spousal pairs at $462, and sole proprietors at $261. Keep in mind, that among

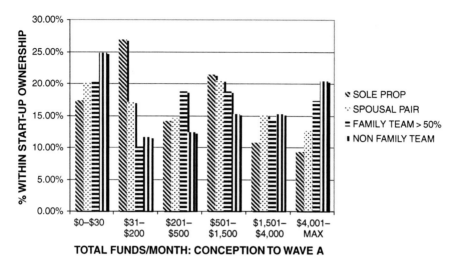

Fig. 4.4 Total funds per month per team since conception: six categories

those who reached new firm status in PSED II, a median of $466 per month was invested in the start-up since conception.

These data illustrate that nonfamily teams appear to be more aggressive in terms of hours contributed with 46.7% giving over 151 hours per month. This may be due to the difference in team size and/or family boundary issues between work and family. With regard to total funds per month, once again 35.7% of nonfamily teams report contributing greater than $1,501 per month. This may be due, in part, to the fact that nonfamily teams are slightly larger in terms of team size (average of 2.77) when compared to family teams (average of 2.66), spousal pairs (average of 2.00), or sole proprietors (average of 1.00). Also, this is interesting to note since spousal teams report that 62% of their funding comes from personal funds, while family teams greater than half report 51% coming from personal funds, nonfamily teams report 50% from personal funds, and sole proprietors report 43.8% from personal funds. Future research needs to more fully explore these patterns and relationships especially given the emphasis on sources of capital and availability of time to devote to venture start-ups.

4.8 Conclusion

Over the past two decades, there has been a renewed and invigorated interest and call for a more synergistic collaboration between entrepreneurship and family business research (Brockhaus, 1994; Muntean, 2008). This chapter answers this call showing that the presence of a family business background is associated with significant differences in the consciousness of motivations for greater flexibility in life, building a business which kids can inherit someday, and in continuing the family tradition. This analysis also shows that such differences in motivational consciousness are intensified with work experience in a parent's business for both men and women. Finally, expectations for sales growth appear to be relatively strong and consistent, while expectations for job growth is somewhat tentative and inconsistent.

In order to more fully address fundamental questions surrounding the antecedents and influential factors in nascent entrepreneurial activity, the intersection of family business and entrepreneurship research is a particularly attractive space to explore. To that end, well-conceived rigorously executed empirical research is needed to provide data to address these fundamental questions. The PSED II research initiative provides considerable data on a number of variables of interest in that intersection including but limited to family role models, the role of financial support acquired throughout family and friends, and the motivations of family life and legacy.

The main focus of this chapter is on the influence of family background on nascent entrepreneurial activity. Indeed, it responds to the continued call for, "more research on how family systems affect opportunity emergence and recognition, the new venture creation decision, and the resource mobilization process" (Aldrich & Cliff, 2003, p. 593). Reciprocally, there is need for future research to examine the role that venture creation can have on family systems (Aldrich & Cliff, 2003). To that end, the longitudinal nature of the PSED II database lends itself to a better understanding of both phenomena and promises to raise the bar for future research.

Notes

1. To minimize impact of outliers, informal sources of funding greater $52,000 are recoded at the top end. Overall, 90% of cases fall between $12 and $52,000 for all sources of funds.
2. Data for this descriptive analysis is not weighted.
3. This could be attributed to one nascent enterprise receiving $1.4 million from informal family funding, therefore, influencing the group mean.

References

Aldrich, H., & Cliff, J. (2003). The pervasive effects of family on entrepreneurship: Toward a family embeddedness perspective. *Journal of Business Venturing, 18*(5), 573–596.

Aldrich, H., Elam, A. B., & Reese, P. R. (1996). Strong ties, weak ties and strangers: Do women business owners differ from men in their use of networking to obtain assistance? In S. Birley & I. MacMillan (Eds.), *Entrepreneurship in a global context*. London: Routledge.

Aldrich, H., & Ruef, M. (2006). *Organizations evolving*. London: Sage.

Astrachan, J. H., & Shanker, M. C. (2003). Family businesses' contribution to the U.S. economy: A closer look. *Family Business Review, 16*(3), 211–219.

Brockhaus, R. (1994). Entrepreneurship and family business research: Comparisons, critique, and lessons. *Entrepreneurship Theory & Practice, 19*(1), 25–38.

Brockhaus, R., & Horwitz, P. (1986). The psychology of the entrepreneur. In D. L. Sexton & R. W. Smilor (Eds.), *The art and science of entrepreneurship*. Cambridge, MA: Ballinger.

Dyer, W. (1992). *The entrepreneurial experience*. San Francisco: Jossey-Bass.

Dyer, W., & Handler, W. (1994). Entrepreneurship and family business: Exploring the connections. *Entrepreneurship Theory & Practice, 19*(1), 71–83.

Family Firm Institute. (2005). Facts and perspectives on family business around the world. http://www.ffi.org/genTemplate.asp?cid = 186#us

Katz, J. (1992). A psychosocial cognitive model of employment status choice. *Entrepreneurship Theory & Practice, 17*(1), 29–37.

Krueger, N. (1993). The impact of prior entrepreneurial exposure on perceptions of new venture feasibility and desirability. *Entrepreneurship Theory & Practice, 18*(1), 5–21.

Matthews, C., & Human, S. (2004). Family background. In W. Gartner, K. Shaver, N. Carter, & P. Reynolds, (Eds.), *Handbook of entrepreneurial dynamics: The process of business creation*. Thousand Oaks, CA: Sage Publications.

Matthews, C., & Moser, S. (1995). Family background and gender: Implications for interest in small firm ownership. *Entrepreneurship & Regional Development, 7*, 365–377.

Matthews, C., & Moser, S. (1996). A longitudinal investigation of the impact of family background and gender on interest in small firm ownership. *Journal of Small Business Management, 34*(2), 29–44.

Muntean, S. (2008). Analyzing the dearth in family enterprise research. In P. H. Phan & J. E. Butler (Eds.), *Theoretic developments and future research in family business*. Charlotte, NC: Information Age Publishing, Inc.

Reynolds, P., & Curtin, R. (2008). Business creation in the United States: Panel Study of Entrepreneurial Dynamics II initial assessment. *Foundations and Trends in Entrepreneurship, 4*(3), 155–307.

Rogoff, E., & Heck, R. (2003). Evolving research in entrepreneurship and family business: Recognizing family as the oxygen that feeds the fire of entrepreneurship. *Journal of Business Venturing, 18*(5), 559–566.

Ruef, M., Aldrich, H., & Carter, N. (2003). The structure of founding teams: Homophily, strong ties, and isolation among U.S. entrepreneurs. *American Sociological Review, 68*, 195–222.

Scott, M. G., & Twomey, D. F. (1988). The long-term supply of entrepreneurs: Students' career aspirations in relation to entrepreneurship. *Journal of Small Business Management, 26*(4), 5–13.

Shapero, A., & Sokol, L. (1982). The sociology of entrepreneurship. In C. A. Kent, D. L. Sexton, & K. H. Vesper (Eds.), *Encyclopedia of entrepreneurship*. Englewood Cliffs, NJ: Prentice-Hall.

White, R., Thornhill, S., & Hampson, E. (2007). A biosocial model of entrepreneurship: The combined effects of nurture and nature. *Journal of Organizational Behavior, 28*(4), 451–466.

Part II
Start-Up Teams

Chapter 5
Owner Contributions and Equity

Amy E. Davis, Kyle C. Longest, Phillip H. Kim, and Howard E. Aldrich

5.1 Introduction

Given that persons starting new ventures often share ownership with one or more persons (Ruef, Aldrich, & Carter, 2003), determining the distribution of ownership among team members and how members contribute various sources to their startups has become more complicated. Teams are recognized as having larger pools of potential resources, including time, money, ideas, and social connections. For teams to be effective, members must synthesize their shared assets enough to compensate for the extra time and effort that coordination, delegation, and consensus making can take (Aubert & Kelsey, 2003; Erez & Somech, 1996; Faraj & Sproull, 2000). Startup teams differ from top management teams, classroom teams, and work teams because they are typically self-selected, self-directed, and composed of individuals sharing close relationships (such as kinship ties). Prior to the PSED I and PSED II, researchers had little empirical information regarding how startup team members activated their pooled resources to pursue business formation. Now that the two studies are publicly available, information on equity and contributions can be used to address at least four important concerns regarding startup processes in teams: access to resources, helpfulness (willingness to contribute), equality, and role differentiation.

5.2 Team Processes

The first of these issues concerns the extent to which the teams access resources through their members. Entrepreneurs must assemble a variety of goods and services for their ventures, from physical resources such as equipment or retail space to contacts in the financial services industry. Further, entrepreneurship requires many diverse skills that are rarely held by only one person, including

---

A.E. Davis (✉)
College of Charleston, 5 Liberty Street, Charleston, SC 29401, USA
e-mail: davisae@cofc.edu

creativity, marketing skills, financial acumen, and industry-specific knowledge. Teams composed of two or more persons potentially can utilize the pooled resources of the participating individuals, and therefore the startup's resources should be assessed at the team level (Aram & Morgan, 1976; Foo, Wong, & Ong, 2005; Olivera & Straus, 2004). From the perspective of access, a four-person team in which each member contributed one resource is just as well positioned for entrepreneurial success as a team in which one member contributed four resources. Moreover, both teams would be better positioned for successful launch relative to a venture started by a solitary owner or team in which no member had contributed a particular resource. Researchers can assess variation in members' access to resources through their teams by measuring the number of different resources possessed by one or more team members as well as the sum of all contributions.

Access provides useful information about the resources available within teams, but provides limited information regarding team effectiveness. A team could have exceptional access to resources but nonetheless have low levels of functioning. For example, a two-person team in which everyone contributes two resources may function better and thus be able to establish an operational business better than a four-person team in which three members contribute one resource and one person contributes five resources, even though the latter team has greater access to resources. An individual contributing five resources may become frustrated as a result of their relative over-contributions. Alternatively, a team in which the majority of the contributions are generated by one individual is not taking advantage of the synergy possible in startup teams in which collaboration of members generates better solutions than those of any one individual.

Even though a team with one high-contributing member has excellent access to resources, the presence of low-contributing members may depress the performance of the entire team and generate negative results, a phenomenon often called "process losses" (Aubert & Kelsey, 2003). Although access leaves many questions unanswered, the same variables used to measure access can be configured to better measure team functioning, either in terms of the average number of resources provided by team members (helpfulness) or the extent to which team members contribute the same number of resources (equality).

The second concern is the helpfulness of team members: how willing and able are team members to offer time and other assistance to help with the business startup. Helpfulness is most likely to emerge from teams with high levels of trust and commitment because each has a positive effect on information and resource exchange (Baldwin, Bedell, & Johnson, 1997; Caldwell & O'Reilly, 2003; Carron et al., 2004; Chansler, Swamidass, & Cammann, 2003; Edmondson, Bohmer, & Pisano, 2001; Jehn & Mannix, 2001; Talaulicar, Grunderi, & Werder, 2005). If they suspect that team members may betray them or doubt their team will be able to collaborate to build a viable business, members may be unwilling to contribute their time and effort, not to mention their human, financial, and social capital to teams (Bray, 2004; Eby & Dobbins, 1997; English, Griffith, &

Steelman, 2004; Halfhill et al., 2005; Shepherd & Krueger, 2002; Smith et al., 1994; Whiteoak, Chalip, & Hort, 2004). Whereas concerns of access can be determined by the summation of pooled contributions among team members and number of unique resources contained within the team, helpfulness is better measured by determining how many resources each member provides. That is, a team in which one member provides several types of resources has a high level of access but a low level of helpfulness if all the remaining members fail to provide contributions. Similarly, a team of two persons in which each contributes three resources has a lower level of access than a team of four in which each person contributes two resources. However, the two-person team has a higher level of helpfulness.

The third concern with regard to contributions and equity distribution among startup team members is the level of equality within startup teams. A team in which members contribute the same number of resources and devote similar numbers of hours may perform better than a team in which contributions are uneven. The level of equality in the distribution of ownership within a startup team can be conceptualized in several ways. Ruef (2003) noted that ownership may be divided equally, regardless of contribution, resulting in a condition he called "objective equality." Objective equality would consist of all team members sharing equal amounts of ownership, such as a 50–50 split in a two-person team. He used the term "equity" to describe ownership shares distributed proportionally to contributions. A three-person team in which one person has a 10% ownership lacks objective equality but has equity if the person owning 10% contributes 10% of the work effort and resources. Alternatively, contributions and ownership may be distributed unequally, a condition that might be associated with a team's demographic characteristics or the relationships among team members (Ruef, 2003).

The fourth concern is the extent of role differentiation within startup teams. Teams differ in how they divide up tasks required for business creation. Some teams have all members working in multiple roles: performing various functions from marketing to operations to accounting; and contributing multiple resources from ideas to training to contacts. Other teams may have some members working in multiple roles and other members specializing in one or more functions and contributing particular types of resources. Finally, some teams may have all members focused mainly on one area of expertise and contributing complimentary resources.

Differentiation may reflect the stage of a startup's development. Initially, team members may have generalized roles that overlap, whereas specialized roles, including leadership roles, may develop over time (Clarysse & Moray, 2004). Teams may benefit from differentiation because role ambiguity is minimized. Bray and Brawley (2002) found that high role clarity improved overall performance and also strengthened the relationship between role efficacy and role performance effectiveness. Foo, Sin, and Yiong (2006), who studied startup teams, found that teams with an established leader, one in which all members agreed which member was the leader, reported higher levels of satisfaction than did teams lacking a distinct leader (see also Clarysse & Moray, 2004).

5.3 Team Processes in the PSED I and PSED II

5.3.1 Features of the PSED I and PSED II Team Data

Collecting information on interactions and exchanges within startup teams is difficult, and therefore most research on entrepreneurial teams is based on homogeneous, single-site studies with fewer than 200 teams (Foo et al., 2005, 2006). In fact, research on small groups in general often involve business students participating in group projects or groups created in laboratory settings (for examples, see Robinson & Smith-Lovin, 2001; Van Der Vet, Bunderson, & Oosterhof, 2006). Because the PSED I and PSED II are nationally representative, results of statistical analyses of these data provide better insight into team processes occurring in new ventures throughout the United States.

All data on startup teams in the PSED I and PSED II come from one team member, the respondent. The respondent provides information on all team members, and the other team members were not contacted to provide their perspectives. This type of data structure is often called egocentric network data (Marsden, 2002) as opposed to complete network data. Complete network data is only possible for a well-defined population with a complete roster of all members, such as a single organization.

5.3.2 Research Opportunities

Contributions and equity measures can be important predictors of entrepreneurial outcomes. Researchers can determine how helpfulness, equality, and differentiation increase the chances of establishing a business or decrease the chances of abandoning the startup effort. Such findings could demonstrate, for example, the most effective ways of distributing equity among team members.

Researchers can also study how the characteristics of team members influence the equity and contribution measures. A study of relationships among team members could shed light on the level of diversity within team types. The largest category of teams in the PSED I and PSED II are spouse teams, but a great deal of variation may exist within this category. Researchers may seek to empirically establish whether levels of diversity of equity, contributions, and commitment are greater between team types or within them. Not only may these contributions vary between team types, but the value of different contributions may vary, depending on the source of the contribution (Kim, Longest, & Aldrich, 2008). Alternatively, researchers may seek to determine whether demographic (gender, age, and race) or human capital (experience) characteristics influence commitment, contributions, and distribution of ownership.

Finally, some researchers may analyze differences among different team members. For example, scholars might examine differences between team members who are independent individuals and team members who represent an organization (referred to as a legal entity in the PSED). Alternatively, a scholar might attempt to discover why particular team members make given contributions or receive particular levels of ownership. For this sort of analysis, the data need to be reconfigured such that the team member is the unit of analysis rather than the respondent or team. In this instance, teams with four members will have four observations whereas teams with two members will have two observations. This type of analysis is possible in STATA using the "reshape, long" command and in SPSS using "varstocases". For examples, using PSED I, see Ruef (2003) and Davis (2007).

5.3.3 Review of Findings from PSED I

Researchers using data from the PSED I generated insights into the issues of access, helpfulness, and equality. For example, Davis (2007) found that helpfulness, measured by the average number of contributions provided by team members, was a better predictor of subsequent startup outcomes than was access, measured by the number of unique contributions provided by team members. Ruef (2003) found that equity often was distributed equally among team members, particularly among teams with close ties or relationships among members. Kim, Longest, and Aldrich (2008) found that assistance from team members (and helpers) reduced odds of discontinuing entrepreneurial activities, especially when the assistance type aligned with role expectations.

5.4 Questionnaire Items in PSED II

Table 5.1 displays the questionnaire items in the PSED II regarding contributions and equity. When applicable, we listed the PSED I items that best correspond to the PSED II items. The items concern team size, expected distribution of equity, member contributions of hours, full-time work, and six individual assistance contributions toward the new businesses. The six assistance types are introductions, information, training, access to financial assistance, physical resources, and business services.[1] The * indicate that respondents were asked about each of their team members, including themselves. As a result, each item appears up to five times for each respondent in the data. For example, a respondent on a three-person team would have valid responses for AG6_1–AG6_3.[2] The wording of AG5_* and Q210e_* differ, with AG5_*

Table 5.1 Questionnaire items for assessing start-up team contributions and equity

PSED II variable name	PSED I variable name	Question[1]
AG5_*	Q210e_*	Is [NAME] acting on their own behalf or does [NAME] represent a business, financial institution, government agency, or other legal entity?
AG6_*	Q207_0*C	Once this business is operational, what proportion of the ownership will (you/[NAME]/all the others) have? (Please remember that the total ownership should add up to 100%.)
AG12	None	Which of the owners would be considered in charge of day to day operations of the new business – you or (G4 OWNER #2) or (G4 OWNER #3) or (G4 OWNER #4) or (G4 OWNER #5)?
AH14_*	Q211_*	How many hours in total (have you/ has [NAME]) devoted to this new business?
AH17_*	None	(Have you/Has [NAME]) begun to work 35 hours or more per week on this new business?
AH19_*	None	What is (your/[NAME]'s) primary role in the new business – say it is general management, sales, marketing, or customer service, finance or accounting, technical or science related, such as research or engineering, manufacturing or operations, or is it administration or human resource management?
AH23_*	Q221_*	In addition to time and personal investments of money, in what other ways (have you/has [NAME]) helped with this new business? First, (have you/has [NAME]) provided **introductions** to other people?
AH24_*	Q222_*	Have you/Has [NAME] provided **information** or advice to help with this new business?
AH25_*	Q223_*	(Have you/Has [NAME]) provided **training** in business related tasks or skills (to help with this new business)?
AH26_*	Q224_*	(Have you/Has [NAME]) provided access to **financial assistance**, like equity, loans or loan guarantees (to help with this new business)?
AH27_*	Q225_*	(Have you/Has [NAME]) provided **physical resources**, use of land, space, buildings or equipment (to help with this new business)?
AH28_*	Q226_*	(Have you/Has [NAME]) provided **business services**, such as legal, accounting or clerical assistance (to help with this new business)?

[1] Questions are displayed in PSED II wording, although the wording in PSED I is similar.
* indicates that the variable appears five times in the data, numbered 1–5 for each team member. However, for AG5_*, this question was not asked of the respondent, team member 1.

asking if a team member is acting independently or on behalf of a legal entity and Q210e_* asking if a team member is a person or nonperson.

We note that contribution reports are from one owner's (the respondent's) perspective. Therefore, various social psychological factors might influence reports of contributions and equity shares. Davis (2007) found that respondents characterized their own contributions substantially differently from the contributions of their teammates in PSED I. Respondents are perhaps more aware of their own contributions relative to the contributions of their co-owners and thus may underreport the contributions of their teammates.

5.5 Key Methodological Considerations

5.5.1 Cases to Keep or Drop

Ideally, the PSED II aimed to capture individuals engaged in entrepreneurial activities that met a few criteria. First, the nascent entrepreneurs should not be owners of infant businesses, those businesses that have positive cash flow exceeding expenses including managers' salaries. In fact, 66 of the 1,214 respondents in the PSED II are infant businesses and should be excluded. Several other respondents in the PSED II are problematic and should be dropped, depending on the research questions under consideration. Ten respondents reported that their first entrepreneurial activity occurred more than 10 years before the interview, and they are therefore not recent nascent entrepreneurs. Other potential disqualifiers include reporting only one startup activity in a 12-month period and reporting fewer than three startup activities (Reynolds & Curtin, 2008). For this analysis, we only excluded the 66 respondents reporting positive cash flow prior to their first interview.[3]

5.5.2 Team Versus Teammates

Some researchers may restrict their investigations to the teammates of the respondents and thus exclude respondents from team-level measures of contributions, equity, and commitment. By contrast, our chapter presents data on team characteristics, and therefore our measures include the respondents. The respondent in PSED II is always team member 1. However, in PSED I, researchers need to use item q210b_* to determine which team member is the respondent.

5.5.3 Team Size

Over 97% of respondents in the PSED II are solo owners or on teams with four or fewer members. Even when solo owners are excluded, more than 93% of respondents are on teams of four or fewer members. The PSED II contains detailed information for all members of teams with up to five members. But for teams with more than five members, the wording of particular questions creates missing information on the fifth member or contains a value that summarizes the characteristics of team members 5 through the total number of members. For demographic information such as gender (ah1_5), respondents with teams of more than five individuals were not asked to provide information on their fifth member. For other types of information, respondents were asked to provide a summary response that applied to their fifth member and all the remaining members. For example, for teams with exactly five members ag6_5 represents the proportion of the business that the fifth team member will own, but if a team has seven members, this question represents the collective proportion of the business team members 5–7 will own. As a result, there is more complete and precise information from respondents on five-person teams than from respondents on teams larger than five.

Researchers must decide how to handle respondents on teams of five or more individuals. One option is to drop the 21 cases of teams with six or more members (i.e., restrict the analyses to teams with five or fewer members).[4] We prefer, however, to keep all respondents but use data from only the first four team members listed by respondents, as this method provides a similar set of possible questions across all teams. The information we present is based on the first four team members the respondent lists, regardless of total team size. We assume, and the data suggest, that these are the four most important team members for those teams with five or more members. In PSED I, detailed information was collected about the five most important team members. However, to maintain consistency with PSED II, we restrict team size to the first four most important team members for the PSED I comparison measures.

5.5.4 Missing Values

Respondents did not always provide complete information about the contributions and equity distributions of their team members. Researchers must then decide whether nonresponses should be assumed to be zero, coded as missing and dropped, or imputed in some way. We make our decision based on the complexity of the question. For assistance contributions, equity, and whether members devoted full-time hours to startup activities, we only code as missing those respondents with no valid responses across their four team members. Otherwise, if respondents provided information on these characteristics for some members but not others, we assumed the values for the missing responses were 0. We decided that this coding was a reasonable assumption because the contribution questions and the full-time effort questions have yes or no responses (e.g., "Have you/Has [NAME] provided *information* or advice to help with this new business?") We assume that respondents certain that their team members provided a particular type of assistance will likely report it, whereas respondents who did not provide an answer are not confident that a team member has done so. Similarly, although not dichotomous, equity ranges from 0 to 100 and thus has a fixed range of possible responses. Even if a formal agreement has not been made, respondents can generate a rough estimate of ownership shares based on the simple calculation of 100 divided by team size.

By contrast, the number of total hours team members contribute to startup activities has a much larger range of possible responses, from one to thousands of hours. In addition, as demonstrated in Table 5.3, the standard deviation shows incredible variability in this measure. Therefore, we were unsatisfied with

5 Owner Contributions and Equity

coding nonresponses as zero for hours contributed to startup activities because nonresponses might result from respondents being unable to provide reasonable estimates of hourly contributions. For example, 15 respondents did not report the number of hours they themselves contributed to their startup but recorded the hours that other team members contributed. Although we cannot be positive, this pattern would suggest a situation in which respondents cannot even calculate the number of hours they have contributed and thus are unwilling to even provide an estimate. Assuming nonresponses for hours to be zero probably leads investigators to underestimate the actual hours contributed by team members.

Rather than losing observations with partial information by dropping them or possibly underestimating hours by coding missing values as 0, we imputed missing hours based on the median quotient between different team members' contribution of hours. To make this imputation, we begin with the understanding that each progressive team member contributes fewer hours. The available data supports this assumption: in every case with full team member data, the respondent reported to have put in the most work hours followed by declining hours reported for each subsequent teammate. The median quotient resulting from dividing hours contributed by team member 1 by hours contributed by team member 2 is 1.25. Therefore, we imputed the missing values for hours contributed by team member 1 by multiplying the hours contributed by team member 2 by 1.25. Conversely, we imputed the missing values for hours contributed by team member 2 by dividing the hours contributed by team member 1 by 1.25. We provide all the median quotients between two team members in Table 5.2 to demonstrate how missing hours were imputed. We used median rather than mean quotients because they are more conservative and the distribution of hours is right-skewed.

Table 5.2 Median quotients of hours contributed to startup activities between team members in PSED II

Member 1 and Member 2	1.25
Member 1 and Member 3	2.00
Member 1 and Member 4	3.23
Member 2 and Member 3	1.13
Member 2 and Member 4	1.67
Member 3 and Member 4	1.00

The result of our data transformation in this instance did not change the overall n of 1,062. This n is identical to the n if any respondent with any valid value for hours for any team member is counted. However, we were able to get more information for team members. Instead of 1,047 for team member 1, we have 1,062, instead of 474 for team member 2, we have 525, instead of 118 for team member 3, we have 143, instead of 59 for team member 4, we have 74. The means change an average of 10 hours with the imputation of the missing values.

We presented one simple method of imputing missing data, but researchers may elect to use multiple imputations to address missing data (PROC MI in SAS). Regardless of whether researchers elect to code missing values as 0, drop cases with missing information, or use some method of imputation, we recommend testing for differences in results among the different techniques.

Because we do not present multivariate analysis in this chapter, we present the maximum N for each variable. Because respondents occasionally did not provide valid answers for questions, the Ns vary in Tables 5.3 and 5.4. Initially, the N for PSED II is 1148: 550 team entrepreneurs and 598 solo entrepreneurs.

Table 5.3 Constructed measures of startup team contributions and equity: PSED I, II

	N	Weighted mean	Weighted standard deviation
Access			
Team size, capped at 4			
PSED II, full sample	1,148	1.69	0.88
PSED I, full sample	817	1.74	0.88
PSED II, teams only	550	2.43	0.73
PSED I, teams only	411	2.41	0.72
PSED II, solos only	598	1.00	0.00
PSED I, solos only	406	1.00	0.00
Number of legal entities, capped at 4			
PSED II, full sample	1,142	0.05	0.31
PSED I, full sample	817	0.02	0.18
PSED II, teams only	544	0.11	0.44
PSED I, teams only	411	0.04	0.27
PSED II, solos only	598	0.00	0.00
PSED I, solos only	406	0.00	0.00
Number of unique contributions provided across the team			
PSED II, full sample	1,147	2.03	2.33
PSED I, full sample	816	2.33	2.45
PSED II, teams only	549	4.19	1.47
PSED I, teams only	410	4.47	1.40
PSED II, solos only	598	0.00	0.00
PSED I, solos only	406	0.00	0.00
Total number of contributions provided across the team			
PSED II, full sample	1,147	3.59	4.50
PSED I, full sample	816	4.13	4.76
PSED II, teams only	549	7.41	3.68
PSED I, teams only	410	7.89	3.69
PSED II, solos only	598	0.00	0.00
PSED I, solos only	406	0.00	0.00
Total number of hours provided across the team			
PSED II, full sample	1,062	2,119.79	6,229.38
PSED I, full sample	772	1,551.00	2,663.38

5 Owner Contributions and Equity

Table 5.3 (continued)

	N	Weighted mean	Weighted standard deviation
PSED II, teams only	525	2,423.05	6,783.39
PSED I, teams only	398	1,884.66	3,222.28
PSED II, solos only	537	1,811.00	5,599.05
PSED I, solos only	374	1,162.91	1,733.67
Helpfulness			
Average number of contributions provided per person			
PSED II, full sample	1147	1.51	1.81
PSED I, full sample	816	1.72	1.88
PSED II, teams only	549	3.11	1.34
PSED I, teams only	410	3.29	1.27
PSED II, solos only	598	0.00	0.00
PSED I, solos only	406	0.00	0.00
Average number of hours provided per team member			
PSED II, full sample	1062	1434.98	4573.22
PSED I, full sample	772	944.00	1454.35
PSED II, teams only	525	1065.71	3229.42
PSED I, teams only	398	755.80	1130.49
PSED II, solos only	537	1811.00	5599.05
PSED I, solos only	374	1162.91	1733.67
Equality			
Difference between highest and lowest equity owner			
PSED II, full sample	1143	6.06	16.48
PSED I, full sample	814	6.35	17.62
PSED II, teams only	545	12.57	21.96
PSED I, teams only	408	12.15	22.89
PSED II, solos only	598	0.00	0.00
PSED I, solos only	406	0.00	0.00
Difference between highest hours and lowest hours			
PSED II, full sample	1062	406.81	2119.86
PSED I, full sample	772	384.88	1036.03
PSED II, teams only	525	806.33	2931.38
PSED I, teams only	398	715.76	1327.07
PSED II, solos only	537	0.00	0.00
PSED I, solos only	374	0.00	0.00
Difference between most contributions and least contributions			
PSED II, full sample	1147	0.76	1.22
PSED I, full sample	816	2.00	2.18
PSED II, teams only	549	1.57	1.35
PSED I, teams only	410	3.84	1.42
PSED II, solos only	598	0.00	0.00
PSED I, solos only	406	0.00	0.00

Table 5.3 (continued)

	N	Weighted mean	Weighted standard deviation
Specialization			
Proportion of contributions that are unique (nonredundant)			
PSED II, full sample	1147	0.30	0.34
PSED I, full sample	816	0.32	0.22
PSED II, teams only	549	0.62	0.19
PSED I, teams only	410	0.61	0.18
PSED II, solos only	598	0.00	0.00
PSED I, solos only	406	0.00	0.00

Table 5.4 Team contribution variables only available in PSED II

	N	Weighted mean	Weighted standard deviation
Access			
Number of team members contributing full-time hours			
Full sample	1,146	0.40	0.63
Teams only	550	0.52	0.76
Solos only	596	0.30	0.46
Helpfulness			
Proportion of team members contributing full-time			
Full sample	1,146	0.26	0.40
Teams only	550	0.22	0.32
Solos only	596	0.30	0.46
Equality			
Diversity of devotion of full-time hours to business			
Full sample	1,146	0.14	0.35
Teams only	550	0.30	0.46
Solos only	596	0.00	0.00
Specialization			
Number of different primary roles in the team (maximum of one per person)			
Full sample	n/a		
Teams only	547	1.78	0.69
Solos only	n/a		

Six respondents who said that they were starting a business with their spouse or someone else (ag1 = 2 or 3) did not report any further information of their team members. Three of these respondents were two-person teams, two on three-person teams, and one on a team of four or more members. Because these respondents provided information about themselves, they are all included in the contributions measures. However, because respondents were not asked if they were acting on behalf of a legal entity, these six respondents have missing values

5 Owner Contributions and Equity   83

for the number of legal entities in the team and therefore the N is 544. One respondent who did report the number of legal entities in their team did not report any contributions by any team member, including himself. Thus, the N is 549 for contributions measures. Researchers should decide what sorts of criteria to use for these seven respondents with regard to whether they should be included with their values coded as zero or if they should be excluded. One might argue, for example, that because 598 solo entrepreneurs were not asked the contributions they had provided to their own startups, the six respondents who only reported their own contributions should either be dropped from the analysis or should have their contributions reported as 0 to make them comparable with solo entrepreneurs.

5.5.5 Weights

The PSED I and II are nationally representative samples of nascent entrepreneurs, when weights are applied. The weight we use for PSED I is autwt, which corrects for the women and minority oversamples in the PSED I, whether entrepreneurs are fully or partially autonomous, and is based on the 817 respondents left after running KScleans, which eliminates problematic cases (Shaver, 2006). For the analyses of PSED II, we used wt_wavea. Any time we deleted cases, we recentered weights so that the sum of the weight equaled the n and the mean weight equaled one.

5.5.6 Solo Owners

Finally, researchers must decide whether to include solo owners in their analyses of team variables. A research question that is bounded by a comparison within teams, such as "do teams with family members contribute fewer forms of assistance than do teams with friends, colleagues, or strangers," does not require the analysis of solo owners. In such situations, the 598 solo owners should be excluded from the analysis. Research objectives that seek to answer questions concerning all startups, such as "are team-based startup efforts better positioned to establish operational businesses than solo startup efforts," requires the inclusion of solo owners. Thus the unit of analysis and overall study aims help determine how to handle solitary entrepreneurs.

We present descriptive statistics for the entire sample, teams only, and solos only in Table 5.3. We would not recommend or expect that any researcher would conduct analysis of the variables in this chapter on only solo entrepreneurs. We wanted to show, however, which variables had legitimate values for solitary owners (as is the case for hours), which variables have a mean and standard deviation of 0 for solitary owners (as is the case for contributions), and finally which variables have a mean of 1 and a standard deviation of zero for solitary owners (as is the case for team size). In addition, we wanted to demonstrate how the descriptive statistics were affected by the inclusion or exclusion of solo owners.

5.6 Data Transformations

Measures of equity and contributions can be configured in different ways, depending on whether researchers are primarily concerned with access, helpfulness, equality, or differentiation. We present our measures in Table 5.3.

5.6.1 Hours

We measured access to sweat equity by summing the hours contributed by all members. To measure helpfulness, we divided the sum by team size to calculate the average number of hours contributed. To measure equality, we calculated the range between the highest and lowest number of hours contributed within teams. With this measure, low numbers represent relative equality whereas high numbers indicate relative inequality of effort.

5.6.2 Assistance Contributions

We chose not to present measures concerning the specific individual contributions (introductions, information, training, physical resources, financial assistance, and business assistance). Instead, to measure access, we show the number of unique contributions provided by team members (0–6) and the total number of contributions provided by up to four of most important members of the collective team (0–24). To measure helpfulness, we divide total contributions by team size to calculate the average number of contributions provided. To measure equality, we calculate range between the highest and lowest number of contributions provided. To measure differentiation, we calculate the proportion of contributions provided within teams that are not repeated and are therefore unique. High numbers indicate that team members are relatively specialized and do not overlap in their contributions to startup activities, whereas low numbers indicate that team members are generalists, with members contributing similar types of assistance.

5.6.3 Equity

Another way in which we measured equality was the difference between the highest and lowest percentage of ownership, with low numbers indicating relative equality and high numbers indicating relative inequality.

5.7 Findings

5.7.1 Descriptive Statistics of Measures Available in PSED I and II

Table 5.3 demonstrates that the team process characteristics are remarkably consistent between PSED I and PSED II. In particular, team size and the difference between highest and lowest equity owner have virtually identical means. The most noticeable difference between PSED I and II is the number of hours devoted to startup activities, with respondents in PSED II reporting several hundred hours more than respondents in PSED I. In addition, the total number of contributions provided by startup teams was slightly higher in PSED I than in PSED II. As a result, the differences between the most and least contributions within teams were higher in PSED II than in PSED I. The incidence of legal entity members is twice as high in PSED II relative to PSED I, but we attribute this difference in part to differences in wordings regarding legal entity members.

The other phenomena of interest in Table 5.3 is the differences in descriptive statistics for contributions, depending on whether the theoretical construct is access, helpfulness, equality, or differentiation. On average, respondents on teams have access to more than seven resources, four of them being unique. Each team member contributes an average of just over three assistance types, a measure of helpfulness. On average, the difference between the highest contributor and the lowest contributor is 1.58 assistance types for PSED II and 3.84 assistance types for PSED I, which suggests that PSED II teams experience greater equality in contributions to the startup than did those from PSED I. Finally, the proportion of assistance types that are unique is just over 0.6 for both PSED I and PSED II, indicating a relatively high level of differentiation and low level of redundancy within teams.

A careful examination of the various measures of hours contributed also reveals interesting findings. For example, although solo owners have fewer total hours dedicated to startup activities, they have a higher average number of hours devoted than members of teams. This result warrants further investigation, but could suggest the presence of social loafing in teams, the ability for members of teams to devote fewer hours to their businesses relative to solo owners, or that maintaining status as a team member may not require "sweat equity."

5.7.2 Measures in PSED II Only

PSED II provides opportunities to better gain insight into the differentiation of roles among team members. In particular, respondents in PSED II indicated who was in charge of day-to-day operations of the business and the primary role of each member. These variables are unique to large scale national datasets of entrepreneurs. Previous researchers have only been able to surmise or allude to such roles. For example Budig (2006) found that marriage increased women's odds of entering self-employment but had no effect on men's entry into self-employment. Further, she found that many self-employed, married women had self-employed spouses. Often, these women reported having a clerical occupation, suggesting that the women did not initiate entrepreneurial activity but instead served a secondary role in their spouses' businesses. Because Budig used the National Longitudinal Study of Youth (NLSY), she was unable to definitively establish that the husbands and wives were co-owners of the same business, much less that women took a nonprimary role in their self-employment.

In PSED II, respondents reported whether team members had begun devoting at least 35 hours per week to startup activities. As was the case with hours, the mean for number of members contributing full-time hours is higher for respondents on teams than solo owners, but the proportion of team members contributing full-time to startup activities is lower for respondents on teams than solo owners.

With regard to differentiation, the number of different primary roles in teams is 1.79. The mean team size for members of teams is 2.42. This pattern suggests that although some members of teams have identical primary roles, there is a moderate level of role differentiation among team members.

We wanted to also demonstrate a correlation between the number of contributions and whether someone was working full-time on the new business. Table 5.5 shows the weighted Pearson's r correlation coefficients for each team member. Those working full-time on business creation clearly contribute more resources than team members not working full-time, with correlations ranging from 0.12 to 0.38. However, contributions and full-time devotion to startup are not synonymous and reveal different elements of commitment by team members. Interestingly, the correlation between full-time effort and contributions is relatively low for the respondent. Although proportionally more respondents who had not devoted full-time reported providing zero contributions (3% versus 1.54% of full-time respondents), 15% of respondents reported providing 5 contributions, whether they had devoted full-time to their startup or not (see Table 5.6).

Table 5.5 Weighted correlations between contributions provided and full-time devotion to startup

	r	N
Team member 1	0.19	550
Team member 2	0.30	513
Team member 3	0.38	130
Team member 4	0.12	64

The results are much different when respondents are reporting the contributions of their first alter. Only 1% of respondents reported that member 2 working full-time on their startup contributed zero or one resource, whereas 18% of respondents with member 2 not working full-time on the startup

5 Owner Contributions and Equity   87

Table 5.6 Weighted percentages for contributions and full-time devotion to startup

Contributions	Respondent No	Respondent Yes	Total	Team member 2 No	Team member 2 Yes	Total
0	3.08	1.54	2.67	4.49	0.00	3.55
1	9.08	3.31	7.56	13.90	1.01	11.19
2	21.35	8.82	18.06	18.01	8.28	15.96
3	23.99	25.88	24.49	23.08	19.41	22.31
4	22.19	31.08	24.52	20.78	27.38	22.17
5	15.06	15.51	15.18	14.06	25.81	16.54
6	5.25	13.86	7.51	5.67	18.10	8.29
	100	100	100	100	100	100

Table 5.7 Weighted descriptive statistics for contributions and full-time devotion to start-up

	Respondent No	Respondent Yes	Team member 2 No	Team member 2 Yes
Mean	3.19	3.84	3.07	4.23
Standard deviation	1.46	1.36	1.56	1.25

contributed either zero or one resource. This finding suggests that entrepreneurs' contributions may go unrecognized by other team members unless they contribute full-time working hours to startup activities (Table 5.7).

5.7.3 Startup Contributions and Entrepreneurial Outcomes in the PSED II

We present the results of bivariate analysis in the form of cross-tabulations of team contribution and equity variables on the 12-month outcome in PSED II in Table 5.8. Respondents' startups were classified as discontinued, ongoing, or established businesses according to criteria outlined in Reynolds and Curtin (2008). Established businesses are those that respondents reported generated revenues in excess of expenses, including salaries, for more than six months and reported that their business was an established business (see items be13, be15, be17, and ba41). Discontinued startups reported at one point in the interview that they were no longer actively pursuing the business (items ba15 and ba42). All other respondents who answered the 12-month wave B follow-up survey are classified as startups. For count and continuous variables, we recoded the variables into "high" or "low" based on the median responses. For example, the median number of average contributions provided by team members is 3, so we coded below 3 as "low" and 3–6 as high. Because it is unusual for respondents to report that team members have differences in ownership shares, we simply created a variable for whether there was a difference in equity ownership (1) or not (0).

Table 5.8 Weighted cross-tabulations between contributions and 12-month outcomes for PSED II

		Team			Any legal entities		
		No	Yes	Total	No	Yes	Total
New firm	Percent	11.67	10.13	10.88	11.10	2.67	10.83
	Frequency	50.21	46.13	96.34	94.81	0.75	95.56
Continues startup	Percent	64.65	63.45	64.03	63.65	76.75	64.06
	Frequency	278.12	288.90	567.02	543.63	21.51	565.14
Quit	Percent	23.68	26.42	25.09	25.26	20.58	25.11
	Frequency	101.85	120.29	222.14	215.80	5.77	221.56
Total	Frequency	430.17	455.33	885.49	854.24	28.02	882.26

Indicators of access and helpfulness
Any devoted to full-time

		Solo			Team		
		No	Yes	Total	No	Yes	Total
New firm	Percent	6.81	18.59	10.15	8.60	16.99	11.67
	Frequency	22.19	23.94	46.13	23.44	26.77	50.21
Continues startup	Percent	62.68	65.72	63.54	62.66	68.10	64.65
	Frequency	204.28	84.62	288.90	170.80	107.32	278.12
Quit	Percent	30.51	15.69	26.31	28.74	14.91	23.68
	Frequency	99.42	20.20	119.61	78.35	23.50	101.85
Total	Frequency	325.89	128.76	454.65	272.59	157.58	430.17

Average contributions (no solos)

		Low (0–2.999)	High (3–6)	Total
New firm	Percent	9.09	13.36	11.68
	Frequency	15.37	34.83	50.21
Continues startup	Percent	63.40	65.40	64.62
	Frequency	107.17	170.51	277.68
Quit	Percent	27.50	21.23	23.70
	Frequency	46.49	55.36	101.85
Total	Frequency	169.02	260.71	429.73

Average hours contributed

		Solo			Team		
		Low (0–299)	High (300–60,000)	Total	Low	High	Total
New firm	Percent	6.87	14.67	10.95	9.77	14.08	11.72
	Frequency	13.24	30.93	44.17	22.12	26.35	48.47
Continues startup	Percent	56.93	68.30	62.87	61.13	70.91	65.56
	Frequency	109.65	144.03	253.68	138.39	132.73	271.12
Quit	Percent	36.19	17.03	26.18	29.10	15.01	22.72
	Frequency	69.71	35.92	105.63	65.87	28.10	93.97
Total	Frequency	192.60	210.88	403.48	226.38	187.18	413.56

5 Owner Contributions and Equity   89

Table 5.8 (continued)

Indicators of role differentiation and equality
Different roles on team (no solos)

		No	Yes	Total
New firm	Percent	8.83	13.43	11.70
	Frequency	14.30	35.90	50.21
Continues startup	Percent	67.01	63.29	64.69
	Frequency	108.54	169.14	277.68
Quit	Percent	24.16	23.28	23.61
	Frequency	39.13	62.20	101.33
Total	Frequency	161.97	267.24	429.21

Difference in hours contributed among team members (no solos)

		Low (0–174)	High (175–51760)	Total
New firm	Percent	9.83	13.91	11.72
	Frequency	21.82	26.65	48.47
Continues startup	Percent	60.90	70.96	65.56
	Frequency	135.17	135.95	271.12
Quit	Percent	29.29	15.13	22.72
	Frequency	64.98	28.99	93.97
Total	Frequency	221.98	191.58	413.56

Difference in percent owned among team members (no solos)

		No	Yes	Total
New firm	Percent	11.97	11.41	11.74
	Frequency	30.40	19.80	50.21
Continues startup	Percent	66.63	62.33	64.88
	Frequency	169.16	108.21	277.38
Quit	Percent	21.40	26.26	23.37
	Frequency	54.32	45.59	99.92
Total	Frequency	253.89	173.61	427.50

Examining the relationships between contributions or equity and startup outcomes with bivariate analyses does not allow us to isolate the net effects of access, helpfulness, differentiation, or equality. Our results show some positive effects of contributions on entrepreneurial outcomes, but these effects may simply reflect the effects of having a more or less developed startup at the time of the initial interview on 12-month outcomes. For example, respondents that reported differentiation in the form of different roles were more likely to have established businesses and less likely to have discontinued businesses. Rather than empirically establishing that differentiation is a favorable team process, this result may also reflect that individuals in teams with established roles are further along in the startup process than respondents without differentiated roles and therefore are more likely to have favorable 12-month outcomes.

Consider the effect of hours contributed on startup outcomes: teams with high differences in the contribution of hours also had favorable outcomes. However, this likely is an artifact of the positive effect of hours. The hours contributed results are positive with regard to outcomes and are also similar for teams and solo entrepreneurs, with the effect of hours slightly stronger on entrepreneurial outcomes for solo entrepreneurs.[5] In fact, inequality of hours is unlikely to have a favorable effect net of other factors, given that respondents that reported inequality in ownership were more likely to report discontinued businesses and less likely to report established businesses. Multivariate analysis will be required to test hypotheses regarding contributions and startup outcomes. In particular, researchers will want to control for the stage of business formation either in the form of length of hours, months, or years, or milestones achieved.

5.7.4 Not Studying Teams?

A great deal of research on entrepreneurs only considers the characteristics of respondents and ignores the characteristics of other owners. In datasets in which the firm is the unit of observation and the primary owner is the respondent, other owners are of less concern. One of the strengths of the PSED I and PSED II is that by locating respondents in their homes, secondary entrepreneurs who would not be captured using other survey instruments are represented in the sample. These types of entrepreneurs are sometimes called hidden entrepreneurs because they are rarely included in studies of entrepreneurship and their characteristics and contributions are therefore rarely empirically measured (Dhaliwal, 2000; Hurley, 1999). Given that the PSED I and PSED II include both primary and secondary owners, researchers not examining team factors should consider using one or more of the indicators shown in Table 5.9 to control for the respondents' roles in their businesses.

First, respondents are asked the percentage of the business they will own once the business becomes operational. We recoded that variable to generate the following categories: solo owner, respondent as majority owner, respondent

Table 5.9 Controls to consider for nonteam analysis

	PSED II		PSED I	
	Weighted frequency	Weighted percent	Weighted frequency	Weighted percent
Respondent's relative ownership share				
Solo owner	592.13	51.80	388.62	47.74
Respondent majority owner	112.74	9.86	80.29	9.86
Respondent owns less than expected by team size	56.94	0.50	34.25	4.21
Equal ownership	317.20	27.75	269.37	33.09
Respondent owns 50%, rest split among two or more others	9.88	0.86	6.78	0.83
Respondent owns more than expected, but less than 50%	54.11	4.73	34.70	4.26
Total	1,143	100	814	100

Table 5.9 (continued)

	PSED II Weighted frequency	PSED II Weighted percent	PSED I Weighted frequency	PSED I Weighted percent
Respondent's primary role				
General management; "everything"	318.90	58.73		
Sales/marketing/customer service	88.54	16.31		
Finance/accounting	34.69	6.39		
Technical/research/science engineering	38.08	7.01		
Manufacturing/operations	32.44	5.97		
Administration/human resource management	30.34	5.59		
Total	543	100		
Who is in charge of day-to-day operations				
Solo owner	591.19	52.11		
Respondent in charge	313.77	27.65		
Respondent NOT in charge	172.00	15.16		
Respondent shares	57.64	5.08		
Total	1,134.00	100.00		

The unweighted frequencies for solo owner in both respondent's relative ownership share and who is in charge of day-to-day operations is 598. The small differences result from weighting. Respondent's primary role and who is in charge of day-to-day operations are not available in PSED I. Although respondent's relative ownership share can be calculated in PSED I, researchers must remember that team member 1 is not always the respondent. Team member 1 in PSED I has the largest ownership share. To calculate the respondent's ownership share, researchers must also use the variables q210b_1–q210b_5 to determine which team member is the respondent.
In PSED 1, there are 406 solo entrepreneurs. 388.62 is the weighted frequency.

as minority owner (owning less than 100/team size), equal ownership (respondent owning = 100/team size), respondent owning 50% and the remaining 50% split among two or more others, and respondent owning more than 100/team-size but less than 50%. More than 60 respondents expected to own less than their predicted share based on team size, suggesting that they perhaps occupy a supporting or periphery role in their startup rather than a proactive role that a solitary owner might occupy.

Second, respondents were asked to give the primary role of themselves and other team members. Researchers not interested in team analysis should still consider a control for primary role. More than 200 respondents listed a role other than "general management" or "everything." Notably, 40 respondents characterized their primary role as human resources/administrative, suggesting a support role that is reactive, as opposed to an initiating role in business creation.

Finally, respondents were asked to identify who was in charge of their day-to-day operations. We recoded this variable into the following categories: solo owner, respondent in charge, respondent not in charge, and respondent shares day-to-day control. More than 100 respondents reported not being in charge of daily operations at their business.

5.8 Conclusion

Use of the variables we have described in this chapter will enhance understanding of how startup teams collaborate to work toward business creation. Researchers can better understand how equity distributions and contributions influence entrepreneurial outcomes of nascent entrepreneurs and thus better determine optimal configurations of contributions and equity. In addition, researchers can use various characteristics of respondents and their teammates to predict equity distributions and contribution characteristics. For example, in our preliminary analysis we found that team members' willingness and ability to contribute hours, full-time effort, and other resources were positively associated with favorable 12-month outcomes. In addition, while we found that different roles among team members and differences in hourly contributions were positively associated with favorable 12-month outcomes, differences in ownership shares were negatively associated with entrepreneurial outcomes.

Given the breadth and depth of the information collected in PSED II, each of these avenues of research would surely shed new light on the entrepreneurial process. Even our preliminary analyses showed nuanced relationships between teams and short-term startup outcomes. Further specifying the ways in which access, equality, differentiation, and helpfulness uniquely and jointly contribute to the functioning and success of nascent entrepreneurs will provide a more complete understanding of the origins of new businesses.

Notes

1. In PSED I, respondents were also asked about personal services (assistance with childcare and housework) and "other" types of assistance. We exclude those assistance types for this chapter to enhance the comparability across the two datasets.
2. In PSED II, the respondent is always team member 1. Respondents were not asked whether they are acting on their own behalf or as a representative of another organization and therefore AG5_1 does not exist.
3. In analyses not shown here, we also ran descriptive univariate statistics on the entire sample of 1,214 respondents. The differences between the 1,214 respondents and the 1,148 were very small. For example, mean number of unique contributions using the entire sample was 2.07 (s.d. = 2.35) and the mean with infant businesses excluded 2.03 (s.d. = 2.33).
4. Using all 1,214 respondents generates 22 respondents on teams with more than 5 members.
5. This interaction is not surprising given that the success or failure of a solo business depends on the owner, along with interactions in the environment whereas the success or failure of a team-based startup depends on each team members' assets and efforts, the interactions among the team, and the environment.

References

Aram, J. D., & Morgan, C. P. (1976). The role of project team collaboration in R&D performance. *Management Science, 22*, 1127–1137.

Aubert, B. A., & Kelsey, B. (2003). Further understanding of trust and performance in virtual teams. *Small Group Research, 34*, 523–556.

Baldwin, T. T., Bedell, M. D., & Johnson, J. L. (1997). The social fabric of a team-based M.B.A. program: Network effects on student satisfaction and performance. *Academy of Management Journal, 40*, 1389–1397.

Bray, S. R. (2004). Collective efficacy, group goals, and group performance of a muscular endurance task. *Small Group Research, 35*, 230–238.

Bray, R. M., & Brawley, L. R. (2002). Role efficacy, role clarity, and role performance effectiveness. *Small Group Research, 33*, 233–253.

Budig, M. J. (2006). Intersections on the road to self-employment: Gender, family, and occupational class. *Social Forces, 84*, 2223–2239.

Caldwell, D. E., & O'Reilly, C. A., III. (2003). The determinants of team-based innovation in organizations: The role of social influence. *Small Group Research, 34*, 497–517.

Carron, A. V., Brawley, L. R., Eys, M. A., Bray, S., Dorsch, K., Estabrooks, P., et al. (2004). Do individual perceptions of group cohesion reflect shared beliefs? An empirical analysis. *Small Group Research, 34*, 468–496.

Chansler, P. A., Swamidass, P. M., & Cammann, C. (2003). Self-managing work teams: An empirical study of group cohesiveness in "natural work groups" at a Harley-Davidson Motor Company Plant. *Small Group Research, 34*, 101–120.

Clarysse, B., & Moray, N. (2004). A process study of entrepreneurial team formation: The case of a research-based spin-off. *Journal of Business Venturing, 19*, 55–79.

Davis, A. E. (2007). *More (or less) than the sums of their parts? Status, teams, and entrepreneurial outcomes.* Unpublished doctoral dissertation, University of North Carolina, Chapel Hill.

Dhaliwal, S. (2000). Entrepreneurship—a learning process: The experience of Asian female entrepreneurs and women in business. *Education and Training, 48*, 445–452.

Eby, L. T., & Dobbins, G. H. (1997). Collectivistic orientation in teams: An individual and group-level analysis. *Journal of Organizational Behavior, 18*, 275–295.

Edmondson, A. C., Bohmer, R. M., & Pisano, G. P. (2001). Disrupted routines: Team learning and new technology implementation in hospitals. *Administrative Science Quarterly, 46*, 685–716.

English, A., Griffith, R. L., & Steelman, L. A. (2004). Team performance: The effect of team conscientiousness and task type. *Small Group Research, 35*, 643–665.

Erez, M., & Somech, A. (1996). Is group productivity loss the rule or the exception? Effects of culture and group-based motivation. *The Academy of Management Journal, 39*, 1513–1537.

Faraj, S., & Sproull, L. (2000). Coordinating expertise in software development teams. *Management Science, 46*, 1554–1568.

Foo, M. D., Sin, H., & Yiong, L. (2006). Effects of team inputs and intrateam processes on new venture team effectiveness. *Strategic Management Journal, 27*(4), 389–399.

Foo, M. D., Wong, P. K., & Ong, A. (2005). Research note: Do others think you have a viable business idea? Team diversity and judges' evaluation of ideas in a business plan competition. *Journal of Business Venturing, 20*, 385–402.

Halfhill, T., Sundrstrom, E., Lahner, J., Calderone, W., & Nielsen, T. M. (2005). Group personality composition and group effectiveness: An integrative review of empirical research. *Small Group Research, 36*, 83–105.

Hurley, A. (1999). Incorporating feminist theories into sociological theories of entrepreneurship. *Women in Management Review, 14*(2) 54–62.

Jehn, K. A., & Mannix, E. A. (2001). The dynamic nature of conflict: A longitudinal study of intergroup conflict and group performance. *Academy of Management Journal, 44*, 238–251.

Kim, P. H., Longest, K. C., & Aldrich, H. E. (2008, August). *Can you lend me a hand? Social support, network structure, and entrepreneurial action.* Paper presented at the annual meeting of the American Sociological Association, Boston.

Marsden, P. V. (2002). Egocentric and sociocentric measures of network centrality. *Social Networks, 24,* 407–422.

Olivera, F., & Straus, S. G. (2004). Group-to-individual transfer of learning: Cognitive and social factors. *Small Group Research, 35,* 440–465.

Reynolds, P. D., & Curtin, R. T. (2008). Business creation in the United States: Panel Study of Entrepreneurial Dynamics II: Initial assessment. *Foundations and Trends in Entrepreneurship, 4*(3), 155–307.

Robinson, D. T., & Smith-Lovin, L. (2001). Getting a laugh: Gender, status, and humor in task discussions. *Social Forces, 80,* 123–158.

Ruef, M. (2003). *Norms of group-generalized exchange in formal organizations.* Unpublished manuscript.

Ruef, M., Aldrich, H. E., & Carter, N. M. (2003). The structure of founding teams: Homophily, strong ties, and isolation among U.S. entrepreneurs. *American Sociological Review, 68,* 195–222.

Shaver, K. G. (2006). *Cleaning of ERC data from ISR web site.* Retrieved September 12, 2008, from http://www.cofc.edu/%7Eshaverk/kscleans06.sps.

Shepherd, D. A., & Krueger, N. F. (2002). An intentions-based model of entrepreneurial teams' social cognition. *Entrepreneurship Theory and Practice, 27,* 167–185.

Smith, K. G., Smith, K. A., Olian, J. D., Sims, H. P, Jr., O'Bannon, D. P., & Scully, J. A. (1994). Top management team demography and process: The role of social integration and communication. *Administrative Science Quarterly, 39,* 412–438.

Talaulicar, T., Grundei, J., & Werder, A. V. (2005). Strategic decision making in start-ups: The effect of top management team orientation and processes on speed and comprehensiveness. *Journal of Business Venturing, 20,* 519–541.

Van Der Vet, G. S., Bunderson, J. S., & Oosterhof, A. (2006). Expertness diversity and interpersonal helping in teams: Why those who need the most help end up getting the least. *Academy of Management Journal, 49,* 877–893.

Whiteoak, J. W., Chalip, L., & Hort, L. K. (2004). Assessing group efficacy: Comparing three methods of measurement. *Small Group Research, 35,* 158–173.

Chapter 6
Business Owner Demography, Human Capital, and Social Networks

Martin Ruef, Bart Bonikowski, and Howard E. Aldrich

6.1 Introduction

While early work on the topic of entrepreneurship tended to portray entrepreneurs as heroic individuals (e.g., see Raines & Leathers, 2000, on Schumpeter's description), more recent perspectives have come to recognize that new business activity is often initiated by groups of startup owners. Starting in the late 1980s and early 1990s, a new generation of scholars in the entrepreneurship field called for a systematic program of research that would document the prevalence of startup teams, describe their properties, and assess their impact on business performance (e.g., Gartner, Shaver, Gatewood, & Katz, 1994; Kamm, Shuman, Seeger, & Nurick, 1990). In a review of developments in entrepreneur research and theory, Gartner et al. (1994) noted that "the 'entrepreneur' in entrepreneurship is more likely to be plural, rather than singular" (p. 6). They offered an expansive definition of startup teams, which included owners, investors, organizational decision-makers, family members, advisors, critical suppliers, and buyers as possible candidates for the role of "entrepreneur."

In this chapter, we focus on one of these candidate roles—that of the owner—in describing the demography and network structure of new business startups in the United States (subsequent chapters consider key nonowners and other helpers). Why do some startup owners go it alone, while others recruit spouses, kin, co-workers, friends, or even strangers to join them? What social processes impact the composition of entrepreneurial teams? To provide some preliminary insight on these questions, we begin with a theoretical overview of mechanisms that have been widely studied as affecting the formation and composition of entrepreneurial and management teams. Next, we turn to the quantitative information on solo startup owners and teams offered by the PSED II, paying particular attention to potential differences from both the general population and the PSED I, an earlier representative survey of

---

M. Ruef (✉)
Department of Sociology, Princeton University, Plainsboro, NJ, USA
e-mail: mruef@princeton.edu

nascent entrepreneurs. We also consider what changes can be observed among startup owners in the PSED II across waves, as some owners abandon their startup efforts and new owners are recruited to join existing teams. Finally, we address the timing of owner recruitment and the features of owner team structure that may impact the duration of group emergence.

6.2 Mechanisms Affecting Owner Team Formation

Following previous research on founding team formation (e.g., Ruef, Aldrich, & Carter, 2003), we discuss three general mechanisms that may influence the composition of owner teams: (a) *homophilous affiliation*, or recruitment on the basis of similarity in readily observed socio-demographic characteristics; (b) *functional diversification*, or recruitment on the basis of complementary (and nonoverlapping) competencies and expertise; and (c) *network constraint*, or recruitment on the basis of existing social ties, particularly those involving strong interpersonal bonds.[1] The first of these mechanisms is primarily social psychological in character, the second has been considered more so in strategic perspectives on entrepreneurial activity, and the third is drawn from a broad array of studies on group formation in structural sociology.

Homophilous affiliation refers to a tendency of individuals to collaborate based on shared socio-demographic characteristics. Although homophily can occur on the basis of similarity in values, beliefs, tastes, or other underlying dispositions (Lazarsfeld & Merton, 1954), visible social identities offer the simplest source of attachment to groups. Three processes help to explain the prevalence of homophily in organizational settings. First, individuals often assume that others who have a common social identity tend to think as they do, even if this perception results from a misattribution of shared understanding (McPherson, Smith-Lovin, & Cook, 2001). Second, the visible similarity of individuals also tends to dispose them toward a greater level of interpersonal attraction and trust, an idea referred to in some studies as the similarity-attraction principle (e.g., Boone et al., 2004). Third, the homophilous recruitment of colleagues can serve as a political mechanism to ensure loyalty and to perpetuate personal power.

Within established organizations, all three processes have been observed, contributing to what Kanter (1977)—studying male managers—famously referred to as "homosocial reproduction." Within entrepreneurial groups, the fine-grained qualitative or quantitative evidence required to adjudicate among these processes remains largely absent. In the aggregate, however, gender and ethnicity appear to be potent drivers of homophilous affiliation in founding teams (Aldrich & Ruef, 2006, pp. 72–73).

Functional diversification refers to a desire to seek out collaborators with diverse and complementary skills that lie beyond the abilities of an individual. Studies of functional diversification can be traced back to the 1950s, when a host of experiments were deployed to analyze the process of role differentiation in small task groups (e.g., Slater, 1955). Within the entrepreneurship field, studies of functional diversity are more recent. Eisenhardt and Schoonhoven (1990) considered the impact of heterogeneity in industry tenure among founding team members on the growth of semiconductor manufacturing startups. They posited that growth would increase with functional heterogeneity, reflecting the ability of diverse entrepreneurial teams to avoid "groupthink" and elicit distinct contributions from members to solve the problems faced by startup enterprises. In his examination of functional diversity among the *Inc. 500* companies, Ensley (1999) offers a slightly different perspective. In contrast to Eisenhardt and Schoonhoven, he conceptualized team heterogeneity as having an *indirect* effect on performance and growth, mediated by cognitive and affective conflict within the group. On the one hand, team members with diverse skills were expected to evidence more debates and disagreements around ideas (*cognitive conflict*), a process that would ultimately lead to the formulation of better business strategies for new enterprises. At the same time, Ensley also hypothesized that skill diversity would be associated with frustrations directed at individual persons within the team (*affective conflict*), a process that could adversely impact consensus around common strategic goals.[2]

A third mechanism, that of *network constraint*, addresses how the formation and dynamics of social groups are limited by pre-existing social networks, particularly those that involve kinship, marital, or romantic relationships. It follows a well-established sociological literature that has called attention to the *embeddedness* of economic actors within social networks (Granovetter, 1985), but departs from this tradition in one notable respect. While much of the literature has argued for the "strength" of weak network ties in searches for job and business opportunities (Granovetter, 1995; see Mouw, 2003, for a critique) or in the strategic manipulation of structural holes (Burt, 1992), the perspective offered here is that the importance of strong network ties often trumps that of weak ties in an entrepreneurial context. This holds true for startup owner teams, in particular, because members have an enduring desire for trust, despite the instrumental advantages that may accrue from weak tie networks, in terms of structural autonomy or the acquisition of novel information.

When spatial or labor market constraints limit the availability of potential business partners, the three mechanisms also offer distinct explanations for solo entrepreneurship. Considering homophilous affiliation, for instance, we would expect to see more single-owner enterprises in neighborhoods where entrepreneurs are clearly in the demographic minority and, therefore, find it difficult to locate partners that conform to in-group biases. By the same token, the principle of functional diversification anticipates that single owner business startups become more likely when co-founders with complementary skills are hard to recruit, perhaps owing to tight labor market conditions. The mechanism of network constraint predicts that solo entrepreneurship will be especially prevalent for owners who are unmarried, romantically unattached, and who do not have family members living nearby.

Homophilous affiliation, functional diversification, and network constraint need not be mutually exclusive. Nevertheless, an important question posed for studies of owner team structure is how these mechanisms may conflict with one another. The network constraints imposed by existing strong ties can lead to nepotism and "satisficing" recruitment decisions, rather than the creation of teams with diverse entrepreneurial knowledge or skills. When demographic characteristics are correlated with distinct dimensions of human capital, then the development of an owner team with a high degree of similarity in age, gender, or ethnicity will also contribute to a lack of functional heterogeneity. Homophily can undermine the role of strong network ties in the creation of founding teams—as may be the case when male owners prefer to collaborate with other males, rather than their spouses—and, conversely, social ties can mitigate in-group biases, as predicted by the extensive literature on the contact hypothesis (e.g., Allport, 1954; Pettigrew & Tropp, 2006).

6.2.1 Owner Team Questions in the PSED II

Items concerning the composition of owner teams can be found in sections G, H, J, and K of the PSED II. Table 6.1 summarizes the items asked in Wave A of individual owners with respect to owner demography, human capital, and interpersonal networks (note that owner contributions are addressed separately in Chapter 5 of this Handbook). Taken as a whole, these questions provide researchers with a valuable opportunity to explore the mechanisms of homophilous affiliation, functional diversification, and network constraint in a nationally-representative sample of social groups.

Two initial items—AG1 and AG2 (not shown in the table)—address the overall size of the business owner teams. AG1 asks whether the new business will only be owned by the respondent, by the respondent and the respondent's spouse, or by the respondent and some other people or businesses. AG2 elicits the total number of people, businesses, or financial institutions that will share ownership of the new business. In Wave A, subsequent items collected information for each respondent and up to four other owners within the nascent enterprise's founding team.

Question AG5 distinguishes between individual persons and representatives of institutional owners. The remaining information in the table was collected only for those business owners acting on their own behalf; institutional owners were addressed separately in section K of the PSED II ("Legal Entity Owners"). Items AH1 through AH6 provide information on the gender, age, ethnicity, marital status, and education of the business owners. The next three items (AH7–AH9) were only asked for owners aside from the respondent. Questions AH7 and AH8 consider the duration and nature of the relationship of all other

Table 6.1 Selected PSED II interview items for business owners, Sections G, H, and J (Wave A)

Summary of variable	Focal respondent	Other owners
Type of owner (person, institution)		AG5_*
Gender	AH1_1	AH1_*
Age	AH2_1	AH2_*
Hispanic/Latino	AH3_1	AH3_*
Non-Hispanic ethnicity	AH4x_1	AH4x_*
White (x = 'a')		
Black/African American ('b')		
American Indian ('d')		
Asian ('e')		
Pacific Islander ('f')		
Other ('z')		
Marital status/living arrangements	AH5_1	AH5_*
(married, living with partner, separated, divorced, widowed, never married)		
Education	AH6_1	AH6_*
(up to 8th grade, some HS, HS degree, technical degree, some college, community college, bachelors, some graduate, masters, doctoral)		
Years they have known respondent		AH7_*
Relationship with respondent		AH8_*
(spouse, cohabiting partner, cohabiting relative, other relative, co-worker, other acquaintance / friend, stranger, non-cohabiting partner)		
Month and year they became involved in business	[AA8]	AH9_*
Occupation (3-digit code, 2000 census classification)	AH10_1	AH10_*
Years of experience (in same industry as startup)	AH11_1	AH11_*
Other businesses started (#)	AH12_1	AH12_*
Other businesses owned (#)	AH13_1	AH13_*
Relationship with other owner (non-respondent)		AJ2_**

* varies from 2 to 5 to accommodate other owners; ** varies from 23 to 45 to accommodate all possible (symmetrical) dyads among other owners. Items for ethnic identification are not mutually exclusive.

owners to the respondent. Question AH9 identifies the month and year that those owners became involved in the business venture (for the focal respondent, this can be inferred from an earlier question, AA8). Other items in section H apply to both respondents and other owners, identifying their occupation, industry tenure, number of startups, and number of other businesses owned (items AH10–AH13).

The information on social relationships included in section H is limited to interpersonal networks involving the focal respondent. In section J, the respondents were also questioned about the relationship between all of the other owners they had identified. By combining these sets of items, a complete image of the social network within each nascent startup can be constructed.

The items on owner demography, human capital, and networks were generally developed with an eye toward comparison with questions in the PSED I.

In the descriptive statistics below, we tabulate figures for the first wave of each panel study and note topics where differences in operationalization may lead to issues of comparability.

6.2.2 Characteristics of Startup Owners

The demographic characteristics and human capital of business startup owners are summarized in Table 6.2, considering data from the first waves of both the PSED I (1998–2000) and PSED II (2005–2006). The overwhelming majority of owners (97–98%) in both surveys are individuals working on their own behalf, as opposed to representatives of businesses, financial institutions, government agencies, or other legal entities. While much of the management literature has called attention to the active role of venture capital firms and other financial intermediaries in entrepreneurial activity, they are not numerically prevalent as owners in general samples of nascent enterprises. In 2005–2006, for instance, PSED II estimates suggest that existing businesses (or their representatives) account for 1.8% of all startup owners, banks account for 0.7%, and venture capital firms only include 0.3% of owners. Moreover, in almost 50% of those cases where an organization does serve as an owner, its representatives have no active decision-making or advisory role in the startup where it holds an equity stake.

The attributes of individual owners reflect some of the diversity of the American population. Relative to the population as a whole, women are under-represented among startup business owners and minorities (particularly, African Americans) are over-represented. Business owners are less likely to have been employed in management or professional occupations and are more likely to have a bachelor's or advanced degree than members of the general population. Marriage rates among owners of startup businesses are slightly less than those observed more generally among adults in the United States.[3]

As reflected in the statistical comparison of the PSED I and II samples, the characteristics of business owners have been fairly stable across time. There is no indication that the demographic composition (with respect to gender, age, or ethnicity) of startup owners has changed significantly, nor has there been any general shift in human capital (considering industry and startup experience).[4] In both the context of the startup boom period of the late 1990s and the less euphoric environment several years later, the "average" owner of a new business enterprise was a 39-year-old white male, with roughly 7–8 years of work experience in the same industry as his startup and a history of one previous startup effort.

There is some indication of a shift over time in the occupational background of owners. In the PSED I, owners of nascent enterprises were more likely to have a professional or technical background. Detailed occupational statistics

Table 6.2 Descriptive statistics for individual owners: Panel Study of Entrepreneurial Dynamics, I (1998–2000) and II (2005–2006)

Variable	Response	PSED I Cases	PSED I Weighted %/mean	PSED II Cases	PSED II Weighted %/mean	Significant sample difference?
Type	Person	1,446	97.8	2,038	96.7	No
	Institution		2.2		3.3	
Gender	Male	1,419	63.0	1,981	62.6	No
	Female		37.0		37.4	
Age	(Years)	1,381	38.7	1,962	39.3	No
Ethnicity[1]	White	1,367	71.5	1,957	71.4	No
	Black		16.5		18.3	No
	Hispanic		8.1		6.4	No
	Asian/Pacific		2.1		1.3	No
	Other		1.8		2.6	No
Industry tenure	(Years)	1,413	8.2	1,958	7.2	No
Other startups	(Count)	1,379	1.3	1,946	0.9	No
Occupation	Professional	1,351	27.7	1,965	20.3	$p < 0.01$
	Administrative		26.6		26.0	No
	Sales/service		19.0		21.0	No
	Production		19.0		20.2	No
	Other[3]		7.6		12.6	$p < 0.01$
Education[2]	No HS degree	815	2.6	1,962	5.4	$p < 0.01$
	HS degree		17.5		23.7	$p < 0.01$
	Some college[4]		41.3		34.7	$p < 0.01$
	BA/BS		23.9		23.0	No
	Postgraduate		14.7		13.2	No
Marital Status[2]	Married	813	55.6	1,971	53.3	No
	Never married		18.0		23.1	$p < 0.01$
	Cohabiting		11.6		11.0	No
	Other[5]		14.8		12.6	No

[1] Due to changes in operationalization, statistics for ethnicity may not be strictly comparable in the PSED I and II. "Other" category includes Native American, mixed ethnicity (non-Hispanic and non-White), and other (unspecified). "Hispanic" category refers to non-white Hispanics.
[2] Statistics for PSED I limited to respondent only.
[3] Includes students, homemakers, retirees, the self-employed, and the unemployed.
[4] Includes vocational and community college degrees.
[5] Includes separated, divorced, or widowed.

reveal that some of this shift can be accounted for by the greater prevalence of computer scientists and kindred workers (e.g., system analysts, programmers, etc.) among startup owners during the period of the dot-com boom. Specifically, around 4% of all owners had a professional background in a computing field in 1998–2000; by 2005–2006, that number had dropped to 1.8%.[5] Compensating for this decline, homemakers, students, and the unemployed were increasingly likely to become owners of business startups, representing 7.5% of all owners in the PSED I, but 9.5% of the total in the PSED II. These trends suggest a declining technical barrier-to-entry for nascent startups, particularly among businesses that rely heavily on electronic commerce.

To some extent, a declining barrier-to-entry is also apparent in the educational credentials of business owners. In 1998–2000, around 80% of all startup owners had some education beyond the level of a high school diploma. By 2005–2006, this number had decreased to 71% of startup owners. Consistent with the shift in occupational demography, this trend may reflect the lower technical threshold that some individuals now face in becoming entrepreneurs, especially in the field of internet-based selling.[6] Alternatively, it may also reflect the increasing labor market disadvantage of job-seekers without a post-secondary education, a trend that can contribute to "survivalist" entrepreneurship in tight labor markets (cf. Boyd, 2000). Like the findings for changes in the occupational background of entrepreneurs, the statistical significance of these trends should be subjected to further scrutiny. By applying multiple two-sample tests to categories within a single nominal variable, the statistics in the table are likely to overstate change over time.

A final difference between the 1998–2000 and 2005–2006 samples involves marital status. In the PSED II data, startup owners were significantly less likely to ever have been married. While this does not have any immediate bearing on the composition of entrepreneurial groups, it does raise questions as to whether startup businesses have lowered their reliance on spousal or intimate ties and, more generally, whether entrepreneurs are more likely to pursue business ventures on their own.

These questions can be pursued directly by examining the socio-demographic composition of teams of startup owners, as summarized in Table 6.3. The size distribution of these teams is highly skewed, with roughly half of all nascent startups involving only a single owner, more than a third involving two owners, 7% with three owners, and only a handful (c. 3%) featuring five or more business owners. Restricting attention to the enterprises with more than a single owner, we see that the majority are mixed gender teams, but that another substantial percentage (nearly 30%) are comprised solely of men. The tendency toward demographic homogeneity is more striking in the case of ethnicity, with 86% of all teams in the PSED II sample falling exclusively into one of the five ethnic categories noted in Table 6.2. Diversity within the owner teams is primarily evident in the case of occupational composition. The majority of multi-owner teams (nearly 72% in the PSED II) draw on more than one of the major occupational categories, thereby mixing professional, administrative, service, production, or other skills.

Relationships within the teams of startup owners are enumerated in a simple (dichotomous) fashion in the table. Despite the apparent increase in entrepreneurs who have never been married (cf. Table 6.2), intimate ties remain an important bond within entrepreneurial groups. Over half of all multi-owner teams include at least one couple who are either married or co-habiting. About a fifth of the owner teams rely on other kinship ties, including both affinal and consanguineal relationships. Teams with former co-workers are slightly less

Table 6.3 Descriptive statistics for teams of owners: Panel Study of Entrepreneurial Dynamics, I (1998–2000) and II (2005–2006)

Variable	Response	PSED I Cases	PSED I Weighted % / mean	PSED II Cases	PSED II Weighted % / mean	Significant sample difference?
Size	One owner	830	47.1	1,214	51.2	No
	Two owners		38.3		35.0	No
	Three owners		7.0		7.1	No
	Four owners		4.2		4.0	No
	Five + owners		3.4		2.7	No
Gender composition[1]	Mixed gender	412	63.2	557	65.0	No
	All male		29.7		29.3	No
	All female		7.1		5.7	No
Age[1]	(Standard deviation)	385	5.4	553	5.2	No
Ethnic composition[1]	Single ethnicity	381	84.5	534	86.0	No
	Multiple ethnicities		15.5		14.0	
Industry tenure[1]	(Standard deviation)	411	5.2	547	5.2	No
Other Startups[1]	(Standard deviation)	395	0.9	542	0.7	No
Occupational composition[1]	Single occupational class	376	26.8	551	28.3	No
	Multiple occupational classes		73.2		71.7	
Relational composition[2]	With spouses/live-in partners	412	54.7	586	51.5	No
	With nonspouse family member		18.0		19.6	No
	With business associates		20.2		16.4	No
	With other friends/ associates		25.1		24.5	No

Size distribution includes individuals who are not acting on their own behalf (representing a business, bank, or other legal entity). All other statistics are limited to autonomous individuals.
[1] Excludes single-owner firms or firms that only have relevant data for a single owner.
[2] Indicates whether relationship is present for *any* pair of owners. Excludes single-owner firms.

common (16% in the PSED II), while those with friends or acquaintances who have not worked together are slightly more common (25%). Notably, there are *no* teams of owners that *only* involve collaborations among strangers (with no prior ties before initiating the startup effort) among the nascent businesses surveyed in 2005–2006.

The trend over time in the owner teams can be summarized very succinctly—there is no evidence of any significant change in the composition of teams formed in 1998–2000 and those formed in 2005–2006. Considered in the aggregate, the size distribution, demographic composition, and relational composition of these teams are statistically equivalent for the measures noted in Table 6.3. There is also a remarkable level of stability for within-team variation in human capital, as measured by industry tenure and prior startup experience. Despite dramatic changes in the economic context of the late 1990s and that of 2005–2006, these statistics hint that the underlying mechanisms of entrepreneurial group formation may be relatively similar across the two periods.[7]

Based on these descriptive statistics, some readers may be tempted to make more precise inferences regarding the mechanisms that lead to the formation of entrepreneurial groups. For instance, the high level of ethnic homogeneity among owner teams may be taken as an indication of a strong in-group bias along this demographic dimension, with white entrepreneurs preferring to collaborate with other whites, African-American entrepreneurs preferring other blacks, and so forth. By contrast, the lower level of homogeneity observed for the occupational composition of teams may be taken to suggest that functional diversity also plays a role in collaboration among business co-owners. Although these mechanisms are theoretically plausible, it should be cautioned that their existence cannot be intuited from our descriptive data alone, for several methodological reasons. First, the aggregate descriptions of owner team composition do not take any account of the marginal distribution of business owner characteristics, as shown in Table 6.2. Considering ethnic composition, for example, the relatively large proportion of white business owners in these samples yields a considerable amount of homogeneity, even in the absence of in-group bias. Thus, one would expect the majority of owner dyads (51%) to consist of two white entrepreneurs under conditions of random mixing ($p = 0.714 \times 0.714$). Second, statistical expectations regarding owner team composition also depend on group size. In the absence of an in-group bias, the expected percentage of teams that are exclusively white drops to 36% for three owners ($p = 0.714 \times 0.714 \times 0.714$), 26% for four owners, and 18.5% for five owners. Finally, these univariate statistics do not account for other factors that may contribute to group homogeneity or heterogeneity along some dimension. It is plausible, for instance, that ethnic homogeneity among these owner teams is at least partially attributable to the reliance of entrepreneurs on kinship ties and that occupational diversity may be reduced, in part, when business owners recruit former co-workers as startup participants.

While a more nuanced examination of the mechanisms of owner team composition lies beyond the purview of this handbook chapter, results from multivariate models of group structure can be summarized briefly (see Ruef, 2002, for further details on methodology). Relative to a model of random mixing, the level of ethnic homogeneity observed among owners in the PSED II is extremely high—around 120 times random expectations for white owners and 383 times expectations for minorities (Ruef, in press, chap. 3); rates of in-group bias among men, women, professionals, and nonprofessionals also exceed random expectations, but by a much lower amount (with odds ratios ranging from 2 to 6). Some of these tendencies toward homophilous affiliation, particularly gender in-group bias, are sensitive to the inclusion of controls for strong network ties within the owner teams (unsurprisingly, the presence of spousal or cohabitation relationships dramatically increases gender heterogeneity). Similar results for the PSED I (see Ruef et al., 2003) suggest that homophilous affiliation on the basis of ethnicity and gender is a strong and stable propensity in owner founding teams, that functional diversification is limited, and that network constraints from relationships with strong ties have a pronounced impact on owner group composition.

6.3 Changes in Owner Team Composition Over Panel Waves

Given the remarkable stability of the demographic and human capital characteristics of startup owners between the PSED I and II, we would expect to find few statistically significant changes in team composition between the two waves of the PSED II, collected one year apart. The descriptive statistics presented in Table 6.4 support this prediction. Two-sample proportion tests comparing the characteristics of teams that took part in both waves of the study do not reveal any statistically significant compositional shifts. Although 8.2% of the teams lost at least one owner between the two waves and 4.3% recruited new owners, the turnover does not appear to have had a major impact on the teams' aggregate characteristics.

A number of small differences between the two waves do exist, though we cannot rule out that they result from essentially random variations. The team size distribution in both waves is positively skewed but becomes slightly more peaked in Wave B, with the proportion of single-owner teams increasing from 50.9 to 52.9% (which corresponds to a decline in mean team size from 1.7 to 1.6). This change, along with the net loss of owners in the sample as a whole, may be an early indicator of team decline resulting from the "liability of newness" (Stinchcombe, 1965). Those entrepreneurial projects that fail to achieve their objectives in the first few months of operation may begin losing members, leaving behind only those most committed to the enterprise. It appears that such decline is not offset by growth among successful teams in our sample.

Minor changes can also be observed in the demographic composition of the startup teams. The proportion of mixed gender and all-male teams declines between the waves, while the proportion of all-female teams increases from 4.8 to 7.0%. Teams in Wave B are less diverse in terms of ethnicity but more diverse in terms of age. The proportion of friend and acquaintance ties among the nascent entrepreneurs declines by 3.1 percentage points (from 20.4 to 17.3%), while the proportion of spousal, kin, and business ties increases.

Owing to sample attrition, the data used for the cross-wave comparisons consist of 473 fewer startup firms than the complete Wave A sample summarized in Table 6.3. However, the results of a series of two-sample tests, which are reported in Table 6.4, suggest that the 741 firms in the reduced sample do not differ significantly from the 1,214 teams in the full sample. Consequently,

Table 6.4 Changes in owner team statistics based on sample attrition: Panel Study of Entrepreneurial Dynamics II, Waves A (2005–2006) and B (2006–2007)

Variable	Response	PSED II Wave A Cases	PSED II Wave A Weighted % / mean	PSED II Wave B Cases	PSED II Wave B Weighted % / mean	Significant sample difference? (Wave A remaining vs. full)	Significant sample difference? (Wave A vs. B)
Size	One owner	741	50.9	741	52.9	No	No
	Two owners		37.1		36.7	No	No
	Three owners		5.8		5.7	No	No
	Four owners		3.9		3.0	No	No
	Five + owners		2.4		1.7	No	No
Gender composition[1]	Mixed gender	341	68.4	346	66.5	No	No
	All male		26.8		26.4	No	No
	All female		4.8		7.0	No	No
Age[1]	(Standard deviation)	338	5.0	327	5.2	No	No
Ethnic composition[1]	Single ethnicity	331	86.5	320	87.5	No	No
	Multiple ethnicities		13.5		12.5		
Industry tenure[1]	(Standard deviation)	335	6.1	325	6.1	No	No
Other startups[1]	(Standard deviation)	331	0.7	322	0.7	No	No
Occupational composition[1]	Single occupational class	336	28.4	326	28.4	No	No
	Multiple occupational classes		71.6		71.6		
Relational composition[2]	With spouses/live-in partners	361	57.9	346	58.8	No	No
	With nonspouse family member		18.9		19.3	No	No
	With business associates		14.9		16.3	No	No
	With other friends/associates		20.4		17.3	No	No

Size distribution includes individuals who are not acting on their own behalf (representing a business, bank, or other legal entity). All other statistics are limited to autonomous individuals.
[1] Excludes single-owner firms or firms that only have relevant data for a single owner.
[2] Indicates whether relationship is present for *any* pair of owners. Excludes single-owner firms.

sample attrition does not appear to systematically bias the demographic composition or human capital of the owner teams.

Thus far, we have examined turnover within entrepreneurial teams by comparing aggregate team attributes at two points in time. However, this approach does not give us insight into the particular characteristics of the lost and recruited owners nor of teams that have been affected by member turnover. In order to better understand changes in team composition, we must combine individual-level data, including variables that flag lost and recruited owners, with data on team-level attributes. Table 6.5 shows the exploratory results of such an analysis.

The first column of the table lists the individual-level variables that describe the owners who have left and joined the sample. The second column contains the team-level variables which have been cross-tabulated with the owner characteristics. In addition to sample sizes and weighted percentages, the table reports the expected percentage for each cell of the table along with a p-value from a two-sample proportion test. The analysis includes data from Wave A for all firms that were reinterviewed in Wave B, including single-owner enterprises.

Of the 1,209 owners (including respondents and others) present in the reduced Wave A sample, 57 left the startup firms prior to the Wave B reinterviews. In the same time period, 29 new owners were recruited, for a total of 1,181 owners in Wave B. Of the latter, 60.5% joined single-owner teams and 39.5 joined multiple-owner teams. This proportion was not significantly different from what one would expect based on the marginals in the sample. The same is true of the distribution of male owners who left mixed-gender (69.3%) and all-male (30.7%) startups. However, new male owners recruited between Waves A and B joined all-female teams in disproportionately high numbers (10%) but were under-represented among teams that had already been composed of both genders (15.8%). Of the male recruits, 74.2% joined all-male teams, which was not significantly different from the expected proportion. This finding suggests that gender homophily continues to play an important role for men in the early stages of startup formation, while firms owned by women may become more gender-diverse. Whether this choice is dictated by preference or by perceived necessity is an important empirical question, but one that is outside of the scope of this chapter. The loss of female owners, much like that of their male counterparts, does not differ significantly from the expected distribution. The recruitment of women follows a different path: a large proportion of new female owners join all-male teams, while considerably fewer join mixed-gender or all-female teams. However, this result should be viewed with caution, given the very small number of female recruits in the sample ($N = 7$).

Small sample size also poses a problem for interpreting the breakdown of lost and recruited owners by ethnicity. African American entrepreneurs seem to withdraw disproportionately from mixed-ethnicity teams, which could stem from negative experiences with owners from other ethnic backgrounds (in contrast, the majority of those recruited join all-black firms). However, given that only seven black owners leave the sample and only four join it, such conclusions are

Table 6.5 Owners who joined or left teams between waves: Panel Study of Entrepreneurial Dynamics II (2005), Waves A and B

Owner variable	Team composition (Wave A)	Owners lost				Owners recruited			
		Number of cases	Weighted % / mean	Expected %	Significant difference?	Number of cases	Weighted % / mean	Expected %	Significant difference?
All owners	Single-owner teams[1]	57	0.0	0.0	–[2]	29	60.5	50.9	No
	Multiple-owner teams		100.0	100.0			39.5	49.1	
Gender: Male	Mixed-gender teams	42	30.7	38.9	No	22	15.8	38.9	<0.05
	All-male teams		69.3	61.1			74.2	61.1	No
	All-female teams		0.0	0.0			10.0	0.0	<0.001
Gender: Female	Mixed-gender teams	15	61.4	55.2	–	7	5.7	55.2	–
	All-male teams		0.0	0.0			78.1	0.0	
	All-female teams		38.57	44.8			16.1	44.8	
Age	All teams	57	43.7	41.2	No	29	37.9	41.2	No
Ethnicity: White	Single-ethnicity teams	41	87.2	94.2	No	23	87.7	94.2	No
	Mixed-ethnicity teams		12.8	5.9			12.3	5.9	
Ethnicity: Black	Single-ethnicity teams	7	18.6	87.5	–	4	100.0	87.5	–
	Mixed-ethnicity teams		81.4	12.5			0.0	12.5	
Ethnicity: Hispanic	Single-ethnicity teams	6	64.9	79.2	–	0	0.0	–	–
	Mixed-ethnicity teams		35.1	20.8			0.0	–	
Industry tenure	All teams	56	9.7	8.2	No	28	8.1	8.2	No
Other startups	All teams	53	1.1	0.9	No	28	0.9	0.9	No
Education: less than BA	Highest level: less than BA	36	68.0	74.8	No	12	65.7	74.8	–
	Highest level: BA or higher		32.0	25.3			34.3	25.3	
Education: BA or Higher	Highest level: less than BA	19	0.0	0.0	No	2	0.0	0.0	No
	Highest level: BA or higher		100.0	100.0			100.0	100.0	

All statistics include single-owner firms.
[1] 1.0% of all teams both lost *and* recruited owners between Waves A and B.
[2] Tests for sample differences not carried out due to small sample size.

speculative at best. Among a similarly small sample of Hispanic owners ($N = 6$), 64.9% exit single-ethnicity teams, which is consistent with the expected distribution. White owners who leave ($N = 41$) and join ($N = 23$) the startups also do so in similar proportions to what one would expect based on the full sample marginals.

The mean age of owners who leave firms is slightly higher than that of the full sample: 43.7 years compared to 41.2 years. In contrast, newly recruited owners tend to be younger, with an average age of 37.9. However, neither difference is statistically significant. The younger age of the recruits may partly explain their shorter average industry experience. Owners who leave the sample have an average of 9.7 years of experience, while those who join it have an average of 8.1 years (compared to a full sample mean of 8.2 years). The same logic may also explain differences in prior entrepreneurship experience: on average, owners who leave the sample have helped start 1.1 businesses, while the figure for new recruits is 0.9 (compared to a full sample mean of 0.9).

Finally, owners who do not possess a bachelor's degree are somewhat more likely to leave teams co-owned by members who hold a B.A. or graduate degree (32%) than one would expect based on the marginals (68%). Still, the proportion of newly recruited owners with less than a B.A. who join these teams is quite similar (34.3%). Given that only two newly recruited owners have a bachelor's degree, the data do not allow us to draw conclusions about the role played by functional diversification in the turnover of startup owners.

6.4 Time Taken to Organize the Owner Team

A final analysis considers how long entrepreneurs take to organize their owner teams, based on the lag time between the date of initial owner involvement and the date of the last owner's recruitment (Table 6.6). To minimize sample attrition, attention here is limited to Wave A of the PSED II. As suggested by the preceding analyses, the number of cases where new owners are recruited to (or leave) these business startups between the two waves is relatively small. Moreover, the overall median lag time for multi-owner team formation in Wave B of the PSED II is identical to that observed in Wave A (2 months).

The descriptive results in the table suggest several differences in the median organizing times depending on owner team composition. Predictably, the duration of team formation rises monotonically with the number of owners, from just a single month (on average) for two-owner teams to nearly a year for teams with five or more owners. There is also some indication that the involvement of institutional owners adds to this phase of the startup process, with the median lag time for new ventures with institutional owners being triple that of ventures without institutional involvement. Notably, this difference is observed even though the majority of institutional owners already have an existing business or personal relationship with these nascent entrepreneurs, rather than being contacted via formal applications, referrals, or other means.

Table 6.6 Median time required to recruit all owners (from date of initial owner involvement): Panel Study of Entrepreneurial Dynamics II (2005–2006), Wave A

Variable	Sub-category	Median (months)	Significant difference?
(Overall sample)		2	–
Size	Two owners	1	$p < 0.001$
	Three owners	3	
	Four owners	7	
	Five + owners	11	
Institutional owners	None	2	$p < 0.05$
	Some	6	
Gender composition	Mixed gender	2	No
	All male	3	
	All female	1	
Ethnic composition	Single ethnicity	2	$p < 0.01$
	Multiple ethnicities	6	
Occupational composition	Single occupational class	2	No
	Multiple occupational classes	2	
Relational composition[1]	With*out* spouses/live-in partners	3	$p < 0.05$
	With nonspouse family member	6	$p < 0.001$
	With business associates	1	No
	With other friends/associates	4	$p < 0.05$
Sample size		$N = 555$	

All statistics exclude single-owner firms. Statistical significance of timing differences is evaluated over sub-categories within variables using non-parametric tests (Mann–Whitney test for two sub-categories, Kruskal–Wallis test for three or more).
[1]Tests of timing differences are conducted with respect to a reference category in which a particular relationship is present (spouses/live-in partners) or absent (all other relations).

A demographic analysis reveals some variation in the duration of owner team formation. All-female owner teams appear to take slightly less time to become organized than mixed-gender teams, which, in turn, take slightly less time than all-male teams. These differences, however, are not statistically significant. More dramatic is the gap between homogeneous ethnic groups, which average two months for team formation, and heterogeneous ethnic groups, which average half a year. The reasons for this gap are difficult to infer from simple bivariate associations. Respondents in the PSED II report that the amount of time they have known co-ethnic partners (mean of 18.9 years) is substantially higher than the amount of time they have known partners who do not share their ethnic identity (10.1 years, $t = 5.22$, $p < 0.001$). One plausible explanation, then, is that co-ethnic owners require less time to develop the trust needed to secure mutual involvement in a business venture, owing to higher levels of a priori familiarity. Alternatively, one might posit that the increased lag time in heterogeneous teams reflects an in-group bias, in which entrepreneurs first approach potential co-ethnic partners for their business ventures and, when faced with a lack of enthusiasm among co-ethnics, only later turn to business partners that do not match their ethnic background.

The table also offers estimates of the effect of social network characteristics on the duration of owner team formation. The involvement of spouses or cohabiting partners appears to accelerate the process of team formation slightly (two month median duration versus three months for owner teams without this relational tie). This cannot be taken to imply that the existence of intimate ties within the owner teams is generally correlated with rapid recruitment. Teams involving kinship relations appear to require relatively long to form, while those among former co-workers emerge quickly. The duration of team formation among owners with ties of friendship or acquaintanceship outside the workplace lies between these two extremes.

As in the case of aggregate figures on the structure of owner teams, some caution should be employed in interpreting these descriptive statistics. The calculated duration of owner team formation is sensitive to the problem of *right-censoring*—i.e., the possibility that more owners could be recruited to any given startup after the interview date and that the "end" of team formation is not truly observed in these cases. In addition, none of the statistics reported in Table 6.6 control for other variables and should therefore not be taken as a basis for causal inferences.

6.5 Discussion

Data on owner teams in the PSED II offer researchers a rare opportunity to observe the extent of stability in group formation over time, addressing the degree to which processes such as homophilous affiliation, functional diversification, and network constraint continue to impact the way that entrepreneurs become linked to one another. Our descriptive results are consistent with the intuitions that in-group biases by ethnic identity strongly affect the formation of owner teams in the United States and that a majority of entrepreneurial groups are constructed on top of pre-existing networks, particularly those involving spouses or live-in partners. Not only are these owner teams more numerically prevalent than other entrepreneurial groups, but they also appear to form more rapidly. There is less clear evidence in favor of the claim that startup owners seek (or are able to achieve) functional diversification in affiliating with other entrepreneurs. However, all of these results should be viewed as preliminary and subject to further investigation with multivariate models of group composition (e.g., Ruef, 2002; Ruef et al., 2003).

Considered in historical context, the changes observed in owner team characteristics between the PSED I and PSED II are remarkably limited. While one survey was conducted during the heart of the "startup boom" of the late 1990s and the other was conducted in the midst of a developing credit crisis, these environmental changes do not seem to have had much impact on the fundamental features of entrepreneurial group formation, either with respect to size, demography, human capital, or interpersonal networks. Within the PSED II panel itself, there is also very little change in owner characteristics between the first two waves (2005–2006 and 2006–2007). Few owners have left the nascent businesses that remain in the sample and fewer still have been recruited as new owners between survey waves.

In conclusion, we will acknowledge a number of data limitations that affect the analysis of owner demography and networks in the PSED II. Perhaps the most salient is that all compositional features of owner team demography and networks are based on the reports of a single entrepreneur. Prior work on perceptions of social network structure have suggested that there can be considerable variation on socio-metric observations between individuals within entrepreneurial organizations; moreover, accuracy in cognition appears to be correlated with interpersonal power in such contexts (Krackhardt, 1990). As a consequence, measurement error in the PSED II network module may be high when these items are elicited from owners who lack much influence in the startup process.

A parallel caveat applies to the application of demographic categories, especially ethnicity. When predictions regarding group processes are dependent on the *self-categorization* of entrepreneurs, then only the respondent's answers to the demographic items serve as valid measures of personal identity. This is especially true for studies that anticipate that in-group biases will be influenced more by internalized perceptions of group membership, rather than externally ascribed status characteristics (see Oldmeadow et al., 2003).

Despite these limitations, the PSED I and II offer a unique resource for researchers that seek to understand the demographic and network composition of business owner teams in the United States. Arguably, these are the only data sets that offer a nation-wide, representative sample of small groups and isolates involved in a common type of social activity. Future scholarship should unpack in greater detail how different mechanisms of group formation (homophily, functionality, and networks) interact in this context, how these processes unfold over time, and what impact they have on metrics of efficacy and fairness within entrepreneurial groups.

Notes

1. Other mechanisms reviewed in the literature, such as *status-driven recruitment* (the effort of entrepreneurs to affiliate with high-status alters) or *ecological constraint* (the limitations imposed by the number of available entrepreneurial partners in the same region or industry), will not be addressed here (see Ruef et al., 2003, for further discussion).
2. Like some of the recent work on top management teams (e.g., Boone et al., 2004), these conflicting processes lead to ambiguity as to whether startup teams will *evolve* to become more functionally diverse, even in the face of environmental pressures. Our discussion of owner turnover and recruitment over time, below, sheds some preliminary light on this issue.

3. For one basis of comparison, see the *Statistical Abstract of the United States* (US Department of Commerce, 2008), Tables 6, 55, 217, and 598.
4. Some caution should be observed in comparing the statistics for ethnicity in the PSED I and PSED II data sets. The former survey relies on a mutually exclusive categorization of owners' ethnic identity, while the latter allows respondents to select as many categories as they feel are appropriate. Comparisons are sensitive to the treatment of multi-ethnic owners.
5. For purposes of calculating these statistics, "computing professionals" are defined as individuals with a three-digit occupational code ranging from 100 ("computer scientists and systems analysts") to 111 ("network systems and data communication analysts"), using the 2000 Census schema.
6. The PSED II data suggest that the proportion of startup owners with a high school education (or less) who are involved in internet or direct selling is equal to that of owners with an education beyond the high school level (z-test statistic = 0.57, no significant difference).
7. A comparison of the PSED I statistics in Table 2 with previously published descriptive findings (e.g., Ruef, Aldrich, & Carter, 2003: Table 2) may appear to indicate some minor discrepancies. These differences result entirely from two methodological considerations: (1) previously published results tend to use slightly more restrictive sampling criteria (e.g., removing cases in which legal entities will own more than 50% of a startup venture); and (2) the number of cases reported within the tables in this chapter are always unweighted.

References

Aldrich, H., & Ruef, M. (2006). *Organizations evolving* (2nd ed.). London: Sage.
Allport, G. (1954). *The nature of prejudice*. Reading, MA: Addison-Wesley.
Boone, C., van Olffen, W., van Witteloostuijn, A., & De Brabander, B. (2004). The genesis of top management team diversity: Selective turnover among top management teams in Dutch newspaper publishing, 1970–94. *Academy of Management Journal, 47*, 633–656.
Boyd, R. (2000). Race, labor market disadvantage, and survivalist entrepreneurship: Black women in the urban North during the Great Depression. *Sociological Forum, 15*, 647–670.
Burt, R. (1992). *Structural holes: The social structure of competition*. Cambridge, MA: Harvard University Press.
Eisenhardt, K., & Schoonhoven, C. B. (1990). Organizational growth: Linking founding team, strategy, environment, and growth among U.S. semiconductor ventures, 1978–1988. *Administrative Science Quarterly, 35*, 504–529.
Ensley, M. (1999). *Entrepreneurial teams as determinants of new venture performance*. New York: Garland.
Gartner, W., Shaver, K., Gatewood, E., & Katz, J. (1994). Finding the entrepreneur in entrepreneurship. *Entrepreneurship Theory and Practice, 18*, 5–9.
Granovetter, M. (1985). Economic action and social structure: The problem of embeddedness. *American Journal of Sociology, 91*, 481–510.
Granovetter, M. (1995). *Getting a job: A study of contacts and careers* (2nd ed.). Chicago: University of Chicago Press.
Kamm, J., Shuman, J., Seeger, J., & Nurick, A. (1990). Entrepreneurial teams in new venture creation: A research agenda. *Entrepreneurship Theory and Practice, 14*, 7–17.
Kanter, R. M. (1977). *Men and women of the corporation*. New York: Basic Books.
Krackhardt, D. (1990). Assessing the political landscape: Structure, cognition and power in organizations. *Administrative Science Quarterly, 35*, 342–369.
Lazarsfeld, P., & Merton, R. (1954). Friendship as a social process: A substantive and methodological analysis. In M. Berger, T. Abel, & C. Page (Eds.), *Freedom and control in modern society* (pp. 18–66). New York: Octagon Books.

McPherson, J. M., Smith-Lovin, L., & Cook, J. (2001). Birds of a feather: Homophily in social networks. *Annual Review of Sociology, 27*, 415–444.

Mouw, T. (2003). Social capital and finding a job: Do contacts matter? *American Sociological Review, 68*, 868–898.

Oldmeadow, J., Platow, M., Foddy, M., & Anderson, D. (2003). Self-categorization, status, and social influence. *Social Psychology Quarterly, 66*, 138–152.

Pettigrew, T., & Tropp, L. (2006). A meta-analytic test of intergroup contact theory. *Journal of Personality and Social Psychology, 90*, 751–783.

Raines, J. P., & Leathers, C. (2000). Behavioral influences of bureaucratic organizations and the Schumpeterian Controversy. *Journal of Socio-Economics, 29*, 375–388.

Ruef, M. (2002). A structural event approach to the analysis of group composition. *Social Networks, 24*, 135–160.

Ruef, M. (in press). *The entrepreneurial group: Social relations, identities, and collective action.* Princeton, NJ: Princeton University Press.

Ruef, M., Aldrich, H., & Carter, N. (2003). The structure of founding teams: Homophily, strong ties, and isolation among U.S. entrepreneurs. *American Sociological Review, 68*, 195–222.

Slater, P. (1955). Role differentiation in small groups. *American Sociological Review, 20*, 300–310.

Stinchcombe, A. (1965). Social structure and organizations. In J. G. March (Ed.), *Handbook of organizations* (pp. 142–193). Chicago: Rand McNally.

U.S. Department of Commerce. (2008). *Statistical abstract of the United States: The national data book.* U.S. Government Printing Office.

Chapter 7
Owner Founders, Nonowner Founders and Helpers

M. Diane Burton, Phillip C. Anderson, and Howard E. Aldrich

7.1 Introduction

Rarely are successful ventures founded by a lone individual without any assistance from others (Shane, 2003, pp. 237–239). Instead, starting a new venture typically involves mobilizing resources from a number of different stakeholders. Unfortunately, previous research has tended to privilege one set of stakeholders: "founders." Consequently, other stakeholders have been relatively ignored. As interest in the characteristics of founding teams has grown, the field's attention must now turn to the question of who exactly should be counted as a member of the "founding team" and how we should describe the other contributing stakeholders. The PSED II data is uniquely suited to address questions about the constellation of people involved in starting a new venture, including their characteristics, relationships, and the kinds of contributions they make.

Although the legal definition of a "business owner" is quite specific, the definition of a "business founder" is ambiguous. As a result, entrepreneurship scholars have had to develop their own definitions. Some have assumed that being a founder is a socially defined category and have relied on self-reports from individuals involved in start-ups to identify the people who were considered to be founders (Baron, Burton, & Hannan, 1996; Roberts, 1991; Wasserman, 2003). Others have limited their definition of founder to a priori criteria such as holding an executive position at the time of legal incorporation (Eisenhardt & Schoonhoven, 1990) or working full-time by some pre-defined time period (Francis & Sandberg, 2000). Still others have limited their definition of "founder" to those who hold ownership stakes in the enterprise (Kamm, Shuman, Seeger, & Nurick, 1990; Reynolds, 2000).

In this chapter we describe the characteristics and contributions of key nonowners and helpers in an effort to further our understanding of founding teams. (Chapter 10 is devoted to describing owners and is an important complement to our work.) In this chapter we place primary emphasis on PSED II;

M.D. Burton (✉)
School of Industrial and Labor Relations, Cornell University, Ithaca, NY, USA
e-mail: burton@mit.edu

however, whenever possible, we compare data from PSED I and PSED II and critically evaluate the usefulness of "founder" as a conceptual category. We conclude with a preliminary analysis relating founding team characteristics to nascent venture outcomes.

7.2 Survey Questions

We begin with a description of the precise survey questions regarding owners, key nonowners, and helpers. For each category, respondents were first asked for the total number of persons/entities. Respondents were then asked for the first names of up to four owners other than themselves, up to three key nonowners, and up to three helpers. For each named person, the survey included a battery of questions that gathered data on demographic characteristics and contributions.

Because prior research indicated that a large fraction of nascent businesses are started by individuals or spousal pairs, the opening question (G1) first identified the new businesses that were expected to be owned by the respondent, the respondent with a spouse, and the respondent and others.

> *G1: As you know, the creation of a new business often involves contributions of many individuals. We would like to start with a list of those people who expect to share ownership of the new business, including any other business or financial institutions that expect an ownership share. Will the new business be owned only by yourself, only by yourself and your spouse, or by yourself and some other people or businesses?*

Solo entrepreneurs can then be coded as having a single owner and spousal pairs as having two owners. Respondents who indicate that their business is being started with others are asked how many others in question G2:

> *G2: [IF the business will be owned by others in addition to the respondent and his/her spouse, ask] "How many total people or other businesses or financial institutions will share ownership of the new business?"*

Although the reported size of the ownership team ranged from 1 to 95, the vast majority of respondents to the survey were either solo entrepreneurs (51%) or spouse/partner pairs (21%). Of the 1,214 respondents to the survey, 27% indicated they were part of a team that included someone other than their spouse and only 1% of the respondents reported having an ownership team of 6 or more individuals. Thus, for 99% of the teams in the survey we were able to collect complete information on individual owners' characteristics by asking demographic and network questions for up to five named owners.

> *G13: "How many other people, who will* not *have an ownership share, have made a <u>distinctive</u> contribution to the founding of this new business, such as planning, development, financial resources, materials, training, or business services?"*

From the 1,191 respondents who answered question G13, the reported number of "other people" ranged from 0 to 95. While a majority, 60% of the sample, reported no one, a full 40% of the sample stated one or more individuals were involved in launching the new venture. Detailed information, including demographic characteristics, network relationships, and kinds of contributions, was collected for up to three named individuals who were identified as making distinctive contributions. Only 6% of the respondents indicated that four or more people made distinctive contributions. Thus, by asking for detailed information for up to three individuals, we were able to obtain information for the great majority of nonowner founders.

> G18: "How many other people, who will <u>not</u> have an ownership share, have provided significant support, advice, or guidance on a <u>regular basis</u> to this new business?"

Question G18 was asked after the series of questions naming individuals who had made distinctive contributions and was intended to generate additional names of "helpers." Among the 1,196 respondents to this question, we found that nearly two-thirds (65%) responded "zero" and the remaining 35% identified the number of helpers as ranging from 1 to 50. Only 5% of the teams indicated that 4 or more people provided significant support, advice, or guidance to the new business. Thus, as with nonowner founders, by asking for detailed information for up to three individuals, we obtained information about the great majority of helpers.

The specific items asked of owners, key nonowners, and helpers, including question wording and identifiers, are presented in Table 7.1.

The questions described in Table 7.1 generate data on a set of individuals who were affiliated with, and contributed to, the nascent venture. This set of individuals is comparable in many respects, but not all, to the individuals who were identified in PSED I as owners and helpers. In PSED I, after respondents were asked to name the "start-up team" which was defined as "those who would expect to own the business," they were asked the following question: "Are there other people, those that would NOT be on the start-up team, who have been particularly helpful to you in getting the business started?" and allowed to name up to five individuals. Note that this question did not mention the *ownership status* of possible persons named as helpers and thus is not directly comparable to the question asked in PSED II.

In the remainder of this chapter, we provide an overview of the basic data that was collected in PSED II and compare the PSED II findings with those from PSED I. We analyze alternative definitions of founding team and then conclude by relating founding team characteristics to venture status after 12 months.

7.3 PSED II Descriptive Statistics

In Table 7.2 we present more detailed descriptive statistics for all three categories of start-up team "affiliates," a term we use to capture the full set of persons who might be owners, key nonowners, and helpers. We use the term "affiliate" because it does not presume an equity-based relationship between the

Table 7.1 PSED II questionnaire items for named individuals associated with the new venture

Question phrase	Owner question IDs (up to 5)	Key nonowner question IDs (up to 3)	Helper question IDs (up to 3)
Is [name] acting on their own behalf or does [name] represent a business, financial institution, government agency, or some other legal entity?	G5 Asked of named individuals other than respondent	G15	G20
Has [name] personally accepted responsibility for any critical components of the start-up process	n/a	G16	G21
Does [name] expect to have a managerial or supervisory role in the new business—participating in day-to-day operation decisions?	n/a	G17	G22
Demographics			
Is [name] male or female?	H1	M2	N2
How old (are you/is [name])?	H2	M3	N3
Are you/Is [name] Hispanic or Latino?	H3	M4	N4
Are you/is [name] White, Black or African American, American Indian, Asian, Pacific Islander, or of Mixed Racial Background	H4	M5	N5
What is your/[name]'s current marital status or living arrangement—married, living with a partner but not married, separated, divorced, widowed or never married?	H5	M6	N6
What is the highest level of education (you have/[name] has completed)?	H6	M7	N7
How many years have you known [name]?	H7	M8	N8
How would you describe your relationship with [name]—are you spouses, partners sharing a household, relatives living in the same household, relatives living in different households, friends or acquaintances from work, friends or acquaintances you have not worked with, strangers before joining the new business team, or do you have some other type of relationship?	H8	M9	N9

7 Owner Founders, Nonowner Founders and Helpers 119

Table 7.1 (continued)

Question phrase	Owner question IDs (up to 5)	Key nonowner question IDs (up to 3)	Helper question IDs (up to 3)
What is your/[name]'s primary occupation	H10	M10	N10
How many years of work experience have you/has [name] had in the industry where this new business will compete?	H11	M11	N11
How many other businesses have you/has [name] helped to start as an owner or part-owner?	H12	M12	N12
Contribution	n/a (asked about each type of contribution in a separate question.)	What was the primary contribution of [name] to this new business—financial, making introductions, providing advice, providing training, physical resources, business services, personal services or what? M13	What was the primary contribution of [name] to this new business—financial, making introductions, providing advice, providing training, physical resources, business services, personal services or what? N13
Employment exclusivity	In terms of current work activity, are you/is [name] working for others for pay? H15	Is [name} an employee or an exclusive subcontractor of this new business? M14	Is [name} an employee or an exclusive subcontractor of this new business? N14
Hours	Have you/has [name] begun to work 35 hours or more per week on this new business? H17	Does [name] work for pay on the new business 35 hours or more per week? M15	Does [name] work for pay on the new business 35 hours or more per week? N15

Table 7.2 Descriptive statistics for owners, key nonowners and helpers

Teams	Owners Cases	%	Key non-owners Cases	%	Helpers Cases	%
Number of individuals named	1,214		1,191		1,196	
Zero		0		60		65
One		51		18		14
Two		35		10		11
Three		7		6		5
Four		4		1		1
Five or more		2		5		4
At least one member from an institution	1,214	3	1,191	9	1,196	10
At least one individual who is an employee or exclusive subcontractor			1,191	11	1,196	6
At least one individual working 35+ hours per week for the venture	1,214	35	1,191	3	1,196	2
Within-category demographics (inc. solos)	1,214		416		339	
Gender composition						
All female		24		28		29
All male		46		43		47
Mixed gender		30		28		24
Ethnic composition	1,202		412		335	
All white		67		66		62
All nonwhite (single ethnicity)		16		16		17
Multiple ethnicities		18		18		21

Individuals	Owners Cases	%	Key non-owners Cases	%	Helpers Cases	%
Working on own behalf	2,038	93	852	84	754	79
Personally accepted responsibility			853	35	756	18
Expects to have a management role			850	25	754	14
Employee or exclusive subcontractor			690	26	590	16
Working 35+ hours per week for the venture	1,972	26	168	21	84	29
Years of industry experience:	1,958		668		578	
Mean		7.2		7.3		7.7
Standard deviation		(9.3)		(10.6)		(11.7)
Range		0–54		0–70		0–88
Years of mgmt experience:	1.940					
Mean		8.3				
Standard deviation		9.1				
Range		0–60				
Prior startups:	1,946		630		533	
Mean		0.8		1.7(7.1)		1.8
Standard deviation		(1.6)		0–95		(7.5)
Range		0–25				0–95

7 Owner Founders, Nonowner Founders and Helpers 121

Table 7.2 (continued)

Individuals	Owners Cases	%	Key non-owners Cases	%	Helpers Cases	%
Years known by respondent:	760		693		589	
Mean		15.6		14.9		13.7
Standard deviation		(13.2)		(13.3)		(13.2)
Range		1–73		1–62		1–58
Relationship to respondent:	764		695		587	
Spouse/partner		39		12		7
Relative		20		35		31
Business associate		12		17		24
Friend		25		27		30
Stranger		5		9		7
Gender (male)	1,981	62	696	58	592	59
Age:	1,962		676		565	
Mean		39.0		42.1		43.4
Standard deviation		(12.9)		(15.2)		(14.9)
Range		15–86		9–95		7–86
Ethnicity:	1,957		686		584	
White		72		72		70
Black		12		13		14
Hispanic		3		6		4
Asian		1		1		1
American Indian		2		1		3
Pacific Islander		0		1		1
Mixed/Other		9		8		7
Education:	1,962		640		533	
Up to high school		30		36		40
Some college		35		21		20
Bachelors degree		23		24		25
Graduate school		13		16		15

Responses have been weighted.
For team statistics, the number of cases represents the total number of respondent teams answering the question. For the individual statistics, the number of cases represents the aggregated total number of all responses for up to five owners, up to three key nonowners and up to three helpers per team.

person named and the venture. The table is divided into two sections. In the top section, the unit of analysis is the nascent venture. In the bottom section, the unit of analysis is the individual. Data describing each nascent venture contains up to five owners (including the respondent), up to three key nonowners and up to three helpers. The individual statistics aggregate across these individuals within each category of affiliate.

In Table 7.2 we see that most of the nascent ventures have very few affiliates. Most of the ventures are started by a solo owner (51%) or a two-person ownership team (35%) and the prevalence of key nonowners and helpers is relatively low. Very few teams have affiliates who are employees or exclusive contractors and the numbers are further diminished when we consider affiliates who are working full-time for the venture. We note that only 35% of the ventures have at least one owner for whom the venture is a full-time endeavor.

In Table 7.2 we also see that across the three categories, it is clear that owners, key nonowners and helpers are demographically quite similar, a high degree of status homophily. They are most commonly white, middle-aged men who have slightly over seven years of industry experience and have done one or more start-ups before. All three categories of venture affiliates tend to have long-standing relationships with the respondent. In addition, when we average across all individuals, the gender, age, race, and education profiles are quite similar. Although the age range of key nonowners and helpers seems odd (from 7 to 95), it reflects the tendency of some respondents to name their young children and aged relatives in answer to these questions. At the same time, owners appear to differ from key nonowners and helpers in several ways. Owners are slightly younger and tend to have less prior start-up experience. In addition, there are a large number of spousal pairs who intend to jointly own the nascent venture.

Of special note is the low frequency with which "strangers" are named as affiliates of the start-up team. Indeed, when reporting on their relationships with owners, key nonowners and helpers, respondents rarely described these affiliates as strangers. Instead, these affiliates were drawn from the ranks of friends and family.

While most affiliates were working on their own behalf, a nontrivial proportion represented institutions. Unfortunately, if an individual affiliate was representing an institution, we have limited information about him/her. The numbers are higher at the individual level (7% of the owners, 16% of key nonowners, and 21% of helpers) than they are at the team level. For key nonowners and helpers we asked whether they had "personally accepted responsibility for any critical components of the start-up process" and whether they "expected to have a managerial or supervisory role in the new business." Interestingly, these two questions begin to suggest ways that key nonowners differ from helpers, as key nonowners are more involved than helpers, although the differences are not great. Key nonowners seem to be more likely to have personally accepted responsibility for a critical component of the start-up process than helpers (35% versus 18%). Key nonowners are more likely to expect to participate in day-to-day operations than helpers (25% versus 14%) and are more likely to be employees or exclusive subcontractors (25% versus 16%).

Given the question wording and sequencing, it seemed likely that different people would come to mind as key nonowners and as helpers. This was confirmed by cross-tabulating the use of key nonowners and the use of helpers for each nascent venture. We found that 38% of the teams use neither, 13% of the teams use both, 27% of the teams use key nonowners but not helpers, and 22% of the teams use helpers but not key nonowners.

Although we observe some demographic similarity between owners and the two nonowner categories of key nonowners and helpers, these affiliate categories differ in ways that broaden, to a limited extent, the diversity of the

7 Owner Founders, Nonowner Founders and Helpers

Table 7.3 Gender and ethnic homophily when either key nonowners or helpers are included with owners

	Owners and key nonowners		Owners and helpers	
	Cases	%	Cases	%
Gender composition	416		339	
All female		11		11
All male		20		26
Mixed gender		69		63
Ethnic composition	410		331	
All white		57		54
All nonwhite (single ethnicity)		10		9
Multiple ethnicities		33		37

founding team. We pursue this issue more fully in Table 7.3, where we examine the demographic similarity of owners to key nonowners and helpers. In this analysis, we consider the subset of teams where we have available demographic data on one or more owners and one or more affiliates.

As Table 7.3 reveals, when we look at the composition of each group when owners are included with one of the two affiliate groups—key nonowners or helpers—we see less homophily than the within-group levels that were reported in Table 7.2. For example, although only 30% of the ownership teams were of mixed gender, owners and key nonowners comprise a mixed gender group 69% of the time, and owners and helpers comprise a mixed gender group 63% of the time. Ethnic homophily, while strong in all situations, seems slightly weaker when looking at groups of owners and key nonowners or groups of owners and helpers. The proportion of mixed ethnicity groups increases from 18% when looking at owners alone to 33% for owner/key nonowner groups and 37% for owner/helper groups. This strong ethnic homophily is likely driven by the fact that there are a large number of spousal pairs and family members involved in these nascent ventures. It is also consistent with prior research on homophily among voluntary relationships (Ruef, Aldrich, & Carter, 2003).

As a first step in understanding family relationships and contributions to nascent ventures in Table 7.4 we present a simple analysis of nonowner and helper contributions, by the type of ownership team and the gender of the respondent.

We are intrigued by the gender differences revealed in Table 7.4. Given the long-standing fact that men are more likely to become entrepreneurs than women, it is not surprising that there are more male respondents (761 of 1,214, 63%) than female respondents (453 of 1,214, 37%) in the sample. However, we see that among men and women entrepreneurs, there appear to be different patterns of co-ownership and collaboration (Aldrich, Elam, & Reese, 1996; Renzulli, Aldrich, & Moody 2000). The majority of both men (446 of 761, 59%) and women (299 of 453, 66%) report having a spouse or partner. But, among the nascent entrepreneurs who are working with one or more others, female respondents are much more likely to be launching a venture

Table 7.4 Tabulation of key nonowners and helpers by gender and owner team type

Respondent gender	No. of cases	% using key nonowners	% using helpers	No. of respondents with spouse/ partner	% Reported spouse/ partner as key nonowner	% Reported spouse/ partner as helper
Female						
Owner team type						
Solo	244	48	33	131	27	7
Spouse/partner	118	30	39	117	1	0
Other	91	33	30	51	7	5
Total	453			299		
Male						
Owner team type						
Solo	384	39	38	163	15	9
Spouse/partner	150	37	34	147	0	2
Other	227	39	32	136	9	5
Total	761			446		

The percentages are weighted but the number of cases are not weighted.
A few respondents who reported that the second owner is a spouse/partner (question H8) did not report their current living arrangement status as *married* or *living with a partner* (question H5).

with their spouse or partner as a co-owner (27% of the women as opposed to 18% of the men); whereas the male respondents are more likely to be launching a venture with other family members, friends, or business affiliates (32% of the men as opposed to 20% of the women). In addition, the female solo entrepreneurs are much more likely to credit their spouse as a key nonowner (27%) than are the male solo entrepreneurs (15%). We see that there is some small potential overlap across the individuals who are affiliated with a nascent venture in the fact that 1% of the female respondents who reported that their spouse or partner was a co-owner also listed that person as a key nonowner. Similarly 2% of the male respondents who indicated they were in a venture that was jointly owned by them and their spouse/partner also listed their spouse/partner as a helper.

Understanding the role of immediate and extended family members in nascent entrepreneurship as well as possible gender differences is an important topic that should be studied in more detail.

7.4 Comparing PSED I and PSED II

The PSED II data included two categories of nonowner affiliates: key nonowners and helpers. PSED I only included a single helper category. As shown in Table 7.5, we find that 63% of the nascent ventures in PSED I had one or more

Table 7.5 Comparing PSED I helpers with PSED II key non-owners and helpers

	PSED I Helpers	PSED II combined categories	PSED II disaggregated categories Key nonowners	PSED II disaggregated categories Helpers
Maximum per team	5	6	3	3
Teams using outside assistance	63%	62%	40%	35%
Relationship to respondent				
Spouse/partner	6%	9%	12%	7%
Relative	24%	33%	35%	31%
Business associate	26%	20%	17%	24%
Friend	41%	29%	27%	30%
Teacher	3%			
Stranger		8%	9%	7%
Contribution to the venture				
Financial support	8%	11%	16%	5%
Physical resources	6%	7%	10%	7%
Business services	8%	9%	10%	9%
Advice	37%	44%	36%	53%
Providing introductions	21%	7%	7%	7%
Training	14%	9%	9%	8%
Personal services	6%	10%	10%	10%
All of the above		1%	1%	1%
Gender (male)	63%	58%	58%	59%
Age	42.4	42.7	42.1	43.4
Years known by respondent	16.6	14.4	14.9	14.0
Ethnicity				
White	75%	71%	72%	70%
Black	15%	13%	13%	14%
Hispanic	6%	5%	6%	4%
Asian	1%	2%	1%	1%
American Indian	1%	1%	1%	3%
Pacific Islander	1%	1%	1%	1%
Mixed/Other	1%	7%	8%	7%

Responses have been weighted

helpers; whereas key nonowner and helper assistance in PSED II was used by 40% and 35% of teams, respectively. However, if we combine PSED II key nonowners and helpers into a single category, under the assumption that this may be what respondents in PSED I were doing when they answered the "helper" question, we can ask about the fraction of nascent ventures that acknowledge any kind of assistance. We calculate that 62% of PSED II teams use either key nonowners or helpers or both. Thus, we can take some comfort in the fact that the overall rates of outside assistance are comparable across the two samples (63% versus 62%). Distinguishing key nonowners from helpers begins to reveal differences across the categories in their relationship to the respondent and in the nature of contributions to the nascent venture. Family ties tend to be more prevalent in the key nonowner than in the helper category, but the differences are not dramatic. The notable differences between key nonowners and helpers arise in descriptions of the kinds of contributions they made. Key nonowners are more likely to have contributed tangible assets (financial support, physical resources, business services) than those identified as helpers; whereas, helpers are more likely to be giving advice.

PSED II entrepreneurs appear to rely more heavily on family and less heavily on friends than PSED I entrepreneurs. In addition, the PSED II entrepreneurs appear to receive fewer introductions from their helpers. While the general pattern of contributions to the venture appears similar across the two surveys, it is worth noting that distinguishing key nonowners from generic helpers reveals that key nonowners are more often contributing material resources, especially financial support, than are helpers. Instead, the most common contribution of helpers is in providing advice.

7.5 What Does It Mean to Be a Founder?

We opened this chapter with the conceptual problem of defining the term "founder." This is an important problem for the field of entrepreneurship because it shapes how we interpret our findings and what recommendations our research implies. For example, there is an oft-invoked research finding that larger founding teams are advantaged over smaller founding teams (Beckman, Burton, & O'Reilly, 2007; Carter, Aldrich, & Ruef, 2004). The theorized mechanism is one of accumulated human capital, with more people bringing more skills to a venture (Cooper, Gimeno-Gascon, & Woo, 1994). However, if a founding team is defined in terms of ownership and the owners are disproportionately passive investors, then their accumulated human capital is not really the key resource they bring to the team, as their human capital is not being used in an operational way. Instead, they provide an advantage to the venture through the assets they bring to what is apparently an already promising venture. If, on the other hand, the founding team is defined in terms of employment status, then the founders' human capital is more directly tied to the performance of the venture on an ongoing basis. If the founding team includes both of these categories of founders, we cannot cleanly separate these two mechanisms by which team size translates into firm performance.

The rich data collected about individuals affiliated with the start-up process in the PSED II allows us to empirically explore some of the consequences of different definitions of the term. In Table 7.6 we present descriptive statistics for nascent venture "founding teams" based on four different definitions of founder: (1) Owners: any named owner, (2) All affiliates: any individual named as

7 Owner Founders, Nonowner Founders and Helpers

Table 7.6 Comparing alternative definitions of founding teams

	(1) Owners		(2) All affiliates		(3) Owner-workers		(4) Affiliate-workers	
Team size (self-report):	1,214		1,214		419		514	
Mean		1.8		3.8		2.0		4.5
Standard deviation		2.5		5.7		4.0		8.0
Range		1–95		1–146		1–95		1–146
Team size (detailed data collected):	1,214		1,214		419		514	
Mean		1.6		2.8		1.2		1.5
Standard deviation		0.8		1.5		0.5		1.0
Range		1–5		1–9		1–4		1–7
% Solo entrepreneurs	1,214	53%	1,214	22%	419	81%	514	68%
% of teams with institutional member(s)	1,214	3%	1,214	19%	419	0%	514	0%
Industry experience	1,211		1,212		419		514	
Average years		7.6		7.8		9.1		9.0
Standard deviation		8.4		8.1		9.6		9.8
Range		0–47		0–50		0–50		0–50
% No industry experience		16%		12%		12%		13%
Start-up experience	1,213		1,213		417		506	
Average startups		0.8		1.0		0.9		1.0
Standard deviation		1.5		2.9		1.9		2.2
Range		0–20		0–82		0–25		0–25
% No start-up experience		51%		36%		55%		51%
Maximum education level	1,212		1,213		417		510	
High school		21%		17%		29%		29%
Some college		38%		31%		38%		35%
Bachelors degree		24%		28%		22%		24%
Some graduate school		16%		24%		10%		12%
% No college degrees		60%		48%		68%		64%
Age	1,203		1,205		414		508	
Average age of group		38.9		40.7		38.4		38.2
Standard deviation		12.0		11.1		12.0		11.9
Range		18–81		18–81		18–78		17–78
Homophily (*for teams with 2+ members*)								
Gender homophily	557		935		78		157	
All female		6%		9%		7%		7%
All male		29%		22%		44%		41%
Mixed gender		65%		69%		49%		52%
Ethnic homophily	552		927		78		156	
All white		64%		58%		71%		55%
		11%		10%		8%		10%

Table 7.6 (continued)

	(1) Owners	(2) All affiliates	(3) Owner-workers	(4) Affiliate-workers
All nonwhite (single ethnicity)				
Multiple ethnicities	25%	32%	21%	35%
Family relationships	556	934	78	122
No family	29%	30%	49%	48%
Some family	9%	31%	1%	9%
All family	62%	39%	51%	43%

Responses have been weighted.

playing a role in the creation of a nascent venture including owners, key nonowners, and helpers, (3) Owner-workers: only those owners who are reported to be working full-time on the venture, and (4) Affiliate-workers: owners who are reported to be working full-time on the venture plus key nonowners and helpers who are described as either employees or exclusive sub-contractors.

Most striking in Table 7.6 is that by changing the operational definition, we generate very different descriptions of founding teams. We first consider team size and present two different calculations: size based on the number of owners, key nonowners and helpers reported by the respondent and size based on the capped number of owners, key nonowners, and helpers for which we collected detailed data. Note that the number of valid cases is dramatically smaller when we require labor inputs from founding team members. If we consider the founding team to include only "Owner-workers" (column 3), we lose the 795 cases where none of the owners were working full-time at the venture. We lose 700 cases if we allow all "Affiliate-workers" (column 4) —owners and nonowners—to be members of the team.

If we consider only ownership (column 1), we would conclude that just over half of the nascent ventures (53%) are founded by solo entrepreneurs. But by broadening the definition to include other contributions (column 2), we would assume, instead, that entrepreneurship is rarely a solitary activity. If we consider all owners, key nonowners, and helpers as members of the founding team, then only 22% of the nascent ventures are being pursued by solo entrepreneurs and the average team size nearly doubles. The percentage of solo entrepreneurs increases to 81% for owners only and 68% for all affiliates if we require tangible labor of founders; however, as noted above, these narrower definitions substantially reduce the set of respondents classified as starting "nascent firms." An interesting question for future research would be to explore the characteristics and outcomes for truly solo entrepreneurs as compared to more socially embedded nascent entrepreneurs.

Not surprisingly given the demographic similarity of owners, key nonowners and helpers reported in Table 7.2, there are relatively small differences in age, industry experience and educational background revealed across different definitions of the founding team. However, the average length of within industry experience increases when the definition of founder is limited to those contributing labor (Columns 3 and 4) and the proportion of teams without any start-up experience or without any college degrees is smallest under the most expansive definition of founder (Column 2).

Depending on our definition of founder, we see different patterns of gender and ethnic homophily. We observe more gender diversity when we include as members of the founding team those affiliates who are not actually working at the venture. We observe more ethnic diversity when we consider nonowners to be members of the founding team. A second noteworthy difference across alternative definitions of founding team is the extent to which the nascent venture is a family endeavor. If we use the least restrictive definition of a founding team by including all owners and affiliates, regardless of whether they are working in the venture, the fraction of founders who are related either by blood or marriage is quite high. This might suggest that nascent ventures gain diversity through weak as opposed to strong ties. However, if we narrow the definition of a team to only those persons actually contributing labor, the fraction of family founders drops substantially. Because prior research suggests that diversity is an important contributor to entrepreneurial success, it would be useful for scholars to further explore the factors that are associated with increased levels of diversity.

7.6 Are All "Founders" Equal?

While varying the operational definition of founding team is an interesting academic exercise, the pressing question for entrepreneurs—and for those who are training and advising entrepreneurs—is whether and how different kinds of affiliates contribute to the ultimate performance of the venture. What configurations of founding teams are most likely to launch successful ventures? The longitudinal nature of the PSED II sample will, someday, allow researchers to address this question more definitively. As of this writing, the first follow-up round has been completed; thus we can offer some preliminary findings relating founding teams to venture performance.

For the 961 cases that completed both the original survey and the first follow-up survey (conducted 12 months after the initial survey), we can observe three different possible states of the nascent venture: (1) a new operational firm exists, (2) the start-up effort continues, or (3) the start-up effort has been abandoned. We follow Reynolds and Curtin (2008) in defining a new operational firm as an entity where the business generates revenues that cover all expenses (including owner's salaries) for 6 or more of the past 12 months. We define the start-up to have been abandoned when the respondent reports to be "disengaged from the business effort discussed a year ago." In Table 7.7 we report simple logistic regression analyses predicting new firm emergence and abandonment as a function of founding team characteristics. We pay particular

Table 7.7 Nascent venture outcomes for 961 Wave B (12-month) respondents: logistic regression analysis reporting odds ratios and standard errors

	New firm (1)	New firm (2)	Abandonment (1)	Abandonment (2)
Founding team size (all affiliates w/demographic data)	0.97 (0.08)	0.96 (0.11)	0.95 (0.06)	1.01 (0.07)
Number of owner-workers	1.75*** (0.24)	1.71*** (0.24)	0.51*** (0.10)	0.51*** (0.10)
Number of KNO/helper-workers	1.08 (0.15)	1.09 (0.15)	1.06 (0.18)	1.02 (0.17)
Has institutional member(s)		0.81 (0.24)		0.88 (0.20)
Female team member(s)		0.61† (0.18)		1.03 (0.21)
Non-white team member(s)		0.49 (0.21)		0.89 (0.22)
College degree(s)		1.41 (0.33)		0.71† (0.13)
No non-family member(s)		1.14 (0.34)		0.66† (0.14)
Industry experience		1.44 (0.57)		0.56* (0.14)
Start-up experience		0.89 (0.24)		0.73 (0.15)
Owner(s) with management experience		1.93 (1.04)		1.43 (0.46)
Constant	0.12*** (0.03)	0.06*** (0.04)	0.50*** (0.09)	1.06 (0.42)
Chi-square	17.94	32.21	13.56	26.66

† $p<0.10$, * $p<0.05$, ** $p<0.01$, *** $p<0.001$

attention to the employment and ownership status while controlling for basic demographic characteristics. With the exception of our team size variables (Founding team size, Number of owner-workers, Number of KNO/helper-workers) which are measured as integers, each of our measures is a simple binary variable indicating whether anyone on the founding team meets the criteria. Of course, this is an extremely simplistic representation of our measures, but given the small team sizes and the relative homogeneity within teams, the binary representation goes a long way towards capturing the key differences across teams. (Interested readers can refer to Table 7.6 where we report the percentage of teams that have female members, nonwhite members or that have no college degrees, family ties, industry experience or start-up experience.) Moreover, given our analytic strategy of using logistic regression models and reporting odds-ratios, the bivariate independent variables can be easily interpreted as the influence of having some versus none of a characteristic on the relative odds of either having a new firm or abandoning the venture effort by the time of the one-year follow-up interview.

In Table 7.7 we report four models: two for each of our two outcomes. The first model is a baseline model that simply accounts for team size and affiliate employment status. The second model includes a range of demographic indicators including whether the team has any members from an institution such as a bank or venture capital firm; whether the team has any female or nonwhite members; whether the venture does not contain nonfamily members; whether at least one member of the team has a college degree, experience in the industry, experience in a start-up; and whether any of the owners has any prior managerial experience.

The most striking finding is that the single strongest correlate of performance—both in the positive sense that a new firm has been created and in the negative sense of the nascent venture has been abandoned—is having owners who are working full-time. Overall team size and the number of nonowning workers are both irrelevant. This finding is an important corrective to our understanding of team size and entrepreneurship. At least in the earliest days of a nascent venture, the most important actors are the owners who are committed full-time to the endeavor.

In Table 7.7 we also see some interesting suggestive evidence that the demographic characteristics of the founding team may contribute to the performance of a nascent venture. For example, having female team members seems to lower the likelihood that a new firm emerges during the 12-month observation period, although this effect is only marginally statistically significant. This may reflect higher levels of conflict that often arise on demographically diverse teams. An important question for future research is whether there is actually a lower rate of new firm emergence, or whether demographically diverse teams take longer. Additionally, it would be important to examine other performance indicators as there is evidence that diverse teams, particularly those that overcome interpersonal conflict, can be higher performing in the long run.

Teams with higher levels of human capital in the form of college degrees and industry experience are less likely to abandon the nascent venture. Teams that involve family members in the nascent venture also appear to be less likely to abandon the effort within the 12-month observation period. An important question for future research is to understand the interplay between social and human capital in nascent ventures. Are the teams with more education and/or family support able to persist longer because they have better material resources or better psychological and social resources? Why are entrepreneurs who have experience in the same industry as that of their new venture more persistent?

7.7 Conclusion

The PSED II data could be used to address a number of important questions about entrepreneurship. Why do some entrepreneurs seek the assistance of others whereas others do not? How do solo entrepreneurs differ from more social entrepreneurs? What are the costs/benefits of obtaining assistance from nonowners? What types of teams are more likely to successfully launch a new venture? Can inexperienced owners compensate by having experienced affiliates?

The PSED II survey asked nascent entrepreneurs to identify owners, key nonowners, and helpers. The goal of these different questions was to understand "founding" as opposed to "owning" or "helping." In asking these questions we were particularly interested in exploring the association between contributions of labor and/or capital and the socially defined category of "founder." Although we did not directly ask about founder status, we can use information about ownership, employment, and contribution to compare and contrast the alternative definitions of founder that appear in the literature. For example, how do the characteristics of founders change if we exclude passive investors? What are the characteristics of founders if we require full-time employment? Including questions about key nonowners as well as helpers, the nature of their contributions, as well as their demographic characteristics and social ties, will allow scholars to have a clearer portrait of the constellation of actors who are involved in launching nascent ventures. The more detailed questions asked in PSED II allow us to differentiate "key nonowners" from "helpers" and represent a conceptual advance over PSED I, which only collected data on "owners" and "helpers."

While our analyses are merely suggestive, future waves of the PSED II data will provide an invaluable resource for addressing the questions that we have posed as well as many others. We hope that future scholars will employ more sophisticated analyses to disentangle the relative contributions of owner, key nonowner, and helper human and social capital to nascent ventures.

References

Aldrich, H. E., Elam, A., & Reese, P. R. (1996). Strong ties, weak ties, and strangers: Do women business owners differ from men in their use of networking to obtain assistance? In S. Birley and I. MacMillan (Eds.), *Entrepreneurship in a global context* (pp. 1–25). London: Routledge.

Baron, J. N., Burton, M. D., & Hannan, M. T. (1996). The road taken: The origins and evolution of employment systems in high-tech firms. *Industrial and Corporate Change, 5*(2), 239–275.

Beckman, C. M., Burton, M. D., & O'Reilly, C., III. (2007). Early teams: The impact of team demography on VC financing and going public. *Journal of Business Venturing, 22*(2), 147–173.

Carter, N. M., Aldrich, H. E., & Ruef, M. (2004). Entrepreneurial teams. In W. B. Gartner, K. G. Shaver, N. M. Carter, & P. D. Reynolds (Eds.), *The handbook of entrepreneurial dynamics: The process of organizational creation* (pp. 299–310). Thousand Oaks, CA: Sage.

Cooper, A. C., Gimeno-Gascon, F. J., & Woo, C. Y. (1994). Initial human and financial capital as predictors of new venture performance. *Journal of Business Venturing, 9*, 371–395.

Eisenhardt, K. M., & Schoonhoven, C. B. (1990). Organizational growth: Linking founding teams, strategy, environment and growth among U.S. semi-conductor ventures. *Administrative Science Quarterly, 28*, 274–291.

Francis, D. H., & Sandberg, W. R. (2000). Friendship within entrepreneurial teams and its association with team and venture performance. *Entrepreneurship Theory and Practice, 25*(2), 5–25.

Kamm, J. B., Shuman, J. C., Seeger, J. A., & Nurick, A. J. (1990). Entrepreneurial teams in new venture creation: A research agenda. *Entrepreneurship Theory and Practice, 14*(4), 7–17.

Renzulli, L. A., Aldrich, H. E., & Moody, J. (2000). Family matters: Gender, networks, and entrepreneurial outcomes. *Social Forces, 79*(2), 523–546.

Reynolds, P. (2000). National study of U.S. business start-ups: Background and methodology. In Jerome Katz (Ed.), *Advances in entrepreneurship, firm emergence and growth* (Vol. 4, pp. 153–228). Stamford, CT: JAI.

Roberts, E. B. (1991). *Entrepreneurs in high technology: Lessons from MIT and beyond.* New York: Oxford University Press.

Ruef, M., Aldrich, H. E., & Carter, N. (2003, April). The structure of organizational founding teams: Homophily, strong ties, and isolation among U.S. entrepreneurs. *American Sociological Review, 68*(2), 195–222.

Shane, S. (2003). *A general theory of entrepreneurship: The individual-opportunity nexus.* Cheltenham, UK: Edward Elgar.

Wasserman, N. (2003). Founder-CEO succession and the paradox of entrepreneurial success. *Organization Science, 14*(2), 149–172.

Part III
The Start-Up Process

Chapter 8
Institutional Isomorphism, Business Planning, and Business Plan Revision: The Differential Impact on Teams Versus Solo Entrepreneurs

Benson Honig, Jianwen (Jon) Liao, and William B. Gartner

8.1 Introduction

This chapter uses an institutional perspective (Powell & DiMaggio, 1991; Meyer & Rowan, 1977) to offer insights into why nascent entrepreneurs are likely to undertake the process of business planning. A considerable amount of time and effort is devoted to the business planning process during venture creation. Gumpert (2002), for example, estimates that over 10 million business plans are written each year. So, does the process of business planning, then, result in the creation of new ventures? One perspective on business planning suggests that planning is an important tool for obtaining investment capital, facilitating entrepreneurial thought and action, establishing organizational goals and objectives, providing insight into competitive markets, and assisting with environmental analysis (Delmar & Shane, 2003; Gartner & Liao, 2007; Gruber, 2007; Kuratko & Hodgetts, 2001; Lambing & Kuehl, 2000; Liao & Gartner, 2006; Stevenson, Grousbeck, Roberts, & Bhidé, 1999; Timmons, 1999; Wickham, 2001). From this perspective, planning matters and nascent entrepreneurs should engage in the business planning process in order to increase their chances for successfully starting new ventures.

Another perspective suggests that individuals engage in planning because of the social pressures to plan, regardless of the actual value that business planning might provide (Honig & Karlsson, 2004). This perspective would marshal evidence that the research record on planning is somewhat mixed (Castrogiovanni, 1996; Stone & Brush, 1996). One study found that only 28% of a sample of *Inc.* 500 firms had completed a formal classic business plan, and only 4% conducted a systematic search (Bhidé, 2000). When planning is conducted, it appears to be a rather cursory activity. For example, 63% of *Inc.* 500 firms took only a few months to plan, and only 9% took more than a year (Bhidé, p. 55). Another study, examining the literature of both nonprofit and entrepreneurial firms, found that although planning was not widespread, it was frequently

---

B. Honig (✉)
Wilfrid Laurier University, Ontario, Canada
e-mail: bhonig@wlu.ca

utilized in order to gain external legitimacy or resources (Stone & Brush, 1996). This suggests that planning activities may frequently be conducted for other than reasons of efficiency; rather, they may be a product of ritual and conformity (Meyer & Rowan, 1977).

Further, these two perspectives are at odds regarding the relationship between planning and success. For example, some studies supporting the planning paradigm highlight a strong relationship between planning and persistence in the venture development process (Delmar & Shane, 2003, 2004; Gartner & Liao, 2007; Liao & Gartner, 2006; Shane & Delmar, 2004). The other perspective suggests that persistence may not be an indicator of success; rather, it may reflect the inability to recognize failure and begin anew (Honig & Karlsson, 2004) and studies examining other performance criteria typically show weak or nonexistent results (Haber & Reichel, 2007).

In this paper, we will use the institutional perspective to empirically examine the impact of institutional forces on business planning behavior for nascent entrepreneurs, differentiating teams, and solo self-employed, using the PSED II database, during a 1-year period in the venture creation process. We distinguish between the extensiveness of planning: comparing informal planning, informally written, and formally written plans. And, this study is also able to examine those individuals who, after 1 year in the business formation process, rewrote their business plans.

Our findings suggest that institutional forces have a strong influence on whether nascent entrepreneurs engage in business planning during the venture creation process and develop more formal business plans. There appeared to be no indication that institutional forces affected whether nascent entrepreneurs modified their business plans.

8.2 Institutional Theory and Business Planning Activity

Institutional theory focuses on understanding the forces that generate stability in social forms and the meanings associated with them (DiMaggio, 1991; Meyer & Rowan, 1977). Our interest is to understand social forms that take the shape of nascent ventures, which may evolve into new firms. As these new organizations come into existence, we test how and why business plans are developed and implemented, with a focus on what accounts for isomorphic planning behavior.

Nascent organizations maintain a liability of newness, leaving them highly susceptible to institutional pressures (Aldrich & Fiol, 1994; Aldrich & Reuf, 2006; Stinchcombe, 1965). These pressures force them to establish new networks to the business world (Suchman, 1995) to show credibility, and to establish necessary exchanges. Business plans may assist them with this requirement (Honig & Karlsson, 2004).

From an institutional perspective, DiMaggio and Powell (1983) argue that three forces drive the processes in which firms and organizations become similar, determined by what they call isomorphic pressures. These three isomorphic pressures are: (1) coercive, (2) regulative and (3) mimetic. For the coercive (regulative ingredient of institution) force, organizations adopt structures or procedures because they are forced to do so, e.g., laws or formal regulations. Although business planning is not seen as an activity highly influenced by the legal system, it is often placed as a requirement for obtaining financial capital by bankers, lenders, venture capitalists (VCs) and even certain angel investors. We suggest:

> H1: Coercive forces, such as exposure to financial institutions, are positively related to the likelihood of business planning.

Normatively, organizations adopt structures or procedures because they are assumed to be superior. Norms refer to how things should be done. If norms are applicable to selected types of actors, they give rise to roles. These normative systems can be both constraining and enabling. When trying to exploit a business opportunity, normative systems come in many forms. Social pressure is found in organizations which work with startups; it occurs while taking entrepreneurial classes, when learning about business routines, and through management experience. Normative forces will increase the likelihood of business planning. Our second hypothesis reflects normative forces as follows:

> H2: Normative forces, such as those produced through general education, or assistance programs, are positively related to the likelihood of business planning.

Finally, we have the mimetic (cultural-cognitive ingredient) force. Organizations copy or mimic one another, often due to uncertainty, and to model themselves after perceived success. Mimetic behavior is influenced by the *cultural-cognitive element:* the shared conceptions that constitute the nature of social reality and the frames through which meaning is made. Culture in this framework is treated as part of a symbolic system. For example, if entrepreneurs are socially supported by their peers, it is likely that peers have business plans and the mimetic forces will lead to the production of more business plans. In combining these forces, institutional theory maintains a key focus regarding how social relationships and actions become taken for granted, and how our cognitive set of shared meanings and possible actions are constructed (Aldrich, 1999). Much work has demonstrated that similar organizations in a particular industry copy procedures, structures, characteristics, and behaviors (Fligstein, 1985; Mizruchi & Fein, 1999). Our third hypothesis is stated as follows:

> H3: Mimetic forces, such as those propagated in particular industries, are positively related to the likelihood of business planning.

8.3 The Impact of Institutional Forces on Team Versus Individual Planning Behavior

Institutional theory has generally held that individual rational choice is constrained by the social structure under which actors operate (Meyer, Boli, & Thomas, 1987). Meyer et al. (1987) remind us that the individual perspective is limiting when it comes to understanding contemporary social processes, including labor markets, elections, and educational institutions. Social forces constitute the glue that keeps society together—with culture establishing normative patterns that include the possibility and probability of starting a social enterprise or business. Understanding how these social forces operate on and by individuals is critical for explaining which choices are made according to individual preferences, and which are made according to institutional systems, norms, and controls (Powell, 1991). Powell calls for "much more sophisticated analysis of how institutions, by precluding some options and facilitating others, shape individual identities and public discourse" (Powell, p. 189). Thus, although individuals are susceptible to social forces, groups or collectives of individuals should be even more susceptible to isomorphism. For example, collective organizational thought may be embodied in standard operating procedures (March & Simon, 1958). For an entrepreneurial organization, writing a business plan may be one of those procedures. Stated as a hypothesis:

> H4: Institutional forces related to business planning, including normative, coercive, and mimetic, will be more evident in team-based startups than in individual solo entrepreneurial activities.

8.4 Research Methods

8.4.1 Sampling Procedures

The data for this study were obtained from the Panel Study of Entrepreneurial Dynamics II (PSED II). The PSED II is a longitudinal data set of individuals in the process of starting businesses who were identified from a random digit dialing telephone survey of 31,845 adults in the United States. An overview of the PSED II research process is provided in Reynolds and Curtin (2008). Additional details of the survey process and descriptions of specific items in the questionnaires used for the initial and follow-up interviews can be found at http://www.psed.isr.umich.edu/psed/documentation.

To qualify as "nascent entrepreneurs," that is, individuals who were in the process of starting a business, respondents answered "yes" to any of the following three questions: (1) Are you, alone or with others, currently trying to start a new business, including any form of self-employment or selling any goods or services to others? (2) Are you, along or with others, now trying to start a new business or a new venture for your employer, an effort that is part of your normal work? (3) Are you, alone or with others, currently the owner of a business you help manage, including self-employment or selling any goods or services to others? In addition, nascent entrepreneurs needed to satisfy four criteria (answering "yes" to one of the three screening items above, reporting startup activity in the past year, were expected to own all or part of the firm, and did not yet have an on-going business). In addition, nascent entrepreneurs who reported positive monthly cash flow covering expenses and salaries prior to the first interview were excluded from the sample as they were considered on-going firms. There were 36 individuals who did not appear very committed to the startup process (e.g., reported only one or two startup activities, did not complete more than one activity in any 12-month period, and did not report any startup activity within 10 years of the detailed interview) who were excluded from the sample. Based on these selection criteria, the number of nascent entrepreneurs available for analysis was 1,214. A follow-up survey was conducted 12 months after the initial interview. Missing data reduced the number of respondents studied, as reported in the findings section.

The PSED II dataset comes with post-stratification weights for each respondent based on estimates from the U.S. Census Bureau's Current Population Survey. The post-stratification scheme was based on gender, age, ethnic background, and income. Applying these weights for analyses are essential for the generalizability of any studies related to the PSED II data set. According to Curtin and Reynolds (2004, p. 492) "Weights should be used in all types of analyses." As per their suggestions for using these weights, we adjusted the weights to reflect the reduction in the number of cases due to missing and not applicable responses.

8.4.2 Measures

8.4.2.1 Business Planning

Over one wave of data collection, nascent entrepreneurs were asked three related questions about business planning: presence, formality, and modifications. For *business planning presence* (D1), nascent entrepreneurs were asked:

> A business plan usually outlines the markets to be served, the products or services to be provided, the resources required—including money—and the expected growth and profit for the new business. (Have/Had) you already begun preparation of a business plan for this new business, (will you prepare one in the future), or (is/was) a business plan not relevant for this new business?

Responses with "No, not yet" or "No, not relevant" were coded with "0"; and with "Yes" coded as "1".

For *business planning formality* (D2), nascent entrepreneurs were asked "What is the current form of your business plan—is it unwritten or in your head, informally written, or formally prepared?" Responses with "unwritten" or "informally written" were coded as "1", "formally written" as "2". For *business planning modification* [Wave B only—D5a (D30)], nascent entrepreneurs were asked "Since last year, (has/had) the business plan been modified or updated (before your involvement ended)?" Responses with "Yes" were coded as "1", "No" as "0".

8.4.2.2 Institutional Isomorphism

The institutional variables were deducted from institutional theory, c.f. DiMaggio and Powell (1983) and Scott (2001). Asking for funding (E1), seeking bankers' help (P8) are indicative of *coercive* pressure, which may likely increase the probability of producing a formal plan. Our indicators of *mimetic* forces consisted of becoming a member of a trade association (E22) and the industry sector (i.e., tech versus nontech) (S6) with "1" for high-tech and "0" for nontech. Following Fligstein (1985), we predicted that nascent entrepreneurs in the high-tech industry and being part of a trade association would subject them more to the mimetic influence of business planning. We used "contact with government for support" (P7) "parents ran own business" (Z8) and "know someone involved in the startup" (T7) to proxy normative isomorphism. All coercive, mimetic, and normative forces were coded as dummy variables with the presence of these behaviors coded as "1", otherwise "0".

8.4.2.3 Control Variables

Prior studies argue that the likelihood of business planning depends on the founder's human capital and social capital (e.g., Honig & Karlsson, 2004). Following Shane and Delmar (2004) and Honig and Karlsson (2004), we control for the effect of human capital in several ways: education, experience in the industry of startup, prior startup experience, working experience, managerial experience and growth orientation. For *education*(H6_1), nascent entrepreneurs were asked "what is the highest level of education you have completed so far?" Responses were coded on an ordinal scale from 0 to 9, with 0—"up to eighth grade" to 9—"LLD, MD, Ph. D and EDD degree." We then converted these scales into their related years of education. We measured *industry experience* (H11_1) as the total years of full-time paid work experience in any field within the industry these nascent entrepreneurs were starting their emerging firms in. For *prior startup experience* (H12_1), nascent entrepreneurs were asked to respond to the question of "How many other businesses (have you/has [NAME]) helped to start as an owner or part-owner?" Responses with 1 or more were coded as "1", otherwise 0. *Work experience* (H20_1) was measured by the years of full-time, paid working experience. For *managerial experience* (H21_1), nascent entrepreneurs were asked the question: "For how many years, if any, have you had managerial, supervisory, or administrative responsibilities?" For *growth orientation* (T1), nascent entrepreneurs were asked to choose among two statements. "I want this new business to be as large as possible, or

I want a size I can manage myself or with a few key employees?" The choice of the former statement was coded as "1", while the latter was coded as "0".

8.4.2.4 Solo Startup Versus Team Startup

Lechter (2001) in a review of research on ventures formed by teams versus solo-founders indicated that teams are more successful. We examine how the influence of institutional forces on various dimensions of business planning varies across samples of solo startup and team startup. A dichotomous variable was created with "1" for solo startup and "2" for a startup team with more than one founding members, and regressions run separately for teams and individuals.

8.4.3 Models

We used a series of hierarchical multiple logistic regression models to determine the impact of institutional forces on business planning presence, formality, and modification across two nascent samples: solo startup and team startup. Binary logistic regression was used because it restricts the range of the dependent variable to a value between 0 and 1, which is appropriate for investigating various dimensions of business planning, which are all dichotomous variables. We first created a base model of logistic regression, which includes all our control variables of human capital. We subsequently added variables related to mimetic, coercive, and normative forces.

Overall, we followed the method developed by Hosmer and Lemeshow (1989) using maximum likelihood estimators to give logistic probabilities, where the computed matrix of covariates and dependent variables are assigned logistic probabilities. All models were run for both samples of solo and team startup and were appropriately weighted.

8.5 Results

Of the 1,214 nascent entrepreneurs studied, 609 (50.2%) indicated they had written a business plan. For those that had written business plans, 124 (20.4 %) were unwritten, 282 (46.2%) were informally written, and 203 (33.4%) were formally written. Of the individuals who have planned, 408 were still in the longitudinal study after 1 year. Of these, 224 (54.4%) indicated that they had changed or modified their business plan in the previous year. When these individuals were asked why they modified their plans, 15% did so to obtain financing, 42% to assist with organizing, and 39% in order to have a plan that better reflected their market and competition.

Table 8.1 shows descriptive statistics for all the variables. Table 8.2 shows *T*-tests for relevant variables regarding the propensity to plan and the changes

Table 8.1 Descriptive statistics and correlation matrix

Variables	Mean	Std	1	2	3	4	5	6	7	8	9	10	11	12	13	14	15	16
1 Years of education	5.369	2.079	1															
2 Years of experience in industry of startup	7.918	9.367	0.081***	1														
3 Prior startup Experience	0.399	0.490	0.183***	0.119***	1													
4 Years of full time working experience	17.269	11.775	0.170***	0.430***	0.291***	1												
5 Years of managerial experience	8.543	8.873	0.258***	0.358***	0.341***	0.665***	1											
6 Growth orientation	0.239	0.427	0.009	−0.93***	0.010	−.123***	−0.051	1										
7 Industry (Tech vs Nontech)	0.240	0.427	0.012	0.039	−0.036	−0.054*	−0.020	0.112***	1									
8 Become a member of trade association	0.078	0.269	0.149***	0.020	0.067**	0.043	0.127***	−0.019	0.008	1								
9 Ask for funding	0.146	0.353	0.102***	0.048*	0.108***	0.0.25	0.094***	0.071**	−0.019	0.134***	1							
10 Bankers help new business started	2.831	1.057	0.024	0.020	−0.048	0.083***	0.102***	−0.025	0.047	−0.008	−0.026	1						
11 Government support for starting new business	3.149	1.109	−0.022	−0.025	−0.067**	0.046	−0.013	−0.025	−0.004	0.003	0.001	0.400**	1					
12 Parents Ran own business	0.507	0.500	0.034	0.004	0.062**	−0.018	0.080***	0.008	−0.015	0.062(*)	0.027	0.047	0.015	1				
13 Know someone involved in startup	0.684	0.465	0.065**	0.025	0.113***	−0.029	0.004	0.027	0.059**	0.036	0.023	−0.016	0.024	0.070**	1			
14 Business plan presence (Y/N)	0.507	0.500	0.138***	0.021	0.049	−0.022	0.034	0.095***	−0.016	0.094***	0.145(**)	−0.070(*)	−0.053	0.032	0.100(**)	1		
15 Business plan formality	1.334	0.472	0.156***	0.057	0.077	−0.002	0.040	0.135***	0.071	0.171***	0.218***	0.002	0.050	−0.007	0.056	.(a)	1	
16 Business plan modification	0.549	0.498	0.042	0.128***	0.092	0.039	0.030	0.024	0.012	0.065	0.009	−0.037	−0.017	−0.022	0.104(*)	.(a)	0.048	1

*** Correlation is significant at the 0.01 level (2-tailed).
** Correlation is significant at the 0.05 level (2-tailed).
* Correlation is significant at the 0.1 level (2-tailed).
a Cannot be computed because at least one of the variables is constant.

8 Institutional Isomorphism, Business Planning, and Business Plan Revision

Table 8.2 *T*-tests: business planning and business plan modification

Variables		Business plan (1 – Yes/0 – No) Means	*T* value	Business plan modification (1 – Yes/ 0 – No) Mean	*T* value
Gender (1- male; 2-female)	0.00	1.39	0.744	1.47	3.331***
	1.00	1.37		1.31	
Highest level of education	0.00	5.09	–4.816***	5.84	–0.844
	1.00	5.66		6.02	
Years of experience in industry	0.00	7.71	–0.724	6.93	–2.608***
	1.00	8.10		9.58	
Startup experience (number of business helped start)	0.00	0.37	–1.698*	0.39	–1.870*
	1.00	0.42		0.48	
Years of managerial experience	0.00	8.23	–1.189	9.39	–0.604
	1.00	8.83		9.97	
Years of full-time experience	0.00	17.55	0.760	17.68	–0.766
	1.00	17.03		18.60	
New business high-tech?	0.00	0.25	0.539	0.22	–0.249
	1.00	0.23		0.23	
Growth orientation (size of business: large or small)	0.00	0.20	–3.320***	0.25	–0.478
	1.00	0.28		0.27	
Solo startup versus team startup	0.00	1.41	1.4993	1.48	–0.446
	1.00	1.50		1.51	

*** Correlation is significant at the 0.01 level (2-tailed).
* Correlation is significant at the 0.1 level (2-tailed).

in business plan. As Table 8.1 indicates, those nascent entrepreneurs with higher levels of formal education are significantly more likely to plan than those with less education. Those who have started businesses previously are also more likely to plan, as are those who have strong growth orientation and begin as a team versus solo entrepreneurs. Additionally, Table 8.2 shows the *t*-tests for a range of variables in this study related to those who modified their business plans. Women were shown to be less likely to modify their plans than men. Those with more years of industry experience were also more likely to modify their plans, as were those with previous startup experience.

Table 8.3 shows logistical regressions examining the propensity to plan, comparing solo startups to team startups.

Chi-squares were significant in both equations, with cell prediction rates of 62% and 59%, respectively. Models 1a and 2a (Table 8.3) include control variables only. Formal education was a good statistically significant predictor of business planning for both individuals and teams. Growth orientation was an even stronger indicator for both groups, suggesting a relationship between high growth objectives and planning behavior. The coefficient for growth orientation increased the probability of writing a plan by 1.8 for the solo entrepreneurs (0.597 e^x) and by 1.4 for the team startups (0.39 e^x). Models 1b and 2b examined the likelihood of planning using the institutional variables under consideration.

Table 8.3 Solo versus team startups: institutional forces and the likelihood of business planning

	Solo startups				Team startups			
	Model 1a		Model 1b		Model 2a		Model 2b	
	β	Exp(β)	β	Exp(β)	β	Exp(β)	β	Exp(β)
Years of education	0.133***	1.142	0.129***	1.138	0.140***	1.151	0.121**	1.129
Years of experience in industry of startup	−0.012	0.988	−0.013	0.987	0.026**	1.026	0.022*	1.022
Prior startup experience	0.125	1.133	−0.029	0.971	0.264	1.302	0.145	1.156
Years of full-time working experience	−0.017	0.983	−0.013	0.987	−0.012	0.989	−0.007	0.993
Years of managerial experience	0.007	1.007	0.007	1.007	0.009	1.009	0.007	1.007
Growth orientation	0.597***	1.816	0.573***	1.774	0.391***	1.479	0.392*	1.480
Industry (tech versus nontech)			−0.533***	0.587			0.309	1.362
Become a member of trade association			0.305	1.357			0.592	1.808
Ask for funding			0.983***	2.673			0.505**	1.656
Bankers help new business started			−0.132	0.876			−0.149	0.862
Government support for starting new business			0.060	1.062			−0.132	0.876
Parents ran own business			−0.002	0.998			0.274	1.316
Know someone involved in the startup			0.300	1.350			0.355*	1.426
−2-log likelihood		802.805		776.559		647.385		654.061
Model chi-square		29.885***		56.131***		24.326***		44.649***
Df		6		13.000		6.000		13.000
Overall hit rate (%)		62.900		64.500		59.500		63.900
Cox & Snell R-square		0.048		0.089		0.047		0.084
N		600		600		505.000		505.000

*** Correlation is significant at the 0.01 level (2-tailed).
** Correlation is significant at the 0.05 level (2-tailed).
* Correlation is significant at the 0.1 level (2-tailed).

8 Institutional Isomorphism, Business Planning, and Business Plan Revision

Asking for funding was statistically significant in both models, accounting for an increased odds of 2.6 for the solo startups and 1.6 for the teams. H1 postulated that coercive forces, such as exposure to financial institutions, are positively related to the likelihood of business planning. Thus, H1 was upheld by the analyses.

Models 1b and 2b also include variables testing the normative and mimetic isomorphic pressures exerted on nascent entrepreneurs. Normative pressures were measured according to assistance through government programs as well as their experience with parents who ran a business and friends within their network who were involved in startups. Although government support programs were not shown to be a predictor of business planning activities, both solo entrepreneurs and team startups demonstrated statistically significant results with regard to education. We interpret this as confirmation of Hypothesis 2, which stated that normative forces, such as education, are positively related to the likelihood of business planning. Finally, we examined the mimetic forces due to specific industries. Interestingly, the relationships were significant and fairly strong for solo entrepreneurs, whereby technology oriented ventures decreased the odds of planning by 0.413. This variable was not significant for the team startups, suggesting that institutional forces operate differently for these two groups. We interpret this finding as supporting Hypothesis 3, which stated that mimetic forces, such as those propagated in particular industries, are positively related to the likelihood of business planning, but only in the case of solo entrepreneurs, and not for teams.

Table 8.4 shows the results of similar nested models examining the formality of business planning, whereby plans formally prepared for external use were coded as 1, and those informally written or those unwritten were the referent.

As can be seen from Table 8.4, model chi-squares are statistically significant, and the predicted cell matrix ("hit rate") is slightly improved over the previous model. Years of industry experience is statistically significant for the solo-startups in models 3a, and 4a, as well as the extended model 3b. Education was not significant in the full model 4b examining the team startups. Further, industry (technology-based) was also statistically significant in 3b, improving the probability of producing a formal plan by 1.7, but not in 4b, affecting the team startups. Asking for funding, our coercive variable, was found strong for both teams and individuals.

Finally, Table 8.5 shows the regressions for those that modified their business plans after one year.

Model 5a shows the first variables examined influencing the probability of modifying a business plan. Only years of experience was weakly statistically significant in models 5a and 6a. For the full models in 5b and 6b, only solo entrepreneurs who knew someone involved in a startup demonstrated a strong and statistically significant result, increasing the odds of modifying a business plan by 2.3.

When examining the differences between the solo and team-based startups in Tables 8.4 and 8.5, we found significant differences between the way institutional

Table 8.4 Solo versus team startups: institutional forces and the formality of business planning

	Solo startups				Team startups			
	Model 3a		Model 3b		Model 4a		Model 4b	
	β	Exp(β)	β	Exp(β)	β	Exp(β)	β	Exp(β)
Years of education	0.126**	1.134	0.104	1.110	0.159**	1.172	0.105	1.110
Years of experience in industry of startup	0.036**	1.037	0.031*	1.031	0.012	1.012	0.010	1.011
Prior startup experience	0.225	1.253	0.063	1.065	0.401	1.493	0.570*	1.767
Years of full-time working experience	−0.009	0.991	0.006	1.006	−0.025	0.976	−0.031	0.969
Years of managerial experience	−0.014	0.986	−0.026	0.974	0.009	1.009	0.008	1.008
Growth orientation	0.419	1.521	0.368	1.444	0.819***	2.268	0.905***	2.472
Industry (tech versus nontech)			0.536*	1.710			0.162	1.176
Become a member of trade association			0.677	1.968			1.458***	4.299
Ask for funding			0.921***	2.513			1.075***	2.930
Bankers help get new business started			−0.095	0.910			−0.039	0.962
Government support for starting new business			0.112	1.118			0.114	1.120
Parents Ran own business			0.027	1.027			−0.193	0.825
Know someone involved in the startup			0.348	1.417			0.053	1.054
−2-log likelihood	350.141		333.959		339.848		313.955	
Model chi-square	11.293**		27.475		19.043***		44.972***	
Df	6		13.000		6.000		13.000	
Overall hit rate (%)	67.400		69.800		66.900		72.100	
Cox & Snell R-square	0.04		0.094		0.066		0.148	
N	272		272		275.000		275.000	

*** Correlation is significant at the 0.01 level (2-tailed).
** Correlation is significant at the 0.05 level (2-tailed).
* Correlation is significant at the 0.1 level (2-tailed).

8 Institutional Isomorphism, Business Planning, and Business Plan Revision 149

Table 8.5 Solo versus team start-ups: institutional forces and business plan modification

	Solo start-ups				Team start-ups			
	Model 5a		Model 5b		Model 6a		Model 6b	
	β	Exp(β)	β	Exp(β)	β	Exp(β)	β	Exp(β)
Years of education	−0.069	0.933	−0.054	0.948	0.076	1.079	0.083	1.087
Years of experience in industry of startup	0.034*	1.034	0.033*	1.034	0.035**	1.036	0.037**	1.037
Prior startup experience	0.247	1.281	0.204	1.226	0.436	1.547	0.592	1.807
Years of full-time working experience	−0.007	0.993	0.000	1.000	−0.005	0.995	−0.007	0.993
Years of managerial experience	0.001	1.001	−0.004	0.996	−0.026	0.974	−0.018	0.982
Growth orientation	0.288	1.333	0.498	1.645	−0.048	0.953	−0.243	0.784
Industry (tech versus nontech)			−0.057	0.944			0.409	1.505
Become a member of trade association			0.471	1.601			0.383	1.466
Ask for funding			−0.122	0.886			−0.477	0.621
Bankers help get new business started			0.019	1.019			−0.186	0.830
Government support for starting new business			0.031	1.032			0.202	1.224
Parents ran own business			0.012	1.012			−0.191	0.826
Know someone involved in the startup			0.849***	2.336			−0.436	0.647
−2-log likelihood	255.393		247.534		248.278		242.546	
Model chi-square	5.367		13.325		8.584		14.517	
Df	6		13.000		6.000		13.000	
Overall hit rate (%)	56.900		61.000		60.600		60.200	
Cox & Snell R-square	0.028		0.068		0.045		0.074	
N	194		194		196.000		196.000	

*** Correlation is significant at the 0.01 level (2-tailed).
** Correlation is significant at the 0.05 level (2-tailed).
* Correlation is significant at the 0.1 level (2-tailed).

variables acted upon teams versus solo entrepreneurs. In general, the results were stronger for individuals than for groups. H4 stated that institutional forces related to business planning, including normative, coercive, and mimetic, would be more evident in team-based startups than in individual solo entrepreneurial activities. As we found the opposite to hold true, H4 was rejected.

8.6 Discussion

The objective of this study was to understand if, and to what extent, institutional forces impacted entrepreneurial planning behavior, comparing individual actors to team-based startups. Our research confirmed the influence of institutional factors on business planning behavior. As with other scholarships conducted on nascent entrepreneurs in Sweden (Honig & Karlsson, 2004; Karlsson & Honig, 2009), we found evidence that institutional forces influenced entrepreneurs in their decision to plan for both individuals and team-based startups. Specifically, we observed that nascent entrepreneurs with more years of formal education were more likely to plan than those with less, in both solo and team-based startups. Formal education is seen by institutional theorists as a significant platform for the dissemination of cultural beliefs (Meyer, Ramirez, & Soysal, 1992; Meyer & Rowan, 1977). Education accounts for much of our socialization regarding established norms, beliefs, and behaviors. Further, it provides legitimacy to the nascent entrepreneur, which might be transferred to nascent organizations (Aldrich & Fiol, 1994; Stinchcombe, 1965). Individuals exposed to increased institutional forces should be expected to behave in culturally representative ways. For entrepreneurs, we suggest that this entails writing of a business plan.

Business planning is frequently asserted to assist entrepreneurs in obtaining financial resources. Further, business planning "reconstructs what it is that is being produced and for whom and defines the value of the product" (Oakes, Townley, & Cooper, 1998). Bankers, venture capitalists, angel investors, and even relatives frequently insist upon reviewing a business plan before investing capital in a nascent enterprise. While the business plan itself may never be critically reviewed by these parties, entrepreneurs may acquiesce to the coercive demands of institutional forces, producing a business plan even if their intentions are to loosely couple their activities from their plans (Karlsson & Honig, 2009). We hypothesized and confirmed that those entrepreneurs who requested capital, both in teams and as individuals, were more likely to plan than those who did not. In this study we examined entrepreneurs who asked financial institutions, or others, for funding, to see if they were more likely to plan than those who did not. We interpreted this as evidence of coercive isomorphism (DiMaggio & Powell, 1983). The results upheld our hypothesis that coercive forces would increase the likelihood of planning. In short, those entrepreneurs that asked for funding were more likely to plan than those who did not.

In addition to the normative and coercive institutional elements, we examined mimetic forces, in our case, those associated with high-technology industries. Organizations are influenced by institutional fields, which serve as models for nascent organizations to emulate. They mimic successful organizations in an established field in order to obtain critical legitimacy behaviors (Fligstein, 1985; Mizruchi & Fein, 1999). Thus, in new ventures, and in particular those that occupy newer organizational fields, legitimacy is pursued in an attempt to maintain an alignment with the changing institutional environment (Suddaby & Greenwood, 2005). We found the influence of this mimetic force for high-technology startups to be strong for technology-oriented solo entrepreneurs. However, the relationship did not hold true for team-based startups.

While we expected to see institutional forces more evident for team-based startups than for solo entrepreneurs, the opposite held true. Our initial expectation was that the more individuals involved as team members, the more opportunities there would be for institutional forces to influence each of the team members, collectively. While one nascent entrepreneur might start a business ignorant of the institutional forces for producing a business plan, the probability of a team not being so exposed would seem remote. That our hypothesis was unsupported suggests an alternative explanation, perhaps linked to the liability of newness (Stinchcombe, 1965). Nascent entrepreneurs may be more susceptible to institutional forces because of their greater need for legitimacy. Legitimacy in consumer markets, for example, is critical for successfully introducing new products and overcoming the consumer's fear of the unknown (Aldrich & Fiol, 1994; Hargadon & Douglass, 2001). New organizations must also construct a collective identity through cooperative action for the purpose of legitimizing their activities towards other actors and institutions (Swaminathan & Wade, 2001). The use of relevant (modified) and formally written business plans may be one way of accomplishing this legitimacy, both toward internal uses (employees) and external demands (customers, industry collaborators).

We also examined the formality of business planning in this study. Of the 50% of nascent entrepreneurs who wrote plans, only 33% of our total population completed formally written ones. We tested the same institutional variables to examine formally written plans versus informal or unwritten plans. Formal education, our normative variable, increased the probability of formal planning for both solo nascent entrepreneurs and teams. The same relationship held true for those that asked for funding—they were more likely to formally plan. We did uncover differences, however, between the two groups. For team startups, having a high growth orientation was a strong and statistically significant predictor of having a formally written business plan for external use. Members of trade associations and business groups were more likely to formally plan when in teams, but not for the solo startups. For solo startups, high-growth orientation appeared to make no difference in degree of plan formality.

Finally, we examined those nascent entrepreneurs who indicated they modified their original business plans, for both individuals and teams. Years of industry experience was the one variable that demonstrated a strong and consistently significant impact on modifying plans. While the effects were small, there was clear evidence that those nascent entrepreneurs with previous startup experience were more likely to modify their plans, whether they were in teams, or not. As with the formality of planning, we discovered considerable variation regarding the modification of plans between the solo entrepreneurs and the team startups. Knowing someone who has started a business was a very strong predictor of solo startup modification. It had no influence, and even a negative coefficient, for the team-based startups.

We believe that to be irrelevant (Mintzberg, 1994a, b). Plans that are not modified lend themselves to constraining organizational flexibility and preserving the status quo (Mintzberg, 1994a). The findings that modification of a business seems to occur independently of the institutional variables supports the perspective that business plans are produced for reasons of legitimacy, coercion, and mimetic opportunities. We posit that these findings suggest that those nascent entrepreneurs who modified their plans did so for very different reasons than the reasons that inspired them to create their plans in the first place. For planning to be effective, it must adapt to changes in the environment, least the plan be irrelevant and out of date (Honig, 2004). We found that only a very small percentage of nascent entrepreneurs appear to modify their plans, despite their obvious enthusiasm for the planning project. We suggest that this finding indicates that many nascent entrepreneurs loosely couple their planning activities from their organizational activities, that is, they go through the motions of planning in response to institutional forces, but fail to implement or pay much attention to their plans (modify them), in order to survive and grow as new organizations (Karlsson & Honig, 2009).

8.6.1 Limitations of the Research

This study involved a comparatively short time period of new venture creation activity—1 year. Additional waves of data collection need to be conducted to either support or refute these initial findings. We encourage government agencies and foundations concerned with developing knowledge and policy about the venture creation process to fund additional data collection waves for PSED II. Our study took place in the USA during one period of time—different cultural and economic environments may yield correspondingly different results. The measures for business plan formality and business plan modification are somewhat crude evaluations of the business planning process. Qualitative studies are required to fully examine issues of both business plan quality and the process of business plan revision. Finally, this study focused on the relationship of institutional forces on business plan activity (presence, formality, and modification) and not on whether business planning activity was correlated to the creation of new ventures. It might be plausible that responding

8 Institutional Isomorphism, Business Planning, and Business Plan Revision

to institutional forces by creating a business plan might actually lead to business creation success.

8.7 Conclusions

Institutional forces play a significant role in determining whether nascent entrepreneurs engage in the process of business planning. Each of the three isomorphic pressures (coercive, normative, and mimetic), as operationalized in this study, affect business planning. Nascent entrepreneurs seeking funding from financial institutions (a coercive force) were more likely to engage in business planning as well as develop a more formal business plan. Nascent solo entrepreneurs with higher levels of education (a normative force) were more likely to engage in business planning as well as develop a more formal business plan, while teams with higher levels of education were more likely to engage in business planning, but not more likely to develop a more formal plan. Finally, industry factors (a mimetic force) were more likely to influence nascent solo entrepreneurs to engage in business planning and develop a more formal business plan, while teams were less likely to engage in a business plan, but were more likely to develop a formal business plan, if they did. None of the three isomorphic pressures were correlated with whether solo or team nascent entrepreneurs modified their business plans.

The PSED II dataset, because of its longitudinal characteristics, and because of the breadth of questions asked about the venture formation process, can play an important role in generating insights into what factors significantly impact venture creation success. This chapter focused on how institutional forces affect business planning, per se. Further research on the factors influencing the creation, formalization, and modification of business plans during the venture creation process can be undertaken to determine the relationship between business planning and success at starting and growing new ventures.

We suggest the "debate" between the two planning perspectives is important to continue to explore through more empirical studies. Not only are more studies of the venture creation process using quantitative datasets such as PSED I and PSED II needed, but more effort needs to be devoted to in-depth qualitative research that more specifically tracks nascent entrepreneur reasons (over time) for why certain startup behaviors are undertaken, or not. Assuming that entrepreneurs not only respond to their situations, but also work to create and modify their environments, scholarship that can better ascertain how and why individuals act, react, and interact will prove to be of major importance in furthering entrepreneurial activity.

Note

1. There are two waves of data. For Wave A, for example, the D1 item would be AD1, for Wave B, the item would be BD1

References

Aldrich, H. (1999). *Organizations evolving*. London: Sage.
Aldrich, H. E., & Fiol, M. (1994). Fools rush in? The institutional context of industry creation. *Academy of Management Review, 19*, 645–670.
Aldrich, H. E., & Reuf, M. (2006). *Organizations evolving* (2nd ed.). London: Sage.
Bhidé, A. (2000). *The origin and evolution of new businesses*. New York: Oxford University Press.
Castrogiovanni, G. J. (1996). Pre-startup planning and the survival of new small businesses: theoretical linkages. *Journal of Management, 22*(6), 801–822.
Curtin, R., & Reynolds, P. (2004). PSED background for analysis. In Appendix B of W. B. Gartner, N. Carter, & P. Reynolds (Eds.), *Handbook of entrepreneurial dynamics: The process of business creation* (pp. 477–494). Thousand Oaks, CA: Sage.
Delmar, F., & Shane, S. (2003). Does business planning facilitate the development of new ventures? *Strategic Management Journal, 24*, 1165–1185.
Delmar, F., & Shane, S. (2004). Legitimating first: Organizing activities and the survival of new ventures. *Journal of Business Venturing, 19*(3), 385–410.
DiMaggio, P. J., & Powell, W. W. (1983). The iron cage revisited: Institutional isomorphism and collective rationality in organizational fields. *American Sociological Review, 48*(2), 147–160.
DiMaggio, P. (1991). Constructing an organizational field as a professional project: US art museums, 1920–1940. In W. Powell & P. DiMaggio (Eds.), *The new institutionalism in organizational analysis* (pp. 267–292). Chicago: University of Chicago Press.
Fligstein, N. (1985).The spread of the multidivisional form among large firms, 1919–1979. *American Sociological Review, 50*, 377–391.
Gartner, W. B., & Liao, J. (2007). Pre-venture planning. In C. Moutray (Ed.), *The small business economy for data year 2006: Report to the president* (pp. 212–264). Washington, DC: U. S. Small Business Administration Office of Advocacy.
Gruber, M. (2007). Uncovering the value of planning in new venture creation: A process and contingency perspective. *Journal of Business Venturing, 22*, 782–807.
Gumpert, D.E. (2002). *Burn your business plan*. Needham, MA: Lauson Publishing.
Haber, S., & Reichel, A. (2007). The cumulative nature of the entrepreneurial process: The contribution of human capital, planning and environment resources to small venture performance. *Journal of Business Venturing, 22*, 119–145.
Hargadon, A. B., & Douglas, Y. (2001). When innovation meets institutions: Edison and the design of the electric light. *Administrative Science Quarterly, 46*, 476–501.
Honig, B. (2004). Entrepreneurship education: Toward a model of contingency-based business planning. *Academy of Management Learning and Education, 3*, 258–273.
Honig, B., & Karlsson, T. (2004). Institutional forces and the written business plan. *Journal of Management, 30*(1), 29–48.
Hosmer, D. W., & Lemeshow, S. (1989). *Applied logistic regression*. New York: John Wiley & Sons.
Karlsson, T., & Honig, B. (2009). Judging a business by its cover: An institutional perspective on new ventures and the business plan. *Journal of Business Venturing, 24*(1), 27–45.
Kuratko, D. F., & Hodgetts, R. M. (2001). *Entrepreneurship: A contemporary approach*. Orlando: Harcourt.
Lambing, P., & Kuehl, C. R. (2000). *Entrepreneurship*. Upper Saddle River, NJ: Prentice Hall.
Lechter, T. (2001). Social interaction: A determinant of entrepreneurial team venture success. *Small Business Economics, 16*(4), 263–278.
Liao, J., & Gartner, W. B. (2006). The effects of pre-venture plan timing and perceived environmental uncertainty on the persistence of emerging firms. *Small Business Economics, 27*, 23–40.
March, J., & Simon, H. (1958). *Organizations*. New York: John Wiley.

Meyer, J., Boli, J., & Thomas, M. (1987). Ontology and rationalization in the Western Cultural Account. In G. Tomas, J. Meyer, F. Ramirez, & J. Boli (Eds.), *Institutional structure: Constituting the state, society and the individual* (pp. 12–37). Newbury Park: Sage.

Meyer, J., Ramirez, F., & Soysal, Y. (1992). World expansion of mass education, 1870–1980. *Sociology of Education*, 65(2), 128–149.

Meyer, J. W., & Rowan, B. (1977). Institutionalized organizations: Formal structure as myth and ceremony. *American Journal of Sociology*, 83(2), 340–363.

Mintzberg, H. (1994a). Rethinking strategic planning part I: Pitfalls and fallacies. *Long Range Planning*, 27, 12–21.

Mintzberg, H. (1994b). *The rise and fall of strategic planning*. New York: The Free Press.

Mizruchi, M. S., & Fein, L. C., (1999). The social construction of organizational knowledge: A study of the uses of coercive, mimetic and normative isomorphism. *Administrative Science Quarterly*, 44, 653–683.

Oakes, L., Townley, B., & Cooper, D. (1998). Business planning as pedagogy: Language and control in a changing institutional field. *Administrative Science Quarterly*, 43, 257–292.

Powell, W., & DiMaggio, P. (1991). *The new institutionalism in organizational analysis*. Chicago: The University of Chicago Press.

Powell, W. (1991). Expanding the scope in institutional analysis. In W. Powell & P. DiMaggio (Eds.), *The new institutionalism in organizational analysis* (pp. 183–203). Chicago: University of Chicago Press.

Reynolds, P. D., & Curtin, R. T. (2008). Business creation in the United States: Panel Study of Entrepreneurial Dynamics II initial assessment. *Foundations and Trends in Entrepreneurship*, 4(3), 155–307.

Scott, R. (2001). *Institutions and organizations*. Thousand Oaks, CA: Sage.

Shane, S., & Delmar, F. (2004). Planning for the market: Business planning before marketing and the continuation of organizing efforts. *Journal of Business Venturing*, 19, 767–785.

Stevenson, H. H., Grousbeck, H. I., Roberts, M. J., & Bhidé, A. (1999). *New business ventures and the entrepreneur*. Boston: McGraw-Hill.

Stinchcombe, A. L. (1965). Social structure and organizations. In J. G. March (Ed.), *Handbook of organizations* (pp. 153–193). Stanford, CA: Rand McNally.

Stone, M. M., & Brush, C. G. (1996). Planning in ambiguous context: The dilemma for meeting needs for commitment and demands for legitimacy.*Strategic Management Journal*, 17, 633–652.

Suchman, M. C. (1995). Managing legitimacy: Strategic and institutional approaches. *Academy of Management Review*, 20, 571–610.

Suddaby, R., & Greenwood, R. (2005, March). Retorical strategies of legitimacy. *Administrative Science Quarterly*, 50, 35–67.

Swaminathan, A., & Wade, J. B. (2001). Social movement theory and the evolution of new organizational forms. In C. B. Schoonhoven & E. Romanelli (Eds.), *The entrepreneurship dynamic: Origins of entrepreneurship and the evolution of industries* (pp. 286–313). Stanford, CA: Stanford University Press.

Timmons, J. A. (1999). *New venture creation: Entrepreneurship for the 21st century* (5th ed.). Irwin, CA: McGraw Hill.

Wickham, P. (2001). *Strategic entrepreneurship: A decision-making approach to new venture creation and management*, Harlow: Pearson. Available at www.psed.isr.umich.edu/psed/documentation

Chapter 9
The Role of Human and Social Capital and Technology in Nascent Ventures

Mark T. Schenkel, Diana M. Hechavarria, and Charles H. Matthews

Research on human and social capital derives from the ideas that actors are both shaped by and contribute to the shaping of their respective economic contexts (e.g., Aldrich & Zimmer, 1986; Burt, 1992; Coleman, 1988; Davidsson & Honig, 2003; Granovetter, 1985). From a human capital perspective, individuals develop "corridors" of knowledge (Ronstadt, 1988) from information exposure and practical experience that lead them to being alert to new venture opportunities that they could not see previously (Kirzner, 1979). Such exposure also provides better preparation to engage in successful efforts to exploit new business venture opportunities (Becker, 1993; Davidsson & Honig, 2003). Similarly, from a social capital perspective individuals presumably develop social relationships throughout time that play a significant role in the enhancement of their alertness to entrepreneurial opportunity (Singh, 2000). Such relationships also allow individuals to engage more effectively efforts to form new ventures because of the socially constructed (Larson & Starr, 1993) and continuously evolving (Aldrich & Zimmer, 1986) nature of the new venture formation process over time.

Despite the insights provided by early research, our understanding about how capital influences the new venture creation process remains relatively limited for several reasons. First, although a stream of literature focusing on prefirm issues has begun to emerge, much of the prior study of business founders has typically been conducted via the use of retrospective accounts, leaving the interpretation of such findings open to the possibility of being systematically influenced by survivor bias (Delmar & Davidsson, 2000). Second, much of this work focuses predominantly on intentions rather than behavior (Davidsson & Honig, 2003). Third, although there is some work that focuses generally on the multidimensionality of human and social capital (e.g., Davidsson & Honig), there is little by contrast that focuses explicitly on the notion of multidimensionality as being context dependent (see Liao & Welsch, 2005, for an exception). Each of these limitations leaves open the

---

M.T. Schenkel (✉)
Belmont University, 1900 Belmont Boulevard, Nashville, TN 37212-3757
e-mail: mark.schenkel@belmont.edu

possibility that the entrepreneurial potential of various capital resources may not always evolve into new entrepreneurial ventures along the same lines as a nascent entrepreneur initially intends (Krueger & Brazeal, 1994). For example, such a distinction draws attention to the possibility social systems or processes may bias individuals to unnecessarily over-invest in human capital on the assumption that more is always better, or utilize a given form of capital in favor of another without a full upfront understanding of the relative tradeoffs involved in such decisions (Davidsson & Honig, 2003). The PSED II data provide an opportunity to address these and other important issues.

9.1 Capital Forms and Concepts

The contemporary study of entrepreneurship tends to be driven by a behavioral view of entrepreneurs as those who specialize "in taking judgmental decisions about the coordination of scarce resources" in the creation of new ventures (Casson, 2003, p. 225). Consistent with such a view, capital researchers generally distinguish between two complementary types of capital resources thought to influence the new venture creation process: (1) those that are derived from the individual's own personal background or experience and (2) those that arise are derived from the individual's unique position in a larger set of social relations.

9.2 Human Capital

The origins of new venture activity can be traced in part to observations that information related to economic opportunity is distributed unevenly across marketplace participants (e.g., Hayek, 1945). Judgments for the use of economic information are complex and it is rarely, if ever, possible to simply plug such information into a scientific formula and take action on the basis of some discrete result. Moreover, the costs of acquiring additional information frequently inhibit making optimal economic decisions (Casson, 2003). Consequently, it has been argued that individuals develop human capital in the form of unique "corridors" of knowledge (Ronstadt, 1988) that produce a unique state of readiness, or "absorptive capacity" (Cohen & Levinthal, 1990). Such corridors provide a foundation for some individuals to be generally more alert to new venture opportunities and generate a greater range of implementation possibilities than those without such corridors (Kirzner, 1979). In sum, implicit within human capital theory is the presumption that the cognitive ability of individuals is increased by the accumulation of information and knowledge stocks such that it allows some individuals to perceive and act more efficiently and effectively in the marketplace through new venturing activity than others (Kirzner, 1999; Shane, 2000).

9.2.1 Information: Personal Background and Life Context

As a result of the theoretical emphasis on information access, accumulated knowledge stocks, and the enhanced ability to process new information in the economic context, one stream of research has sought to generate a greater understanding of why and how life context and personal background distinctions may systematically influence the new venture creation process. Perhaps given a long history of intuitive association, it should come as no surprise that three specific characteristics of interest have emerged to become particularly ubiquitous in this regard: (1) age, (2) sex, and (3) ethnicity.

Age intuitively bears a relationship to the amount of information related to economic activities to which a person could be exposed. It follows that age is also likely to be directly related to an individual's cumulative knowledge base. After all, most formal educational systems are designed to expose individuals to the nature of economic systems, as well as provide them with "building blocks" for designing and actively shaping their career path within such systems. Beyond such formal systems, exposure to new venture creation as a potential career path also comes through norms acquired as to the age appropriateness of such significant life judgments. Accordingly, age is expected to be an important underlying factor to the extent that it can be expected to expose an individual to a critical quantity of information related to engaging in entrepreneurism.

However, it is important to note that interpreting age-related findings remains difficult because its influence is likely to overlap that of other human capital characteristics (e.g., stamina, perseverance). It is also likely that beyond a certain point, the benefit of career-related information goes beyond age alone and depends upon a wider range of influential individual and contextual circumstances. Indeed, data from PSED I show that in comparison to the general population, there is a modest, yet significant difference between nascent entrepreneurs and the general population. Specifically, there are a significantly greater number of young adults (i.e., between 25 and 44 years of age) engaged in nascent venturing activities than in the general population. Such findings suggest that the role of age in new venture creation activity is likely to be best considered in conjunction with other factors.

Sex is also a characteristic widely viewed as bearing a direct relationship to the exposure and accumulation of information and knowledge stocks over time. For example, the participation rate of women in business ownership has historically been far less than that of men (Brush, 1992). Yet despite this historically low level of participation observed, growth in majority of women-owned firms has continued over the past two decades at around two times the rate of all firms. Consequently, the overall share of women-owned firms (i.e., those where women ownership is 50% or more) now accounts for 41% of all privately held firms (Center for Women's Business Research, 2008). Such evidence suggests that while shifts in educational and political institutional structures may not have fully eliminated the barriers, females can increasingly be characterized as holding enough human capital in the form of information and knowledge stocks to make self-employment a more feasible and desirable a career choice.

Ethnicity is a third personal background characteristic that has received wide interest in the extant literature with respect to its influence on human capital development and entrepreneurial activity. The empirical evidence to date suggests that there is not only a significant amount of variation in participation among different ethnic groups (e.g., Reynolds & White, 1997), but also that there is a significant amount of variation in the growth rate of entrepreneurial activities in recent years (cf., Greene & Chaganti, 2003). This observation is particularly interesting in light of business ownership statistics that have generally shown the contrary (e.g., Clinton, 1998, pp. 120–128). Data from PSED I showed Black and Hispanic respondents reported being engaged in the process of starting a new venture at significantly higher rates than White respondents. This finding suggests that while the lack of information and knowledge reflect an ongoing and systematic influence on facilitating self-employment as a career choice in certain ethnic groups, the nature of such influence may be evolving with time.

The discussion above suggests life context and personal background do appear to have some degree of systematic influence on the new venture creation process, in part, by providing access to information related to economic opportunity. However, it also suggests an important weakness of this stream of research. Specifically, it suggests that the study of characteristics such as age, sex, and ethnicity are likely be limited in advancing our understanding with respect to the otherwise "black boxes" of why and how information is actually used to form entrepreneurial judgments (Davidsson & Honig, 2003). In other words, it leaves important questions as to how and to what extent such characteristics can be considered proxies for the underlying cognitive activities likely to be more directly responsible for new venture creation. As a result, the evidence suggests greater focus needs to be turned toward the role knowledge plays as a source of cognitive capital more directly.

9.2.2 Knowledge: A Source of Cognitive Capability

The study of human capital influences in entrepreneurship derives from the idea that entrepreneurs develop and employ different knowledge structures than nonentrepreneurs do. From this perspective, knowledge structures may be likened to sources of competitive advantage (Barney, 2002) for some individuals in that they enhance the cognitive capability of some individuals to recognize opportunities by allowing the "connecting the dots" more effectively among various market forces than others (Baron, 2006). Empirical studies tend to support this view. For instance, comparison study has shown that serial entrepreneurs tend to identify more opportunities than novice entrepreneurs (Ucbasaran & Westhead, 2002). Similarly, studies suggest that education is generally associated with positive economic return when pursuing nascent entrepreneurial activity (Bates, 1995; Davidsson & Honig, 2003).

However, careful examination of knowledge as a source of human capital also suggests that one way of deepening our understanding of the origins of nascent activity revolve around gaining greater insight into the qualitative role knowledge plays in forming entrepreneurial expectations and judgments. For example, a significant and growing literature that evolved in recent years focuses on the role of knowledge in the recognition of opportunity and exploitation. Much of this work draws on observations that knowledge may be distinguished as being of either an explicit or tacit nature (Polanyi, 1966). Explicit knowledge refers to readily codified aspects of information, or that which can be articulated or transmitted in formal, symbolic language. Tacit knowledge, by contrast, refers to "know how," or that which is context-specific, more challenging to articulate as it is represented by the absence of agreed-upon language. Shane (2000), for instance, examined eight sets of entrepreneurs at MIT who presented with the same invention. He found that individual entrepreneurs tended to "discover" opportunities related more to the tacit types of information these individuals already possessed. Similarly, Davidsson and Honig (2003) observed prior start-up experience to be the strongest knowledge-based form of human capital to distinguish nascent entrepreneurs from the larger Swedish population, suggesting that start-up experience was a more tacit form of knowledge than formal education.

Closely related to this stream of research, there is a group of studies that focused on how individuals search for information related to entrepreneurial opportunity. These studies stimulated directions for theoretical development by generating new and potentially interesting empirical observations, but also raised new questions as to the role of important factors such as the existence of prior knowledge in the opportunity recognition process. For example, an early empirical comparison of entrepreneurs and nonentrepreneurs suggested that entrepreneurs spend significantly more time searching for information in their off hours and through nonverbal scanning (Kaish & Gilad, 1991). However, subsequent research has failed to replicate these findings (Busenitz, 1996). Given this lack of replication and suggestions such as individuals not being able to search for an opportunity without first knowing what they are searching for (Kirzner, 1997), it appears reasonable to conclude that important questions for this theoretical line of inquiry persist.

Recent research suggests that the formation of future expectations associated with entrepreneurial opportunity varies based on the presence of both external (i.e., market-based) *and* internal (i.e., self-based) knowledge sources. In other words, these studies illustrate that entrepreneurism occurs at the nexus of individual knowledge and external information about economic opportunity (Shane & Eckhardt, 2003). For example, Smith, Matthews and Schenkel (2009) draw upon the explicit-tacit knowledge distinction to examine how relative differences in the degree of "opportunity" tacitness relate to the process of opportunity identification. They found that a relatively high degree of opportunity codifiability with respect to market-based characteristics leads to a greater likelihood of identification through systematic search efforts, whereas a relatively high degree of opportunity tacitness leads to a greater likelihood of identification through prior experience. Similarly, and consistent with the tacitness argument and prior research suggesting that entrepreneurs disproportionately rely on decision-making heuristics (e.g., Busenitz & Barney, 1997), a recent study finds that the possession of a greater need for cognitive closure was positively associated with new venture activity (Schenkel, Matthews, & Ford, 2009). These authors reasoned that cognition is motivated and tactical in nature (Sorrentino & Roney, 2000), and that the need for closure provides a cognitive means for dealing with the opened-ended nature of opportunity pursuit by enabling information that might otherwise be considered "irrational" to be incorporated meaningfully into existing knowledge structures.

Taken as a whole, the research to date appears clearly to support the premise that the knowledge structures accumulated through various types of information serve as an important source of human capital in the creation of new ventures. It also appears to suggest that not only do important questions remain with respect to its influence, but also that such influence may be both complemented and constrained by a larger social context. We now turn attention to sources of capital originating in social relations.

9.3 Social Capital

9.3.1 Information: Tie Strength

Research suggests that while approximately one half of entrepreneurs recognize ideas for new ventures through their personal capital, the other half recognizes such ideas through their social contacts (Hills, Lumpkin, & Singh, 1997; Koller, 1988). Such evidence clearly suggests that the beginnings of new venture creation activity may not always occur in a "vacuum" devoid of social influence. It also suggests that a key source of information leading to entrepreneurial activity is located in the various types of social relations maintained.

The informational value of social capital has historically been suggested to vary based on the strength of the social relation, or tie. Weak ties are forms of social capital typically present in relationships such as infrequent acquaintances. Granovetter's (1973) seminal work emphasized the importance of possessing an extended network of weak ties to obtaining information resources. Because such ties tend to be based on relatively loose relationships among individuals, they are proposed to increase, or act as a bridge to information and resources that individuals may otherwise be unable to gain access (Davidsson & Honig, 2003). For example, weak ties may expose individuals to different world views, or novel ideas that provide them a wider frame of information or inspiration for reference (Aldrich & Zimmer, 1986). An implicit assumption of this perspective is that because the connectivity is "weak," it is likely to be limited with respect to information redundancy. A lack of redundancy, in turn, provides the holder of such a relationship additional chances to garner more information about entrepreneurial opportunities that he or she might not otherwise have, but need, in order to exploit them.

By contrast, strong ties are forms of social capital typically present in relationships with individuals such as close friends or relatives. Strong ties have been argued to bond actors via mechanisms such as trust, reciprocity and the threat of future censure from exchange (Burt, 1992; Davidsson & Honig, 2003). The quality of information resources in strong relationships is thought to be of higher caliber, as well as more consistently available because strength leads to a sense of embeddedness among those it connects (Granovetter, 1985). This implies that opportunity identification might be enhanced because the quantity *and/or* quality of information with respect to a given opportunity are likely to be more robust. Collectively, this discussion suggests that one reason social capital, both weak and strong alike, increases the likelihood for new venture activity is because it increases the overall probability that opportunities for creating economic value will be identified in the first place (Singh, 2000).

9.3.2 Knowledge: Conceptualizing Capability in Social Capital

Gaglio and Katz (2001) have reviewed the literature and concluded that people likely vary in their ability to understand the workings of economic, social, and physical processes, deconstruct causal relationships, see cross-linkages, critically evaluate information and challenge assumptions, and engage in counterfactual thinking. Yet others have pointed out that social ties strength also appears particularly important with regard to capability development in new ventures because it fosters progress through the process (Larson & Starr, 1993). Strong ties are often developed over time and through multiple transactions. Consequently, they are more likely to be based on reciprocity, trust, and emotional closeness, and less so on short-term calculations of self-interest (e.g., Granovetter, 1993). Research suggests that bond strength is directly associated with the transfer of tacit knowledge, and also allows each member to develop a greater degree of informal control over the other in the relationship (Jones, Heterly, & Borgatti, 1997). However, strong ties development also has limits because the development of strong ties involves substantial effort be devoted to the creation and maintenance. Therefore, the marginal benefit is likely to decline with each new tie sought because the entrepreneur's time is ultimately limited. Indeed, empirical research backs such an interpretation. Research on entrepreneurial networks, for instance, has shown that a majority of business owners report somewhere between three and ten strong ties (e.g., Aldrich, Reese, & Dubini, 1989).

Drawing on the previous research of Nahapiet and Ghoshal (1998), Liao and Welsch (2005) note that a broader conceptualization of social capital takes into account not only the strength of social relationships but also the qualitative nature norms and values that are associated with such relationships. Yet these researchers point out that social capital theory has been limited with respect to how the concept has been explored in this regard, particularly in the new venture creation context. Consequently, this leaves important theoretical questions yet to be considered fully with respect to the dimensionality of social capital. For example, given that new organizations are viewed at least in part as socially constructed (Granovetter, 1985), one question of interest revolves around how various forms of social capital act to complement or inhibit an individual's personal knowledge capital. Another revolves around if and how specific types of new venture context act to influence the role of various sources of human and social capital. We now turn our attention to technology as one important source of context differentiation.

9.4 Technology as a Context Differentiator

Although what constitutes high versus low technology is ambiguous in the literature, research clearly suggests that entrepreneurship researchers believe technology "matters" with respect to considering the influence of human and social capital (Stearns & Reynolds, 1994). For example, studies focusing on human capital have shown that technical entrepreneurs tend to be well educated as reflected by having at least a master's degree (e.g., Cooper, 1973). Similarly, researchers focusing on social capital have argued that technology ventures, particularly in economic sectors that are considered knowledge-intensive, place greater emphasis on knowledge accumulation and learning to a far greater extent than nontechnology ventures (Liao & Welsch, 2005).

Liao and Welsch's (2005) recent work provides some interesting insights into how the study of social capital can be refined using technology as a context differentiator. For instance, by comparing the structural, relational, and cognitive forms of social capital among nascent entrepreneurs and nonentrepreneurs, they found that what differentiated high-tech entrepreneurs from other entrepreneurs was the benefit received from relational capital. Specifically, they found that high-tech entrepreneurs benefit greatly from trustfulness in the relationships, as well as the information and knowledge made possible by such relationships. In short, they found an amplification effect for one form of social capital that appears particularly important when technology is involved.

Given the human capital work reviewed above in conjunction with Liao and Welsch's (2005) work on the social capital, the literature appears to clearly suggest that one question confronting entrepreneurship researchers revolves around more fully exploring the dimensionality of knowledge as a human

9 The Role of Human and Social Capital and Technology in Nascent Ventures 165

capital resource in the creation of new ventures, particularly in the technological context. For example, one question of interest might consider whether other forms of human capital (e.g., work experience) are required at some critical threshold level to complement formal education when entrepreneurial activity involves a technological context. Similarly, this review also suggests there is much to be gained by exploring how the dimensionality of knowledge from a human capital standpoint combines with the dimensionality of that from a social capital standpoint, both generally and in terms of more specific contexts. For example, given the counterintuitive findings of Liao and Welsch (2005) with respect to the impact of social capital on new venture creation, one question researchers might consider is the extent to which human and social capital persist in the development of new ventures, and whether or not such pattern differences extend to various types of venture performance.

9.5 Capital Measures Available in PSED II

The following describes items that reflect a range of approaches available for measuring human social capital in PSED II. This description is not intended to be exhaustive, but rather provide a sense of measures that might be employed given current questions of theoretical interest and debate in the literature.

9.5.1 Human Capital

9.5.1.1 Explicit Knowledge

Explicit knowledge is described as that which derives from information that is codifiable in nature. Following this description, item AH6_1 reflects the highest level of education completed by survey respondents, suggesting it can be employed to measure the explicit dimension of the knowledge. Response options are categorized as follows: (1) up to eighth grade; (2) some high school; (3) high school diploma; (4) technical or vocational degree; (5) some college; (6) community college degree; (7) bachelor's degree; (8) some graduate training; (9) master's degree; (10) law, MD, PHD, EDD, degree; (98) DK; (99) NA.

9.5.1.2 Tacit Knowledge

Given that tacit knowledge is postulated to be intrinsically more difficult to codify, measures are likely to vary with respect to the degree to which they approximate it. There are several items available in PSED II to measure tacit knowledge. One item, AH11_1, asks respondents to report the number of years of work experience they've had in the industry where the new business will compete. A second item, AH21_1, asks respondents to report the number of years, if any, for which they've held managerial, supervisory, or administrative responsibilities. Responses for both of these items are categorized as follows: actual number of years (0–95), with the answer verified if the respondent would have been under 18; (98) DK; (99) NA. A third item, AH12_1, asks respondents to report the number of other businesses they've helped to start as an owner or part-owner. Responses for this item are categorized as follows: actual number of businesses started (0–95); (95) 95 or more businesses; (98) DK; (99) NA.

9.5.1.3 Knowledge of Self

Researchers have suggested that the concept of self-efficacy can apply to a range of specificity levels from the execution of tasks to career choice (Wood & Bandura, 1989). Research further suggests that when tasks are considered interrelated among a given set of choices, including those pertaining to career or occupation, self-efficacy can become a powerful predictor of such choices (Gist, 1987). Entrepreneurial self-efficacy has been defined as the strength of a person's belief that he or she is capable of successfully performing the various roles and tasks of entrepreneurship (Boyd & Vozikis, 1994; Chen, Greene, & Crick, 1998; Krueger & Dickson, 1994). This work suggests that entrepreneurial self-efficacy is clearly concerned with the carrying out of a specific action, not its outcome.

PSED II includes a series of items designed to measure self-efficacy from the specific perspective of the venture being pursued. The first item, AY6, asks respondents to report the overall degree to which they believe their skills and abilities will help them start this new business. The second item, AY7, asks respondents to report if they believe their past experience will be very valuable in helping them start this new business. The third item, AY8, asks respondents to report the extent to which they are confident they can put in the effort needed to start this new business. Responses for each of these items are categorized as follows: (1) strongly agree; (2) agree; (3) neither; (4) disagree; (5) strongly disagree; (8) DK; or (9) NA.

9.5.1.4 Life Context and Personal Background

As previously discussed, several life context and personal background characteristics have been suggested and shown not only to reflect the amount and nature of human capital possessed but also to influence the potential ways in which it is used to create new ventures (cf., Davidsson & Honig, 2003; Delmar & Davidsson, 2000). Accordingly, several life context and personal background items are useful to consider as comparative focal points, particularly as these variables may serve as important control variables for investigating the various influences of human and social capital variables described above and social capitals that follow below. The first item, AH2_1, asks respondents to report their age in years. Responses for this item are categorized as follows: number of years from 18 to 97 (respondent must be 18 or older to participate in the study); (98) DK; (99) NA. The second item, AH1_1, asks respondents to report their sex. Responses for this item are categorized as follows: (1) male; (2) female;

(8) DK; (9) NA. A series of additional items (AH3_1, AH4a_1, AH4b_1, AH4d_1, AH4e_1, AH4f_1, AH4z_1) asks respondents to report their race or ethnicity. Responses for this item can be categorized based on the following options presented to survey respondents: Hispanic or Latino; Black/African American; American Indian; Asian; Pacific Islander; Other.

9.5.2 Social Capital

PSED II also contains variables reflecting explicit and tacit knowledge variables that parallel prior research focusing on the role of human capital (e.g., Davidsson & Honig, 2003; Delmar & Davidsson, 2000; Schenkel, 2005). In addition, it also provides an opportunity to measure structural, relational, and cognitive aspects of social capital parallel recent research utilizing PSED I data that focuses on furthering the understanding of social capital dimensionality (Liao & Welsch, 2005).

9.5.2.1 Explicit Knowledge

As in the case of item AH6_1 for human capital, items AH6_2–5, AM7_1–3 and AN7_1–3 reflect the highest level of education reported among owners, key nonowners, and helpers, respectively. These items can be employed to measure the explicit dimension of the knowledge present among the collective ownership and other key stakeholders of the new business. Similarly, response options for these items are categorized as follows: (1) up to eighth grade; (2) some high school; (3) high school diploma; (4) technical or vocational degree; (5) some college; (6) community college degree; (7) bachelor's degree; (8) some graduate training; (9) master's degree; (10) law, MD, PHD, EDD, degree; (98) DK; (99) NA.

9.5.2.2 Tacit Knowledge

As in the case of item AH11_1 for human capital, items AH11_2–5, AM11_1–3 and AN11_1–3 asks respondents to report the number of years of work experience of other owners, key nonowners, and helpers, respectively, in the business have had in the industry where the new business will compete. A second set of items, AH12_2–5, AM12_1–3 and AN12_1–3, asks respondents to report the number of other businesses that other owners, key nonowners, and helpers helped to start, respectively, as an owner or part-owner. Responses for this item are categorized as follows: actual number of businesses started (0–95); (95) 95 or more businesses; (98) DK; (99) NA.

9.5.2.3 Structural Capital

Items AP10 and AP11 reflect the relationships respondents report while starting this new venture that are consistent with Liao and Welsch's (2005) conceptualization of structural capital. These are strong ties in that the structure of bonds (i.e., close personal relationships) covers those with similar background experience, experience to which the nascent entrepreneur aspires, and structural incentive for continuing the tie beyond the venturing activity alone. Specifically, these items ask respondents if many of their friends (AP10) or relatives (AP11) have started new businesses. Response options are categorized as follows: (1) strongly agree; (2) agree; (3) neither; (4) disagree; (5) strongly disagree; (8) DK; or (9) NA.

9.5.2.4 Relational Capital

Four items are consistent with the underlying aspects of trust and trustfulness that is reflected in Liao and Welsch's (2005) conceptualization and prior empirical study of relational capital. Specifically, item AP6 asks respondents if young people in their community are encouraged to be independent and start their own businesses. Item AP7 asks respondents if state and local governments in your community provide good support for those starting new businesses. Item AP8 asks respondents if bankers and other investors in your community go out of their way to help new businesses get started. Item AP9 asks respondents if community groups provide good support for those starting new businesses. Response options for each of these items are categorized as follows: (1) strongly agree; (2) agree; (3) neither; (4) disagree; (5) strongly disagree; (8) DK; or (9) NA.

9.5.2.5 Cognitive Capital

Five items are consistent with the notion of shared norms reflected in Liao and Welsch's (2005) conceptualization of cognitive capital. Specifically, these items ask respondents if the social norms and culture of the community where you live: (AP1) are highly supportive of success achieved through one's own personal efforts; (AP2) emphasize self-sufficiency, autonomy, and personal initiative; (AP3) encourage entrepreneurial risk-taking; (AP4) encourage creativity and innovativeness; and (AP5) emphasize the responsibility that the individual has in managing his or her own life. Response options for each of these items are categorized as follows: (1) strongly agree; (2) agree; (3) neither; (4) disagree; (5) strongly disagree; (8) DK; or (9) NA.

9.5.3 Technology Context

PSED II provides several means of capturing technological context. One item, AS6, asks respondents to report whether or not they consider the business to be high-tech. Response options are categorized as follows: (1) yes; (5) no; (8) DK; or (9) NA. In addition, item AD11 asks respondents to report whether or not this new business has developed any proprietary technology, processes, or procedures that no other company can use, will it develop proprietary technology, processes, or procedures in the future, or is this not relevant to the new business. Response options are categorized as follows: (1) yes; (2) no, not yet; will in the future; (5) no, not relevant; (8) DK; or (9) NA. Items AS3 and AS4 are also available. These items ask respondents to report if the technologies or procedures required for this product or service were generally available more than a year ago, and more than five years ago, respectively? Response options are categorized as follows for these items: (1) yes; (5) no; (8) DK; (9) NA. Finally, it is also important to note that the data provide ample opportunity for creating categorization or index variables along technological lines. For example, item AA1 asks respondents to categorize the kind of business the new venture represents based on NAICS code.

9.6 Preliminary Statistics and Implications for Future Research

Descriptive statistics for questions related to selected dimensions of human and social capital are presented in Table 9.1. These data provide insight into a variety of issues associated with human and social capital in the nascent venture context. In some cases, these insights act to enrich previous thought. For example, frequency counts suggest that the explicit knowledge dimension of human capital in the form of formal education, particularly at the collegiate level, is indeed positively related to entrepreneurial activity as observed in previous studies (e.g., Davidsson & Honig, 2003). Findings also suggest the relationship between explicit knowledge and nascent entrepreneurial activity appears to hold regardless of the technological context. However, the results also appear to contradict previous research to some extent with respect to the nature of this association. Specifically, these descriptive findings suggest the relationship between explicit knowledge such as human capital in the form of formal education may be indicative of a nonlinear relationship with respect to nascent venturing activity. That is, formal education appears to be associated increasingly with entrepreneurial activity up to the completion of a bachelor's degree. Beyond that point, the relationship appears to decline. This raises new questions as to the role of explicit knowledge as a source of capital in new venturing. For example, it is possible that formal education is associated with the use of logic focusing on direct value added up to a point in the new venturing process beyond which focus shifts toward assessing value from a "real options" investment perspective against more traditional forms of employment as an alternative (e.g., McGrath & MacMillan, 2000).

Another interesting observation in Table 9.1 is reflected in a comparison of human capital reported by nascents directly in the form of tacit knowledge to that reported with respect to the social capital involved in the venturing effort. Specifically, social capital in the form of start-up experience reported among

Table 9.1 Descriptive statistics for items reflecting human and social capital

Construct Dimension Item no. and description	Total no. of responses	Item response rate (%)	Unit of analysis	Mean¹(σ)	AS6: High-tech context Yes Mean(σ)	No(σ)
Human capital						
Explicit knowledge						
AH6_1 Highest level of formal education (in continuous proxy measure form)	1,036	99.5	Continuous (proxy)	5.50 (2.16)	5.58 (2.25)	5.48 (2.23)
AH6_1 Highest level of formal education			Categorical	N/A	Count²	Count
– Up to eighth grade	5	0.5			2	3
– Some high school	45	4.3			9	36
– High school diploma	209	20.1			47	162
– Technical or vocational degree	54	5.2			18	36
– Some college	295	28.3			70	224
– Community college degree	47	4.5			11	36
– Bachelor's degree	216	20.7			43	173
– Some graduate training	31	3.0			6	25
– Master's degree	93	8.9			26	66
– Law, MD, PHD, EDD, degree	41	3.9			14	27
Tacit knowledge						
AH11_1 Industry-specific work experience	1,033	99.2	Years	9.48 (10.73)	10.65 (11.39)	9.15 (10.51)
AH21_1 Managerial, supervisory, or administrative responsibility	1,038	99.7	Years	10.97 (10.18)	10.87 (10.79)	10.97 (9.98)
AH12_1 Start-up experience.	1,041	100	No. of businesses	1.02 (1.96)	1.15 (1.96)	0.98 (1.96)
Knowledge of self (self-efficacy)						
AY6, 7, 8 Mean: Believe skills, abilities and past experience will help to start this business, and confident effort can be put forth.	1,041	100	Level of Agreement (1–5)	1.53 (0.54)	1.47 (0.51)	1.54 (0.55)

Table 9.1 (continued)

Construct Dimension Item no. and description	Total no. of responses	Item response rate (%)	Unit of analysis	Mean¹(σ)	AS6: High-tech context Yes Mean(σ)	No(σ)
Social capital						
Explicit knowledge						
AH6_2-5 Mean: Highest level of formal education (in continuous measure form) among remaining owners	470	41.2	Categorical	5.44 (2.09)	5.67 (2.14)	5.37 (2.07)
AM7_1-3 Mean: Highest level of formal education (in continuous measure form) among key non-owners	360	31.6	Categorical	5.41 (2.17)	5.13 (2.01)	5.50 (2.22)
AN7_1-3 Mean: Highest level of formal education (in continuous measure form) among helpers	269	23.6	Categorical	5.21 (2.12)	5.31 (2.15)	5.18 (2.11)
Tacit knowledge						
AH11_2-5 Mean: Industry specific work experience among remaining owners	469	41.1	Years	7.31 (10.24)	7.87 (12.55)	7.16 (9.45)
AM11_1-3 Mean: Industry specific work experience among key non-owners	281	24.6	Years	8.10 (10.39)	7.38 (9.41)	8.35 (10.73)
AN11_1-3 Mean: Industry specific work experience among helpers	363	31.8	Years	7.86 (9.80)	7.86 (9.51)	7.86 (9.90)
AH12_2-5 Mean: Start-up experience among remaining owners	463	40.6	No. of businesses	0.96 (1.43)	0.89 (1.17)	0.99 (1.51)
AM12_1-3 Mean: Start-up experience among key non-owners	347	30.4	No. of businesses	1.26 (2.04)	1.08 (1.92)	1.31 (2.07)

Table 9.1 (continued)

Construct Dimension Item no. and description	Total no. of responses	Item response rate (%)	Unit of analysis	Mean¹(σ)	AS6: High-tech context Yes Mean(σ)	No(σ)
AN12_1-3 Mean: Start-up experience among helpers	271	23.8	No. of businesses	1.29(2.09)	1.24(1.57)	1.31(2.25)
Structural capital						
AP10 Have many friends that have started businesses	1,032	90.5	Level of Agreement (1–5)	3.06 (1.13)	2.94 (1.16)	3.10 (1.12)
AP11 Have many relatives that have started businesses	1,036	90.9	Level of Agreement (1–5)	3.13 (1.18)	3.07 (1.20)	3.16 (1.17)
Relational capital						
AP6 Young people in their community are encouraged to be independent and start their own businesses	1,025	89.9	Level of Agreement (1–5)	2.79 (1.15)	2.72 (1.20)	2.82 (1.14)
AP7 State and local governments in your community provide good support for those starting new businesses	1,018	89.3	Level of Agreement (1–5)	2.85 (1.10)	2.83 (1.16)	2.86 (1.09)
AP8 Bankers and other investors in your community go out of their way to help new businesses get started	1,016	89.1	Level of Agreement (1–5)	3.08 (1.07)	3.00 (1.16)	3.10 (1.04)
AP9 Community groups provide good support for those starting new businesses	1,019	89.4	Level of Agreement (1–5)	2.64 (0.99)	2.54 (0.99)	2.68 (1.00)
Cognitive Capital						
AP1 The social norms and culture of the community where you live are highly supportive of success	1,038	91.1	Level of Agreement (1–5)	2.18 (1.03)	2.20 (1.08)	2.18 (1.01)

9 The Role of Human and Social Capital and Technology in Nascent Ventures

Table 9.1 (continued)

Construct *Dimension* Item no. and description	Total no. of responses	Item response rate (%)	Unit of analysis	Mean[1](σ)	AS6: High-tech context Yes Mean(σ)	No(σ)
achieved through one's own personal efforts						
AP2 The social norms and culture of the community where you live emphasize self-sufficiency, autonomy, and personal initiative	1,038	91.1	Level of Agreement (1–5)	2.17 (0.97)	2.23 (1.02)	2.15 (0.95)
Cognitive Capital						
AP3 The social norms and culture of the community where you live encourage entrepreneurial risk-taking	1,033	90.6	Level of Agreement (1–5)	2.36 (1.08)	2.29 (1.07)	2.39 (1.08)
AP4 The social norms and culture of the community where you live encourage creativity and innovativeness	1,037	91.0	Level of Agreement (1–5)	2.29 (1.05)	2.22 (1.06)	2.31 (1.05)
AP5 The social norms and culture of the community where you live emphasize the responsibility that the individual has in managing his or her own life	1,037	91.0	Level of Agreement (1–5)	2.03 (0.89)	1.99 (0.86)	2.04 (0.90)

[1] Actual means and standard deviations (where applicable) are reported for all individual variables. In order to foster generalizability to the larger population, PSED II principal investigators recommended that these observations be weighted in order to correct for a missing case data weighted based on the nature of the research question under consideration and specific data requirements for the given data analysis technique employed. Thus, generalizability implication discussed in Footnote 1 also applies here. In addition, it should be pointed out that the total frequency counts for technology as a context consist of fewer than the overall number of cases for individual variables due to missing case data for item AS6.

[2] Actual item counts are reported for technology context.

remaining owners is consistently less than that reported for key nonowners and helpers in both high- and low-tech contexts. In addition, social capital in the form of start-up experience reported among remaining owners is also less than for the nascent entrepreneur in the high-tech context, but comparable in the low-tech context. Collectively, this evidence raises interesting questions for future research as to the role of social capital providers. For example, one possible interpretation of the disparate findings observed for tacit knowledge in terms of start-up experience is that owners with minimal start-up experience are sought out for funding purposes, whereas key nonowners and other helpers are sought out with greater experience for some type of operational or other strategic reason. For instance, nascents might prefer owners to have enough start-up experience to have some comfort with early stage performance variations, but not so much that they seek to exert too strong an influence on early strategic decision-making directly as compared to other key nonowners and helpers. Such a possibility is consistent with trying to offset the adverse effects of judgment given the risk of direct financial investment (Kahneman & Tversky, 1979). It also raises interesting questions from a strategic perspective with respect to the timing of key talent additions to nascent ventures.

One way of addressing questions associated with the strategic contribution of human and social capital resources is to examine the pattern of associations between various human and social capital variables with the decisions to launch, continue, and discontinue new venture creation activities. In order to explore the potential for additional insights offered by such an approach, we conducted a series of analyses using Multivariate Analysis of Variance (MANOVA) as a statistical technique to compare groups of individuals by outcomes reported in during follow-up interviews. Specifically, we compared groups of individuals on a number of dependent variables based on their reporting starting a new firm, continuing in the start-up process, and quitting on the new business start-up process at the time of first follow-up. The MANOVA technique is preferable when comparing multiple variables simultaneously because it reduces the overall error rate relying on a series of fragmented univariate tests leads to, accounts for important information in the form of correlations among the variables considered, and has the potential to reveal sets of variables that may reliably differentiate the groups in cases where such groups may not significantly differ on any of the variables individually (Stevens, 2002). Tables 9.2–9.4 present the results of these analyses.

These data reveal a number of insights into a variety of issues associated with human and social capital in the nascent venture context beyond those provided in Table 9.1. For example, Table 9.2 shows significant multivariate F-ratio statistic for the set of human capital variables that focus on individuals' sets of knowledge resources. Consistent with the descriptive findings in Table 9.1, the MANOVA results also suggest that explicit knowledge in the form of formal education is generally associated with the new business creation efforts. However, the results in Table 9.2 extend to those in Table 9.1 by further suggesting that explicit knowledge in the form of formal education generally

Table 9.2 MANOVA results predicting outcome by human capital knowledge variables

Dimension Item no. and description	Full sample New firm (n=103) Mean[2]	Full sample Start-up continues (n=519) Mean	Full sample Quit (n=199) Mean	High-tech sample New firm (n=18) Mean	High-tech sample Start-up continues (n=132) Mean	High-tech sample Quit (n=41) Mean	Low-tech sample New firm (n=85) Mean	Low-tech sample Start-up continues (n=385) Mean	Low-tech sample Quit (n=158) Mean
Explicit knowledge									
AH6_1 Highest level of formal education	6.04†	5.75	5.43	6.50	5.68	5.44	5.94	5.77	5.43
Tacit knowledge									
AH11_1 Industry-specific work experience	11.30**	10.61	7.84	17.28†	10.67	10.77	10.04**	10.64	7.08
AH21_1 Managerial, supervisory, or administrative responsibility	15.15***	11.89	9.57	17.11†	11.19	10.46	14.73***	12.07	9.34
AH12_1 Start-up experience.	1.13	1.15	0.99	1.11	1.30	1.15	1.13	1.10	0.95
Knowledge of self									
AY6, 7, 8 Mean: self-efficacy	1.46*	1.50	1.61*	1.33	1.49	1.57	1.61*	1.50	1.61
Multivariate F ratio statistic[1]	3.30***			1.29			2.91***		

† $p < 0.10$ * $p < 0.05$ ** $p < 0.01$ *** $p < 0.001$
[1] Multivariate significance test value based on Wilks lambda (Λ) test statistic.
[2] Univariate test significance level is reported in this column for the variables contributing to overall multivariate significance across outcome groups.

Table 9.3 MANOVA results predicting outcome by knowledge social capital variables among owners

Dimension Item no. and description	Full sample			High-tech sample			Low-tech sample		
	New firm ($n=46$) Mean[2]	Start-up continues ($n=236$) Mean	Quit ($n=90$) Mean	New firm ($n=9$) Mean	Start-up continues ($n=62$) Mean	Quit ($n=18$) Mean	New firm ($n=37$) Mean	Start-up continues ($n=172$) Mean	Quit ($n=72$) Mean
Explicit knowledge									
AH6_2-5 Mean level of formal education among other owners	5.30	5.74	5.37	5.85	5.77	5.94	5.17	5.74	5.23
Tacit knowledge									
AH11_2-5 Mean level industry-specific work experience among other owners	8.76*	7.56	4.97	10.63	6.98	4.66	8.30†	7.82	5.04
AH12_1 Mean level of start-up experience among owners	0.77	1.00	0.89	1.44	0.90	0.94	0.61	1.05	0.88
Multivariate F ratio statistic[1]	1.82†			0.52			2.11*		

† $p<0.10$ * $p<0.05$ ** $p<0.01$ *** $p<0.001$.
[1] Multivariate significance test value based on Wilks lambda (Λ) test statistic.
[2] Univariate test significance level is reported in this column for the variables contributing to overall multivariate significance across outcome groups.

Table 9.4 MANOVA results predicting outcome by structural, relational, and cognitive social capital variables

Dimension Item no. and description	Full sample New firm (n=100) Mean[2]	Full sample Start-up continues (n=492) Mean	Full sample Quit (n=187) Mean	High-tech sample New firm (n=16) Mean	High-tech sample Start-up continues (n=128) Mean	High-tech sample Quit (n=39) Mean	Low-tech sample New firm (n=84) Mean	Low-tech sample Start-up continues (n=363) Mean	Low-tech sample Quit (n=148) Mean
Structural capital									
AP10 Have many friends that have started businesses	2.92*	2.96	3.23	3.06	2.93	3.00	2.89*	2.98	3.29
AP11 Have many relatives that have started businesses	2.98	3.13	3.25	3.06	3.08	3.23	2.96	3.15	3.26
Relational capital									
AP6 Young people in their community are encouraged to start their own businesses	2.73	2.73	2.86	3.06	2.62	2.74	2.67	2.77	2.89
AP7 State and local governments in your community provide good support for those starting new businesses	2.87	2.81	2.91	3.19	2.75	2.80	2.81	2.83	2.95
AP8 Bankers and other investors in your community go out of their way to help new businesses get started	2.92	3.08	3.06	2.75	3.02	3.05	2.95	3.11	3.07
AP9 Community groups provide good support for those starting new businesses	2.72	2.63	2.62	2.88	2.48	2.54	2.69	2.68	2.64

Table 9.4 (continued)

Dimension Item no. and description	Full sample outcome			High-tech sample outcome			Low-tech sample outcome		
	New firm ($n=46$) Mean[2]	Start-up continues ($n=236$) Mean	Quit ($n=90$) Mean	New firm ($n=9$) Mean	Start-up continues ($n=62$) Mean	Quit ($n=18$) Mean	New firm ($n=37$) Mean	Start-up continues ($n=172$) Mean	Quit ($n=72$) Mean
Cognitive capital									
AP1 The social norms and culture of the community where you live are highly supportive of success achieved through personal efforts	1.92*	2.16	2.24	1.81	2.19	2.28	1.94	2.15	2.22
AP2 The social norms and culture... emphasize self-sufficiency, autonomy, and personal initiative	1.98	2.10	2.19	1.94	2.23	2.31	1.99	2.05	2.16
AP3 The social norms and culture... encourage entrepreneurial risk-taking	2.21	2.31	2.40	2.25	2.19	2.54	2.20	2.35	2.37
AP4 The social norms and culture... encourage creativity and innovativeness	2.22	2.21	2.34	2.38	2.15	2.36	2.19	2.23	2.34
AP5 The social norms and culture... emphasize individual responsibility	1.94	1.96	2.11	2.13	1.89	2.10	1.91	1.99	2.11
Multivariate F ratio statistic[1]	1.22			0.92			1.04		

†$p < 0.10$ * $p < 0.05$ ** $p < 0.01$ *** $p < 0.001$
[1] Multivariate significance test value based on Wilks Lambda (Λ) test statistic
[2] Univariate test significance level is reported in this column for the variables contributing to overall multivariate significance across outcome groups.

9 The Role of Human and Social Capital and Technology in Nascent Ventures 179

differentiates those who report launching a new venture from those who continue and those who quit, but does not distinguish those who choose to continue from those who choose to quit.

Table 9.2 shows a similar pattern for tacit knowledge suggesting that both industry specific work experience and managerial experience differentiates the various groups. Results suggest that this relationship is particularly robust with respect to differentiating those who start and continue when compared to those who quit. Moreover, this relationship holds across both high and low technological contexts. In sum, these findings suggest that greater amounts of explicit and tacit knowledge may bear a systematically stronger influence on the choice to launch new ventures than it does on choices of persistence. Table 9.2 also shows that the mean score for self-efficacy does vary significantly among the groups, but in reverse from the other forms of knowledge. Specifically, greater self-efficacy is reported in conjunction with the decision to start and continue with new businesses, than with the decision to quit. Collectively, these findings raise interesting questions for future research. For example, it remains unclear whether the combination of less education and experience combined with greater self-efficacy is associated with a premature decision to quit a potentially viable new business, or reflects an otherwise mindful decision to avoid a potential state of overconfidence that leads to staying with a venture that otherwise may not have such promising potential (Geroski, 1995). This suggests the need for research to consider more systematically how the knowledge patterns observed in Table 9.2 relate to longer-term measures of venture performance. It is also important to note that because these groupings reflect only discrete states of choice with no naturally occurring metric between the groups, strong attention should be directed toward developing strong theoretical connections as such patterns are investigated.

Table 9.3 focuses on explicit and tacit knowledge reflected in the social capital reported among others maintaining an ownership interest in the new business beyond the founder. In contrast to the findings for human capital, the multivariate F-ratio statistic for the set of social capital variables that represent individuals' sets of knowledge resources fails to reach significance. This finding could suggest that there is no difference among the groups with respect to the average level of explicit or tacit knowledge possessed by owners beyond the founder. However, it is important to note that industry specific work experience among other owners did exhibit a similar and statistically strong pattern in differentiating the various groups. This suggests that the lack of multivariate significance and significance for other socially-based knowledge variables could reflect the limited power associated with the small sample size. It is also possible that the broad lack of observed differences is systematically related to the amount of time between the initial and follow-up data collection. Both possibilities suggest caution is warranted in interpreting these results, as well as the need for further study to address these possibilities.

Table 9.4 focuses on structural, relational, and cognitive aspects of social capital from the founder's perspective and provides some insight to extend previous research. For example, utilizing PSED I data Liao and Welsch (2005) found that what differentiated entrepreneurs from others overall is their ability and capacity to create social capital, particularly in the form of relational capital. This difference was observed to be amplified in the high-technology context. Because the nascent venture activity may be characterized as a developmental process occurring over a significant period of time (Ardichvili, Cardozo, & Ray, 2003), an interesting area of inquiry revolves around the idea that some resources may be more influential at certain times during the process, but less influential at others. Following this line of reasoning, Liao and Welsch suggest one question of interest is to explore how structural, relational, and cognitive capital each contributes to transitions across the new business creation process. While it remains important to note that the three outcomes illustrated in Table 9.4 do not reflect a naturally progressive metric, Liao and Welsch's findings suggest that relational capital may be expected to be disproportionately associated with new business start and continuance when compared to quitting. Table 9.4, by contrast, does not support such an expectation. Specifically, the results of Table 9.4 show no difference in the association of relational capital to the various outcomes reported in PSED II. In addition, these results do suggest that structural capital in the form of having friends with start-up experience, as well as cognitive capital in the form of social norms and culture in the surrounding community that are supportive of success achieved through personal efforts differs across the groups. However, it does not do so in the direction that would be expected. Greater perceived cognitive capital in this form was reported by those who reported quitting than by those reporting start-up or continuing the new business.

One possibility for failing to support the earlier relational capital finding could be that something in the broader economic climate or marketplace has changed. As a result, it is possible that the role of relational capital is less prominent in the more recent PSED II sample than in PSED I, in part, because the broader situational context demands as such. Capital theory combined with breadth of contextual data available in PSED II and PSED I provides opportunities to address issues of this nature. In the process, it also makes use of the opportunity to enhance existing research through close real-world approximation without artificially precluding and without sacrificing conceptual parsimony (Coleman, 1988). For example, PSED II and PSED I provide comparative opportunities for developing finer grained insights into the temporal aspect of decisions associated with social capital additions (e.g., team members with certain "key" skill sets, when they choose to join the venture "full time" i.e., greater than 35 hours per week). Addressing such questions may provide a foundation for extending our existing understanding of the factors identified to be related to longer-term metrics of new venture performance. Another interesting possibility for future research would be to compare these and other findings presented in this chapter to those in similar PSED studies in other countries.

The items reviewed in the preceding tables are potentially limited in some respects. For example, although from an intuitive standpoint explicit knowledge may frequently be conceptualized as a capital resource that is linear in nature, it is important to note that the actual measurement of this variable in PSED II is categorical in nature. Thus, because item AH6_1 is categorical, it remains possible that the conversion or interpretation of this measure as a quasi-linear implicitly reflects assumptions about the value of differing levels of education that could have an adverse biasing effect on associations observed in statistical tests. Similarly, it should be reinforced that some of the social capital measures identified in Tables 9.1 and 9.4 (e.g., structural, relational, and cognitive capital) reflect approximations of theoretical constructs in previous research (i.e., Nahapiet & Ghoshal, 1998). In other words, the measurement of these constructs reflects researchers' efforts (i.e., Liao & Welsch, 2005) to develop proxy measures for testing theoretical extensions subsequent to the data design and collection efforts of PSED I. It remains possible that such efforts could have a systematic biasing effect on the interpretation of previous tests based on the use of PSED I data, as well as the paralleling descriptive findings depicted in this chapter. We see opportunity here for future research. For example, future research could be conducted to validate the dimensionality of social capital as a construct presented here. Such work could prove integral to advancing theory on social capital influences by illustrating how separating the influence of trust in the form of relational capital from shared norms in the form of cognitive capital helps to understand nascent venture creation activity. Beyond this example, we also believe the collective evidence discussed above illustrates many other potentially fruitful directions for future research efforts.

References

Aldrich, H., Reese, P. R., & Dubini, P. (1989). Women on the verge of a breakthrough? Networking among entrepreneurs in the United States and Italy. *Entrepreneurship & Regional Development, 1*(4), 339–356.

Aldrich, H., & Zimmer, C. (1986). Entrepreneurship through social networks. In D. L. Sexton & R. W. Smilor (Eds.), *The art and science of entrepreneurship* (pp. 3–23). Cambridge, MA: Ballinger.

Ardichvili, A., Cardozo, R., & Ray, S. (2003). A theory of entrepreneurial opportunity identification and development. *Journal of Business Venturing, 18*(1), 105–123.

Barney, J. B. (2002). *Gaining and sustaining competitive advantage* (2nd ed.). Upper Saddle River, NJ: Prentice Hall.

Baron, R. A. (2006). Opportunity recognition as pattern recognition: How entrepreneurs "connect the dots" to identify new business opportunities. *The Academy of Management Perspectives, 20*(1), 104–119.

Bates, T. (1995). Self-employment entry across industry groups. *Journal of Business Venturing, 10*(2), 143–156.

Becker, G. S. (1993). *Human capital: A theoretical and empirical analysis, with special reference to education* (3rd ed.). Chicago: The University of Chicago Press.

Boyd, N. G., & Vozikis, G. S. (1994). The influence of self-efficacy on the development of entrepreneurial intentions and actions. *Entrepreneurship Theory & Practice, 18*(4), 63–77.

Brush, C. G. (1992). Research on women business owners: Past trends, a new perspective and future directions. *Entrepreneurship Theory & Practice, 16*(4), 5–30.

Burt, R. S. (1992). *Structural holes: The social structure of competition.* Cambridge, MA: Harvard University Press.

Busenitz, L. W. (1996). Research on entrepreneurial alertness. *Journal of Small Business Management, 34*(4), 35–44.

Busenitz, L. W., & Barney, J. B. (1997). Differences between entrepreneurs and managers in large organizations: Biases and heuristics in strategic decision-making. *Journal of Business Venturing, 12*(1), 9–30.

Casson, M. (2003). Entrepreneurship, business culture and the theory of the firm. In Z. J. Acs & D. B. Audretsch (Eds.), *Handbook of entrepreneurship research: An interdisciplinary survey and introduction* (Vol. I, pp. 223–246). Boston: Kluwer Academic Publishers.

Center for Women's Business Research. (2008). *Key facts about women owned businesses.* Retrieved April 2008, from http://www.nfwbo.org/facts/index.php

Chen, C. C., Greene, P. G., & Crick, A. (1998). Does entrepreneurial self-efficacy distinguish entrepreneurs from managers? *Journal of Business Venturing, 13*(4), 295–316.

Clinton, W. J. (1998). *The state of small business: A report of the President.* Retrieved July 2008, from http://www.sba.gov/advo/research/stateofsb1998.pdf

Cohen, W. M., & Levinthal, D. A. (1990). Absorptive capacity: A new perspective on learning and innovation. *Administrative Science Quarterly, 35*(1), 128–152.

Coleman, J. S. (1988). Social capital in the creation of human capital. *The American Journal of Sociology, 94*, S95–S120.

Cooper, A. C. (1973). Technical entrepreneurship: What do we know? *Research and Development Management, 3*(2), 59–64.

Davidsson, P., & Honig, B. (2003). The role of social and human capital among nascent entrepreneurs. *Journal of Business Venturing, 18*(3), 301–331.

Delmar, F., & Davidsson, P. (2000). Where do they come from? Prevalence and characteristics of nascent entrepreneurs. *Entrepreneurship & Regional Development, 12*(1), 1–23.

Gaglio, C. M., & Katz, J. A. (2001). The psychological basis of opportunity identification: Entrepreneurial alertness. *Small Business Economics, 16*(2), 95–111.

Geroski, P. A. (1995). What do we know about entry? *International Journal of Industrial Organization, 13*, 421–440.

Gist, M. E. (1987). Self efficacy: Implications for organizational behavior and human resource management. *Academy of Management Journal, 12*, 472–485.

Granovetter, M. (1985). Economic action and social structure: The problem of embeddedness. *American Journal of Sociology, 91*(3), 481–510.

Granovetter, M. (1993). The nature of economic relationships. In R. Swedberg (Ed.), *Explorations in economic sociology.* New York: Russell Sage.

Granovetter, M. S. (1973). The strength of weak ties. *American Journal of Sociology, 78*(6), 1360–1380.

Greene, P. G., & Chaganti, R. (2003). Levels of resources for ethnic entrepreneurs. In C. H. Stiles (Ed.), *Structure and process* (Vol. 4, pp. 59–74). New York: Elsevier Science.

Hayek, F. A. (1945). The use of knowledge in society. *American Economic Review, 35*(4), 519–530.

Hills, G. E., Lumpkin, G. T., & Singh, R. P. (1997). Opportunity recognition: Perceptions and behaviors of entrepreneurs. *Frontiers of Entrepreneurship Research, 15*, 105–117.

Jones, C., Heterly, W. S., & Borgatti, S. P. (1997). A general theory of network governance: Exchange conditions and social mechanisms. *Academy of Management Review, 22*(4), 911–945.

Kahneman, D., & Tversky, A. (1979). Prospect theory: An analysis of decision under risk. *Econometrika, 47*(2), 263–291.

Kaish, S., & Gilad, B. (1991). Characteristics of opportunities search of entrepreneurs vs. executives: Sources, interests, general alertness. *Journal of Business Venturing, 6*(1), 45–61.

9 The Role of Human and Social Capital and Technology in Nascent Ventures

Kirzner, I. M. (1979). *Perception, opportunity, and profit: Studies in the theory of entrepreneurship.* Chicago: University of Chicago Press.

Kirzner, I. M. (1997). Entrepreneurial discovery and the competitive market process: An Austrian approach. *Journal of Economic Literature, 35*(1), 60–85.

Kirzner, I. M. (1999). Creativity and/or alertness: A reconsideration of the Schumpeterian entrepreneur. *Review of Austrian Economics, 11,* 5–17.

Koller, R. H. (1988). *On the source of entrepreneurial ideas.* Paper presented at the Frontiers of Entrepreneurship Research, Wellesley, MA.

Krueger, N., Jr., & Dickson, P. R. (1994). How believing in ourselves increases risk taking: Perceived self-efficacy and opportunity recognition. *Decision Sciences, 25*(3), 385–400.

Krueger, N. F., Jr., & Brazeal, D. V. (1994). Entrepreneurial potential and potential entrepreneurs. *Entrepreneurship Theory & Practice, 18*(3), 91–104.

Larson, A., & Starr, J. A. (1993). A network model of organization formation. *Entrepreneurship Theory & Practice, 17*(2), 5–15.

Liao, J., & Welsch, H. (2005). Roles of social capital in venture creation: Key dimensions and research implications. *Journal of Small Business Management, 43*(4), 345–362.

McGrath, R. G., & MacMillan, I. C. (2000). Assessing technology projects using real options reasoning. *Research Technology Management, 43*(4), 35–49.

Nahapiet, J., & Ghoshal, S. (1998). Social capital, intellectual capital and the organizational advantage. *Academy of Management Review, 23*(2), 242–266.

Polanyi, M. (1966). *The tacit dimension.* Garden City, NY: Doubleday.

Reynolds, P. D., & White, S. B. (1997). Entrepreneurial processes and outcomes: The influence of ethnicity. In P. D. Reynolds & S. B. White (Eds.), *The entrepreneurial process: Economic growth, men, women, and minorities* (pp. 179–204). Westport, CT: Quorum Books.

Ronstadt, R. (1988). The corridor principle. *Journal of Business Venturing, 3*(1), 31–40.

Schenkel, M. T. (2005). *New enterprise opportunity recognition: Toward a theory of entrepreneurial dynamism.* Unpublished doctoral dissertation, University of Cincinnati, Cincinnati, OH.

Schenkel, M. T., Matthews, C. H., & Ford, M. W. (2009). Making rational use of 'irrationality'? Exploring the role of need for cognitive closure in nascent entrepreneurial activity. *Entrepreneurship & Regional Development, 21*(1), 51–76.

Shane, S. (2000). Prior knowledge and the discovery of entrepreneurial opportunities. *Organization Science, 11*(4), 448–469.

Shane, S. A., & Eckhardt, J. T. (2003). The individual-opportunity nexus. In Z. J. Acs & D. B. Audretsch (Eds.), *Handbook of entrepreneurship research: An interdisciplinary survey and introduction* (pp. 161–191). Boston: Kluwer Academic Publishers.

Singh, R. P. (2000). *Entrepreneurial opportunity recognition through social networks.* New York: Garland Publishing.

Smith, B. R., Matthews, C. H., & Schenkel, M. T. (2009). Differences in entrepreneurial opportunities: The role of tacitness and codification in opportunity identification. *Journal of Small Business Management, 47*(1), 38–57.

Sorrentino, R. M., & Roney, C. J. R. (2000). *The uncertain mind: Individual differences in facing the unknown.* Philadelphia: Psychology Press.

Stearns, T. M., & Reynolds, P. D. (1994). *Contextual differences between high tech and low tech firms: An examination of performance.* Paper presented at the Frontiers of Entrepreneurship Research, Wellesley, MA.

Stevens, J. P. (2002). *Applied multivariate statistics for the social sciences.* London: Lawrence Erlbaum Associates Publishers.

Ucbasaran, D., & Westhead, P. (2002). *Does entrepreneurial experience influence opportunity identification?* Paper presented at the Frontiers of Entrepreneurship Research, Wellesley, MA.

Wood, R., & Bandura, A. (1989). Social cognitive theory of organizational management. *Academy of Management Review, 14*(1), 361–384.

Chapter 10
Financing the Emerging Firm: Comparisons Between PSED I and PSED II

William B. Gartner, Casey J. Frid, John C. Alexander, and Nancy M. Carter

10.1 Introduction

This chapter explores whether certain kinds of financing that are both expected and acquired by entrepreneurs during the venture startup process might have an influence on the likelihood that these efforts will lead to ongoing ventures. We look at whether entrepreneurs expect and utilize their own personal funds for business creation, as well as whether entrepreneurs expect and acquire funds from sources external to themselves. We offer a novel way of looking at external funding sources by dividing external funding into two categories: monitored and unmonitored.

Nearly all research in the entrepreneurship area on the process of acquiring financial capital has focused on new ventures rather than on emerging ventures (Astebro & Bernhardt, 2003; Cassar, 2004; Chaganti, DeCarolis, & Deeds, 1995; Ou & Haynes, 2006; Verheul & Thurik, 2001), though some research has been conducted on firm financing using the first Panel Study of Entrepreneurial Dynamics, PSED I (Reynolds, 2007; Stouder, 2002; Stouder & Kirchhoff, 2004). By emerging ventures, we mean those efforts undertaken by individuals to develop an on-going venture. Emerging ventures, therefore, are not ventures per se, but attempts by individuals to develop a venture. The successful outcome from the emerging venture process would be a new venture (Gartner, 1993; Gartner & Brush, 2007).

While Reynolds (2007) and Reynolds and Curtin (2008) offer some insights into some of the broad characteristics of emerging venture finance (e.g., amounts invested by individuals and teams), there appears to be little research on the structure of these financial investments and their relationship to venture creation success. Using theory from research on the sources of funding for new ventures (e.g., Cassar, 2004), we offer a set of hypotheses about the

---

W.B. Gartner (✉)
Spiro Institute for Entrepreneurial Leadership, 345 Sirrine Hall, Clemson University, Clemson, SC 29634, USA
e-mail: gartner@clemson.edu

A version of this chapter, focusing on a portion of the PSED1 data only, was presented in (Gartner, Frid & Alexander, 2008).

types of financial resources that certain kinds of emerging businesses expect to pursue and acquire, and we explore whether entrepreneurs using these expected and acquired funding sources are more likely to create on-going businesses. We test our hypotheses using data from the first Panel Study of Entrepreneurial Dynamics, PSED I (Gartner, Shaver, Carter, & Reynolds, 2004), and the second Panel Study of Entrepreneurial Dynamics, PSED II (Reynolds & Curtin, 2008); both are longitudinal data sets that track the activities of entrepreneurs in the process of starting ventures.

Our findings suggest that entrepreneurs who are able to acquire external financing of any kind (monitored or unmonitored) are significantly more likely to have started a business or remain in the business startup process. Indeed, the use of personal funds only was negatively correlated with startup survival.

10.2 Theory Development and Hypotheses

Entrepreneurs use a variety of financing sources for the development of their ventures: their own personal finances; the finances of their spouses, team members, family and friends; financing by equity investors; debt through personal loans; debt through loans to the business from banks, suppliers, capital financing, etc. Typically, the way that business financing has been understood, is by separating the sources of financial capital into two broad categories: debt or equity (Cassar, 2004; Chaganti et al., 1995). While for certain kinds and sizes of ongoing businesses the categories of "debt" and "equity" might provide meaningful insights into these firms' capital structures, the phenomenon of emerging ventures is different. For example, the nature of debt for an emerging venture can be of various types with various obligations for payment. An entrepreneur can provide a loan of personal funds to the emerging venture. An entrepreneur can have family and friends make loans to the emerging venture. An entrepreneur could acquire a bank loan to fund the emerging venture. We believe that the obligations to a debt holder who might be a family member or a friend would be very different than the obligations an entrepreneur would have for a bank loan. We believe that the label "debt," then, has very different consequences and implications for both the entrepreneur and the emerging venture when debt is acquired personally, from family or friends, or from banks and sophisticated investors.

We would offer the same logic for surmising that equity in emerging ventures may have different obligations to shareholders than in established organizations. An equity investment provided by family and friends to an emerging venture may have less of a claim on present or future earnings or have fewer obligations regarding control of the corporation compared to equity held by venture capitalists (VCs) or professional investors.

10.2.1 Personal, Monitored, and Unmonitored Financing Sources

We suggest that a better way to differentiate among various sources of financial capital used for creating new ventures is to consider the level of oversight and involvement the provider of a source of capital might require. First, we note that nearly all entrepreneurs are likely to use their own personal financial resources, and that they will also use personal funds from other team members. In terms of acquiring resources from others outside the venture team, we posit that there are two broad categories of funding sources that have different levels of oversight and involvement: unmonitored and monitored financial sources. Unmonitored sources of funds include funds from a second mortgage, credit cards, spouses, friends, and family. These funds are provided to the entrepreneur with little to no overview of the business plan or operations. For example, an entrepreneur can acquire capital through a credit card, and these funds are not strictly monitored in terms of what the funds are used for, and how these funds will eventually be paid off. In contrast, monitored sources of funding include loans from a bank, finance company, current employer, the Small Business Administration, and venture capital. These funds are provided after a thorough understanding of the business plan and operations have been achieved. A bank loan would require entrepreneurs to provide an indication of how the funds were to be used, and, to show how and when the funds would be paid back.

This categorization scheme of external financial resources into monitored and unmonitored is not without some concerns. Certainly it is possible that our categorization of various sources of financial capital into these two broad sources of funding may, at times, fall into the opposite category. A family member might loan money to an entrepreneur and require a business plan, and, continue to review the entrepreneur's efforts over time. Paul Reynolds (in a personal conversation) suggested that family members might monitor their financial investments through "dinner table" conversations, which might be more frequent and thorough than monitoring done by banks or sophisticated investors. And, a loan officer at a bank might provide a business loan without much documentation and oversight. But, we would surmise that the kinds of financial sources we have identified would likely fit into the two types of unmonitored or monitored categories in nearly all circumstances.

It should also be noted that we are interested in the kinds of funding that are expected and acquired *during* the process of venture creation. Our view of monitored and unmonitored funding assumes oversight *during* the venture creation process, and is less oriented towards what possible consequences might occur if these expected (or acquired) funds are not paid back to these external sources. Doug Bosse, in comments made at the Babson Entrepreneurship Research Conference in June 2008, suggested that entrepreneurs seeking outside funding might face either expected contractual consequences or expected social consequences from accepting resources from others. For example, the social consequences of failing to pay back either equity or debt to friends or family might be more serious to an entrepreneur than the failure to pay back funds to a bank or VC, so entrepreneurs may be more likely to insure venture success based on funding from family and friends, than from contractual sources such as banks or VCs. Our constructs of "monitored and unmonitored" are less about expected consequences of a venture investment, and more about whether or not venture investors are likely to pay methodical attention to their investment.

We believe that the "monitored and unmonitored" financing constructs do have some face value, and, therefore, at this initial stage, are worth exploring. We develop hypotheses about how various characteristics of these entrepreneurs and their firms will likely influence these entrepreneurs' expectations of receiving these two types of financing, and whether the actual acquisition of these types of financing will affect successfully starting a new venture. And, we then subsequently provide a way to operationalize these two categories of financing. Further development of these constructs is certainly warranted through in-depth interviews of entrepreneurs to ascertain the ways that various investors actually interacted with these entrepreneurs during the venture creation process.

10.2.2 Characteristics of Funding Source Use

Parts "A" of the first five hypotheses focus on the expectations for funding, and, therefore, are only applicable to data analyzed from PSED I. We suggest that the entrepreneur's expectations of the future size of the new venture will significantly influence whether monitored and unmonitored sources of funds are sought during the startup process. Smaller companies would require less capital. Furthermore, the expectation that a company would be small would likely mean the entrepreneur might be offered less capital, as well. Barriers to entry may exist relative to more sophisticated capital sources, so the access and cost of these funding sources may be too high for entrepreneurs contemplating starting companies that stay small. Larger firms would likely need outside funding for expansion. Finally, the cost to access certain kinds of funding may decline the larger the firm. Ang (1992) finds that the high transaction costs faced by small businesses in securing outside financing may preclude some sources of funding. Cosh and Hughes (1994) and Cassar (2004) find that smaller firms use relatively less outside financing.

> H_{1A}: The expected size of the new firm will be positively related to an expected use of unmonitored and monitored sources of financing as a larger percentage of total resources.
>
> H_{1B}: The expected size of the new firm will be positively related to the acquisition of unmonitored and monitored sources of financing as a larger percentage of total resources.

10 Financing the Emerging Firm

Financial institutions and VCs may consider the form of incorporation to be a signal of the credibility, internal operational quality, and accountability of the proposed business. Operational quality and accountability are often found in successful businesses. Prior evidence by Storey (1994), Freedman and Godwin (1994), and Cassar (2004) suggest a positive relationship between incorporation and leverage and/or bank financing.

> H_{2A}: Emerging firms who are incorporated will be positively related to an expected use of more monitored sources of financing.
>
> H_{2B}: Emerging firms who are incorporated will be positively related to the acquisition of more monitored sources of financing.

Agency conflicts between debt and equity holders tend to be higher for firms that are expected to grow more quickly. This results from the incentive for equity holders to leverage the company, as they are the residual claimants, whereas the debt holders are the fixed claimants. Michaelas, Chittenden, and Poutziouris (1999) find that leverage and debt are positively related to future growth. Cassar (2004) finds that future growth is positively related to the use of bank financing.

> H_{3A}: Entrepreneurs who intend to start firms with higher rates of growth will be positively related to expecting to use more unmonitored and monitored sources of financing as a larger percentage of total resources.
>
> H_{3B}: Entrepreneurs who intend to start firms with higher rates of growth will be positively related to acquiring more unmonitored and monitored sources of financing as a larger percentage of total resources.
>
> H_{4A}: Entrepreneurs who intend to start firms with higher rates of growth will be positively related to expecting to use more monitored sources of financing.
>
> H_{4A}: Entrepreneurs who intend to start firms with higher rates of growth will be positively related to acquiring more monitored sources of financing.

Characteristics of the entrepreneur may affect access to funding. Education and industry experience may provide entrepreneurs access to funding networks that may otherwise not be available. For example, Cleman and Cohn (2000) find that education is positively related to acquiring external loans. While Verheul and Thurik (2001) and Haynes and Haynes (1999) find that gender has no influence on the likelihood of getting a loan, we thought it worth exploring whether gender had an influence on the types of funding sources entrepreneurs are expected to acquire. In general, in terms of the characteristics of the business owner, overall, Cassar (2004) found that once firm characteristics were taken into consideration, the characteristics of the business owner do not affect the financing of the firm.

10.2.2.1 Gender

> H_{5A}: Male entrepreneurs will be more likely to expect to use monitored and unmonitored sources of financing as a larger percentage of total resources than female entrepreneurs.

H_{5B}: Male entrepreneurs will be more likely to acquire monitored and unmonitored sources of financing as a larger percentage of total resources than female entrepreneurs.

10.2.2.2 Race

H_{5C}: White entrepreneurs will be more likely to expect to use monitored and unmonitored sources of financing as a larger percentage of total resources than minority entrepreneurs.

H_{5D}: White entrepreneurs will be more likely to acquire monitored and unmonitored sources of financing as a larger percentage of total resources than minority entrepreneurs.

10.2.2.3 Education

H_{5E}: The higher the entrepreneur's level of education, the greater the proportion of monitored and unmonitored funding the entrepreneur will expect to use.

H_{5F}: The higher the entrepreneur's level of education, the greater the proportion of monitored and unmonitored funding the entrepreneur will acquire.

10.2.2.4 Net Worth

H_{5G}: The higher the entrepreneur's net worth, the greater the proportion of monitored and unmonitored funding the entrepreneur will expect to use.

H_{5H}: The higher the entrepreneur's net worth, the greater the proportion of monitored and unmonitored funding the entrepreneur will acquire.

10.2.2.5 Startup Experience

H_{5I}: The greater the number of prior startups the entrepreneur has been involved in, the greater the proportion of monitored and unmonitored funding the entrepreneur will expect to use.

H_{5J}: The greater the number of prior startups the entrepreneur has been involved in, the greater the proportion of monitored and unmonitored funding the entrepreneur will acquire.

10.2.2.6 Industry Experience

H_{5K}: The greater the number of years the entrepreneur has worked in the same industry as the startup, the greater the proportion of monitored and unmonitored funding the entrepreneur will expect to use.

H_{5L}: The greater the number of years the entrepreneur has worked in the same industry as the startup, the greater the proportion of monitored and unmonitored funding the entrepreneur will acquire.

The critical words in the first five hypotheses are: expected and acquired. Because the data from both PSED I and PSED II looks at individuals who are in the process of starting businesses, it is possible to explore what these individuals expected to do (in PSED I) and, then, subsequently study what they actually did (in PSED I and PSED II). For the final two hypotheses, we examine whether the expectation and acquisition of using monitored sources leads to starting an on-going business. Given that the acquisition of monitored sources of financing is likely to require an entrepreneur to provide a business plan and financial projections, we would assume that these entrepreneurs would be better prepared during the startup process and that they would select the kinds of businesses that would be more likely succeed so as to merit the acquisition of monitored financing.

H_{6A}: Entrepreneurs who expect to use monitored sources of financing are more likely to start an on-going business.

H_{6B}: Entrepreneurs who acquire monitored sources of financing are more likely to start an on-going business.

10.3 Samples and Questions

We used a cleaned sample of 817 cases (Shaver, Carter, Gartner, & Reynolds, 2001) taken from the Panel Study of Entrepreneurial Dynamics I (Gartner et al., 2004) and a sample of 1,214 cases from the Panel Study of Entrepreneurial Dynamics II (Reynolds & Curtin, 2008) to explore the financing expectations and actions of entrepreneurs during the startup process. Analyses were conducted using weights so that these samples might better represent the general population of U.S. working age adults (Reynolds & Curtin, 2004).

There are a number of significant differences in the questions asked about financing in the PSED I and PSED II data sets. Stouder and Kirchhoff (2004) describe the financing questions in PSED I in some detail. Our chapter will therefore, point out how the PSED II financing question were organized, and how these questions differ from PSED I. Financing questions in PSED I are listed in Appendix Tables 10.8–10.10.

Three principal sections of the PSED II deal with emerging firm financing. Section E (Startup Finances) was designed to assess the following: whether or not external financing is sought or is even relevant to the startup; what activities are undertaken that affect both costs and revenues; the level of financial sophistication of the respondent (see Katz & Cabezuelo, 2004); and actions taken related to the official legal registration of the emerging firm.

In sections Q and R of the PSED II, items regarding startup investments and the net worth of the emerging firm are addressed. Similar to the items in PSED I, these two sections examine the sources and amounts of funding acquired by nascent entrepreneurs. However, items in the first wave of the PSED I were about financing *expectations* (such as whether funding was expected to come from source "x", and, how much was expected from this source). Waves 2–4 in the PSED I asked respondents to indicate how much they actually acquired. For the two waves in the PSED II, respondents were asked to indicate how much they actually acquired from each source. Only one item in PSED II deals with financing expectations, and it asks respondents to gauge how much, overall, they expect to acquire to start the business, rather than their expectations of how much they expect to acquire from each financing source.

The logic for focusing on what nascent entrepreneurs actually acquired at each wave in the data collection process in PSED II (and particularly at Wave 1) was to provide more similarity in measuring actual behaviors in financing vis-à-vis other startup behaviors. So, while the PSED I questions ask nascent entrepreneurs what they expected to obtain for various sources of outside financing, the questions in PSED II asked respondents what they actually acquired for various sources of outside financing.

Another difference between the financing questions in PSED I and PSED II, is that questions in PSED II separate financing by whether the emerging venture has been legally registered or not. For many sources of financing a firm must be legally registered in order to acquire that source of funding. In PSED II, Section Q asks respondents about the source of funds from other persons and legal entities acquired *before* registering legally. Section R asks respondents about loans and other financial support received *after* registration. Financing sources are further categorized based on whether contributions are loans to the new business that are expected to be paid back (debt), or are provided as a percentage of ownership (equity).

Stouder and Kirchhoff (2004: 358–366) provide descriptions of finance variable names and interview questions in PSED I, which are reproduced here in Appendix Tables 10.8–10.10. PSED II variable names and interview questions are provided in chapter Appendix Tables 10.11–10.13. The "other choices" column lists associated variables (often the same item is applied to other owners of the emerging firm; i.e. AQ4_1, AQ4_2, AQ4_3, etc.). The final three columns describe the flow of the interview pattern based on responses to specific questions.

In Tables 10.1 (PSED I) and 10.2 (PSED II), we classify questionnaire items into the three categories of personal contributions, unmonitored external sources, and monitored external sources.

Table 10.1 PSED I questions used for personal, unmonitored, and monitored sources

Dependent variable	Wave 1 Expected	Wave 2 Acquired
Personal contributions*	Q198	R656
	Q212_1–5	R678_1–5
	–	R771
	–	R772
Unmonitored external sources		
Spouse	Q268	–
Spouse (of team members)	Q270	–
Family and friends	Q272	–
Family and friends (of team)	Q274	–
2nd Mortgage	Q277a	–
Credit card	Q282a	R779

10 Financing the Emerging Firm

Table 10.1 (continued)

Dependent variable	Wave 1 Expected	Wave 2 Acquired
Family (respondent + team)	–	R773, R773a
Friends (respondent + team)	–	R774, R774a
2nd Mortgage/refinancing car	–	–
Other	Q288a	R780, R781
Monitored external sources		
Employer	Q276	–
Bank	Q279	–
SBA loan	Q281	–
Venture capitalist	Q284	–
Personal finance company	Q286	–
Bank/financial institution/VC	–	R775, R775a
Private investors	–	R776, R776a
Government agencies	–	R777, R777a
Suppliers/subcontractors	–	R778
Personal finance firm	–	–
Other	Q288a	R780, R781

* Personal contributions in Wave 1 are acquired, not expected, by respondents.

Table 10.2 PSED II questions used for personal, unmonitored, and monitored sources

Dependent variable	Wave A	Wave B
Personal contributions		
Personal savings before registration	AQ4_1–5	BQ4_1–5
Personal (+ team) equity after registration	AR4	BR4
Personal loan after registration	AR10	BR10
Start-up team debt loan after registration	AR11	BR11
Unmonitored external sources		
Family and relatives before registration	AQ5_1–5	BQ5_1–5
Friends, employers, colleagues before registration	AQ6_1–5	BQ6_1–5
Credit cards (before registration)	AQ7_1–5	BQ7_1–5
Asset backed (2nd mortgage, car loan) before registration	AQ9_1–5	BQ9_1–5
Lease-backed (property and equipment) after registration	AR7	BR7
Spouses, family of start-up team after registration	AR12	BR12
Employees who will not own, after registration	AR13	BR13
Credit cards (after registration)	AR15	BR15
Monitored external sources		
Bank or financial institution loan before registration.	AQ8_1–5	BQ8_1–5
Asset backed (can be repossessed) before registration	AR6	BR6
Bank credit line after registration	AR8	BR8
Credit from suppliers after registration	AR9	BR9
Bank loan after registration	AR16	BR16
Venture capitalists	AR17	BR17
Government agency (non-SBA)	AR18	BR18
SBA-guaranteed loan	AR19	BR19

It should be noted that, because the PSED II data has only two waves, while the PSED I data has four waves, we will be using only the first two waves in PSED I so as to make similar comparisons over time between the two data sets.

For personal contributions, respondents were asked how much of their own money they had contributed to the business, and how much in personal funds other team members contributed to the business. These were added together to construct the personal contributions variable. For unmonitored and monitored external sources of funding, in PSED I, Wave 1 item numbers list what respondents *expected* they would receive in funding. Wave 2 PSED I item numbers are about what respondents actually *acquired* in external funding. Unmonitored sources of funds include funds from a 2nd mortgage, credit cards, spouses, friends, and family. These funds are provided to the entrepreneur with little to no overview of the business plan or operations. In contrast, monitored sources of funding include loans from a bank, finance company, current employer, the Small Business Administration, and venture capital. These funds are provided after a thorough understanding of the business plan and operations have been achieved.

We also control for firm characteristics such as the expected size of the business (AT2), industry (AB1), legal form (AC1, BC1), team size (AG2, BG2a), expected growth rate (AT1), and characteristics of the nascent entrepreneurs such as industry experience (AH11), prior startup experience (AH12), race (AH3, AH4), education (AH6), gender (qsex), and household net worth (AZ36x).

The startup outcome measure was determined using questions from Wave B, Section A. Efforts undertaken by nascent entrepreneurs were categorized as a *new firm* if all of the following conditions were met in more than 6 of the past 12 months: the new business received money from the sale of goods (BA30); monthly revenue was greater than monthly expenses (BA32); and salaries or wages of owners who were active in managing the business were included in monthly expenses (BA34).[1] Startup efforts were categorized as *active startups* if respondents answered "no" to any one of these conditions. Active startups also include efforts where the respondent devoted more than 160 h of full-time work to the startup during the past year, and expected to spend more than 80 h over the next 6 months (BA37, BA38); the respondent considered the startup to be a major focus of his or her work career (BA40); and he or she declared active involvement in the startup (BA42). Startup efforts were categorized as *quit* if respondents declared disengagement from the process (BA15 or BA42).

10.4 Comparisons of PSED I and PSED II

In this section of the chapter, we examine the effects of individual and emerging firm characteristics on the type and amount of funding used during the venture creation process. We compare the initial interview and first follow-up results from Waves 1 and 2 in PSED I to the Waves A and B in PSED II. It is worth noting how methodological differences in the finance sections between the two data sets affect statistical comparisons and analysis. In the PSED II data set, determining the amount of funding by source contributed to the emerging firm is straightforward. In Wave A, respondents are asked how much has been contributed; and in Wave B they are asked how much has been contributed overall (Wave A + Wave B). In addition, respondents are asked to confirm if the amount given is indeed correct. A manual examination of the financing variables will reveal that in almost all cases responses are consistent and that the total amount contributed will correspond to the value listed in the most recent wave of data collection, for each respondent.

In the PSED I, it is less clear whether question items are asking for a cumulative amount of money contributed to the emerging firm. In addition, questions differ between waves. Some sources of funding are reworded, combined with other sources of funding, or dropped altogether. After manually examining the data it appears that some respondents report how much "total, so far" has been contributed to the startup, while others report how much was contributed specifically for that particular wave.

We dealt with this in the following manner. First, most of the discrepancies show up in the later waves (S and T). Because this study looks only at Wave Q versus Wave R, we don't have this problem. All the Wave Q questions ask about expectations, and all the Wave R questions ask "How much has X put into the business." At Wave Q, if respondents indicated that they have already asked the source, and the source said "yes," that dollar amount was included in the acquired category. For example: Q266 asks if spouse was asked for funding. Q266a asks if the answer was "yes or no" or "will fund." Q268 asks how much was expected. If Q266a was "yes," then the amount from Q268 would be acquired.

There is no problem with determining unmonitored funding sources between items in Waves Q and R. Wave Q separates respondent friends, family, team friends, and team family into four separate items. Wave R combines respondent and team friends, and respondent and team family. As per the categorization scheme in Table 10.1, all of these sources are grouped together as "unmonitored." To explore funding of *only* friends or *only* family, we would combine the respondent and team items from Wave Q and compare these to Wave R. The logic for the monitored sources similarly applies. We are comparing total monitored at Wave Q to total monitored at Wave R. So while the bank/ financial institution/ VC are all combined into one question in Wave R, but separated into three items for Wave Q, we only run into problems when we want to compare *only* bank financing, or *only* VC financing. Similarly, questions regarding funding from private investors, government agencies, and suppliers/ subcontractors are asked in Wave R but not in Wave Q, which could inflate the values in the Wave R "acquired" category when compared to "expectations." But, the number of responses and funding provided for these categories was minimal [i.e., private investors (R776): 3 total, $12,000, $2,000, and $100; government agencies (R777): 2 total; $100,000 and $115,000; subcontractors (R778): 2 total; $30,000 and $10,000]. We also looked at the open-ended questions regarding expected financing in Wave Q, "other funding sources," and categorized these responses into either monitored or unmonitored. Presumably, if funding from private investors, government agencies, and subcontractors was expected, it would have shown up in the responses to the "other funding sources" item.

The logic underlying the finance questions in PSED I were meant to measure financing expectations, followed by what actually occurred. Wave 1 asks for *expected* amounts by source and Waves 2–4 ask for *acquired* amounts. None of this is to say that determining funding amounts in PSED I is impossible. Indeed, analyzing financing expectations and then seeing what actually occurred is a major benefit to using PSED I. What it does mean, however, is that comparisons between PSED I and PSED II are not as straightforward as one might expect.

PSED II values are all acquired funding, but, respondents are asked to reveal funding behavior before and after legal registration of the nascent venture. It appears that the logic for exploring "before and after" legal registration is that the failure to obtain legal registration may be a significant barrier to acquiring certain funding sources, and, that certain types of funding might only be given to legally registered businesses, rather than provided to the founders. (In hindsight, it might have been valuable to ask respondents whether they had also personally co-signed for any debt obligations made to the legal entity.)

Table 10.3 describes the frequency, mean, and median dollar amounts for each type of funding used (personal funds, personal funds only, unmonitored, and monitored) in PSED I and PSED II. Frequency counts for the type of funding used (personal funds, personal funds only, unmonitored, and monitored) indicate that there are significant differences in the distributions of sources of financing acquired between the two samples ($p < 0.001$ for personal, personal contributions only, and unmonitored funding). More respondents in PSED I used personal funds (90.4%) compared to those in PSED II (84.4%). PSED I respondents were less likely to use personal funds only (36.6%) to fund the emerging firm, compared to 46.7% using personal funds only in PSED II. More respondents in PSED I acquired unmonitored funding (59.9%) compared with 33.5% in PSED II. For the acquisition of monitored funding, no significant

Table 10.3 Use of personal and external funding by PSED I or PSED II (weighted)

	PSED I			PSED II		
	Frequency (%)	Mean ($)	Median ($)	Frequency (%)	Mean ($)	Median ($)
Personal contributions	90.4	37,100	8,000	84.4	31,700	5,000
Personal contributions *as the sole source of financing*	36.6	17,475	5,000	46.7	14,212	3,000
Acquired unmonitored	59.1	34,969	6,520	33.5	23,286	4,000
Acquired monitored	18.3	113,274	34,119	15.4	91,370	18,802

10 Financing the Emerging Firm 197

differences were found between nascent entrepreneurs in PSED I and PSED II: 18.3% of PSED I respondents acquired monitored funding, compared with 15.4% of the respondents in PSED II. Finally, it should be noted that Reynolds and Curtin (2008) also found significant differences in the distribution of "total funding by team members" between the PSED I and PSED II data sets. They discussed problems with accounting for "outliers" in the PSED II data set, and suggested that the differences reflect a number of respondents in PSED II who invested either larger or smaller amounts of funding than respondents in the PSED I cohort (Reynolds and Curtin, pp. 217–221).

The average amounts of funding from each source are heavily skewed due to extremely high values. Therefore, the median values in Table 10.3 provide a better measure of central tendency for both samples. Both average and median values are listed here.

To test for differences between the mean dollar amounts acquired for each source of funding in the two samples, we ran a series of independent-samples t-tests. Again, a number of methodological issues arose while making this comparison due to differences in questions between the two data sets. Reported funding amounts for monitored and unmonitored funding in Wave 1 of PSED I were recoded as actually having been acquired if the respondent indicated that funding for the emerging firm was complete, or if the funding source actually contributed the money. Comparisons of the mean funding amounts represent acquired funding only, not expectations, in PSED I and PSED II.

Also, financial data in both the PSED I and PSED II data sets are highly skewed. In both data sets, a few respondents and their respective team members made personal contributions in millions of dollars, while a large number of respondents made personal contributions of less than $5,000. Many respondents also reported acquiring zero dollars of external unmonitored and monitored funding, contributing to these skewed distributions. Following the logic of Reynolds and Curtin (2008), all high values were reset to three standard deviations above the mean. We also do not include the zero values in the analysis, since we are interested only in those nascent entrepreneurs who acquired funding.

Table 10.4 shows results from the tests, comparing the mean dollar amounts acquired by respondents in PSED I and PSED II. We report the means comparisons for the log—transformed variables for personal contributions, personal contributions only, acquired unmonitored, and acquired monitored funding. All values from the PSED I, collected in 1999, are adjusted for inflation to the 2005 PSED II values using the consumer price index (see Reynolds & Curtin, 2008). The analysis is also weighted.

Statistically significant differences were found between respondents in the PSED I and PSED II regarding the mean dollar amount in all four categories of funding sources. However, whether differences between the means for the two samples are substantive may be open to interpretation (see Table 10.3). The average amount of personal contributions from nascent entrepreneurs to their startups in the PSED I was 6% greater than in PSED II (PSED I mean = 3.890;

Table 10.4 Independent samples t-tests for differences in mean dollar amount acquired between PSED I and PSED II (log-transformed, weighted)

Source	PSED I N	Mean	SD	PSED II N	Mean	SD	Difference	t-test	df	p
Personal	712	3.890	0.835	998	3.666	0.810	0.224	5.546	1501	0.000
Personal *only*	293	3.658	0.816	552	3.509	0.798	0.149	2.555	583	0.011
Acquired unmonitored	374	3.803	0.828	404	3.614	0.837	0.189	3.164	773	0.002
Acquired monitored	98	4.635	0.896	185	4.231	0.885	0.404	3.631	196	0.000

Equal variances not assumed.
PSED I financing amounts adjusted for inflation using Consumer Price Index.

PSED II mean = 3.666) with a t-test statistic of 5.546, 1,501 degrees of freedom, and an associated P value of $p=0.000$.

Nascent entrepreneurs in the PSED I who used only personal sources to fund their emerging ventures contributed 4% more money than nascent entrepreneurs in PSED II (PSED I mean = 3.658; PSED II mean = 3.509) with a t-test statistic of 2.555, 583 degrees of freedom, and an associated P value of $p=0.011$.

The average amount of funding from unmonitored sources acquired in PSED I was 5% greater than in PSED II (PSED I mean = 3.803; PSED II mean = 3.614) with a t-test statistic of 3.164, 773 degrees of freedom, and an associated P value of $p=0.002$.

The average amount of funding from monitored sources acquired in PSED I was 9% greater than in PSED II (PSED I mean = 4.635; PSED II mean = 4.231) with a t-test statistic of -3.631, 196 degrees of freedom, and an associated P value of $p=0.000$.

A comparison of the median amounts of financing contributed in PSED I and PSED II using a nonparametric test (Mann–Whitney U Test), also found significant differences between the two samples for each of the four funding categories.

10.4.1 Sources of Financing Expectations

The amount of each type of funding as a proportion of total financing for the emerging firm was calculated (i.e., expected monitored / (expected monitored + expected unmonitored + personal contributions) for PSED I. Table 10.5 shows the correlations of selected firm- and entrepreneur- level characteristics by *expectations* of receiving funds from monitored and unmonitored sources. Note that personal funds in PSED I are actually acquired. A fourth category labeled "both" is included to show correlations for those entrepreneurs that expected or acquired both monitored and unmonitored sources to finance the emerging firm. Correlations on continuous variables used the Pearson coefficient, and categorical variable correlations used Spearman. Significant correlations are denoted by asterisks.

The findings on expectations of firm size were significantly and positively correlated to *expectations* of acquiring both monitored and unmonitored sources of financing as a greater proportion of total financing. Therefore, H1A was supported. In addition, use of personal funds as the sole means of financing was negatively correlated with larger expected firm size. The findings on incorporation were also significantly and positively correlated to the expected use of monitored and unmonitored sources of financing. Therefore, H2A was also supported. The findings on intentions to start firms with high growth rates were not correlated to expected use of unmonitored, monitored, or the use of both types of financing. Therefore, H3A and H4A were not supported.

Table 10.5 PSED I correlations of nascent firm/entrepreneur characteristics by expected funding source (as a proportion of total financing, weighted)

		Expected funding (PSED I – Wave 1)		
H_{1A} Firm size		Pearson's correlations	Significance	N
	Monitored	0.324***	0.000	619
	Unmonitored	−0.056	0.161	619
	Personal	−0.190***	0.000	619
	Both	0.190***	0.000	619
	Firm size = log of expected first-year sales			
H_{2A} Legal form		Spearman's Rho	Significance	N
	Monitored	0.179***	0.000	675
	Unmonitored	0.078*	0.044	675
	Personal	−0.155***	0.000	675
	Both	0.155***	0.000	675
	0 = Not incorporated; 1 = Incorporated			
H_{3A}/H_{4A} Firm growth		Spearman's Rho	Significance	N
	Monitored	−0.028	0.453	714
	Unmonitored	0.016	0.67	714
	Personal	−0.002	0.962	714
	Both	0.002	0.962	714
	0 = Grow as large as possible; 1 = Size to self-manage			
H_{5A} Gender		Spearman's Rho	Significance	N
	Monitored	−0.149***	0.000	723
	Unmonitored	0.089*	0.016	723
	Personal	0.020	0.598	723
	Both	−0.020	0.598	723
	0 = Male; 1 = Female			
H_{5C} Ethnicity		Spearman's Rho	Significance	N
	Monitored	−0.025	0.514	695
	Unmonitored	−0.048	0.207	695
	Personal	0.052	0.167	695
	Both	−0.052	0.167	695
	0 = White; 1 = Minority			
H_{5E} Education		Spearman's Rho	Significance	N
	Monitored	0.022	0.560	715
	Unmonitored	0.030	0.428	715
	Personal	−0.033	0.376	715
	Both	0.033	0.376	715
	Education = categorical; high-school through post-college			
H_{5G} Entrepreneur's household net worth		Pearson's correlation	Significance	N
	Monitored	0.034	0.429	534
	Unmonitored	−0.046	0.289	534
	Personal	0.012	0.788	534
	Both	−0.012	0.788	535
	Net worth = log of reported value			

Table 10.5 (continued)

	Expected funding (PSED I – Wave 1)			
H_{5I} Prior startup experience		Spearman Rho	Sig.	N
	Monitored	−0.018	0.640	715
	Unmonitored	−0.006	0.867	715
	Personal	0.022	0.560	715
	Both	−0.022	0.560	715
	0 = Zero; 1 = One start-up; 2 = 2 or more			
H_{5K} Industry experience		Pearson corr.	Sig.	N
	Monitored	0.114**	0.008	546
	Unmonitored	−0.127**	0.003	546
	Personal	0.022	0.605	546
	Both	−0.022	605	546
	Industry experience = years worked in same field as startup			
H_{6A} Outcome		Spearman Rho	Sig.	N
	Monitored	0.112*	0.019	442
	Unmonitored	0.048	0.316	442
	Personal	−0.088	0.066	442
	Both	0.088	0.066	442
	0 = Gave up; 1 = Still trying; 2 = In business			

* Significant at .05; ** Significant at .01; *** Significant at .001.

The analyses of entrepreneur characteristics and the expected use of financing sources surfaces a few findings that we suggest are worth pointing out. We found a positive correlation between males and expectations of monitored funding as a greater proportion of total funding (shown as a negative correlation between females and monitored funding in Table 10.5). Therefore, H5A was supported. No correlation was found between ethnicity and expected use of any of the funding sources; nor were any correlations found for education, household net worth, or prior startup experience. H5C, H5E, H5G, and H5I were not supported.

Industry experience is negatively correlated with the expectation of using unmonitored financing sources, but positively correlated to use of monitored sources. H5K, the greater the number of years the entrepreneur has worked in the same industry as the startup, the greater the proportion of monitored and unmonitored funding the entrepreneur will *expect* to use, was partially supported.

Finally, H6A, nascent entrepreneurs who expect to use more monitored sources of funding are more likely to start an ongoing business, was supported.

10.4.2 Sources of Financing Acquired

Tables 10.6 and 10.7 show correlations between firm and entrepreneur characteristics, and the type of funding *acquired* as a proportion of total financing, in PSED I and II, respectively.

Table 10.6 PSED I correlations of nascent firm/entrepreneur characteristics by acquired funding source (as a proportion of total financing, weighted)

	Acquired funding (PSED I - Wave 2)			
H_{1B} Firm size		Pearson's correlations	Significance	N
	Monitored	0.106	0.101	240
	Unmonitored	0.023	0.722	240
	Personal	−0.090	0.166	240
	Both	0.090	0.166	240
	Firm size = log of expected first year sales			
H_{2B} Legal form		Spearman's Rho	Significance	N
	Monitored	0.073	0.243	254
	Unmonitored	0.050	0.431	254
	Personal	−0.053	0.399	254
	Both	0.053	0.399	254
	0 = Not incorporated; 1 = Incorporated			
H_{3B}/H_{4B} Firm growth		Spearman's Rho	Significance	N
	Monitored	0.044	0.471	268
	Unmonitored	0.125*	0.041	268
	Personal	−0.141*	0.021	268
	Both	0.141*	0.021	268
	0 = Grow as large as possible; 1 = Size to self-manage			
H_{5B} Gender		Spearman's Rho	Significance	N
	Monitored	−0.068	0.266	268
	Unmonitored	0.049	0.420	268
	Personal	−0.015	0.810	268
	Both	0.015	0.810	268
	0 = Male; 1 = Female			
H_{5D} Ethnicity		Spearman's Rho	Significance	N
	Monitored	−0.091	0.143	262
	Unmonitored	−0.069	0.264	262
	Personal	0.097	0.118	262
	Both	−0.097	0.118	262
	0 = White; 1 = Minority			
H_{5F} Education		Spearman's Rho	Significance	N
	Monitored	−0.097	0.115	268
	Unmonitored	−0.036	0.561	268
	Personal	0.082	0.180	268
	Both	−0.082	0.180	268
	Education = categorical; high school through post college			
H_{5H} Entrepreneur's household net worth		Pearson's correlation	Significance	N
	Monitored	−0.061	0.392	202
	Unmonitored	−0.101	0.155	202
	Personal	0.109	0.123	202
	Both	−0.109	0.123	202
	Net worth = log of reported value			

Table 10.6 (continued)

	Acquired funding (PSED I - Wave 2)			
$H_{5\,J}$ Prior startup experience		Spearman Rho	Sig.	N
	Monitored	−0.201***	0.001	265
	Unmonitored	−0.206***	0.001	265
	Personal	0.228***	0.000	265
	Both	−0.228***	0.000	265
	0 = Zero; 1 = One start-up; 2 = 2 or more			
H_{5L} Industry experience		Pearson corr.	Sig.	N
	Monitored	0.011	0.878	214
	Unmonitored	0.104	0.131	214
	Personal	−0.080	0.241	214
	Both	0.080	0.241	214
	Industry experience = years worked in same field as startup			
H_{6B} Outcome		Spearman Rho	Sig.	N
	Monitored	0.354***	0.000	268
	Unmonitored	0.496***	0.000	268
	Personal	−0.556***	0.000	268
	Both	0.556***	0.000	268
	0 = Gave up; 1 = Still trying; 2 = In business			

* Significant at .05; ** Significant at .01; *** Significant at .001.

Table 10.7 for PSED II shows that firm size (as measured by expected income in the first year of operations) is positively correlated with the use of monitored funding, and negatively correlated to personal and both monitored and unmonitored together. Table 10.6 for PSED I shows a slightly significant positive correlation (0.106, $p > 0.101$) between a larger expected firm size and use of monitored funding sources. Therefore, H1B had mixed support.

Table 10.7 shows a positive correlation was found between incorporation of the emerging firm and acquiring monitored funding in the PSED II data. A corresponding negative correlation between incorporation and use of personal funds was also found. No correlation was found between incorporation and monitored funding in PSED I. H2B has mixed support.

Table 10.7 shows that the growth aspirations of the entrepreneur in PSED II are not correlated to any one type of financing, but in PSED I (Table 10.6) there were strong positive correlations between high growth aspirations and more use of unmonitored, and a combination of monitored and unmonitored funds. Therefore, H3B and H4B had mixed support.

Gender was not correlated to acquiring any one type of funding in PSED I (Table 10.6), but in PSED II males were positively correlated to the use of more monitored financing than females (Table 10.7). H5B was partially supported. Ethnicity was not correlated to acquiring any one type of funding in PSED I, but in PSED II ethnicity was correlated with using more monitored funding, and less personal funding. Therefore, H5D was not supported. We suggest that these findings on ethnicity for both the PSED I and PSED II data sets are the

Table 10.7 PSED II correlations of nascent firm/entrepreneur characteristics by acquired funding source (as a proportion of total financing, weighted)

	Acquired funding (PSED II – Waves A and B)			
H_{1B} Firm size		Pearson's correlations	Significance	N
	Monitored	0.141***	0.000	955
	Unmonitored	0.007	0.825	955
	Personal	−0.101**	0.002	955
	Both	0.101**	0.002	955
	Firm size = log of expected first year sales			
H_{2B} Legal form		Spearman's Rho	Significance	N
	Monitored	0.202***	0.000	350
	Unmonitored	0.045	0.401	350
	Personal	−0.152**	0.004	350
	Both	0.152**	0.004	350
	0 = Not incorporated; 1 = Incorporated			
H_{3B}/H_{4B} Firm growth		Spearman's Rho	Significance	N
	Monitored	−0.023	0.457	1,018
	Unmonitored	−0.042	0.177	1,018
	Personal	0.038	0.220	1,018
	Both	−0.038	0.220	1,018
	0 = Grow as large as possible; 1 = Size to self-manage			
H_{5B} Gender		Spearman's Rho	Significance	N
	Monitored	−0.074*	0.018	1,025
	Unmonitored	−0.007	0.829	1,025
	Personal	0.039	0.216	1,025
	Both	−0.039	0.216	1,025
	0 = Male; 1 = Female			
H_{5D} Ethnicity		Spearman's Rho	Significance	N
	Monitored	0.075*	0.017	1,008
	Unmonitored	−0.002	0.938	1,008
	Personal	−0.060*	0.056	1,008
	Both	0.060*	0.056	1,008
	0 = White; 1 = Minority			
H_{5F} Education		Spearman's Rho	Significance	N
	Monitored	0.062*	0.049	1,023
	Unmonitored	−0.006	0.855	1,023
	Personal	−0.022	0.477	1,023
	Both	0.022	0.477	1,023
	Education = categorical; high school through post-college			
H_{5H} Entrepreneur's household net worth		Pearson's correlations	Significance	N
	Monitored	0.059	0.102	766
	Unmonitored	−0.037	0.309	766
	Personal	−0.015	0.686	766
	Both	0.015	0.686	766
	Net worth = log of reported value			

10 Financing the Emerging Firm

Table 10.7 (continued)

	Acquired funding (PSED II – Waves A and B)			
$H_{5\,J}$ Prior start-up experience		Spearman's Rho	Significance	N
	Monitored	0.060*	0.056	1025
	Unmonitored	0.057*	0.070	1025
	Personal	−0.066*	0.035	1025
	Both	0.066	0.035	1025
	0 = Zero; 1 = One start-up; 2 = 2 or more			
H_{5L} Industry experience		Pearson's correlations	Significance	N
	Monitored	0.003	0.937	807
	Unmonitored	−0.027	0.452	807
	Personal	0.019	0.600	807
	Both	−0.019	0.600	807
	Industry experience = years worked in same field as start-up			
H_{6B} Outcome		Spearman's Rho	Significance	N
	Monitored	0.130***	0.000	834
	Unmonitored	0.079*	0.023	834
	Personal	−0.099**	0.004	834
	Both	0.099**	0.004	834
	0 = Gave up; 1 = Still trying; 2 = In business			

* Significant at .05; ** Significant at .01; *** Significant at .001.

result of using two waves of data, only, for analyses. When emerging ventures are tracked for longer periods of time in the PSED I data set (across Waves 1 through 4), Gartner, Frid, and Alexander (2008) found that minority nascent entrepreneurs were less likely to acquire monitored and unmonitored sources of funding as a proportion of total funding, and more likely to use personal funds as the sole source of venture financing.

Education was not correlated with use of any of the funding types in PSED I, but in PSED II higher levels of education was correlated with higher use of monitored funding. H5F was partially supported. The entrepreneur's household net worth was not correlated to acquiring any type of funding in either PSED I or PSED II. Therefore, H5H was not supported. Regarding the entrepreneur's prior startup experience, in PSED I strong negative correlations were found between having prior startup experience and use of monitored and unmonitored funding. It seems that the more prior startups, the greater the amount of personal funds as the sole source of funding was used in PSED I. In PSED II we find just the opposite (albeit with weak correlations). Table 10.7 shows that more prior startup experience is positively correlated with use of monitored and unmonitored funding, and negatively correlated with use of personal funds only. H5J is therefore partially supported. Industry experience was not correlated with types of funding in either PSED I or II, so H5L was not supported.

In both PSED I and PSED II, venture survival ("in business" or "still trying to start a business") was positively correlated with whether the nascent entrepreneur acquired monitored and unmonitored sources of capital. Negative correlations were found between venture survival and use of personal funds only in both PSED I and PSED II as well. Therefore, H6B was supported.

10.5 Discussion and Conclusions

The results of these analyses hinges on this observation: One time period is too short a time frame to determine what entrepreneurs actually do. As Reynolds (2007) points out in his analyses of the PSED I data set, the determination of whether an emerging venture will become an on-going venture, on average, takes over 24 months to ascertain. Since the analyses for this study looked at a time period of less than this, in both PSED I and PSED II, the mixed findings on the acquisition of various financing sources is likely to be due to the short time frame. We would encourage government agencies or foundations interested in supporting research that seeks to understand the venture development process to consider funding efforts to collect additional waves of data for PSED II. As we noted earlier, when a longer time frame is used to evaluate nascent entrepreneur financing activities and their outcomes, significant differences in what these individuals actually accomplish begin to appear (Gartner et al., 2008).

Since we are more confident of the findings generated from analyses from a longer period of time and with a more narrowly defined cohort of similar emerging ventures (Gartner et al., 2008), we will emphasize only one insight into the findings generated for this chapter that correspond to the findings from our other work.

The acquisition of outside funding, either monitored or unmonitored, is significantly correlated with venture survival. About 90% of entrepreneurs who are able to acquire outside financing were either in business or continuing to develop their emerging businesses compared to only 40% of entrepreneurs who depended on personal financing sources, only. This finding will be discussed further in the next section.

10.5.1 Directions for Future Research

We suggest that there is likely to be significant interactions among such characteristics of emerging ventures as the quality of the opportunity pursued, the "quality" of the entrepreneurs pursuing these opportunities, the kinds of efforts undertaken to develop these opportunities, and, the sources of financing that these entrepreneurs both expect and are able to acquire. An entrepreneur's expectation of acquiring outside funding (both unmonitored and monitored) is likely to have some correlation to the entrepreneur's perceptions of the quality of the opportunity being pursued, but, these perceptions are likely to be significantly tempered by the entrepreneur's skills and abilities to develop these opportunities. There is a need, then, for very detailed process research on the creation of ventures that follows both the thinking and actions of entrepreneurs more frequently over a period of time. Case research that explores why entrepreneurs select particular high- or low-quality opportunities, and, then pursue various resource acquisition strategies might better ascertain the kinds of barriers entrepreneurs encounter for developing their ventures.

We believe that many entrepreneurs have poor skills in accurately assessing the viability and value of the opportunities they pursue, as well as a poor assessment of their skills and abilities to successfully develop these ventures (Baron, 1998, 2007). Research that explored both the quality of the entrepreneur and the quality of the opportunity might better ascertain which kinds of entrepreneurs and which kinds of opportunities are more likely to receive funding. Given that many entrepreneurs use personal funds only, and that these efforts are more likely to result in failure, we suggest that "poor quality" entrepreneurs and "poor quality" opportunities are likely to be in this funding category.

The categorization of monitored and unmonitored funding sources could be further developed both empirically and theoretically as constructs for discerning among various ways entrepreneurs acquire outside financing. We suggest that detailed case studies need to be undertaken to track the process entrepreneurs undertake to coax others to provide funds, and, then, study what kinds of interaction occur between these entrepreneurs and others regarding these investments. There would also be value at exploring specific funding sources (e.g., use of credit cards, bank loans) to evaluate whether the use of specific funding sources might play a significant role in venture creation.

Since the acquisition of any outside funding (monitored or unmonitored) is a significant predictor of survival, it would be valuable to explore how entrepreneurs went about acquiring these sources of financing *and* whether external funding was the result of having other aspects of the emerging venture in place, beforehand, or not. For example, external funding might be provided if the entrepreneur has accomplished other activities, such as developing a prototype, engaging in marketing efforts, and writing a business plan. External funding, then, might be significantly correlated with emerging ventures that are more complete than other efforts. Or it might be possible that entrepreneurs who are able to acquire external funding are able, then, to subsequently engage in other venture creation activities because they have funding. Exploring when external funding is obtained, vis-à-vis other venture creation activities would provide important insights into whether external funding is the result of other entrepreneurial efforts, or more likely the catalyst for venture emergence.

Finally, while the analyses conducted on the cases in the PSED I and II data sets tended to minimize the influence of outliers and anomalies among various cases in these samples, these outliers might provide important insights into how and why some entrepreneurs are able to use (or not use) financial resources to create new businesses. For example, a number of entrepreneurs started businesses without using any personal funds: What kinds of businesses were started and did any of these businesses grow substantially? Baker and Nelson (2005) suggest that a critical resource utilization skill for many entrepreneurs is "bricolage," the ability to use whatever resources are at hand for the creation and pursuit of new opportunities. While we have shown that those entrepreneurs who would have acquired outside resources were significantly more likely to get into business or continue to pursue business development, there were a substantial number of entrepreneurs who still got into business without external resources. These entrepreneurs are worth knowing more about, particularly if they can offer insights into more effective and efficient ways to use resources at hand.

10.6 Conclusions

The financing data in PSED I and II are, in some respects, initially overwhelming. As can be seen in the appendixes, the number of questions about financing is substantial, and, as we have described earlier, the ways in which questions have been asked in PSED I and II about financing also influence what we can understand about this process. Much more effort needs to be undertaken to explore the nuances in these two data sets. There is much to learn from the outliers and anomalies that our statistical techniques tended to discount.

This chapter took a novel approach to exploring the financing variables. Tables 10.1 (PSED I) and 10.2 (PSED II) describe a variety of ways that nascent entrepreneurs might go about acquiring financial resources for the development of their emerging ventures. We categorized these many different financing activities into three broad approaches: personal, monitored and unmonitored. Our analyses, using our three categorizations of financing, generated mixed results. We believe that the use of only two waves of data for PSED I and PSED II limited the number of insights that could be generated about financing and the venture development process. We believe that when more waves of data are collected for PSED II, better clarity will emerge regarding the relationship of different sources of financing to success at creating new ventures.

We see that between what entrepreneurs believe will occur and what actually occurs in the development of their opportunities is still much of a mystery. Financial support of emerging ventures appears to be critical to their survival, yet it is unclear whether this support is the cause of their survival or the effect of previous activities to both insure survival and funding.

We hope that more attention will be given to the process entrepreneurs undertake to use their own personal funds and the funds of others in the creation of new ventures. Both the PSED I and PSED II data sets remain untapped in regard to the many insights they might produce regarding the venture financing process.

10.7 Appendix

Table 10.8 PSED I finance items: first phone interview (Waves 1 and 2)

Item number		Response	Question
Wave 1	Wave 2		
137	594	Yes/no	Projected financial statements?
138	595	Year	In what year did financial projections begin
138a	595a	Month	And in what month?
139	596	Yes/no	Saving money to invest in this business?
140	597	Finished/in process	Finished saving money, or still in process?
141	598	Intend/finished	Started saving money?
142	599	Year	Year started saving?
142a	599a	Month	And in what month?
143	600	Yes/no	Invested own money
144	601	Year	Year started investing?
144a	601a	Month	And in what month?
145	602	Yes/no	Asked other people or financial institutions?
146	603	Complete/in process	Asking others completed or still in process?
147	604	Others/not relevant	Will others be asked, or not relevant?
148	605	Year	Year seeking funds begin?
148a	605a	Month	And in what month?
149	606	Yes/no	Has credit with a supplier been established?
150	607	Year	Year supplier credit first established?
150a	607a	Month	And in what month?
160	617	Yes/no/existing acct	Opened bank account for new business?
161	618	Year	Year first open a commercial bank account?
161a	618a	Month	And in what month?
162	619	Yes/no	Received money from sales?
162a	620	Year	In what year was the first income received?
162b	620a	Month	And in what month?
163	621	Yes/no	Monthly revenue > monthly expenses?
164	622	Year	In what year did this first happen?
164a	622a	Month	And in what month?
165	623	Yes/no	Owner/manager salaries counted expenses?
166	624	Year	In what year did this first occur?
166a	624a	Month	And in what month?
175	633	Yes/no	Paid state unemployment insurance taxes?
176	634	Year	In what year were the first taxes paid?
176a	634a	Month	And in what month?
177	635	Yes/no	Paid any social security taxes (FICA)?
178	636	Year	Year first social security taxes (FICA) paid?
178a	636a	Month	And in what month?
179	637	Yes/no	Filed a federal income tax return?
180	638	Year	Year first federal return filed?
181	639	Yes/no	Listed with Dun & Bradstreet?
182	640	Year	Year first listed with Dun & Bradstreet?
182a	640a	Month	And what month?

Table 10.9 PSED I investment items: first phone interview (Wave 1)

Item number Wave 1	Response	Question
198	Dollar amount	Amount of own money put in (debt or equity)?
212	Dollar amount	Team personal money (debt or equity)?
224	Yes/no	Has (team) provided access financial assistance?
263	Dollar amount	Total funds needed to become self-sustaining?
264	Dollar amount	Cash needed to operate first 30 days?
265	Dollar amount	$ needed before attracting investors?
266	Yes/no/no	Asked spouse or household partner for funding?
266a	Yes/no/pending	Yes, no, or still pending?
268	Dollar amount	Amount expected from spouse or partner?
269	Yes/no/no	Asked spouses/partners from team members?
269a	Yes/no/pending	Yes, no, or still pending?
270	Dollar amount	Amount expected from team spouse/partner?
271	Yes/no	Asked friends and family for funding?
271a	Yes/no/pending	Yes, no, or still pending?
272	Dollar amount	Amount expected from friends and family?
273	Yes/no	Asked team friends and family for funding?
273a	Yes/no/pending	Yes, no, or still pending?
274	Yes/no/pending	Amount expected from team friends and family?
275	Yes/no/no employ	Asked current employer for funding?
275a	Yes/no/pending	Yes, no, or still pending?
276	Dollar amount	Amount expected from current employer?
277	Yes/no/NA	Taken a 2nd mortgage to fund new firm?
277a	Dollar amount	Amount expected from 2nd mortgage
278	Yes/no	Asked bank for loan?
278a	Yes/no/pending	Yes, no, or still pending?
279	Dollar amount	Amount expected from bank?
280	Yes/no	Asked SBA loan?
280a	Yes/no/pending	Yes, no, or still pending?
281	Dollar amount	Amount expected from SBA loan?
282	Yes/no/no credit cards	Used credit cards?
282a	Dollar amount	Amount expected from credit cards?
283	Yes/no	Asked venture capitalists?
283a	Yes/no/pending	Yes, no, or still pending?
284	Dollar amount	Amount expected from VCs
285	Yes/no	Asked personal finance company?
285a	Yes/no/pending	Yes, no, or still pending?
286	Dollar amount	Amount expected from personal finance co.
287	Yes/no	Asked other sources for funding?
287a	String	What is this other source of funding?
288	Yes/no/pending	Yes, no, or still pending?
289	Month	Months needed to pay back all sources?

10 Financing the Emerging Firm

Table 10.10 PSED I investment items: first follow-up interview (Wave 2)

Item number Wave 2	Response	Question
656	Dollar amount	Amount of own money put in (debt or equity)?
656a	Dollar amount	Team's personal money (debt or equity)?
770	Dollar amount	Total equity from all sources?
770a	Dollar amount	Total debt from all sources?
771	Dollar amount	Personal contributions (equity)?
771a	Dollar amount	Personal contributions (debt)?
772	Dollar amount	Team members' contributions (equity)?
772a	Dollar amount	Team members' contributions (debt)?
773	Dollar amount	Family and relatives (equity)?
773a	Dollar amount	Family and relatives (debt)?
774	Dollar amount	Friends and business associates (equity)?
774a	Dollar amount	Friends and business associates (debt)?
775	Dollar amount	Banks, VCs, institutions (equity)?
775a	Dollar amount	Banks, VCs, institutions (debt)?
776	Dollar amount	Private investors (equity)?
776a	Dollar amount	Private investors (debt)?
777	Dollar amount	Government agencies (equity)?
777a	Dollar amount	Government agencies (debt)?
778	Dollar amount	Suppliers, subcontractors (debt)?
779	Dollar amount	Credit cards?
780	Dollar amount	Other source (equity)?
780a	String	What is this other source of equity money?
781	Dollar amount	Other source (debt)?
781a	String	What was the other source of loans for the business?
782	Dollar amount	Estimated net worth of the business today?
783	Ratio: percent	What % of the firm do you personally own?

Table 10.11 PSED II Section E start-up finances: item overview

Item number Wave A	Wave B		Other choices	Yes/ one or more	No/ not yet	Don't know/ irrelevant
AE1	BE1	Asked others for funds?		E2	E5	E5
AE2	BE2	Month/year first sought				
AE3	BE3	Received outside funds?		E4	E5	
AE4	BE4	Month/year first received				
AE5	BE5	Credit with supplier?		E6	E7	E7
AE6	BE6	Month/year supplier credit established				
AE7	BE7	Paid employees?		E8	E11	E11

Table 10.11 (continued)

Item number Wave A	Item number Wave B		Other choices	Yes/ one or more	No/ not yet	Don't know/ irrelevant
AE8	BE8	Month/year hired				
AE9	BE9	How many work 35+ hours/week?				
AE10	BE10	...less than 35 hours/week?				
AE11	BE11	Bank account for business?	BE11c	E12	E13, BE18	E13, BE18
AE12	BE12	Month/year opened				
AE13		Has business received income?		E14	E18	
AE14		Month/year of first income				
AE15		Has monthly revenue > expenses?		E16	E18	
AE16		Month/year first exceeded				
AE17		Are salaries for owner-managers computed as expenses?				
AE18	BE18	Accountant retained?		E19	E20	E20
AE19	BE19	Month/year retained				
AE20	BE20	Lawyer retained		E21	E22	E22
AE21	BE21	Month/year retained				
AE22	BE22	Has business become a member of a trade or industry association?		E23	E24	E24
AE23	BE23	Month/year joined				
AE24	BE24	Can potential customers contact firm by phone/ email/internet?	BE24c	E25	E26	E26
AE25	BE25	Month/year first listed				
AE26	BE26	Applied for federal EIN or employer ID number?		E27	E28	E28
AE27	BE27	Month/year applied				
AE28	BE28	DBA filed?		E29	E30	E30
AE29	BE29	Month/year filed				
AE30	BE30	State-unemployment insurance paid?		E31	E32	
AE31	BE31	Month/year paid				
AE32	BE32	FICA paid?		E33	E34	
AE33	BE33	Month/year paid				
AE34	BE34	Federal income tax filed?		E35	E36	
AE35	BE35	Month/year filed				
AE36	BE36	Dun & Bradstreet listed?		E37		
AE37	BE37	Month/year filed Go to next section				

10 Financing the Emerging Firm

Table 10.12 PSED II Section Q start-up investments before legal registration: item overview

Item number Wave A	Wave B		Other choices	Yes/ one or more	No/ not yet	Don't know/ irrelevant
AQ4_1	BQ4_1	Personal savings contributed (in $)	_2– _5 (A) _6 – _10 (B) BQ4c			
AQ5_1	BQ5_1	Family and relatives contribution	_2– _5 (A) _6–- _10 (B) BQ5c			
AQ6_1	BQ6_1	Friends, employers, co-workers	_2– _5 (A) _6 – _10 (B) BQ6c			
AQ7_1	BQ7_1	Credit card loans	_2 – _5 (A) _6 – _10 (B) BQ7c			
AQ8_1	BQ8_1	Bank and other financial institution	_2 – _5 (A) _6 – _10 (B) BQ8c			
AQ9_1	BQ9_1	Asset backed (2nd mortgage or car)	_2 – _5 (A) _6 – _10 (B) BQ9c			
AQ10_1	BQ10_1	Other sources	_2 – _5 (A) _6 – _10 (B) BQ10c			
AQ11_1	BQ11_1	What was the source of "other"?				
AQ12x_1	BQ12x_1	Total funding amount	_2 – _5 (A) _6 – _10 (B)			
AQ12_1	BQ12_1	Is this amount correct?	_2 – _5 (A) _6 – _10 (B)	Q13		Q4
AQ13_1	BQ13_1	How much of the above do you expect to be paid back to [you/name]?	_2 – _5 (A) _6 – _10 (B)			
AQ14_1	BQ14_1	Month/year initial investment made	_2 – _5 (A) _6 – _10 (B)			
AQ15	BQ15	Interviewer checkpoint: is business registered?		NEXT (R0)		Q16
AQ16	BQ16	How much additional funding will be needed to be registered as a legal entity?	BQ16c			
AQ17	BQ17	What proportion of this funding will be shares in ownership of the new business? Go to next section	BQ17c			

Table 10.13 PSED II Section R start-up investments after legal registration: item overview

Item number Wave A	Wave B		Other choices	Yes/ one or more	No/ not yet	Don't know/ irrelevant
AR1	BR1	Has business directly received loans from you or others?	BR1c	R2	R26	
AR2	BR2	Month/year received				
AR3	BR3	Did you or others invest equity after the business was registered?	BR3c	R4	R6	
AR4	BR4	How much equity was invested?				
AR5	BR5	What % of total ownership did these investments account for?	BR5c			
AR6	BR6	Debts backed by assets (land, vehicles) that could be repossessed?	BR6c			
AR7	BR7	Debts in form of leases	BR7c			
AR8	BR8	Bank line of credit, or working capital loan?	BR8c			
AR9	BR9	Supplier credit	BR9c			
AR10	BR10	Personal loans	BR10c			
AR11	BR11	Team member loans	BR11c			
AR12	BR12	Spouse and family loans	BR12c			
AR13	BR13	Employee loans	BR13c			
AR14	BR14	Other individual loans	BR14c			
AR15	BR15	Credit card	BR15c			
AR16	BR16	Bank loans	BR16c			
AR17	BR17	Venture capital	BR17c			
AR18	BR18	Government agencies (not SBA)	BR18c			
AR19	BR19	SBA-guaranteed loans	BR19c			
AR20	BR20	Other	BR20c			
AR21x	BR21x	Total dollar amount				
AR21	BR21	Is this correct?		R22	R6	
AR22	BR22	If you sold the business, what would the net value be today?	BR22c			
AR23		Could anyone else claim ownership of the business?		R24	R26	
AR24		Who would claim ownership?				
AR25		What % would they expect?				
AR26	BR26	Additional funding required to complete 1st year of operations?	BR26c			
AR27	BR27	Will funds be loans or equity?				
AR28	BR28	How much additional debt?				
AR30	BR30	What % of total ownership or equity will you (or other owners) account for?				
AR32	BR32	All $ in commercial bank account?		Next	R35	
AR34	BR34	All $ in existing bank account?		Next	R35	
AR35	BR35	Proportion held elsewhere? Go to next section				

Note

1. Additionally, respondents had to answer "yes" to item BA41, which asked if it was agreed that the current status of the business was indeed an operating business.

References

Ang, J. S. (1992). On the theory of finance for privately held firms. *Journal of Small Business Finance, 1*(3), 185–203.
Astebro, T., & Bernhardt, I. (2003). Startup-up financing, owner characteristics, and survival. *Journal of Economics and Business, 55*, 303–319.
Baker, T., & Nelson, R. E. (2005). Creating something from nothing: Resource construction through entrepreneurial bricolage. *Administrative Science Quarterly, 50*, 329–366.
Baron, R. A. (1998). Cognitive mechanisms in entrepreneurship: Why and when entrepreneurs think differently than other people. *Journal of Business Venturing, 13*, 275–294.
Baron, R. A. (2007). Behavioral and cognitive factors in entrepreneurship: Entrepreneurs as the active element in new venture creation. *Strategic Entrepreneurship Journal, 1*, 167–182.
Cassar, G. (2004). The financing of business start-ups. *Journal of Business Venturing, 19*, 261–283.
Chaganti, R., DeCarolis, D., & Deeds, D. (1995). Predictors of capital structure in small ventures. *Entrepreneurship Theory and Practice, 20*(4), 7–18.
Cleman, S., & Chon, R. (2000). Small firms' use of financial leverage: Evidence from the 1993 national survey of small business finances. *Journal of Business Entrepreneurship, 12*(3), 81–98.
Cosh, A. D., & Hughes, A. (1994). Size, financial structure and profitability: UK companies in the 1980's. In D. J. Hughes & D. J. Storey (Eds.), *Finance and the small firm* (pp. 18–63). London: Routledge.
Freedman, J., & Goodwin, M. (1994). Incorporating the micro business: perceptions and misperceptions. In D. J. Hughes & D. J. Storey (Eds.), *Finance and the Small Firm* (pp. 232–283). London: Routledge.
Gartner, W. B. (1993). Words lead to deeds: Towards an organizational emergence vocabulary. *Journal of Business Venturing, 8*(3), 231–240.
Gartner, W. B., & Brush, C. B. (2007). Entrepreneurship as organizing: Emergence, newness and transformation. In T. Habbershon & M. Rice (Eds.), *Praeger perspectives on entrepreneurship* (Vol. 3, pp. 1–20). Westport, CT: Praeger Publishers.
Gartner, W. B., Frid, C. J., & Alexander, J. C. (June, 2008). *Financing the emerging business through monitored and unmonitored sources of funding*. Paper presented at the Babson Entrepreneurship Research Conference, Chapel Hill, NC.
Gartner, W. B., Shaver, K. G., Carter, N. M., & Reynolds, P. D. (Eds.), (2004). *Handbook of entrepreneurial dynamics: The process of business creation*. London: Sage.
Haynes, G. W. & Hanyes, D. C. (1999). The debt structure of small businesses owned by women in 1987 and 1993. *Journal of Small Business Management, 37*(2), 1–19.
Katz, J., & Cabezuelo, A. (2004). Measures of financial sophistication. In W. B. Gartner, K. G. Shaver, N. M. Carter, & P. D. Reynolds (Eds.), *Handbook of entrepreneurial dynamics: The process of business creation*(pp. 372–385). London: Sage.
Michaelas, N., Chittenden, F., & Poutziouris, P. (1999). Financial policy and capital structure choice in U.K. SMEs: Empirical evidence from company panel data. *Small Business Economics, 12*(2), 113–130.

Ou, C., & Haynes, G. W. (2006). Acquisition of additional equity capital by small firms: Findings from the National Survey of Small Business Finances. *Small Business Economics, 27*, 157–168.

Reynolds, P. D. (2007). *Entrepreneurship in the US: The future is now.* New York: Springer.

Reynolds, P. D. & Curtin, R. T. (2004). Appendix A: Collection In W. B. Gartner, K. G. Shaver, N. M. Carter & P. D. Reynolds (Eds.) *Handbook of entrepreneurial dynamics* (pp. 453–476). Thousand Oaks, CA: Sage Publications.

Reynolds, P. D., & Curtin, R. (2008). Business creation in the United States in 2006: Panel study of entrepreneurial dynamics II. *Foundations and Trends in Entrepreneurship, 4*(3), 155–307.

Shaver, K. G., Carter, N. M., Gartner, W. B., & Reynolds, P. D. (2001). Who is a nascent entrepreneur? Decision rules for identifying and selecting entrepreneurs in the panel study of entrepreneurial dynamics. In W. D. Bygrave, E. Autio, C. G. Brush, P. Davidson, P. G. Greene, P. D. Reynolds, & H. J. Sapienza (Eds.), *Frontiers of entrepreneurship research.* Babson Park, MA: Babson College.

Storey, D. J. (1994). The role of legal status in influencing bank financing and new firm growth. *Applied Economics, 26*(2), 129–136.

Stouder, M. D. (2002). *The capital structure decisions of nascent entrepreneurs.* Unpublished doctoral dissertation, Rutgers, The State University of New Jersey, Newark.

Stouder, M. D., & Kirchhoff, B. (2004). Funding the first year of business. In W. B. Gartner, K. G. Shaver, N. M. Carter, & P. D. Reynolds (Eds.), *Handbook of entrepreneurial dynamics: The process of business creation*(pp. 352–371). London: Sage.

Verheul, I., & Thurik, R. (2001). Start-up capital: Does gender matter? *Small Business Economics, 16*(4), 329–345.

Part IV
Emergence of a New Firm

Chapter 11
Reconceiving the Gestation Window: The Consequences of Competing Definitions of Firm Conception and Birth

Claudia B. Schoonhoven, M. Diane Burton, and Paul D. Reynolds

One of the challenges of organizational scholarship is defining when an organization begins to exist. Although the literature often borrows analogies from the biological realm, there is growing recognition that the notions of conception, gestation, and birth are complex constructs when applied to organizations (Cardon, Zietsma, Saparito, Matherne, & Davis, 2005). There is increasing consensus around the importance of understanding the process of organizational emergence—referred to as *organizational gestation* or *firm creation* in this chapter. The start of the gestation period, or *conception*, can be operationalized several ways. One option is the time (date) reported when an individual first begins to give serious thought to a new business, or as the dictionary defines the concept, "the moment at which an idea starts to take shape or emerge." Conception may also be considered as the point in time (date) when the first action is taken by a founder to start the firm. Another is to identify the time period when a serious effort is made to assemble resources and people (several actions within a relatively short period) to develop the new business. The end of the gestation period is termed an *organizational "birth,"* the point at which a new business entity has been established.[1]

The challenge with the concept of organizational "birth" is that few have created a theoretical rationale for when a new firm birth can be said to exist. Organizational scholars appear to assume that the birth construct itself is self-evident and not problematic. Indeed most analyses fail to address when a new firm can be said to exist (Katz & Gartner, 1988). However, as interest in the gestation process grows, it is time for a more thorough analysis of the concept of new firm birth. In this chapter the data collected as part of the second Panel Study of Entrepreneurial Dynamics (PSED II) project are used to empirically examine the gestation process by comparing alternative definitions of organizational conception and organizational birth. This analysis demonstrates that while a new organizational birth is a complex construct, its component theoretical dimensions can be articulated and measured empirically. These, in turn, have significant consequences for the

---

C.B. Schoonhoven (✉)
University of California, Irvine; Irvine, California, USA
e-mail: kschoonh@uci.edu

proportion of nascent enterprises to be considered new firms and the duration of the gestation period. The analysis reported here implies that scholars and policy makers should carefully consider what is meant by conception, gestation, and birth as they are applied to entrepreneurial organizations. These definitions determine which entrepreneurs are counted, how long it takes to launch a venture, and whether entrepreneurial efforts are deemed a success; variations in the definitions can lead to substantially different conclusions.

Within the entrepreneurship literature there has been progress conceptualizing the process by which start-up activity generates entrepreneurial ventures. One of the first large-scale systematic efforts to explore new firm conception and birth was based on a representative sample of 3,000 new firms in Minnesota and Pennsylvania (Reynolds & Miller, 1992). Data were collected on dates of four key events: the principal entrepreneur's major time commitment to the enterprise, initial hiring, initial financing, and initial sales. In this study, the earliest reported event signaled the firm's conception and first sales revenues marked the firm's birth date. Although 90% of the firms reported a gestation window of less than 3 years, the gestation window varied widely from 1 month to 10 years. This analysis, however, was only of existing firms, and it did not include entrepreneurial efforts that did not produce a new firm.

Another analysis was based on combining data from small representative samples of adults in Wisconsin and the entire United States. (Carter, Gartner, & Reynolds, 1996). Data collected during 1992 and 1993 produced a cohort of 71 nascent entrepreneurs, who completed follow-up interviews a year later. Respondents were asked whether they engaged in any of 14 "start-up activities." The date of the first reported activity was defined as the date of conception of the enterprise and this is a behavioral indicator of firm conception. The definition of a new firm birth was based on the respondent's report that the nascent firm had become operational. The study concluded that entrepreneurs who reported more activities early in the start-up process (closer to the conception date) and who placed more emphasis on developing a presence for the nascent enterprise among external audiences were more likely to establish a new operational firm.

Liao, Welsch, and Tan (2005) used data collected for PSED I between late 1998 and early 2000. Their analysis indicated that the sequencing of various start-up activities is complex and multifaceted. The authors concluded that there is no one best way to define firm conception and that specific sequences of start-up events are highly variable.

In the present analysis data from PSED II[2] are used to explore the implications of three different dimensions of new firm "conception" and four different conceptions of new firm "birth." These latter are derived from four approaches to the study of new firm creation taken by entrepreneurial researchers, organizational ecology scholars, industrial organizational economists, and labor market economists. Each is discussed below.

The entrepreneurship literature emphasizes the process of organizational emergence and the actions of individuals. Organizational ecologists are concerned with the vital rates of new firms (births, deaths), but traditionally have not questioned where new firms and populations come from (Carroll & Hannan, 2000).[3] An organization is assumed to exist when its presence can be detected through an archival record like a trade association registry; such sources are typically used to identify the relevant organizational population in empirical research. Industrial organization economists studying the emergence of new firms often use federal government data sets to identify new firms based on the initial filing of tax documents (Haltiwanger, Lynch, & Mackie, 2007). Finally, labor market economists are not concerned with organizations per se, but are instead concerned with the employment status of individuals. In this tradition, self-employment, franchises, and new establishments that may be subunits of other organizations may all be considered entrepreneurial ventures (Lazear, 2004).

The PSED II dataset provides the opportunity to investigate new firm conception, gestation, and birth with a large, representative sample of U.S. nascent entrepreneurs—over 1,200 cases. Because data were collected on the prevalence and timing of 39 different entrepreneurial start-up activities (or behaviors), it is possible to develop (1) several operational definitions of new firm conception, (2) operational measures of new firm birth consistent with the four different approaches and (3) to compute width of the firm gestation period. This allows for the examination of the firm gestation process and its outcomes based on the four perspectives described above. To foreshadow the results, the analyses indicates a low association between these different indicators of firm birth across each of the four traditions and their substantial impact on both the length of the gestation process and the number of firm births produced.

The following sections discuss the PSED II sample and describe the different start-up activities on which information was collected and the considerable variation in the prevalence of the various activities. Next is a description of how each of the different definitions of firm conception and birth are operationalized. Following this is a review of the impact of alternative operational definitions on the length of time between conception and new firm birth. In the paper's final sections the implications of these results for the study of organizational creation, the business life course, and the emergence of new industries are discussed. The analysis suggests that those relying on government administrate data for policy decisions need to take into account the highly variable number of new firms that are revealed by varying sources of data and that each reveals firms at multiple points in the start-up and operating processes.

11.1 The PSED Sample

The PSED II research protocol is designed to identify individuals actively engaged in new venture creation. Respondents were selected for the PSED II sampling frame if (a) they considered themselves to be trying to *start a new business*; (b) they expected to personally own at least part of the business; and (c) they had engaged in some start-up activities within the past 12 months such as looking for equipment or a location, organizing a start-up team, working on a business plan, beginning to save money, or any other activity that would facilitate a business launch. Existing operating companies, defined as organizations where revenues exceeded expenses (including salaries or wages for owners' active in managing the business) for at least 6 of the prior 12 months, are not included in the sample.

Respondents who met the screening criteria were invited to participate in a 60-minute phone interview; 1,214 nascent entrepreneurs were selected from a nationwide representative sample of 31,845 adults. At the beginning of the detailed Wave A interview, respondents were again asked to confirm that "in the *past twelve months*" they had "taken actions to help start a new business that you will own all or part of." This question limited the sample to only active nascent entrepreneurs. The PSED II screening procedure, however, identifies nascent entrepreneurs at varying points in the firm's gestation process. The sampling procedures captured potential firms which had been gestating for different lengths of time, developing at different speeds, whose entrepreneurs had been working at different levels of intensity to start up the business. Some respondents describe a business idea that had received serious thought within the past year but few start-up activities had been implemented. Others describe a start-up effort they had pursued more than a decade prior to the interview but which had not yet become a profitable activity. Yet other respondents were describing a nascent business they had recently initiated and were in the process of actively pursuing a variety of start-up activities.

In the initial detailed interview information is obtained about 39 different start-up activities. For each activity that has been initiated, the respondent provides the month and year when this occurred. These timing data allow start-up activities to be sorted in chronological order and to determine the length of time between each start-up activities. The detailed interview also captures information about the history of positive monthly cash flow, when it occurs, for the nascent enterprise. The screening procedure gathered information about the previous 12 months alone. Sixty-six of the 1,214 nascent enterprises report positive monthly cash flow more than 12 months prior to the detailed interview. These cases, which are considered to be "reactivated" businesses rather than nascent businesses still in the gestation process, were dropped from the analysis, thereby reducing the sample to 1,148 cases. The sample is further reduced when only cases with a successful follow-up interview in Wave B are included. Missing data will reduce the sample size for some analyses.

11.2 The Start-Up Activities: Descriptive Statistics

In the PSED II interview the respondents report on 39 discrete start-up activities and indicate if it is relevant for their business, if each activity has been undertaken, and, if so, the month and year associated with the activity. Twenty of these activities replicate PSED I activities (Gartner, Shaver, Carter, & Reynolds, 2004) or are enhancements based on earlier assessments by Reynolds and Miller (1992); Gartner and Starr (1993); Gatewood, Shaver, and Gartner (1995); and Carter, Gartner, and Reynolds (1996). Additional items were developed to expand knowledge of several activities, such as details about the team creation process and business registry participation. Table 11.1 presents a summary of these start-up activities, rank ordered by the proportion of cases that report the activity in the initial, Wave A, interview. The item labels are provided in the right column of Table 11.1, and the exact wording is available from the interview schedule available on the project website [www.psed.isr.umich.edu].

Table 11.1 reveals that nascent entrepreneurs report highly variable sets of activities have been initiated. It should be no surprise that all but a few (99%) reported a date when they first started thinking about their businesses. Depending on the state of development and type of business being implemented, there is considerable diversity in reports of initiation. While more than three in five report they had invested their own money in the start-up (79%), began talking to customers (76%), began development of a model or prototype of the produce or service to be sold (65%), initiated the development of a business plan (64%), or began to use physical space (62%), less than 60% report any of the other 32 start-up activities. Many activities may not apply to the specific business at hand. For example, very few of the nascent entrepreneurs in our nationally representative sample consider intellectual property protection to be relevant for their new business. As a result, only 7% reported they had applied for intellectual property protection and only 5% had obtained a patent, trademark, or copyright. It is particularly noteworthy that few nascent entrepreneurs report activities that would include them in a government or industry registry. This highlights the fact that a great deal of entrepreneurial activity, and much of the start-up process, goes undetected when government and industry registries are the sources of data.

11.2.1 Defining and Measuring New Organization Conception

As the dictionary defines it, conception is "the moment at which an idea starts to take shape or emerge." When applied to new firm start-ups, conception is typically associated with a serious effort to assemble resources and people to develop the new business; actions are taken and entrepreneurial behavior implemented. This is consistent with the earliest use of the term "entrepreneur" as one that assembled resources for a profitable business undertaking (Say, 1816).

Excluding studies from the PSED and its direct precursors, historically there has been a paucity of empirical investigations of pre-birth activities, the process that is initiated when new firms are conceptualized. Some scholars have begun to focus attention on where new firms come from or their origins (Schoonhoven & Romanelli, 2001; Sorensen & Sorenson, 2003); however, this focus is on the causal factors accounting for when and where new firm births can be observed. There is a current research stream on academic entrepreneurship that examines

Table 11.1 Start-up activities: item numbers, content, first wave prevalence

Item label[a]	Start-up activity	Wave A report (%)
A8	Serious thought given to the start-up	99
Q14_1	Actually invested own money in the start-up	79
D20	Began talking to customers	76
D6	Began development of model, prototype of product, service	65
D4	Initiated business plan	64
B8	First use of physical space	62
D22	Began to collect information on competitors	62
D18	Purchased materials, supplied, inventory, components	59
E13	Receive income from sales of goods or services	56
E25	Established phone book or internet listing	55
D24	Began defining market for product, service	54
D16	Purchased or leased a capital asset	53
D28	Determined regulatory requirements	53
D9	Began to promote the good or service	49
D1	Business plan completed	41
E11	Open a bank account for the start-up	39
C2	Legal form of business registered	36
D26	Developed financial projections	35
D8	Model, prototype completed	35
H17_1	Began to devote full time to the start-up	28
E5	Established supplier credit	27
E18	Hired an accountant	26
C4	Sought liability insurance for start-up	22
E1	Sought external funding for the start-up	19
E20	Hired a lawyer	18
E3	Received first outside funding	13
E7	Hired an employee	13
E22	Joined a trade association	12
G7_1	Respondent signed equity agreement	10
D11	Proprietary technology under developed	8
D13	Initiated patent, copyright, trademark protection	7
D15	Patent, copyright, trademark obtained	5
E15	Initial positive monthly cash flow	3
Item label	Business registry listings	Wave A report (%)
E26	Acquired federal Employer Identification Number (EIN)	26
E34	Filed initial federal tax return	27
E28	Filed for fictitious name (DBA)	18
E32	Paid initial federal social security (FICA) payment	17
E30	Paid initial state unemployment insurance payment	9
E36	Know that Dun and Bradstreet established listing	5

[a]Item number refers to Wave A questionnaire, available on the project website. The items requesting the date the activity was initiated or occurred generally follow the item number. Sample includes all Wave A except those with significant positive monthly cash flow prior to the initial interview, n = 1,148.

when and how academic scientists move innovations from academic laboratories into new ventures (Murray, 2004); however, these investigations of gestation processes are limited to a very narrow segment of the entrepreneurial population. The PSED studies are the first to empirically measure firm conception from the beginning of the process with representative samples of the U.S. population, and PSED II collected the most extensive number of activities to date. In this chapter the discussion of firm conception and firm birth is confined to indicators available in the PSED II dataset.

The PSED II dataset provides information on the timing of various start-up activities; this provides the potential for three operational indicators of new firm conception. The first is the reported date when the entrepreneur first gave serious thought to the new organization, a measure of managerial cognition and awareness that, according to Table 11.1, is the most commonly reported activity and tends to be the earliest activity entrepreneurs engage in. The second is the date when the entrepreneur reports engaging in an activity other than "thought"—*any* activity— to start up a new business, a behavioral indicator. The third involves attention to the timing and intensity of start-up activities: this measure is referred to as "Recent active nascent entrepreneur" or "Active NE". With this measure, conception is considered to occur only for those entrepreneurs who have reported more than 2 start-up activities, of which at least 2 occurred within the same 12-month period, and the earliest of the first 2 occurred within 12 months but less than 120 months (or 10 years) prior to the first detailed interviews.[4] These are defined as a recent confirmed active nascent entrepreneur or "active NE."

Taken together, these provide three different dates of conception of a nascent enterprise. On average, conception measured as "first thought" tends to occur 37.7 months before the first detailed interview (Wave A). Conception measured as first start-up activity occurs 11.5 months later, and attaining the status of an active nascent entrepreneur occurs 7.5 months after that, but still 18.7 months before the first detailed interview.[5] This indicates that different definitions of new firm conception can affect the length of time required for the start-up process.

11.3 Defining and Measuring Length of the Gestation Period

The gestation period is defined as the elapsed time from conception (using one of the three measures discussed above) until the new firm's birth date. While the indicators in the PSED II data set facilitate alternative definitions of conception, developing alternative measures of firm birth is more complicated. Drawing from the extant empirical literature, four different measures were developed of a firm "birth," each reflecting different conceptual definitions.

Organizational ecologists consider themselves to be corporate and industrial demographers who are concerned with the dynamics of organizational populations (Carroll & Hannan, 2000; Hannan & Freeman, 1977). Scholars in this tradition distinguish between new and existing firms in existing populations in addition to the emergence of a new population of organizations that can have *de novo* entrants—entirely new firms—or *de alio* entrants—firms that move from another industry population into the new population. The first case, referred to as population level analysis, takes as given the time of the first new firm, and it does not attempt to explain the origin of the population or capture important information about the entry process itself. In the case of an absence of an existing population, a larger social unit like an organizational community or a sector of the economy is taken as the originating conditions. This is referred to as "sectoral analysis" which is used to address variation in the flow of entries following the first entry. In both cases, however, ecologists and demographers acknowledge the existence of a new organization only when it is first "recorded" (Carroll & Hannan, 2000, p. 105).[6] The date of a new organizational entry is noted when a formal (written) record of its existence can be obtained from industry directories, listings, legal registrations, and the like. Therefore entrants to a given population likely differ in their organizational age.

PSED II collected data on four indicators that may be used to determine an "ecological" birth date: (1) obtaining a phone book/Internet listing [E25],[7] (2) being listed in a trade association directory listing [E22], (3) a fictitious name for the firm has been registered [E28], and (4) the entrepreneur has legally established an organizational form for the entity [C2], typically with a state government in the United States. Inter-item correlations for these four ecological indicators for a new firm birth range from 0.21 to 0.42. Measures related to the first payment of state unemployment insurance or federal social security payments were excluded as they are only required of firms employing other workers and would not apply to about half of the nascent enterprises. To obtain ecological birth dates for new firms in the PSED data set, the earliest date for any of these four events is taken as the birth date.

Industrial organizational economists are primarily interested in the impact of entrepreneurial firms on the overall economy. They consider the birth of a new business occurs when it participates in economic transactions which can affect the trading price and quantity of any commodity. From the PSED II data the activities chosen to represent active participation in the economy include (1) generating sales revenues [E13], (2) receiving outside funding to help launch and support the business [E3], (3) hiring employees [E7], (4) paying federal social security (FICA) taxes [E32], and (5) paying into a state-mandated unemployment insurance fund for employees [E30]. These latter two are additional indicators that the new firm is actually employing individuals. The dates when each of these five activities occurred were provided by the PSED II entrepreneurs in their interviews. The first of these dates to occur is taken as the earliest indicator of a firm's birth or existence as an economic actor. Inter-item correlations for the five economic indicators range from 0.14 to 0.40.

Labor market economists are interested in the labor market participation of individuals. Their studies of entrepreneurship tend to focus on whether or not individuals choose to become entrepreneurs or continue as employees and the relationship between entrepreneurship and other labor market outcomes such as spells of unemployment, wages, and wage growth. Thus, new firm creation as conceived by labor market economists focuses on the employment status of individuals associated with a new organization. In PSED II there are two labor market indicators of an organization's birth: (1) when the owner(s) begins working full-time for the nascent business [H17_1] and (2) when employee(s) were first hired to work for the firm [E7]. The date reported for the earlier of the first two events can be taken as the birth date of the new firm in PSED II. The correlation for these two items is 0.18 indicating that a relatively low proportion of new firms employ workers other than the owners.

The entrepreneurial process approach defines a new firm's birth when its founder(s) reports a profit (Reynolds, 2007). The entrepreneurial process approach considers a nascent firm to have completed the transition to a new firm when it has sufficient revenue to cover all expenses. These criteria were developed during the PSED research program and first implemented in PSED I based on reports— "Is it now an operating business?"—from the responding nascent entrepreneur (Reynolds, 2007). A more precise measure of profitability was developed for the PSED II procedures and is the basis for determining the nascent firm's status in the follow-up interviews (Reynolds & Curtin, 2008). Firm birth, indicated as initial profitability, occurs when a series of benchmarks are reported during the Wave B interview [items A30–A35]. These include (1) the firm has received income (or revenue) in 6 of the past 12 months, (2) the income covered all monthly expenses, and (3) monthly expenses include the owners' salaries.[8] If all three of these criteria are met, the firm's birth is considered to have occurred in the first month that all expenses and salaries were covered by income or revenue. These are sequential criteria, and all must be met to satisfy the initial profitability standard. Hence, inter-item correlations are not relevant in this case.

The relationships between these four alternative conceptions of a new firm birth are presented in Table 11.2. Reading horizontally at top of the table, the four column headings list each of the four birth approaches, followed by a summary of the measures used to operationalize each new firm conception. The inter-correlations between each of the four constructs are presented in the middle four rows of Table 11.2. Here, each case is coded 0 if it does not meet the birth criteria and 1 if it satisfies the operational definition. In the lower four rows of Table 11.2 are reported the percentage of cases that meet each criterion for birth that also meets the criterion for that row.

In the correlation table, all coefficients are significantly related to all others. But Table 11.2 also clearly reveals that there is no one-to-one statistical correspondence between any of the four definitions of new firm birth. These are highly divergent indicators of new firm birth with relatively low correlations between them, and coefficients range from a low of 0.15 to a very modest 0.45. The two measures, initial profitability and the labor market indicators have the lowest correlations with the other birth indicators. The initial profitability measure has relatively small correlations of only 0.14, 0.26 and 0.17 with the other 3 measures for ecology, economic activity, and labor market participation, respectively. The labor market indicator is more strongly correlated with the ecology and economic activity measures with correlations of 0.25 and 0.30, respectively. The two most strongly correlated approaches are the labor market

Table 11.2 Associations between alternative approaches to new firm birth

| | The four approaches to measuring a new firm birth ||||
	Initial profitability	Labor market participation	Any economic activity	Population ecology
	All must occur	First of any:	First of each	First of each
	Revenue	1. Owners full time work	1. Sales	1. Phone book/internet listing
	Covers monthly expenses	2. Initial hires	2. Hires	2. Trade Assoc membership
	Covers owners salaries		3. FICA payments	3. Fictitious (DBA) name files
	Six of past 12 months		4. Unemp Ins payments	4. Register legal form
			5. Funding received	
Correlations between measures				
Initial profitability	1.00			
Labor market participation	0.14	1.00		
Economic Activity	0.26	0.45	1.00	
Population ecology	0.17	0.25	0.30	1.00
Correspondence between the 4 Approaches (as % of firms co-included)				
Initial profitability (12%)*	100.0%	61.8%	100.0%	84.4%
Labor market participation (40%)	18.8%	100.0%	84.2%	91.9%
Economic Activity (66%)	18.1%	50.1%	100.0%	82.5%
Population ecology (68%)	15.1%	47.9%	81.2%	100.0%

*Proportion of cases meeting the criteria for a firm birth.

and economic activity indicators, at 0.45. This latter case makes intuitive sense as two of the five indicators of major economic activity are mandated by governments (state or federal) for employer firms.

An alternative interpretation of these results can be derived from the bottom set of rows in Table 11.2. We can see that some measures of firm birth include a substantial proportion of cases considered new firms by another definition. For example, while only 12% of all cases would be considered new firms by the initial profitability criteria,[9] 100% of these cases also meet the economic activity criteria. However, only 84.4% of the initial profitability cases (12% of all cases) also meet the population ecology criteria, and only 61.8% of the initial profitability cases also meet the labor market criteria. In contrast, 68% of all cases meet the population ecology birth criteria, but among these only 15.1% meet the initial profitability criteria, about half (47.9%) meet the labor market participation criteria, and 81.2% meet the economic activity criteria.

Given these relatively low measures of association between the four approaches to new firm births, it can be safely concluded that ecologists, economists, process entrepreneurship researchers, and labor market theorists are measuring different kinds of organizations, captured at different stages of the firm creation process. Little wonder the four disciplines arrive at different conclusions about the nature of the entrepreneurial process.

11.4 Alternative Definitions and the Gestation Window

The next question becomes, "What are the consequences of these four different conceptualizations of new firm birth?" While there are numerous consequences, we focus on two: (1) the number of firms considered born by each definition and, (2) the length of time required to complete the new firm creation process—the width of the gestation window. The preliminary analysis for each is presented in Table 11.3.

The first column of Table 11.3 presents the three different measures of firm conception; initial thought, initial behavior, and reaching active nascent entrepreneur status. (Active NE is conception indicated by 2 or more start up activities, with 2 reported within same 12-month period, with the earliest of the first 2 less than 120 months or 10 years prior to first detailed interview.) They are presented in three sets of three rows each, with the first set of rows indicating the number and percentage of cases in the sample; the second set reporting the average number of months for width of the gestation window; and the third set of rows reporting median width of the gestation window. Horizontally across the top of the table are the four conceptions of new firm birth each with a summary of its operationalizations.

The first set of three rows in Table 11.3 present the sample size for each cell followed by the proportion of the sample in each cell. This primarily reflects the proportion of the sample that has met the criteria for a new firm birth after the first follow-up interview. We can see that these range from a low of 12% to a high of 67% after two waves of interviews and an elapsed observation period of 12 months. The largest number of the nascent ventures in our sample is counted as being new firm births when the population ecology approach is applied (67%) followed closely by the economic activity (66%) criteria. But fewer than half of the sample have a labor market impact that would qualify the entity as a new firm birth (39%) and a very small number of cases would be considered new firm births if we require profitability (12%). Specifically, five times more new firm births are created when the population ecology conception of birth is applied (n = 624) compared to the initial profitability conception (n = 111). These differences alone demonstrate that different conceptions of firm birth have major consequences for the cohort size of nascent enterprises that would be considered new firms.

The second set of three rows in Table 11.3 presents the average width of the gestation window (in months) for all possible combinations of measures of conception and firm birth at the end of the data collection period Wave B, 12

Table 11.3 Effect of alternative conceptions of firm birth on gestation duration

Alternative definitions of firm conception	Alternative definitions of firm birth			
	(1) Initial profitability	(2) Population ecology	(3) Any economic activity	(4) Labor market participation
	Profitability All following occur Revenue Covers monthly expenses Covers owners salaries Six of past 12 months	Major registrations First of following: 1. Phone book/internet listing 2. Trade Assoc membership 3. Fictitious (DBA) name files 4. Register legal form	Major econ First of following: 1. Sales 2. Hires 3. FICA payments 4. Unemp Ins payments 5. Funding received	Owners, employees First of following: 1. Owners full time work 2. Initial hires
Number of cases[a]				
1. Active NE	111 (12%)	614 (66%)	605 (65%)	353 (38%)
2. Initial behavior	111 (12%)	624 (67%)	614 (66%)	365 (39%)
3. Initial thought	110 (12%)	619 (67%)	608 (66%)	364 (39%)
Width of gestation window (mean months)[b]				
1. Active NE	14.0 (7)	6.9 (10)	8.7 (8)	7.8 (8)
2. Initial behavior	19.8 (8)	13.7 (9)	16.2 (7)	14.7 (7)
3. Initial thought	25.4 (11)	20.0 (6)	21.7 (7)	21.0 (7)
Width of gestation window (median months)				
1. Active NE	13.0	3.0	4.0	4.9
2. Initial behavior	14.0	3.0	5.9	5.0
3. Initial thought	17.0	6.0	8.0	8.0

[a] Each conception's number of cases, by birth definition, and % (in parentheses) of total Wave B sample size (where $n = 972$).
[b] For width of the gestation windows, T-tests for significant differences are reported for all 66 paired comparisons of the mean values, which yield 11 comparisons for each cell with all other cells. Number in parentheses indicates the number of statistically significant differences at 0.05 or better for each cell. Number of significant differences ranges from 0 to 11 per cell. Of 66 possible comparisons, 50 are statistically significant: 39 beyond 0.001, 7 at 0.01, and 4 at 0.05.

11 Reconceiving the Gestation Window 231

cells in all.[10] The table clearly shows that width of the gestation window varies substantially as we modify the operational definitions of conception and birth. The gestation windows range from a low of 6.9 months to a high of 25.4 months.

It is useful to determine if these alternative gestations windows are statistically significantly different. *T*-tests were calculated for all possible pairs of cells in Table 11.3 (66 in all) was computed to determine whether the mean number of months for each of the 12 gestation windows is significantly different when compared to the others. Of these 66 comparisons, 50 were statistically different from one other (two-tailed tests of significance), with 39 significant beyond 0.001, 7 at 0.01, and 4 at the 0.05 level. That is, 75% of the 66 paired comparisons yielded gestation windows that are substantially different lengths of time from the others. Alternatively, only 25% (16) of the 66 paired comparisons yielded gestation windows that are not statistically different from one another.

The longest gestation window is found in the 25.4 months that transpire between the entrepreneurs' initial thought about starting a business and when that business becomes profitable. This long gestation window is also the most statistically different from all of the other 11 gestation windows lengths, and as such it is the most significant outlier when gestation lengths are compared. The shortest gestation window is 6.9 months; this is created when the founder becomes "an active nascent entrepreneur" (indicated by multiple actions taken in a short period of time) and when existense of the firm is formally registered, as required by the population ecology indicator of a new firm birth. It is clear from these comparative data on length of the gestation window that ususlly, 75% of the time, researchers will be working with substantially different estimates of size of the gestation window. Furthermore, as indiccated by the data above on number of cases, there will be a wide disparity in the number of cases that count as "firm births," because of different definitions of a new firm's birth adopted in each study.

One of the consequences of using alternative conceptual definitions and measures of new firm birth for width of the gestation window for new firms is reflected in the data in the middle set of rows of Table 11.3. This provides evidence of the time lag between different events in the start-up sequence. For all four measures of firm birth (profitability, organization ecology registration, economic activity, and labor market participation), the time lag between the founder's initial thought about stating a new business and when he/she takes the first action to start the business, is between 5.5 and 6.3 months. Once the initial action is taken to start the firm, an additional 5.8 to 8.5 months transpires before the founder becomes an actively engaged nascent entrepreneur. Last, once the founder becomes an active nascent entrepreneur, anywhere from 6.9 to 14.0 months transpire before the firm is formally created, depending on which of the four definitions of firm birth applies.

The final set of rows provides the median value, in months, of the gestation window for the same combinations. We can observe that the median values for most entries are smaller than the mean values reported above them, indicating that the distribution is skewed. A small proportion of cases have very wide gestation windows. Overall these data demonstrate that the length of the gestation process is highly variable, with some entrepreneurs completing the firm gestation process in a period of several months with others requiring a number of years (see also Reynolds, 2007, p. 56).

Summarizing from the mean values in Table 11.3, the creation of a new firm from its initial thought to its formal establishment takes anywhere from 20 to 25.4 months, with variation depending upon which of the four conceptions of firm birth is applied. There is a subsequent actions, and furthermore, a nearly 12-month duration transpires between making a serious commitment to starting the enterprise (two or more start-up actions are taken) and the transition to a new firm's birth. These data illustrate that approximately two years prior to the formalization of a new firm's birth, nascent entrepreneurs are busily taking actions to establish the new venture. This period of time is largely unaccounted for in the theoretical literature on entrepreneurship and it is seldom explored in the emperical research.

11.5 Implications for Research: Next Questions

These alternative definitions of a new firm's birth have relevance for at least three issues central to the study of new firms. They are the conception of "firm death," analyses of firm survival rates, and our understanding of firm growth.

The term "firm death" or mortality is sometimes associated with portrayals of dramatic bankruptcies or the closure of long established businesses, which are often the economic foundation of an established community. Images of families in distress, poverty, and local institutions in disarray are common. This implies that the firm, or firms, that are being shut down have had a long period of profitable operations, sometimes for generations, and that the broader community is very dependent on the business. When it is no longer functioning, widespread hardship may ensue. Examples include the closing of coal mines in Applachia, the foreclosure of thousands of family farm businesses in the United States during the 1980s, and collapse of the U.S. mortgage banking industry in 2007–2008.

Conversely, if a firm is defined as one that has engaged in any economic transaction, has been added to a business registry, or received the full-time labor of an owner or employee—regardless of whether or not it has ever generated profits, then "failure" or discontinuance has different consequences. For example, a firm may incorporate as a legal entity, be listed as a business, spend several hundred dollars on legal fees, and be considered a new economic actor. However, if no additional activities are taken to develop the nascent enterprise it could be considered to be disbanded or a "business failure." In effect, a nascent firm whose founder(s) expended minimal energy and whose development received scant external attention would nonetheless be treated statistically as equivalent to a relatively well-developed profit-generating business that is disbanded and whose many employees are thrown out of work.

This latter case could also be treated as the discontinuance of the gestation or business creation process. After preliminary actions were taken to establish a new business, the founders withdrew from further effort. Hence the gestation process was terminated and an organizational abortion could be said to have taken place.

The diverse conceptions of new firm birth discussed above also have implications for survival analyses and in particular our understanding of the relationship between organizational age and the likelihood of surviving. Consider, for example, the prevailing distinction in the organizational ecology literature between the liabilities of "newness" and "adolescence." Early research found support for Stinchcombe's (1965) argument that death rates of young organizations exceed those of older ones. For example, Freeman, Carroll, and Hannan (1983) found this pattern for labor unions, semiconductor firms, and San Francisco newspaper publishers. Referred to as "negative age dependent mortality or death rates," several authors have reviewed the multitude of studies reporting this pattern (Aldrich & Marsden, 1988; Singh & Lumsden, 1990; Hannan, Carroll, Dobrev, & Han, 1998a; and Hannan, Carroll, Dobrev, Han, & Torres, 1998b).

In contrast, other research shows that mortality rates do not always decline monotonically with age after founding. That is, the life chances of organizations do not continuously improve with age. Referred to as the "liability of adolescence," some have found that death rates rise for a brief early portion of the life span before declining over the remainder of the typical life span (i.e., Fichman & Levinthal, 1991). The liability of adolescence assumes that the probability of firm death is low immediately after birth, increases for some time, reaches a maximum at some point during firm adolescence, and then reflects a continuous decline thereafter. These contrasting findings may actually be an artifact of how new firm births are defined and measured.

The same concern is applicable to measures of new firm growth. Measures of growth are sensitive to the scope of activity at the initial point in the trajectory. If growth measures start with the level of activity reported during the initial periods of profitability, growth it is likely to be less substantial than if the origin is based on the level of activity (revenue or employment) when the first listing in a registry or first economic transaction is completed. As a result, much higher rates of initial growth would be recorded for firms when birth is defined using a population ecology or industrial organization economist's definition.

Our analyses demonstrate that differences in the length of the gestation process will be observed when attention is focused on the early phases of the new firm creation process, those events in the first several years, where a difference of 6 to 12 month is a significant portion of time in the nascent entrepreneurship process.

If the focus is on phenomena that take decades to unfold, such as the creation of new industry sectors, the impact on temporally based issues may be less substantial. If, however, the focus is on the rate of firm creation and discontinuance during the early period of creation of a new sector or organizational population, the different counts of initiatives considered "new organizations"—reflecting different definitions of organizational birth—could be significant. Recall that in Table 11.3 the number of new firms identified using the population ecology or industrial organization definitions are five and a half times greater than those using the initial profitability criterion.

In the same way, analyses of activities pursued during gestation will be affected substantially by the definition used for firm birth, which itself would be considered an outcome of the process. Firm birth definitions based on economic activity, initial registrations, or labor force participation will lead to a much shorter gestation period and a much smaller number of start-up activities during gestation when compared to analyses using initial profitability as a measure of firm birth. The number of start-up activities, their sequence of occurrence, as well as the activities considered significant in creating a "firm birth" will be affected in major ways by the definition of firm birth.

In sum, for a wide range of analyses related to the gestation period, the definition of firm birth clearly has major consequences for subsequent analyses and interpretations. For assessments of the outcomes of the early stages of the firm's life course—such as survival and early growth trajectories—the results could also be significant. For assessments of the long-term patterns of the emergence of new industries or organizational forms—which tend to focus on well-established firms or organizations of considerable scope—the impact of alternative definitions of conception and firm birth may be less substantial.

11.6 Implications for Policy

There are several implications for policy and policy makers. Much of the information about firm creation, survival, and impact provided to policy makers is developed from government-based administrative data sets, where new firms are inferred from new registry listings. This is very similar to the population ecology definition of a new firm. Yet the image of a new firm policy makers might have is of a business with at least a minimal level of profits and one which provides jobs, sales, value added, and new tax revenues. This analysis suggests that presentations of data on new firms based on administrative registries should be carefully reviewed to determine the proportion of these new listings that are actually profitable business ventures. If, as implied in the analysis in Table 11.3, only 15% are generating profits, the potential of these new firms to make major contributions to economic growth in the short term is likely to be much less than anticipated.

Governments, at multiple levels and across many countries, seek to assist new firms. One complication has been to identify new firms that may require or welcome assistance. Our analysis suggests than most new "firms" identified through government registries and industry directories will not have achieved profitable operations and that it may be some time before this occurs. In short, governments may find welcoming entrepreneurs if they approach new firm listings with offers of assistance or to provide information about programs designed to enhance their potential. Such approaches will be more effective if implemented shortly after the new listings are identified as the commitments of the start-up teams during the initial gestation periods may be tenuous. Information about the potential for government assistance may have a major impact on encouraging a more substantial commitment to the firm's creation at this early stage. This, in turn, may lead to more profitable new businesses.

11.7 Overview and Conclusions

Two events delineate the gestation of a new firm, conception and birth. While there is agreement on the abstract meaning of both, there is little agreement on the operational definitions of either. New firm conception is an important construct because it signals the beginning of the new firm's gestation process, which ends in either the creation of a new firm—an organizational birth—or withdrawal from the firm creation process. Nonbirth outcomes are of consequence because substantial entrepreneurial effort is expended during the firm gestation process; few economic benefits accrue to the founders and their investors if a firm is not created.

A substantial literature on new firm births has been created by scholars applying the perspectives of entrepreneurship, organizational ecology, industrial and organizational economics, and labor market economics. Within and across disciplines no uniform conception of new firm "birth" has been established. The rich data set developed for PSED II has provided an opportunity to consider the implications of three measures of firm conception: initial serious thought is given, initial start-up actions are taken, and potential founders take sufficient action to be termed "active nascent entrepreneurs."

Four measures of firm birth were developed to reflect different theoretical approaches to the phenomena. Attaining initial profitability reflects an entrepreneurial process approach. Being "registered" reflects the traditions of organizational ecology. Engaging in economic transactions reflects industrial organizational economics, and hiring employees meets the labor market economists' approach to new firm births. Combining three different measures of firm "conception" with four measures of firm "birth" created a matrix of 12 gestation windows of different lengths. All but 3 of the 66 different paired comparisons were significantly different from one another, revealing the power of the different perspectives to alter the number of new firm births observed empirically as well as the lengths of the gestation process.

Three different definitions of firm conception created a significant impact on the width of the gestation window—from 6.9 months to 25.4 months on average. The three definitions of firm conception, however, had little impact on the number of cases considered to have completed the gestation process within the separate definitions of new firm birth. For example, when the three measures of conception are compared using the labor market approach to new firm birth, the number of cases produced was 353, 364, and 365—quite consistent counts.

In contrast, alternative definitions of firm birth had a substantial impact on number of new firm births observed. When birth is defined as attaining profitability, only 12% of the nearly 1,000 cases qualified as new firms. The gestation windows for profitability were approximately 6 months longer on average than when the other three measures of firm birth were applied. These other definitions would result in 38–67% of the cohort being considered new firms, and their respective gestation windows were about 6 months shorter.

These differences in number of new firms and width of the gestation window have substantial implications for any research on the early stages of the firm's life course and inferences about temporal patterns of firm survival and growth. The low proportion of new firms identified as profitable suggests that care be taken in interpreting government administrative data by policy makers. On the other hand, the low proportion of new firms with profitable operations suggests that the residual set of nascent firms may be an important audience for government assistance programs, those programs seeking to provide assistance to young firms that may benefit from assistance.

Notes

1. End of the gestation period can also be (2) the end of the observation period and an event is right-censored or (3) when the gestation activities are suspended, metaphorically an aborted gestating entity.
2. The PSED II cohort was identified between October 2005 and February 2006.
3. The origin of new forms (defined as populations) has been studied recently by Ruef (2000) and others have called for investigations of the origins of new firms (Schoonhoven & Romanelli, 2001).
4. This criterion is designed to prevent the inclusion of those respondents that report very few start-up activities spread over a number of years and do not appear to have a serious commitment to creating a new firm; they appear to be "hobby" nascent entrepreneurs. Such hobbyists are not included in some analysis of the PSED I and II cohorts (Reynolds and Curtin, 2008, p. 169).
5. For a small proportion of cases, these events occur *after* the initial detailed interview (Wave A) and are reported on the first follow-up (Wave B) interview.
6. Analysts ordinarily do not use historical time as the primary clock in analyzing entry processes. Rather they focus on the distribution of interarrival times and control for historic time.
7. This identifies the item number in the Wave A and B questionnaires, which are available on the project website [www.psed.isr.umich.edu].
8. The wording of these criteria is provided in items A32–A35 of the PSED II Wave B interview schedule.
9. See Table 11.3 for number and percentage of cases by birth definition.
10. Because cases are right-censored at the end of the Wave B observation period, it is likely that some of the nascent firms that have not yet completed the gestation process will eventually do so, thereby increasing the average number of months in the gestation window.

References

Aldrich, H. E., & Marsden, P. V. (1988). Environments and organizations. In N. Smelser (Ed.), *Handbook of sociology* (pp. 361–392). Beverly Hills, CA: Sage.

Cardon, M. S., Zietsma, C., Saparito, P., Matherne B. P., & Davis, C. (2005). A tale of passion: New insights into entrepreneurship from a parenthood metaphor. *Journal of Business Venturing, 20*(1), 23–45.

Carroll, G. C., & Hannan, M. T. (2000). The demography of corporations and industries. Princeton, NJ: Princeton University Press.

Carter, N., Gartner, W. B., & Reynolds, P. D. (1996). Exploring start-up event sequences. *Journal of Business Venturing, 11*(3), 151–166.

Fichman, M., & Levinthal, D. A. (1991). Honeymoons and the liability of adolescence: A new perspective on duration dependence in social and organizational relationships. *Academy of Management Review, 16*, 442–468.

Freeman, J., Carroll, G. C., & Hannan, M. T. (1983). The liability of newness: Age dependence in organizational death rates. *American Sociological Review, 48*, 692–710.

Gartner, W. B., Shaver, K. G., Carter, N. M., & Reynolds, P. D. (Eds.). (2004). *Handbook of entrepreneurial dynamics: The process of business creation.* Thousand Oaks, CA: Sage.

Gartner, W. B., & Starr, J. (1993). The nature of entrepreneurial work. In S. Birely and I. C. MacMillan (Eds.), *Entrepreneurship research: Global perspectives* (pp. 35–67). Amsterdam, The Netherlands: North-Holland.

Gatewood, E. J., Shaver, K. G., & Gartner, W. B. (1995). A longitudinal study of cognitive factors influencing start-up behaviors and success at venture creation. *Journal of Business Venturing, 10*(5), 371–391.

Haltiwanger, J., Lynch, L., & Mackie, C. (Eds.). (2007). *Understanding business dynamics: An integrated data system for America's future.* Washington, DC: The National Academies Press.

Hannan, M. T., Carroll, G. R., Dobrev, S. D., & Han, J. (1998a). Organizational mortality in European and American automobile industries, Part I: Revisiting the effects of age and size. *European Sociological Review, 14*, 279–303.

Hannan, M. T., Carroll, G. R., Dobrev, S. D., Han, J., & Torres, J. C. (1998b). Organizational mortality in European and American automobile industries, Part II: Coupled clocks. *European Sociological Review, 14*, 303–13.

Hannan, M. T., & Freeman, J. (1977). The population ecology of organizations. *American Journal of Sociology, 82*, 929–64.

Katz, J. A., & Gartner, W. G. (1988). Properties of emerging organizations. *Academy of Management Review, 13*(3), 429–441.

Lazear, E. P. (2004). Balanced skills and entrepreneurship. *American Economic Review, 94*(2), 208–211.

Liao, J.-W., Welsch, H., & Tan, W.-L. (2005). Venture gestation paths of nascent entrepreneurs: Exploring the temporal patterns. *Journal of High Technology Management Research, 16*(1), 1–22.

Murray, F. (2004). The role of academic inventors in entrepreneurial firms: Sharing the laboratory life. *Research Policy, 33*(4), 643–659.

Reynolds, P. D. (2007). New firm creation in the U.S.: A PSED I overview. *Foundations and Trends in Entrepreneurship, 3*(1), 1–149.

Reynolds, P. D., & Curtin, R. T. (2008). Business creation in the United States: Panel study of entrepreneurial dynamics II initial assessment. *Foundations and Trends in Entrepreneurship, 4*(3), 155–307.

Reynolds, P. D., & Miller, B. (1992). New firm gestation: Conception, birth, and implications for research. *Journal of Business Venturing, 7*(5), 405–417.

Ruef, M. (2000). Emergence of organizational forms: A community ecology approach. *American Journal of Sociology, 105*(3), 658–714.

Say, J.-B. (1816). *A Treatise on political economy.* New York: A.M. Kelly (1964 reprint).

Schoonhoven, K., & Romanelli, E. (Eds.). (2001). *The entrepreneurship dynamic: Origins of entrepreneurship and the evolution of industries.* Stanford, CA: Stanford University Press.

Singh, J. V., & Lumsden, C. J. (1990). Theory and research in organizational ecology. *Annual Review of Sociology, 16*, 161–95.

Sorensen, J. B., & Sorenson, O. (2003). From conception to birth: Opportunity perception and resource mobilization in entrepreneurship. In J. A. C. Baum & O. Sorenson (Eds.), *Advances in strategic management: Geography and strategy* (Vol. 20, pp. 89–117). Amsterdam: JAI Press.

Stinchcombe, A. (1965). Social structure and organizations. In J. March (Ed.), *Handbook of organizations* (pp. 142–193). Chicago: Rand McNally.

Chapter 12
Start-Up Activities and New Firm Characteristics

Tatiana S. Manolova, Candida G. Brush, and Linda F. Edelman

12.1 Introduction

A central activity in entrepreneurship is the creation of new organizations (Aldrich, 1999; Gartner, 1985; Low & Abramson, 1997). Organizations are defined as goal directed, boundary maintaining activity systems that emerge when entrepreneurs take the initiative to engage in founding activities (Gartner, 1985; McKelvey & Aldrich, 1983). While organization theory examines the development of exchange relationships (Stinchcombe, 1965), acquisition of legitimacy (Aldrich, 1999), and mobilization of resources (Scott, 1987) in existing or established organizations, there is considerably less research investigating the ways in which *new* organizations emerge or come into being (Aldrich, 1999; Gartner, 2001; McKelvey & Aldrich, 1983).

Organizational formation is a dynamic process in which activities such as obtaining resources, developing products, hiring employees, and seeking funds are undertaken at different times and in different orders (Gartner, 1985). Empirical studies on organizing activities have found that more organizing activities lead to survival (Carter, Gartner, & Reynolds, 1996; Lichtenstein, Dooley, & Lumpkin, 2006), that new firm survival is enhanced when legitimacy-building activities are engaged in before other types of organizing activities (Delmar & Shane, 2004), and that the concentration and timing of start-up activities lead to new firm formation (Lichtenstein, Carter, Dooley, & Gartner, 2004).

All of these studies, in some way, build on Katz and Gartner's (1988) well-regarded framework which explains organizational formation by outlining the properties of emerging organizations. Starting with the assumption that organizations emerge from the interaction between individuals and the environment, Katz and Gartner posit that four basic properties are central to organizational emergence. These properties are *intentionality*—the purposeful effort involved in organization emergence; *resources*—the tangible building blocks

---

T.S. Manolova (✉)
Bentley University, 175 Forest St., Waltham, MA 02452, USA
e-mail: tmanolova@bently.edu

of an organization; *boundary*—the creation of protected or formalized areas in which emergence occurs; and *exchange*—the crossing of boundaries to secure either inputs (e.g., resources) or outputs of the organization. The authors argue that all four dimensions characterize a "complete organization" (Katz & Gartner, p. 433).

Only a handful of studies have tested the four properties empirically (see Chrisman, 1999; Kundu & Katz, 2003; Reynolds & Miller, 1992; Reynolds & White, 1997, for partial tests of the theoretical framework). Recently, Bush, Manolova, and Edelman (2008) tested the framework in its entirety. They found that all four properties are necessary for firm survival. Our paper builds on Brush, Manolova, and Edelman (2008) by comparing the four properties of emerging organizations across two new venture formation data sets, the Panel Studies of Entrepreneurial Dynamics I (PSED I) and the Panel Studies of Entrepreneurial Dynamics II (PSED II). Building on Delmar and Shane (2004) who examined the timing of activities and the influence of legitimizing activities on survival, our work considers the extent to which the existence and completeness of organizational start-up properties influence the likelihood that the new venture will continue the organizing process.

12.2 Organizational Emergence and the Katz and Gartner (1988) Framework

Organizational emergence involves those activities and events before an organization becomes an organization. This is the period in the life cycle of an organization when it is "in-creation." Referred to as gestation (Reynolds & Miller, 1992), pre-launch (McMullan & Long, 1990), and birth or creation (Quinn & Cameron, 1983), this is the phase where nascent entrepreneur(s) undertakes purposeful actions to construct an organization based on his/her vision (Aldrich, 1999; Baron, 1998, 2000; Bird, 1988).

During emergence, the entrepreneur(s) brings together resources, and engages in activities which will eventually distinguish the business as an entity that is separate from the individual(s) who began the firm (Carter et al., 1996). Firm formation is a social process that occurs over time as entrepreneurs make connections to individuals and organizations, acquire resources outside the newly established boundaries of the firm, and engage critical stakeholders to commit to the concept of the new venture (Low & Abramson, 1997; Shook, Priem, & McGee, 2003). It is the "territory between pre-organization and the new organization" and is defined by four basic characteristics or properties, intentionality, resources, boundary, and exchange (Katz & Gartner, 1988, p. 429). Each of the four emergent properties is discussed below.

12.2.1 Intentionality

Intentionality is "an agent's seeking information that can be applied toward achieving the goal of creating a new organization" (Katz & Gartner, 1988, p. 431). Organizations are created by individual actors acting purposefully (Scott, 1987), and therefore it is the intentions of the entrepreneur(s) that lead to activities involved in creating an organization (Bird, 1988; Shook et al., 2003). There are several recent conceptual and empirical studies about entrepreneurial intentions (for a comprehensive review of the new venture cognition literature, see Forbes, 1999). For example, Kolvereid (1997) found support for the importance of entrepreneurial intentions to start-up success, and Krueger, Reilly, and Carsrud (2000) studied two models of entrepreneurial intentionality finding that the decision to start a business often preceded scanning for an opportunity.

12.2.2 Resources

Resources are the building blocks of an organization. They include human and financial capital, property, and equipment (Katz & Gartner, 1988, p. 432). Resources are the endowments that the entrepreneur brings to the start-up process, such as personal funds, time, and experience (Brush, Greene, & Hart, 2001). The creation of new organizations requires the "marshalling" or "harnessing" of resources (Scott, 1987, pp. 159–160). These resources are then used, combined, and coordinated into the production activities of the new organization (Penrose, 1957). Munificence or scarcity of resources in the environment, as well as availability and specificity can affect firm survival (Becker & Gordon, 1966; Pfeffer & Salancik, 1978). Studies examining the role of resources in new ventures find different resource configurations influence new firm success, that firm resources interact with firm strategies and that entrepreneurs "make do" with resources they have (Baker & Nelson, 2004; Brush et al., 2001; Chandler & Hanks, 1994).

12.2.3 Boundary

Boundary is the "barrier condition between the organization and its environment" (Katz & Gartner, 1988, p. 432). It is the "space" where the organization exerts some control over the resources in its environment. Boundaries can be determined by social relations, time, legal and formal contracts as well as physical and spatial considerations (Scott, 1987). As boundaries coalesce, routines and competencies can be developed within the firm that allows it to compete and cooperate (Aldrich, 1999). Boundaries of the organization are identified by transactions and information flows as the organization develops patterns of exchange (Katz & Kahn, 1978). Boundaries may be formal, as in legal form, or informal, as in the case when the entrepreneur makes a conscious decision to found the business (Learned, 1992). Early boundary defining actions include deciding on which people to hire; how jobs are to be structured, and how new members interact with each other as well as how they interact with others outside the organization (Aldrich, 1999). Studies examining boundaries of new organizations find that in the early phases of organizational evolution structures, practices and boundaries varied widely, but tended to be informal and fluid (Bhave, 1994). Chrisman (1999) found that boundaries were created by nascent ventures early in their formation.

12.2.4 Exchange

Exchange refers to cycles of transactions that occur within the organization (Katz & Gartner, 1988, p. 432). While exchange can occur within the boundaries of an organization, for fledgling firms, most exchanges occur across organizational boundaries. The pattern of exchange usually involves resources or inputs that are transformed into outputs (Katz & Kahn, 1978). Exchanges are inherent in the social contract that employees or participants in the organization agree to perform certain work in exchange for pay, rights, or privileges (Weick, 1979). Resources are acquired through an exchange process while goods and services are produced and exchanged across boundaries of the organization (Scott, 1987).

A significant number of studies have examined individual elements of the Katz and Gartner (1988) framework, or have used the framework as a conceptual anchor. However, only a few researchers have systematically studied the properties of emerging organizations. Reynolds and Miller (1992) examined the gestation (defined as conception to birth) process in new firms. They found significant variation in the length and patterns of gestation. For example, in their sample of over 3,000 established firms, they found that not all of the firms engaged in what they considered to be four key events of gestation: principal's commitment, initial hiring, initial financing, and initial sales. In addition, while the average gestation period was 3 years of less, some firms took as little as one month to start-up while others took up to 10 years.

Building on the Reynolds and Miller (1992) study, Carter et al. (1996) examined the start-up activities of a cross-section of 71 nascent entrepreneurs. They found that fledging firms can be classified according to three activity profiles: started a business; gave up; and still trying. They showed that firms can be distinguished based on the activities of the owner/founder and that the behaviors of successful nascent entrepreneurs are significantly different than the behaviors of those entreprencurs who were less successful. Chrisman (1999) examined three of the properties of emerging organizations in a study of Small Business Development Center clients. He found that 78% respondents created organizational boundaries in their new ventures; that stocks of resources varied by geographic region, and that intentions influenced the creation process. In a complete test of the Katz and Gartner (1988) framework, Kundu and Katz (2003) studied 47 born-international small and medium sized enterprises (SME's). They found that resources, and in particular the human capital of the owner, was a significant predictor of exchange (their dependent variable), which they defined as exports. Finally, Brush et al. (2008) tested the entire Katz and Gartner (1988) framework using 4 years of data from PSED I. They found the four properties lead to a greater likelihood of firm survival and that the more activities in which a firm engaged, the greater the likelihood that the firm would not disband. In sum, we see several studies that examine one or more of the elements of the properties framework but only Kundu and Katz (2003) and Brush, Edelman, and Manolova (forthcoming) have tested the framework in its entirety. In the next section we develop a set of hypotheses to test the basic tenets of the four properties framework across two data sets, PSED I and PSED II. Our goal is to add to the cumulative body of empirical evidence based on the Katz and Gartner (1988) framework, thus enhancing the reliability of the previous studies in this area.

12.3 Hypotheses

When nascent entrepreneurs gain control over resources and shape these into ongoing exchange relations, organizations coalesce as entities (Aldrich, 1999). Similarly, when intentions, resources, boundaries, and exchanges converge into a cohesive manner so that the entity is independent of its founders, the new venture will have a life of its own (Welbourne & Andrews, 1996). Katz and Gartner (1988) note that not all four properties will appear simultaneously in emerging organizations, but some aspects of these four properties must be present to identify the existence of an emerging new entity. Hence, the "four properties characterize a complete organization" (Katz & Gartner, p. 388). In other words, the four properties of an emerging organization do not exist independently. Therefore:

> Hypothesis 1: In both nascent entrepreneur cohorts (PSED I and PSED II), the four properties of emerging organizations are positively associated with the likelihood of continuing the organizing effort. More specifically:
> H1a: Intentionality is positively associated with the likelihood of continuing the organizing effort.
> H1b: Resources are positively associated with the likelihood of continuing the organizing effort.
> H1c: Boundary is positively associated with the likelihood of continuing the organizing effort.
> H1d: Exchange is positively associated with the likelihood of continuing the organizing effort.

Due to the ambiguity that is inherent in the start-up process, new organizations face significant selection pressure (Reynolds & White, 1997). To mitigate this, fledging firms seek to conform to standards and to formalize operations and produce outcomes as a means to gain both socio-political and cognitive legitimacy (Aldrich, 1999). Organizational survival depends on replicating existing roles and competencies and maintaining boundaries and exchanging resources across boundaries (Aldrich). This suggests more visible evidence of organizational dimensions (e.g., structure, resources, facilities, routines) would be better than less. Similarly, research shows that while there are many combinations of start-up activities, occurring in different orders, those nascent firms that carry out more activities are more likely to survive (Carter, Gartner, & Reynolds, 1996). Therefore, the more fully developed the resources, boundaries (or structural elements), exchange, and intentions, the greater the likelihood of survival in fledging firms. Formally:

> Hypothesis 2: In both nascent entrepreneur cohorts (PSED I and PSED II), nascent ventures that manifest greater completeness of the four properties are more likely to continue the organizing effort.

12.4 Methodology

12.4.1 Sample

The data utilized for this comparative study were drawn from both data sets (PSED I and PSED II) of the National Panel Study of Entrepreneurial Dynamics (PSED), a longitudinal study of nascent entrepreneurs started in 1998. Following the classification and weighting scheme developed by Reynolds and Curtin (2007), the initial sample used for the present study included recent active nascent entrepreneurs, who had not reported positive monthly cash flow before the first interview, were involved in more than three start-up activities, had two or more activities in a single 12-month period and had not initiated the nascent enterprise more than 10 years prior to the first interview (n = 747 for PSED I and n = 947 for PSED II). To ensure comparability across the two studies, we included data from the initial and the first follow-up interview for both data sets, which were available for 447 nascent ventures from the PSED I cohort (59.8%) and 774 nascent ventures from the PSED II cohort (81.7%). We eliminated the cases in which the first start-up activity took place 96 months or more prior to the first telephone interview. We felt that in those cases the time between initial activity and the expected outcome (a new business start-up) was unreasonably long (8 years or more) and that other spurious factors could confound our results (see also Brush et al., forthcoming). This resulted in the loss of 88 cases from the PSED I and 48 cases from the PSED II cohorts. We report descriptive statistics for the 359 cases retained in PSED I and the 726 cases retained in PSED II. Missing data on some of the properties and controls left usable sample sizes of n = 304 for PSED I and n = 637 for PSED II, respectively, for which we report the results from the Cox proportional hazard estimations.

12.4.2 Measures

Both nominal and continuous measures are utilized in this study.

12.4.2.1 Start-Up Status

Start-up status in PSED I was measured by a self-reported categorical variable, indicating whether or not the start-up effort was, at the time of the follow-up interviews, an operating business, still an active start-up, an inactive start-up, no longer being worked by anyone, or something else. More specifically, 111 nascent ventures reported that they had reached an operating status, 105 were an active start-up, 72 were inactive start-ups, 65 were no longer being worked by anyone, and 6 reported "something else." Following Delmar and Shane (2003, 2004), we coded the fourth category (no longer being worked on by anyone) as nascent venture disbanding (or failure).

In PSED II, the current status of the start-up was inferred by several items in the follow-up interview schedule (Reynolds & Curtin, 2007). We used a summary variable (interviewer checkpoint), which assessed whether a new firm had emerged (100 cases), the start-up was still active (456 cases), or the nascent entrepreneur had quit (170 cases). We coded the third category (quit) as nascent venture disbanding (or failure).

12.4.2.2 Properties of Emerging Organizations

We explored the four properties of emerging organizations: intentionality, resources, boundary, and exchange, following the definitions provided by Katz and Gartner (1988, pp. 431–433), and used expert opinions to classify the founding activities into the four properties of emerging organizations (see also Brush et al., forthcoming). The data on emerging organizations' properties came from PSED data sets' respective sections on founding activities. PSED I includes questions on 26 founding activities (Carter, Gartner, & Reynolds, 2004), while PSED II includes questions on 34 founding activities (Reynolds & Curtin, 2007). Of these, 22 are utilized in both projects. We did not include the question asking about attainment of positive cash flow, because this question was also used as a screening question, and retained the data on the remaining 21 founding activities in our analysis. Twenty of the activities were measured by self-reported dichotomous variables indicating whether or not nascent entrepreneurs had engaged in that particular activity prior to, or at the time of, the initial and the subsequent phone interviews. One of the activities—new product development—was measured using a four-point ordinal scale. In addition, nascent entrepreneurs who indicated that they had engaged in a particular activity were asked to indicate in which year and in which month they first engaged in the activity. We combined responses from the initial and follow-up waves of phone interviews to track whether or not nascent entrepreneurs had engaged in a founding activity over the entire observation period available at the time of the respective follow-up interview, and, if they did, in which year/month work on that particular activity began.

Nascent entrepreneurs were also asked whether or not they had spent a long time thinking about the new venture, or if the idea came suddenly. Since over 99% of the respondents in both cohorts reported they had thought about the new venture, we excluded this variable from our analysis of emerging organizations' properties, as we felt the lack of variability would unduly confound the effect of intentionality on the continuation of the organizing effort. However, we did retain the time nascent entrepreneurs first thought of their venture and used the time stamp to determine the origin of the event history analysis time scale.

12.4.2.3 Intentionality

To measure intentionality we followed Katz and Gartner's (1988) identification of purposeful actions for seeking information and taking action to start the venture. It was measured by four binary variables. Nascent entrepreneurs were asked to report whether or not they had developed a business plan, identified the business opportunity, developed financial statements, or started working full-time for the nascent venture.

12.4.2.4 Resources

Resources are the building blocks of an organization. They include human and financial capital, building, and equipment (Katz & Gartner, 1988). Resources were measured by seven dichotomous and one ordinal variable. The seven dichotomous variables indicated whether or not nascent entrepreneurs had applied for a patent, acquired raw materials, acquired equipment, invested their own money,[1] asked for funds, obtained credit from suppliers, or hired employees. In addition, the level of new product development was measured by an ordinal variable, ranging from 0 (no work done) to 3 (product or service ready for sale).

12.4.2.5 Boundary

Boundary is the "barrier condition between the organization and its environment" (Katz & Gartner, 1988, p. 432). Boundary was measured by using four self-reported binary measures, indicating whether or not nascent entrepreneurs had opened a separate bank account for the new venture, applied for a phone listing[2] or a Dun & Bradstreet listing, or filed an income tax for their business.

12.4.2.6 Exchange

Exchange refers to cycles of transactions that occur within an organization (Katz & Gartner, 1988, p. 432). Exchange was measured by four dichotomous variables. Nascent entrepreneurs were asked to report whether or not they had started marketing or promotional efforts, received revenues from sales, and paid unemployment insurance taxes or federal social security (FICA) taxes.

12.4.2.7 Property Completeness

Property completeness was measured by summing up the counts across the four categories, ranging from 0 (no indication of any property of an emerging organization) to 20 (all 20 elements). We added new product development to the property completeness score if the nascent entrepreneur reported that some work had been initiated.

12.4.2.8 Control Variables

We controlled for entrepreneur and industry effects.[3] To account for the effect of nascent entrepreneur's demographic characteristics and human capital, we included controls for gender, age, education, and work experience. We also introduced four industry dummies, which measured industry effects relative to the baseline category of consumer services (the most populous business segment). Another aspect of the industry environment we controlled for was the level of competition. In the PSED I analysis, we measured industry competitiveness with an ordinal scale, where $0 =$ expect no competition, $1 =$ expect low competition, $2 =$ expect moderate competition, and $3 =$ expect strong competition. In the PSED II analysis, we measured industry competitiveness with an ordinal scale, where $0 =$ no other business offering the same products or services to potential customers, $1 =$ few competitors, and $2 =$ many competitors.

12.5 Results

12.5.1 Descriptive Statistics

The PSED I and PSED II cohorts were different in gender and race composition because PSED I included oversamples of women and minorities.[4] The two cohorts were similar in other aspects. The nascent entrepreneurs in the PSED II sample were slightly older (mean age 44.77 years compared to 40.50 years in PSED I) and with longer work experience (21.92 years versus 18.06 years, respectively). Fifty-two percent of both samples had at least some college education. The nascent entrepreneurs contemplated entry into five industrial sectors, with the most popular sector being consumer services (51.8% of the nascent entrepreneurial ventures in PSED I and 58.8% of the nascent entrepreneurial ventures in PSED II). Eighteen percent of the nascent businesses in PSED I and 23.4% of the nascent ventures in PSED II had disbanded during the time of the study.

The nascent businesses varied widely in the types of elements and completeness of emerging organizations' properties, with counts in the "Intentionality" and "Resources" categories generally higher than the counts in the "Boundary" and "Exchange" categories. Thus, 91.3% of the nascent entrepreneurs in the PSED I cohort had identified the business opportunity and 71.6% of the nascent entrepreneurs in PSED II had prepared a business plan, but 1 in 12 had applied for a Dun & Bradstreet listing,[5] and 1 in 8 had paid insurance taxes. Over 60% of the nascent ventures in both samples had generated revenues from sales during the period of the study. Overall, nascent ventures in both cohorts had accumulated slightly less than half of the 20 property items we tracked in this study. Of note, however, is that nascent entrepreneurs in the PSED I cohort reported generally higher counts of start-up activities compared to the PSED II cohort. Thus, 91.3% of the PSED I cohort reported identifying a business opportunity, compared to 67.9% of the PSED II cohort, and 81.1% reported buying raw materials, compared to 69.9% of the PSED II cohort. On the other hand, 65.9% of the PSED II cohort reported a separate phone/internet listing of their nascent venture, compared to only 28.3% of the PSED I cohort.

Tables 12.1 and 12.2 present the descriptive statistics for PSED I and PSED II, respectively.

12.5.2 Analytical Procedure

To estimate a model of factors that influence the hazard (or risk) of a nascent venture disbanding, we used the statistical technique of failure time analysis; more popularly known as an event history approach. By taking into consideration both the occurrence and the timing of an event while simultaneously estimating the effects of exogenous factors, event history analyses offers two advantages over multiple regression for the study of longitudinal data. First, it handles censored data, or events that the subjects under observation have not experienced before the end of the observation period. Over 75% of the nascent ventures in the PSED II sample and over 80% of the nascent ventures in the PSED I sample were continuing the organizing effort at the end of the study, but could experience disbanding at some point in the future. Previous research shows that such a large number of censored cases can produce substantially biased estimates (Tuma & Hannan, 1978; Vermunt, 1996). Second, event history analysis effectively handles life-cycle dependent variable measures. The

12 Start-Up Activities and New Firm Characteristics

Table 12.1 Descriptive statistics: PSED I

	N	Min	Max	Mean	SD	Yes	Percent
Dependent variables							
Continue organizing	359	1.00	5.00	2.30	1.13		
Failure time	359	13.00	110.00	43.37	24.01		
Independent variables							
Intentionality							
Prepared business plan	359	0.00	1.00	0.61	0.48	273	60.8
Identified opportunity	359	0.00	1.00	0.91	0.28	410	91.3
Prepared financials	356	0.00	1.00	0.52	0.50	229	51.3
Started working full-time	359	0.00	1.00	0.36	0.48	173	38.5
Resources							
Applied for a patent	357	0.00	1.00	0.14	0.35	70	15.6
Bought raw materials	359	0.00	1.00	0.79	0.40	364	81.1
Bought equipment	358	0.00	1.00	0.58	0.49	273	60.8
Invested money	359	0.00	1.00	0.91	0.28	414	92.2
Asked for funds	358	0.00	1.00	0.30	0.45	137	30.5
Applied for a credit	341	0.00	1.00	0.48	0.50	213	47.4
Hired employees	359	0.00	1.00	0.23	0.42	108	24.1
Level of new product development	356	0.00	3.00	2.22	1.08		
Boundary							
Opened bank account	354	0.00	1.00	0.50	0.50	219	48.8
Applied for a phone listing	359	0.00	1.00	0.29	0.45	127	28.3
Applied for a Dun & Bradstreet listing	342	0.00	1.00	0.07	0.26	32	7.1
Filed income tax	359	0.00	1.00	0.32	0.47	147	32.7
Exchange							
Started marketing efforts	359	0.00	1.00	0.70	0.45	325	72.4
Made sale	359	0.00	1.00	0.60	0.48	277	61.7
Paid social security taxes	357	0.00	1.00	0.20	0.40	94	20.9
Paid insurance taxes	357	0.00	1.00	0.12	0.33	59	13.1
Property completeness	313	0	19	9.62	4.48		
Controls							
Agriculture and mining	353	0.00	1.00	0.03	0.18	17	3.8
Transportation	353	0.00	1.00	0.01	0.11	5	1.1
Manufacturing	353	0.00	1.00	0.07	0.26	41	9.1
Business services	353	0.00	1.00	0.36	0.48	148	33.0
Gender: male	359	0.00	1.00	0.42	0.49	199	44.3
Age	358	18.00	74.00	40.50	10.87		
Education	358	0.00	9.00	4.77	1.96		
Years work experience	357	0.00	53.00	18.06	10.83		
Level of competition	357	0.00	3.00	1.91	0.80		

*Frequencies: Binary variables only.

Table 12.2 Descriptive statistics: PSED II

	N	Min	Max	Mean	SD	Frequencies* Yes	Frequencies* Percent
Dependent variables							
Continue organizing	726	1	3	2.10	0.60		
Failure time	726	12.00	108.00	36.96	21.93		
Independent variables							
Intentionality							
Prepared business plan	726	0.00	1.00	0.72	0.44	555	71.6
Identified opportunity	726	0.00	1.00	0.68	0.46	526	67.9
Prepared financials	726	0.00	1.00	0.45	0.49	349	45.0
Started working full-time	726	0.00	1.00	0.29	0.45	235	30.3
Resources							
Applied for a patent	726	0.00	1.00	0.09	0.28	73	9.4
Bought raw materials	726	0.00	1.00	0.69	0.46	542	69.9
Bought equipment	726	0.00	1.00	0.61	0.48	477	61.5
Invested money	726	0.00	1.00	0.82	0.37	642	82.8
Asked for funds	726	0.00	1.00	0.23	0.42	176	22.7
Applied for a credit	726	0.00	1.00	0.35	0.48	279	36.0
Hired employees	726	0.00	1.00	0.16	0.36	123	15.9
Level of new product development	670	0.00	3.00	2.19	1.02		
Boundary							
Opened bank account	719	0.00	1.00	0.47	0.49	368	47.5
Applied for a phone listing	726	0.00	1.00	0.65	0.47	511	65.9
Applied for a Dun & Bradstreet listing	720	0.00	1.00	0.07	0.26	62	8.0
Filed income tax	726	0.00	1.00	0.40	0.49	322	41.5
Exchange							
Started marketing efforts	726	0.00	1.00	0.61	0.48	476	61.4
Made sale	726	0.00	1.00	0.65	0.47	510	65.8
Paid social security taxes	723	0.00	1.00	0.23	0.42	185	23.9
Paid insurance taxes	726	0.00	1.00	0.11	0.31	88	11.4
Property completeness	657	1.00	20.00	9.15	3.73		
Controls							
Agriculture and mining	725	0.00	1.00	0.05	0.22	41	5.3
Transportation	725	0.00	1.00	0.03	0.19	32	4.1
Manufacturing	725	0.00	1.00	0.10	0.30	85	11.0
Business services	725	0.00	1.00	0.21	0.41	168	21.7
Gender: male	726	0.00	1.00	0.62	0.48	480	61.9
Age	722	18.00	82.00	44.77	12.35		
Education	726	2.00	10.00	5.79	2.08		
Years work experience	719	0.00	56.00	21.92	12.21		
Level of competition	726	0.00	2.00	2.17	0.694		

* Binary variables only.

endogenous variable or "time to event" is specified not in real time, but in time forgone since a triggering event and is often referred to as "waiting", "failure", or "spell" time. In our study, the nascent venture's disbanding is life-cycle dependent, and so is more meaningfully compared in terms of the year and month in the life of the nascent venture than in historical calendar time.

Following similar empirical research (Khavul, 2000; Romanelli, 1989), this study uses the Cox proportional hazards model to estimate the likelihood of an event occurring at any point in the life of the nascent venture, given that the event has not occurred until that point. Compared to parametric models, the semi-parametric Cox proportional hazard model does not require the researcher to specify a baseline relationship between time and failure (event) rates (Allison, 1984), which is an important advantage, given the early stage of theoretical development on pre-founding failure rates (Amburgey & Rao, 1996). Analyses were performed using the Cox Regression Survival procedure in STATA, implementing the Breslow method for ties. Sampling weights were introduced to correct for sampling design (Reynolds & Curtin, 2007).

The general form of the simple one predictor Cox regression is as follows: $h(t) = [h_o(t)] e^{(BX)}$, where X is the independent variable (covariate), B is the regression coefficient and t indicates the time to the event occurring. Here $h_o(t)$ is the baseline hazard function which estimates the expected risk of an event occurring without the presence of the covariate; while $e^{(BX)}$ is the hazard ratio which indicates the shift of the baseline function, or the increase or decrease in the risk of the event occurring when the covariate is included. Individual item HR (Hazard Ratios) report exponentiated coefficients e^b, rather than coefficients b. Computing $100*[e^b-1]$ gives the percentage change in the hazard with each unit change in the explanatory variable. For dichotomous variables, the computation provides the relative hazard for the groups corresponding to values of the dummy variable (Allison, 1984). In addition, Wald's χ^2 statistic tests the omnibus null hypothesis that all regression coefficients are equal to zero. Following Delmar and Shane (2003, 2004), we chose the time of initiation of the first founding activity as the origin of our time scale. The "spell" time is the number of months elapsed from the initiation of the first founding activity to the time of nascent venture disbanding. For the right-censored firms (e.g., those that continued their organizing effort at the end of the observation period), we recorded the "waiting period" or the minimum time for which we know no event occurred. The waiting period, or "failure time," "qualified by the knowledge of whether or not a firm experienced an event" became the dependent variable in the failure time analysis (Schoonhoven, Eisenhardt, & Lyman, 1990, p. 195).

12.5.3 Hypothesis Testing

Hypothesis one predicted that each of the four properties of nascent ventures affected the likelihood of continuing the organizing effort. As the interest here is in the joint significance of the items under each of the property categories, we specified four chi-square (χ^2) tests, each of which checked the probability that the regression coefficients under the corresponding property category are equal to zero (Allison, 1984).

The results from the testing of Hypothesis one are presented in Table 12.3. They suggest that the joint effect of the four properties vary between the two cohorts. Thus, in the PSED I cohort, intentionality does not affect the likelihood of continuing the organizing effort, whereas in the PSED II cohort, it is boundaries that do not appear to affect the likelihood of continuing the organizing effort.

Table 12.3 Cox regression estimates on likelihood of nascent venture disbanding: joint effects of property categories

Variable	PSED I ($n = 304$) Hazard ratio	S.E.	PSED II ($n = 637$) Hazard ratio	S.E.
Controls				
Agriculture and mining	2.995	2.828	**0.193** *	0.136
Transportation	3.683	4.275	0.875	0.318
Manufacturing	0.900	0.627	0.605	0.220
Business services	1.669	0.613	**0.596**†	0.184
Gender: male	1.78	0.748	0.705	0.155
Age	0.988	0.025	**0.972** *	0.013
Education	0.926	0.081	0.937	0.055
Years work experience	1.026	0.025	1.022 †	0.013
Level of competition	1.33	0.355	**1.632** ***	0.233
Intentionality				
Prepared business plan	1.136	0.446	0.843	0.198
Identified opportunity	1.012	0.738	0.907	0.188
Prepared financials	**0.376** *	0.175	**1.650** *	0.375
Started working full-time	0.614	0.242	**0.498** **	0.125
Resources				
Applied for a patent	1.644	0.746	0.766	0.275
Bought raw materials	**0.348** **	0.134	1.035	0.237
Bought equipment	1.204	0.524	0.742	0.162
Invested money	0.850	0.523	0.812	0.205
Asked for funds	**0.384** *	0.181	0.990	0.221
Applied for a credit	0.821	0.313	**0.520** **	0.125
Hired employees	0.608	0.324	1.245	0.359
Level of new product development	1.221	0.196	0.989	0.113
Boundary				
Opened bank account	1.025	0.473	1.334	0.340
Applied for a phone listing	0.627	0.307	0.720	0.171
Applied for a Dun & Bradstreet listing	1.336	1.335	1.222	0.547
Filed income tax	**0.129** **	0.087	**0.566** *	0.150

12 Start-Up Activities and New Firm Characteristics

Table 12.3 (continued)

Variable	PSED I ($n = 304$) Hazard ratio	S.E.	PSED II ($n = 637$) Hazard ratio	S.E.
Exchange				
Started marketing efforts	**0.416 ***	0.152	1.474	0.386
Made sale	0.971	0.471	**0.520 ***	0.145
Paid social security taxes	**4.590 ***	3.025	0.662	0.363
Paid insurance taxes	3.010	2.091	2.002	1.202
Regression function				
Log pseudo likelihood	−235.382		−845.201	
Wald χ^2 (df = 29)	**76.87*****		**118.34 *****	
Joint Effects of Significance	$\chi^2 (df)$			
Intentionality	5.00 (4)		**12.41 (4) ***	
Resources	**18.81 (8) ****		**16.46 (8) ***	
Boundaries	**11.39 (4) ***		6.27 (4)	
Exchange	**17.87 (4) ****		**10.28 (4) ***	

† significant at $p < 0.1$; * significant at $p < 0.05$; ** significant at $p < 0.01$; *** significant at $p < 0.001$.

Hypothesis two predicted that property completeness will be positively associated with the continuation of the organizing effort. As results presented in Table 12.4 show, each additional activity the nascent venture initiates towards the completion of the four properties decreases the hazard of new venture disbanding in any given month the nascent venture has not yet been disbanded by 17.3% for nascent ventures in PSED I and 11.4% for nascent ventures in PSED II. This result lends strong support for Hypothesis two.

In sum, this study shows strong support for the Katz and Gartner (1988) framework in that the more complete the properties, the more likely organizing efforts will continue. At the same time, empirical tests reveal significant variations in the types of activities nascent entrepreneurs undertake both within, and between the two cohorts. In addition, the joint effects of the four properties differ across the two samples. While resource acquisition and product-market activities significantly affected the likelihood of nascent venture disbanding, the effect of intentionality or boundaries was not as ubiquitous. The following section discusses our results.

12.6 Discussion

The objective of this inquiry is to validate the Katz and Gartner (1988) framework by comparing the properties of emerging organizations across two data sets, PSED I and PSED II. Using longitudinal data on nascent organizations we empirically tested the four properties of emerging organizations—intentionality, resources, boundary, and exchange—and their effect on the

Table 12.4 Cox regression estimates on likelihood of nascent venture disbanding: effect of property completeness

Variable	PSED I (n = 304) Hazard ratio	S.E.	PSED II (n = 634) Hazard ratio	S.E.
Controls				
Agriculture and mining	1.814	1.626	**0.202 ***	0.151
Transportation	2.273	2.675	0.957	0.383
Manufacturing	1.052	0.536	0.686	0.224
Business services	1.303	0.426	0.822	0.215
Gender: male	1.595	0.520	0.760	0.153
Age	0.981	0.022	**0.975**†	0.012
Education	0.993	0.074	0.969	0.051
Years work experience	1.021	0.021	1.014	0.012
Level of competition	1.121	0.257	**1.536 *****	0.203
Property completeness	**0.823*****	0.042	**0.886 *****	0.229
Regression function				
Log pseudo likelihood	−254.112		−873.992	
Wald χ^2(df = 10)	**20.11***		**42.70 *****	

† significant at $p < 0.1$, * significant at $p < 0.05$, ** significant at $p < 0.01$, *** significant at $p < 0.001$.

likelihood of continued organizing (Katz & Gartner). We then tested for property completeness, following the logic that firms which engage in a greater number of start-up activities are less likely to fail (Carteret al., 1996). In so doing we have provided empirical verification to the original Katz and Gartner framework.

12.6.1 All Properties Are Necessary for Continuing the Organizing Effort

In the original Katz and Gartner (1988) framework, the authors argue that all four properties are necessary for continuing the organizing effort. The findings from Brush et al. (forthcoming) using 4 years of longitudinal data from PSED I are consistent with the original framework. However, in our empirical test of this framework using 2 years of data we found that for PSED I, only three out of the four properties were significant: resources, boundaries, and exchange, and that "intentions" were not significant. When we replicated the test on the data from PSED II, we again found that only three of the four properties were significant: resources, exchange and intentions, and that "boundary" was not significant.

To understand our findings, we compared the differences between resources and exchange, which are the properties that were significant across both data sets, with intentions and boundaries, each of which was not significant in one of the two data sets. It was clear to us that the properties resources and exchange were operationalized as tangible activities (e.g., bought raw materials or invested money for resources and made sale or paid social security taxes for exchange) in both PSED I and PSED II. In addition, in our tests, we only drew on 2 years of organizing data, hence not only are these tangible activities, but they are activities that are likely to have occurred at the beginning of the new venture creation process.

This differs from intentionality and boundaries which were found to be not significant in PSED I and then PSED II, respectively. While linear logic suggests that the nascent entrepreneur intends to start a business before actually creating the new venture (Hanks, Watson, Jensen & Chandler, 1994) one of the interesting findings from PSED I is that this linear view of organizational creation was not empirically validated (Brush et al., forthcoming). Instead of finding that intentions precede the other properties, Brush et al. (forthcoming) found that intentionality and the other three properties are interrelated, and that intentionality is dependent on the other properties.

Our nonsignificant finding with respect to boundaries may be a function of the short time period in our longitudinal data sets. Many nascent entrepreneurs cannot achieve the level of control necessary to gain mastery over organizational boundaries (Aldrich, 1999). Empirical evidence suggests that only about one half of all founders succeed in creating an operating entity (Duncan & Handler, 1994) and that around one half of all fledgling entrepreneurs are still trying after 18 months (Reynolds & White, 1997). Therefore, it may be that the inconsistency between our findings and those of the original tenets of the Katz and Gartner (1988) framework is a function of our data. Given that Brush et al. (forthcoming) found support for boundaries in their study of properties of emerging organizations using four years of PSED I data, it seems likely that a longitudinal study which includes more years may result in different findings.

12.6.2 Property Completeness

The second finding from this inquiry is that firms which engage in more activities are less likely to disband. This finding is consistent with Carter et al. (1996) as well as with Brush et al. (forthcoming). In both the PSED I and the PSED II data sets, firms which engaged in more activities were more likely to continue the organizing effort. This suggests that entrepreneurs who are actively engaged in the process of starting the venture are likely to end up with a viable new venture in the short run.

12.7 Implications and Conclusions

Using longitudinal data on nascent entrepreneurs, this paper empirically tests the effects of the four properties of emerging organizations—intentionality, resources, boundary, and exchange, as identified by Katz and Gartner (1988), on the likelihood of continued organizing across two data sets, PSED I and PSED II. Our findings suggest that all four properties are necessary for firm survival in the short term and that entrepreneurs who engage in a larger number of start-up activities are more likely to continue the organizing effort in the short term.

We do note a few limitations to our study. In particular, the choice of the underlying categories of the dependent variable is subject to debate. For example, Gartner and Carter (2003) consider four start-up status categories: "operating", "still trying", "currently inactive", and "disbanded"; Lichtenstein et al. (2004) collapse the "currently inactive" and "disbanded" categories into one and consider three categories: "succeeded", "ongoing", and "failed"; Carter at al. (2004) consider "operating" and "still active" versus the other categories. As such, some might argue that a different categorization of groups might be more appropriate. However, we felt that more consistency would be achieved by building on research (Delmar & Shane, 2003, 2004) that analyzed many of the same variables that we used.

Limitations aside, this paper empirically examines the well-regarded Katz and Gartner (1988) properties of emerging organizations' model of organizational emergence. Our findings from two longitudinal nascent entrepreneur data sets, PSED I and PSED II, provide validity for the original model. In addition, our findings lend strong support to the dynamic nature of new venture emergence by validating previous research which suggests that the more activities in which the entrepreneur is engaged, the more likely the continuation of the organizing effort. Organizational emergence plays a central role in the field of entrepreneurship, and empirically verifying the well-regarded Katz and Gartner framework adds to our understanding of this important process.

Notes

1. The item was recoded from a similar, but not identical, question in PSED II.
2. Phone or internet in PSED II.
3. In a related study on emerging organization properties (Brush et al., forthcoming), we also controlled for the legal form and intended strategies of the nascent venture. Because of low response rates in PSED II, we had to exclude those controls from our comparative analysis.
4. Case weights were developed to adjust for the oversampling of women and minorities. For more information on the PSED I case weights, see Gartner, Shaver, Carter, and Reynolds (2004) Appendices B and C.
5. While Dun & Bradstreet may send out a request for information to new ventures, often new firms are added to the data base without any direct action on their part. Therefore, the percentage of new ventures listed on Dun and Bradstreet may be significantly different from the number of firms that applied for a listing.

References

Aldrich, H. (1999). *Organizations evolving*. Thousand Oaks, CA: Sage.

Allison, P. D. (1984). *Event history analysis, regression analysis for longitudinal event data*. Beverly Hills, CA: Sage.

Amburgey, T. L., & Rao, H. (1996). Organizational ecology: Past, present, and future. *Academy of Management Journal, 39*(5), 1265–1286.

Baker, T., & Nelson, R. (2004, August). *Making do with what's at hand: Entrepreneurial bricolage*. Paper presented at the Academy of Management Meetings, New Orleans, LA.

Baron, R. (1998). Cognitive mechanisms in entrepreneurship: Why and when entrepreneurs think differently than other people. *Journal of Business Venturing, 13*(2), 275–294.

Baron, R. (2000). Counterfactual thinking and venture formation: The potential effects of thinking about "What might have been." *Journal of Business Venturing, 15*(1), 79–91.

Becker, S. W., & Gordon, G. (1966). An entrepreneurial theory of formal organizations part I: Patterns of formal organizations. *Administrative Science Quarterly, 11*(3), 315–344.

Bhave, M. (1994). A process model of entrepreneurial venture creation. *Journal of Business Venturing, 9*(3), 233–242.

Bird, B. J. (1988). Implementing entrepreneurial ideas: The case for intention. *Academy of Management Review, 13*(3), 442–453.

Brush, C. G., Edelman, L. F., & Manolova, T. S. (2008). The effects of initial location, aspirations, and resources on likelihood of first sale in nascent firms. *Journal of Small Business Management, 46*(2), 159–182.

Brush, C. G., Green, P.G., & Hart, M. M. (2001). From initial idea to unique advantage: The entreprenurial challenge of constructing a resource base.. *Academy of Management Executive 15*(1).

Brush, C. G., Manolova, T. S., & Edelman, L. F. (2008). Properties of emerging organizations: An empirical test. *Journal of Business Venturing, 23*(5), 547–566.

Carter, N. M., Gartner, W. B., & Reynolds, P. D. (1996). Exploring start-up event sequences. *Journal of Business Venturing, 11*(3), 151–166.

Carter, N. M., Gartner, W. B., & Reynolds, P. D. (2004). Firm founding. In W. B. Gartner, K. G. Shaver, N. M. Carter, & P. D. Reynolds (Eds.), *The handbook of entrepreneurial dynamics: The process of organization creation* (pp. 311–323). Newbury Park, CA: Sage Series.

Chandler, G., & Hanks, S. (1994). Market attractiveness, resource-based capabilities, venture strategies and venture performance. *Journal of Business Venturing, 9*(4), 331–349.

Chrisman, J. (1999). The influence of outsider-generated knowledge resources on venture creation. *Journal of Small Business Management, 37*(4), 42–58.

Delmar, F., & Shane, S. (2003). Does business planning facilitate the development of new ventures? *Strategic Management Journal, 24*(12), 1165–1185.

Delmar, F., & Shane, S. (2004). Legitimizing first: Organizing activities and the survival of new ventures. *Journal of Business Venturing, 19*(3), 385–410.

Duncan, J. W., & Handler, D. P. (1994). The misunderstood rule of small business. *Business Economics, 29*(3), 1–6.

Forbes, D. (1999). Cognitive approaches to new venture creation. *International Journal of Management Review, 1*(4), 415–439.

Gartner, W. B. (1985). A conceptual framework for describing the phenomenon of new venture creation. *Academy of Management Review, 10*(4), 696–706.

Gartner, W. B. (2001). Is there an elephant in entrepreneurship: Blind assumptions in theory development. *Entrepreneurship Theory and Practice, 25*(4), 57–80.

Gartner, W. B., & Carter, N. M. (2003, August). *Still trying after all these years: Nascent entrepreneur "semi-survivor" bias in the Panel Study of Entrepreneurial Dynamics*. Paper presented at the Academy of Management Meetings, Seattle, WA.

Gartner, W. B., Shaver, K. G., Carter, N. M., & Reynolds, P. D. (Eds.) (2004). *Handbook of entrepreneurial dynamics: The process of organization creation.* Newbury Park, CA: Sage.

Hanks, S., Watson, C., Jensen, E., & Chandler, G. (1994). Tightening the life cycle construct: A taxonomic study of growth stage configurations in high technology-organizations. *Entrepreneurship Theory and Practice, 18*(2), 5–29.

Katz, D., & Kahn, R. (1978). *The social psychology of organizations.* New York: Wiley.

Katz, J., & Gartner, W. B. (1988). Properties of emerging organizations. *Academy of Management Review, 13*(3), 429–441.

Khavul, S. (2000). *Money and knowledge: Sources of seed capital and the performance of high-technology start-ups.* Unpublished doctoral dissertation, Boston University, Boston, MA.

Kolvereid, L. (1997). Organizational employment versus self-employment: Reasons for career choice intentions. *Entrepreneurship Theory and Practice, 20*, 23–31.

Krueger, N. F., Reilly, M. D., & Carsrud, A. L. (2000). Competing models of entrepreneurial intentions. *Journal of Business Venturing, 15*(5/6), 411–432.

Kundu, S. K., & Katz, J. (2003). Born-international SME's: Bi-level impacts of resources and intentions. *Small Business Economics, 20*(1), 25–47.

Learned, K. (1992). What happened before the organization? A model of organization formation. *Entrepreneurship Theory and Practice, 17*(1), 39–48.

Lichtenstein, B. B., Carter, N. M., Dooley, K., & Gartner, W. B. (2004, June). Exploring the temporal dynamics of organizational emergence. Paper presented at the Babson Entrepreneurship Research Conference, Glasgow, Scotland.

Lichtenstein, B. B., Dooley, K. J., & Lumpkin, G. T. (2006). Measuring emergence in the dynamics of new venture creation. *Journal of Business Venturing, 21*(2), 153–175.

Low, M., & Abramson, M. (1997). Movements, bandwagons, and clones: Industry evolution and the entrepreneurial process. *Journal of Business Venturing, 12*(6), 435–458.

McKelvey, W., & Aldrich, H. (1983). Populations, natural selection and applied organizational science. *Administrative Science Quarterly, 28*(1), 101–128.

McMullan, W. E., & Long, W. (1990). *Developing new ventures.* Orlando, FL: Harcourt Brace Jovanovich.

Penrose, E. T. (1957). *The theory of growth of the firm.* New York: Wiley and Sons.

Pfeffer, J., & Salancik, G. R. (1978). *The external control of organizations.* New York: Harper Row.

Quinn, R. E., & Cameron, K. (1983). Organizational life cycles and shifting criteria of effectiveness: Some preliminary evidence. *Management Science, 29*(1), 33–51.

Reynolds, P. D., & Curtin, R. T. (2007). *Business creation in the United States in 2006: Panel study of entrepreneurial dynamics II.* Hanover, MA: now Publishers, Inc.

Reynolds, P. D., & Miller, B. (1992). New firm gestation: Conception, birth and implications for research. *Journal of Business Venturing, 7*(5), 405–417.

Reynolds, P.D., & White, S. B. (1997). *The entrepreneurial process: Economic growth, men, women, and minorities.* Westport, CT: Quorum.

Romanelli, E. (1989). Environments and strategies of organization start-up: Effects on early survival. *Administrative Science Quarterly, 34*(3), 369–387.

Schoonhoven, C. B., Eisenhardt, K., & Lyman, K. (1990). Speeding products to market: Waiting time to first product introduction in new firms. *Administrative Science Quarterly, 35*(1), 177–207.

Scott, R. (1987). *Organizations: Rational, natural and open systems* (2nd ed.). Englewood Cliffs, NJ: Prentice Hall.

Shook, C. L., Priem, R. L., & McGee, J. E. (2003). Venture creation and the enterprising individual: A review and synthesis. *Journal of Management, 29*(3), 379–399.

Stinchcombe, A. L. (1965). Social structure and organizations. In J. G. March (Ed.), *Handbook of organizations* (pp. 142–193). Chicago: Rand McNally.

Tuma, N. B., & Hannan, M. T. (1978). Approaches to the censoring problem in analysis of event histories. In K. F. Schuessler (Ed.), *Sociological methodology.* San Francisco: Jossey-Bass.

Vermunt, J. K. (1996). *Log-linear event history analysis: A general approach with missing data, latent variables, and unobserved heterogeneity.* Tilburg, The Netherlands: Tilburg University Press.

Weick, K. (1979). *The social psychology of organizing.* Reading, MA: Addison Wesley.

Welbourne, T. M., & Andrews, A. O. (1996). Predicting the performance of initial public offerings: Should human resource management be in the equation? *Academy of Management Journal, 39*(4): 891–919.

Part V
Cross-Study Comparisons

Chapter 13
PSED II and the Comprehensive Australian Study of Entrepreneurial Emergence [CAUSEE]

Per Davidsson and Paul D. Reynolds

13.1 Introduction

Hundreds of millions are involved in business creation in every part of the world. The Global Entrepreneurship Monitor research program makes clear that participation varies dramatically, from 2/100 adults to over 40/100; most countries have a substantial number of individuals involved (Bosma, Jones, Autio, & Levie, 2008). But individuals pursue firm creation with a wide variation in personal characteristics, social and family contexts, educational and work experiences, support from community and social networks, economic and political structures as well as cultural milieu.

This leads immediately to several major questions:

1. Are there national differences in the tendency of individuals to get involved in business creation?
2. Does the national context affect the way in which individuals go about creating a new firm?
3. Does the national context affect the proportion of start-ups that become operational young businesses?

These are not, however, issues of a purely academic interest.

In some countries, many may enter the firm creation process as nascent entrepreneurs but a relatively small proportion may complete the process with an operating new firm. In other countries, a smaller proportion may elect to pursue new firm creation, but a higher proportion may succeed with a new firm. While the aggregate social cost, total time and funds invested in the start-up efforts, may be similar in the two cases, more of these costs will be borne by those that leave the process before they become owners of new businesses in the first situation. In the second situation, a larger proportion of the nascent

---

P. Davidsson (✉)
Faculty of Business, Queensland University Of Technology, GPO Box 2434, Brisbane Qld 4001, Australia
e-mail: per.davidsson@qut.edu.au

entrepreneurs who bear the costs of business creation are successful in creating a new business; the same individuals are bearing the costs and receiving the benefits.

The first of these questions has been the focus of a major cross-national comparison, the Global Entrepreneurship Monitor program, and some results will be discussed below. Answers to the second and third questions are best provided by longitudinal studies which identify a cohort of nascent entrepreneurs as they go about the business creation process and track this group to identify those that succeed in implementing a new firm. Such panel studies are complex and expensive, but the results are extremely useful for understanding the firm creation process.

This chapter will provide a preliminary comparison related to the second issue, using data from two harmonized longitudinal studies of new venture creation, one implemented in the United States (the second Panel Study of Entrepreneurial Dynamics or PSED II) and the other in Australia (The Comprehensive Australian Study of Entrepreneurial Emergence or CAUSEE). Following the development of PSED I a number of national panel studies were implemented in Argentina, Canada, the Netherlands, Norway, and Sweden.[1] However, there was no conscious effort to harmonize the major features of these projects. In contrast, the PSED II and CAUSEE designs are based on earlier studies completed in the United States and Sweden and share a harmonized conceptualization; there has been a conscious effort to use similar procedures, selection criteria, and interview item wording (Davidsson, Steffens, Gordon, & Reynolds, 2008).

Neither study, as of 2008, had progressed to the point of providing a reliable answer to the third issue, the proportion of start-ups that become new businesses.

A review of the major similarities and differences between the two projects will be discussed in the next section. A summary of the differences in prevalence rates—the proportion of adults that have chosen to enter the start-up process—is provided in the third section. The fourth section provides a comparison of the nascent entrepreneurs and their start-up ventures, based on the data gathered in the initial detailed interviews. The final section provides comments on the success of the effort.

13.2 Comparison of Project Designs

The most important features of the two projects are very similar. Both start with a representative sample of adults, selected from households identified through the use of a Random Digit Dialing (RDD) procedure to locate residential phone numbers. In these cases, the phone numbers are created by a random procedure to overcome the bias from unlisted numbers omitted from public phone directories. In both projects, the first adult contacted in the household that was willing to complete the interview is chosen as the respondent. Both studies attempted to have an equal number of male and female respondents; post-stratification case weights were assigned to create samples that were similar to the adult population.[2]

The wording of the screening items used to identify those adults that would be considered active nascent entrepreneurs was identical. The criteria used to select those that qualified on the basis of responses to screening items are also identical. Large proportions of the CAUSEE initial detailed interview utilized wording and formats identical to the PSED II interview schedule; both studies utilized phone interviews.

But there were also differences, some reflected in the overview presented in Table 13.1 Perhaps the most important procedural difference was the use of two survey operations in the PSED II study and one for CAUSEE. In the United States it was much less expensive to have a commercial survey firm (Opinion Research Corporation of Princeton, NJ) complete the screening interviews, 2,000 each week. At the end of each week, they would relay details of eligible respondents that volunteered for the study to the Institute for Social Research at the University of Michigan. This survey unit completed the initial detailed and all follow-up interviews. This two-stage procedure led to a gap of at least a week between the two initial interviews. The CAUSEE procedure was to have the screening firm (Taylor Nelson Sofres of Australia) initiate detailed interviews as soon as an eligible respondent was identified; a much more efficient procedure. Over 20% of the completed interviews in CAUSEE were done as direct continuation from the screener.

A second procedural difference, related to the study of nascent entrepreneurs, is the presence of a comparison group identified and interviewed in the CAUSEE project. The CAUSEE project took advantage of the screening procedure to complete interviews not only with nascent entrepreneurs but also with the owners of young firms, those who began trading within the last 4 years, since 2004. Those that qualified for both were interviewed as nascent entrepreneurs. About 93% of those contacted for the CAUSEE screening did not qualify as either a nascent entrepreneur or young firm owner. One in 50, or 2%, of this group were selected at random and invited to complete the comparison group interview; 481 accepted. While no explicit comparison group was interviewed in the PSED II project, a large proportion of the interview was used with a comparison group selected and interviewed as part of the PSED I project.

But these procedural differences are unlikely to affect the ability to make precise comparisons and are small compared to the similarities. The sizes of the screening samples are similar, 31,845 for PSED II and 28,383 for CAUSEE. The unweighted prevalence of active nascent entrepreneurs is about 43% higher for the United States, 4.93/100 for PSED II and 3.44/100 for CAUSEE. In the PSED II project there was greater success at getting the first detailed interview completed, 77% compared to 61% for CAUSEE. The screening sections of the interviews were comparable in length, but the PSED II detailed interview was somewhat longer.

Table 13.1 PSED II and CAUSEE: major operational features[1]

	U.S. PSED II	CAUSEE
Population of interest	National sample of noninstitutionalized 18 years and older	National sample of noninstitutionalized 18 years and older
Selection of households	RDD household phones	RDD household phones
Selecting adults from households[2]	First eligible on phone	First eligible on phone
Dates of screening, initial interview	October 2005–February 2006	July 2007–April 2008
Size of initial screening[3]	31,845	28,383
Prevalence initially eligible: #/100	4.93	3.44
Number initially eligible	1,571	977
Proportion eligible completing initial detailed interview	77.3%	60.8%
Number completing initial detailed interview	1,214	594
Criteria for nascent entrepreneur	(1) Consider self-active; (2) Engaged in start-up behavior; (3) Expect some ownership, (4) Start-up not yet an operational new firm	(1) Consider self-active; (2) Engaged in start-up behavior; (3) Expect some ownership, (4) Start-up not yet an operational new firm
Screening interview firm	Opinion Research Corporation, Inc.	Taylor Nelson Sofres, Australia
Detailed interview firm	University of Michigan, Institute for Social Research	Taylor Nelson Sofres, Australia
Length of screening interview, average	2 min	2 min
Length of detailed interview, average	60 min	47 min
Comparison group [4,5]	None	2/100 of not active (n = 481)
Number of variables in initial detailed data set	1,477	657

[1] All counts are unweighted.
[2] Once female quota filled, selected only males from household.
[3] Excludes pretest interviews.
[4] PSED I included a comparison group with many variables identical to the PSED II nascent entrepreneur schedule.
[5] Selected at random from those not qualified as nascent entrepreneurs or young firm owners.

A gross count of variables in the initial detailed data sets, 1,477 for PSED II and 657 for CAUSEE, indicates a substantial difference in length. This reflects, in part, the different topics covered in the two interview schedules.

The PSED II interview schedule involves considerable detail on the multiple owners, participants in the founding team that will not own part of the new business, and those considered part of the helping networks of the nascent entrepreneur; modules not included in the CAUSEE interviews. These sections involve a large number of variables for nascent enterprises with 4- and 5-person teams, but only a small percentage with large start-up teams complete these sections. In addition, there is considerable detail on the financing of the nascent enterprise; again, there are many items for which only a few respondents provided answers. Again these details were not part of the CAUSEE interviews.

On the other hand, the CAUSEE interview schedule includes topics related to the newness and relatedness of the venture idea; resource (dis)advantages: effectuation, and bricolage that are not included in the PSED II interview schedule. These latter terms—effectuation and bricolage—refer to a variety of strategies that may be used to overcome a shortage of resources by applying creative, iterative, and incremental strategies (Baker & Nelson, 2005; Sarasvathy, 2001; Winborg & Landstrom, 2001).

If other features of the samples of nascent entrepreneurs are similar in the two countries, the patterns found in each national study can be assumed to be present in the other. For example, patterns related to the development and incorporation of nonowning founders and the social network found in the U.S. PSED II cohort can be assumed to occur in Australia. The patterns found in the CAUSEE cohort for Australia related to effectuation and bricolage can be assumed to be present in the United States. In this regard, the combination of similarity in basic operational procedures and diversity in details gathered about business creation provides a greater range of information about the business creation process than if both projects were identical in all respects.

13.3 Prevalence Rates: United States Versus Australia

Perhaps the most basic comparison involves the results of the screening procedure, which would be represented in terms of the proportion of adults that appear to qualify as nascent entrepreneurs. These would be individuals that answered yes to one or more of the initial screening items, suggesting they consider themselves involved in a start-up effort or new business. In addition, they will have stated that they have engaged in some start-up activities in the past 12 months, expect to own all or part of the new business, and have not had a positive monthly cash flow for more than 3 months.

The prevalence among all those 18 years and older is presented for the full sample and by gender in Fig. 13.1; these weighted estimates vary slightly from those in Table 13.1. The vertical lines are the 95% confidence intervals; the horizontal bars represent the mean values. If the vertical lines do not overlap, then the difference between the samples would be statistically significant at least at the 0.05 level. The values are provided in the table at the bottom of the chart.

All the differences are both statistically and substantively significant. The overall mean prevalence rate in the U.S. cohort is 5.7/100, compared to 3.2/100

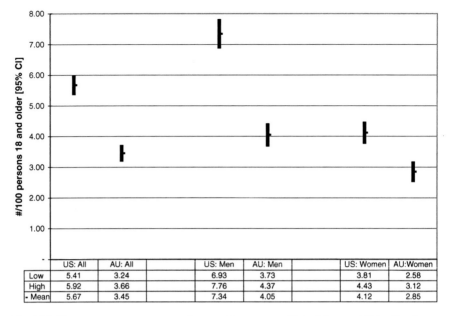

Fig. 13.1 Nascent entrepreneur screening prevalence rates: United States, AU by Gender

for Australia, almost 67% higher. Among men the mean difference is 7.3 versus 4.1/100, the U.S. is 78% higher. Among women the mean difference is 4.1 versus 2.8/100, the U.S. is 46% higher.

These results indicate a somewhat greater difference from that found with the Global Entrepreneurship Monitor (GEM) national surveys; many of the procedures and operational definitions are harmonized with the panel studies (Reynolds et al., 2005). The GEM results for the years 2000 through 2006 are summarized in Table 13.2. In this case the population base are those 18–64 years old, rather than all those over 18 years of age; this has the effect of slightly elevating the prevalence rates. Three measures are presented, the prevalence of nascent entrepreneurs, those owners of new firms up to 42 months old, and a combined measure, the Total Entrepreneurial Activity (TEA) index, now referred to as the early stage activity index. The average values for all years are provided in the bottom row of numbers.

The average values indicate that the GEM procedures indicate that the prevalence of nascent entrepreneurs is 32% higher in the United States than in Australia, 8.2/100 versus 6.2/100. On the other hand, the prevalence of new firm owners is 22% higher in Australia than in the United States, 5.0/100 compared to 4.1/100. As a consequence, the average TEA rates, which combine both measures, are almost identical, at 11.3/100 for the United States and 11.0 for Australia.

Several issues deserve some attention. First, the substantial year to year variation in the GEM results probably reflects the small sample sizes; a total screening sample of 2,000 per year was utilized in most countries. On the other

Table 13.2 Entrepreneurial activity prevalence,[1] GEM: U.S. and AU: 2000–2006

Year	U.S.: Nascents	AU: Nascents	U.S.:New firms	AU:New firms	U.S.:TEA	AU:TEA
2006[2]	7.5	7.3	3.3	5.7	10.0	12.0
2005[3]	8.8	6.5	5.2	4.7	12.4	10.9
2004[4]	–	–	–	–	11.3	13.4
2003[5]	7.9	4.9	3.9	4.7	10.8	9.2
2002[5]	7.0	3.1	4.0	4.5	9.9	7.3
2001[5]	8.2	7.4	3.5	7.2	11.9	13.4
2000[5]	9.8	8.1	4.7	3.3	12.7	10.9
Average	8.2	6.2	4.1	5.0	11.3	11.0

[1] Prevalence as number per 100 persons 18–64 years of age.
[2] Bosma and Harding (2007, p. 7).
[3] Minniti, Bygrave, and Autio (2006, p. 18).
[4] Acs, Arenius, Hay, and Minniti (page 17); 2004 data only.
[5] Reynolds and Hechavarria (2008); analysis using the 2000–2003 consolidated file with harmonized transforms and weights adjusted for 18–64-year-old respondents.

hand, the average values across 6 or 7 years represent over 12,000 interviews and provides more precise comparisons. Second, the much larger samples and more precisely harmonized procedures in the PSED II and CAUSEE projects would suggest these prevalence rates justify more confidence. Nonetheless, the GEM results for nascent entrepreneur prevalence rates are similar, but the difference between the United States and Australia is smaller, 32% compared to 70%. It seems reasonable to assume that participation in new firm creation is more common in the United States than in Australia.

Perhaps the third difference is the most interesting; the 22% higher prevalence rate of new firms owners in Australia than in the United States. New firm owners are those that report a going business that is up to 42 months old. Assuming year-to-year stability in the business creation process in the two countries and a similar average size of the ownership teams, there are at least two patterns that could account for these differences. First, it is possible that a larger proportion of nascent entrepreneurs succeed in launching a new firm in Australia. Second, the death rate of new firms may be lower in Australia than in the United States.

Both processes would help to account for the apparent anomaly in the GEM prevalence rates, higher prevalence rates for nascent entrepreneurs in the United States and higher prevalence rates for new firms in Australia. The presence or relative impact of the two processes can only be determined by the presence of two harmonized longitudinal studies, such as PSED II and CAUSEE.

13.3.1 Characteristics of the Nascent Cohorts

What are the differences, if any, between the nascent entrepreneurs developing new firms in the United States and those in Australia? A number of comparisons provide a partial response to this question. The personal characteristics and background of these individuals are presented in Table 13.3. The column to the right in the following tables presents the level of statistical significance. Because the sample sizes are relatively large, there are often statistically significant differences. In only a few cases, however, are the substantive differences significant.

For example, the proportion of men is almost identical, about 60%, in the two cohorts. While all age groups are represented in both cohorts, they seem to be slightly older in Australia, with fewer under 24 years of age and more 55 years and older. In both countries the majority are of a white, European background, but this is greater in Australia, reflecting the smaller proportion of

Table 13.3 Personal characteristics, background: U.S. vs. Australia

	U.S.:PSED II	AU:CAUSEE	Statistical significance
Number of cases	1,148	977	
Men	61.3%	59.0%	
Women	38.7%	41.0%	(0.143)
18–24 years old	14.5%	6.3%	
25–34 years old	27.1%	23.7%	
35–44 years old	26.3%	30.6%	
45–54 years old	20.2%	24.1%	
55–98 years old	11.9%	15.3%	(0.000)
White, European	70.3%	80.6%	
Black	12.7%		
Hispanic	5.0%		
Indigenous Australian		3.3%	
Asian/Middle East		5.1%	
Mixed, other	11.9%	11.0%	(0.000)
No high school degree	5.8%	17.6%	
HS degree (12 years)	20.5%	15.7%	
Post-HS, no college degree	40.8%	28.9%	
College degree	20.3%	22.2%	
Graduate experience, degree	12.6%	15.6%	(0.000)
Home owner	63.7%	69.1%	
Rent, not a homeowner	36.3%	30.9%	(0.005)
Working (Full-time, Part-time, Self-Employed)	74.4%	85.2%	
Retired	20.1%	3.1%	
Not working now	5.5%	11.7%	(0.000)
Born in the country	93.8%	73.8%	
Born outside the country	6.2%	26.2%	(0.000)
R, Fa, Mo native born	85.1%	52.3%	
R native, 1+ parent not	8.7%	21.5%	
R not native, 1+ parent not	1.0%	1.6%	
R, Fa, Mo not native born	5.2%	24.6%	(0.000)

13 PSED II and the CAUSEE

nonwhite ethnic groups. There seems to be greater diversity in educational attainment among the Australian cohort, with a larger proportion that have not finished high school, 18% versus 6%, but also a greater percentage that have college degrees or graduate experience, 38% versus 33% for the Unitd States. Slightly larger proportions are homeowners in Australia, 69% versus 64%, and slightly larger proportions are working full-time, 85% versus 74%.

There are major differences related to immigration status. Among Australian nascent entrepreneurs, 26% were born outside the country, compared to 6% in the United States. When the birth location of the parents are considered, 52% of the Australian nascents report they and both parents were born in Australia, compared to 85% among U.S nascent entrepreneurs. In other words, 15% of U.S. nascents report that they or one or both parents were born outside the country compared to 48% of Australian nascent entrepreneurs. This reflects a higher proportion of immigrants and immigrant families among the Australian population; there is no strong tendency for those in Australia with immigrant background to be more prone to start firms than others (Davidsson et al., 2008).

The extent of family background in new and small businesses is presented in Table 13.4. While the differences are statistically significant, with 53% of the U.S. nascents reporting parents who were business owners compared to 58% of the Australians, the substantive difference is slight.

There are similar small differences in the extent to which the nascents decision to enter the start-up process was based on a desire to take advantage of an opportunity, rather than a response to poor career options leading to entry into business creation out of necessity. A slightly larger proportion of Australian nascents, 24%, report they were responding wholly or in part to necessity when compared to U.S. nascents, 17%.

Table 13.4 Family background, motivation: U.S. vs. Australia

	U.S.:PSED II	AU:CAUSEE	Statistical significance
Number of cases	1,148	977	
Parents were business owners	52.6 %	58.1 %	
Parents were not business owners	47.4 %	41.9 %	(0.006)
Context: opportunity	82.3 %	75.8 %	
Context: work, seek opportunity	0.3 %	0.0 %	
Context: mixed	3.9 %	15.4 %	
Context: necessity	13.5 %	8.9 %	(0.000)
Idea for business first	38.0 %	47.7 %	
Idea, motivation together	49.3 %	35.6 %	
Entire motivation first	12.7 %	16.7 %	(0.000)
Future: easy management	77.8 %	74.5 %	
Future: maximize growth	22.2 %	25.5 %	(0.069)

The sequence in which the entrepreneurial desire and business ideas occurred varies substantially in both countries; with the largest proportion indicating that the business idea occurred before or at the same time as the desire to become an entrepreneur. A small minority, 13% in the United States and 17% in Australia, report the desire to become an entrepreneur preceded the development of the business idea.

The proportion seeking to maximize the growth of their new business is almost the same in both cohorts, about one in four.

In both countries the largest proportion of the start-ups are one-person efforts. As shown in Table 13.5, about 54% in the United States and 51% in Australia report that only one person will own the firm.[3] The average team size is slightly higher in Australia, 1.75 compared to 1.64 for the United States. In the U.S. cohort 5% report teams of four or more individuals, compared to 7% in the Australian cohort.[4]

In both countries about 40% of the nascent enterprises involve individuals who take a major responsibility for some aspect of the firm creation process although they do not expect to own part of the new firm. These are referred to as nonowning founders; more details on this group and their contributions are available in the PSED II data set.

Some of the characteristics of the nascent enterprise are presented in Table 13.6. At the time of the initial interview, the majority report the legal form as a sole proprietorship, with either a corporate or limited company form more popular than partnership. A substantial proportion report that the legal form has yet to be established.

The most popular location during the start-up stage is a private residence, although a number report that a dedicated location is not yet required. A minority report the nascent enterprise is sharing the site of an existing business or has a location dedicated to this new firm.

A series of three questions are used to determine the technological focus of the nascent enterprise. These three items—related to the technology in use, a focus on research and development, and if the owners consider the business as

Table 13.5 Start-up teams: U.S. vs. Australia

	U.S.:PSED II	AU:CAUSEE	Statistical significance
Number of cases	1,148	617	
Team size, humans (average)	1.64	1.75	(0.016)
Team size: 1 owner	53.8%	50.6%	
Team size: 2 owners	34.2%	35.3%	
Team size: 3 owners	6.8%	7.3%	
Team size: 4 owners	4.6%	2.6%	
Team size: 5+ owners	0.5%	4.2%	(0.000)
Nonowning founders: yes	39.4%	37.6%	
Nonowning founders: no	60.6%	62.4%	(0.244)

Table 13.6 Nascent enterprises: U.S. vs. Australia

	U.S.:PSED II	AU:CAUSEE	Statistical significance
Number of cases	1,148	617	
Sole proprietorship	37.1%	49.4%	
Partnership	8.9%	16.5%	
Ltd (Australia), Corp. (United States)	16.5%	18.1%	
Not determined	37.6%	18.0%	(0.000)
Location: residence	44.1%	66.1%	
Location: exist business	5.9%	9.5%	
Location: dedicated site	8.9%	10.2%	
Location: not needed yet	40.1%	11.1%	
Location: other	1.0%	3.1%	(0.000)
Technology less than 5 years old	22.9%	29.7%	(0.001)
R&D a major focus	25.0%	44.3%	(0.000)
Consider business high-tech	24.3%	31.6%	(0.001)
High-tech index: highest	5.1%	9.2%	
High-tech index: moderate	15.3%	20.4%	
High-tech index: low	25.8%	37.2%	
High-tech index: none	53.8%	33.3%	(0.000)

high technology—are presented at the bottom of Table 13.6. The responses to these three items can be used to create an index and classify nascent enterprises as from no technological focus to the highest level, also shown at the bottom of Table 13.6. There is little question that CAUSEE respondents are reporting a greater emphasis on new technology.

The economic sector and the location of customers for the nascent enterprises are presented in Table 13.7. Comparisons of economic sectors utilize both 4 very general categories and 15 more precise categories.

While the differences between the U.S. and Australian nascent enterprises are statistically significant, the differences are small and probably reflect the differences in the national emphasis on economic sectors. This is particularly true of the larger proportion emphasizing extractive sectors in Australia, 6% compared to 3% for the United States and the larger proportion emphasizing real estate in the United States, 5% compared to 1% for Australia. In both countries a wide range of business activities are represented among the nascent enterprises.

The bottom of Table 13.7 presents the percentage of customers, averaged across all nascent enterprises, expected in different locations. Australian nascent enterprises expect to have somewhat more customers outside the country, 10% compared to 3% for the United States. This is associated with a reduction in customers expected in the immediate region, within 20 miles or 30 km of the business.

These comparisons can be considered in terms of the nature of the nascent entrepreneur and the teams that are attempting to implement new firms and the

Table 13.7 Nascent enterprise sectors, customer orientations: U.S. vs. Australia

	U.S.:PSED II	AU:CAUSEE	Statistical significance
Number of cases	1,148	617	
Extractive sectors	3.2%	6.1%	
Transformative sectors	23.7%	22.3%	
Business markets sectors	29.6%	26.4%	
Consumer markets sectors	43.5%	45.2%	(0.018)
Extractive: Agriculture	3.1%	5.5%	
Extractive: Mining	0.1%	0.6%	
Transformative: Manufacturing	6.5%	8.1%	
Transformative: Construction	10.6%	6.9%	
Transformative: Transport, warehouse	2.3%	1.9%	
Transformative: Utilities	0.0%	0.3%	
Transformative: Communication, information	4.3%	5.0%	
Business: Lodging, food,bars	5.4%	4.8%	
Business: Wholesale	4.4%	2.3%	
Business: Finance,insurance	2.7%	1.8%	
Business: Consultancy, business services	17.1%	7.4%	
Consumer: Retail	19.1%	17.2%	
Consumer: Consumer services, arts, recreation	13.2%	14.0%	
Consumer: Health, social, educational services	6.4%	12.9%	
Consumer: Real estate	4.7%	1.1%	(0.000)
Local customers:	61.3%	50.4%	(0.000)
Regional customers	20.7%	21.2%	(0.608)
National customers	15.7%	18.5%	(0.008)
International customers	3.0%	10.0%	(0.000)

character of the nascent enterprises being implemented. Within the two cohorts of nascent entrepreneurs:

- Gender representation is identical; 60% are men in both countries.
- Nascent entrepreneurs are slightly older in Australia.
- The majority are white, of European descent, in both countries.
- More educational diversity in Australia, with a higher proportion with college and graduate experience and without high school degrees.
- More homeowners in Australia, 69% versus 64%.
- More working while they implement new firms in Australia, 85% versus 74%.
- Substantially greater proportions are immigrant or in an immigrant household in Australia, where 48% of households have a parent or nascent born outside the country, compared to 15% for the United States.

- About the same proportion of nascents, about half, in both countries had parents who were business owners.
- Australian nascents were more likely to be involved out of necessity; about 24% had necessity as part of their motivation, compared to 18% in the United States.
- There were no major differences in the development of business ideas versus motivation to become an entrepreneur.
- About the same proportion in both countries, one in four has a focus on high growth.
- Team sizes were comparable in both countries, perhaps slightly larger teams in Australia.
- Both countries reported nonowning founders involved in about 40% of the nascent enterprises.

In summary, if there is a difference between the nascents, those in Australia appear more likely to be immigrants and also slightly older and better established as employees and homeowners.

The nascent enterprises are also quite similar in the two countries:

- The legal status at the time of the first interviews is similar, with a higher proportion of sole proprietorship in Australia; a larger proportion not determined in the United States.
- Most are located in residences or a location not needed at the first interview.
- Nascent enterprises in Australia appear to have a greater focus on new technology.
- The industry sectors cover a broad range representing the full diversity of economic activity in each country.
- There is a concentration of focus on local customers in both countries, with a slightly higher emphasis on international customers in Australia, 10% compared to 3% for the United States.

In summary, nascent enterprises in the two countries are quite similar and reflect the economic structure in the countries. Australian nascent enterprises may be more focused on new technology and international customers.

13.4 Alternative Interpretation

This preliminary assessment has assumed that the PSED II and CAUSEE procedures identified nascent entrepreneurs at the same stage in the start-up process. A small consistent difference is evidence that CAUSEE nascent entrepreneurs are more established in the community and labor force, more likely to have advanced education, report larger teams, more likely to have a legal form, and have a fixed location for the business. If Australians are, for whatever reason, less likely to indicate they are active in new firm creation at the early stages of the process, it could account for these subtle differences—which are all relatively small; Australians wait until they are further into the process before they report they are nascent entrepreneurs. If entrepreneurial career choices are less socially encouraged in Australia, it may account for this reluctance.

The GEM 2003 cross-national comparisons involved measures of the extent for cultural support for entrepreneurship from interviews completed with the adult population and questionnaires completed by well-informed experts in each country (Reynolds, Autio, & Hechavarria, 2008; Reynolds & Hechavarria, 2008).[5] Both groups indicate a slightly higher level of acceptance of entrepreneurship as a career option in the United States, which may encourage those in the United States to report participating in a business start-up at an earlier stage. Additional analysis will be required using the PSED II and CAUSEE data sets to determine the potential impact of this "willingness to be identified as a nascent entrepreneur" effect.

13.5 Overview and Commentary

The critical features of identifying a representative sample of nascent entrepreneurs actively involved in business creation have been harmonized for the projects underway in the United States and Australia, PSED II and CAUSEE. While there is some variation in the coverage of the detailed interviews, the critical procedures for locating and identifying cohorts of nascent entrepreneurs are identical or very similar. The initial comparisons provide tentative answers to the issues raised in the introduction.

Are there national differences in the tendency of individuals to get involved in business creation?

Both the comparison based on the two longitudinal studies and the use of 6 years of data collected as part of the GEM project suggest a greater propensity among U.S. adults to participate in new firm creation. U.S. adults are about 70% more likely to become involved, reflecting a prevalence rate of 5.7/100 adults over 18 years of age, compared to 3.4/100 for Australians. Our alternative interpretation suggests this difference may be inflated by a higher propensity among Americans to report themselves as "starting a business" at rather tentative stages of venture development. The Australians that do become involved are more likely to be part of an immigrant household and may be more established in the community.

Does the national context affect the way in which individuals go about creating a new firm?

Only limited evidence is available in this assessment related to this question. However, the size of the start-up teams, the economic sectors, the legal form, a major focus on local and regional customers, the aspirations for growth are all similar in the two cohorts of nascent enterprises. Australian nascent firms may have a slightly greater emphasis on new technology and international customers, the latter probably an effect of the smaller home market.

Does the national context affect the proportion of start-ups that become operational young businesses?

There is no data, as yet, from the two longitudinal studies that can be used to respond to this issue. Neither study has collected enough follow-up data to determine the outcomes for these two cohorts of nascent enterprises; other research suggests it may take 5 years for most of the start-ups to reach a resolution.

Data from the GEM annual surveys, however, suggests that the prevalence of new firms is higher in Australia than in the United States, and this is in absolute terms. If so, this may indicate that either a larger proportion of Australian nascent enterprises become new firms, that a survival in the early years is greater for Australian new firms, or that both processes are in operation. When PSED II and CAUSEE have completed follow-ups to track the outcomes for their respective cohorts of nascent enterprises it will be possible to confirm the implications based on the GEM data and estimate the relative impact of these different processes.

It is clear that the benefits of efforts to harmonize the procedures and interview schedules of the PSED II and CAUSEE longitudinal studies will be substantial; well worth the small cost required to achieve compatibility. This suggests that if harmonized longitudinal projects were implemented in other countries, particularly those with different levels of participation in business creation and different economic and social contexts, much new information about factors that affect business creation and its contribution to economic growth could be developed.

Notes

1. Alsos and Kolvereid (1998), Delmar and Davidsson (2000), de Rearte, Lanari, and Atucha (1998), Diochon, Menzies, and Gasse (2007) and van Gelderen, Thurik and Bosma (2005).
2. In the PSED II project, case weights for the entire screening sample were developed to provide a match to the Current Population Studies national samples based on age, gender, ethnicity, and household income. Case weights have as yet not been developed for the Australian sample.
3. In Tables 13.5, 13.6 and 13.7 the number of Australian cases is reduced from 977 to 617, reflected in the weighted count of the reduced number completing the detailed interview.
4. The sample procedure selects individuals participating in a start-up initiative; those initiatives with start-up teams are more likely to be sampled than one-person efforts. This can lead to a larger proportion of team start-ups in the cohorts. No adjustment has been made for this bias, in either the PSED II or CAUSEE data sets. Note that this tendency towards oversampling of team efforts is reduced by the fact that many "teams" are partners sharing the same household (Ruef, Aldrich, & Carter, 2003) so they represent only one sampling unit. It would be more precise, however, to speak of a cohort of nascent entrepreneurs rather than a cohort of nascent enterprises.

5 Both interview schedules involve multiple items that can be used to create an index. Among typical adults there is greater diversity in the United States, with both a higher proportion of US respondents indicating very low and very high cultural acceptance of entrepreneurship. US experts are considerably more positive than Australian experts.

References

Acs, Z., Arenius, P., Hay, M., & Minniti, M. (2004). *Global entrepreneurship monitor: 2004 executive report*. Babson Park, MA and London, UK: Babson College and London Business School.

Alsos, G. A., & Kolvereid, L. (1998). The business gestation process of novice, serial and parallel business founders. *Entrepreneurship Theory and Practice, 22*(4), 101–114.

Baker, T., & Nelson, R. E. (2005). Creating something from nothing: Resource construction through entrepreneurial bricolage. *Administrative Science Quarterly, 50*(3), 329–366.

Bosma, N., & Harding, R. (2007) *Global entrepreneurship monitor: 2006 summary results*. Babson Park, MA and London, UK: Babson College and London Business School.

Bosma, N., Jones, K., Autio, E., & Levie, J. (2008). *Global entrepreneurship monitor: 2007 executive report*. Babson Park, MA and London, UK: Babson College and London Business School.

Davidsson, P., Steffens, P., Gordon, S., & Reynolds, P. (2008). *Anatomy of new business activity in Australia: Some early observations from the CAUSEE project* [working paper]. Brisbane, Australia: Queensland University of Technology.

Delmar, F., & Davidsson, P. (2000). Where do they come from? Prevalence and characteristics of nascent entrepreneurs. *Entrepreneurship and Regional Development, 12*, 1–23.

De Rearte, A. G., Lanari, E., & Atucha, P. (1998). El proceso de creation de empresas; Abordaje methodologico y primeros resultados de un studio regional (The process of firm creation: Methodological approach and preliminary results from a regional study). Argentina: Universidad Nacional de Mar del Plata.

Diochon, M., Menzies, T.V., & Gasse, Y. (2007). From becoming to being: Measuring firm creation. *Journal of Enterprising Culture, 15*(1), 21–42.

Minniti, M., Bygrave, W. D., & Autio, E. (2006). *Global entrepreneurship monitor: 2005 executive report*. Babson Park, MA and London, UK: Babson College and London Business School.

Reynolds, P. D., Autio, E., & Hechavarria, D. (in press 2008). *Global entrepreneurship monitor: Expert questionnaire data: 1999–2003* (ICPSR Archives). Ann Arbor, MI.

Reynolds, P. D., Bosma, N., Autio, E., Hunt, S., De Bono, N., Servais, I., et al. (2005). Global entrepreneurship monitor: Data collection design and implementation: 1998-2003. *Small Business Economics, 24*, 205–231.

Reynolds, P. D., & Hechavarria, D. (2008). *Global entrepreneurship monitor: Adult population survey data sets: 1998–2003* (ICPSR Archive, Project 20320). Ann Arbor, MI.

Ruef, M., Aldrich, H. E., & Carter, N. M. (2003). The structure of organizational founding teams: Homophily, strong ties, and isolation among U.S. entrepreneurs. *American Sociological Review, 68*(2), 195–222.

Sarasvathy, S. (2001). Causation and effectuation: Towards a theoretical shift from economic inevitability to entrepreneurial contingency. *Academy of Management Review, 26*(2), 243–288.

Van Gelderen, M., Thurik, A. R., & Bosma, N. (2005). Success and risk factors in the pre-start-up phase. *Small Business Economics, 24*, 365–380.

Winborg, J., & Landstrom, H. (2001). Financial bootstrapping in small businesses: Examining small business managers' resource acquisition behaviors. *Journal of Business Venturing, 16*(3), 235–254.

Chapter 14
PSED II and the Kauffman Firm Survey

Alicia Robb and Paul D. Reynolds

14.1 Introduction

While new firm creation is an important feature of modern economies, research on major aspects of the early stages of the business life course is hampered by the length and complexity of the process. Conceptual complexity is reflected in the difficulty of developing simple, precise measures of initiating the firm gestation process, or conception, as well as the transition from a nascent enterprise to an operating business – a new firm birth. The length of the process is reflected in the substantial time many nascent enterprises stay in the gestation process. It takes over 5 years after conception for over 90% to reach a resolution as new firms or to be abandoned; one-third seem to continue indefinitely as nascent enterprises (Reynolds, 2007). Once the new firm is operational, it may take another 5–10 years before it is fully established; half usually terminate operations before the fifth year.

It is both expensive and operationally complex to develop, staff, and implement a longitudinal project that may last 10–15 years. Furthermore, it may be more than a decade before major analyses can be implemented. One solution is to simultaneously implement two projects, each focusing on a different stage of the early part of the firm's life course. The second Panel Study of Entrepreneurial Dynamics (PSED II) project, implemented with selection of a cohort of nascent entrepreneurs in 2005, was initiated at about the same time as the Kauffman Firm Survey (KFS) implemented with the selection of a cohort of businesses identified in 2005 as having started in 2004. Both projects involve systematic follow-ups to track the development of their cases—nascent enterprises, new firms—in the subsequent years. There was some harmonization of

---

A number of very useful comments and observations were provided by David DesRoches of Mathematica Policy Research, Inc.

A. Robb (✉)
University of California, Santa Cruz, CA, USA
e-mail: arobb@ucsc.edu

the interview schedules utilized in these two projects to facilitate comparing results for different stages of the firm's life course.

The PSED II project is designed to provide detailed descriptions of a representative sample of nascent entrepreneurs as they move from conception to the implementation of a new firm. The KFS is designed to provide detailed descriptions of a representative sample of new firms from their "birth"—implementation as an operating business—through their early years. The critical overlaps between the projects are the stages associated with the firm's birth transition. Using these two projects to describe the initial stages of the firm's life course is facilitated by matching cases from the two cohorts at this critical transition.

Aside from attempts to capture different stages of the firm's life course, these projects differ in one major regard—the conception of a "new firm." In the PSED II initiative, a new firm is conceptualized as a business activity that is profitable. A nascent enterprise is re-classified as a new firm when it reports a monthly revenue stream that is greater than the monthly expenses, including all salaries, for more than 6 months. Given this criteria, an enterprise engaged in transactions (such as purchases of supplies or components, rental of space, or payment of salary and wages) is in the nascent stage until revenue is greater than the operational expenses. Based on this conceptualization the Internet retail firm, Amazon.com, has been a nascent enterprise for most of its existence; biotech firms that require several decades to develop, test, and gain approval of new medical technology would also be considered nascent enterprises for most of this gestation period.

Much analysis in economics focuses on markets, considered to be exchanges between buyers and sellers of goods and services (National Research Council, 2007, p. 32). There is a major interest in identifying economic actors that will participate in markets, as their participation will affect the supply or demand for goods and services as well as the transaction prices. The extent to which a specific economic actor (a business, person, or household) conducts his/her own affairs to maintain financial solvency is not relevant. This perspective leads to an interest in new firms as new participants in markets, both as a customer for components, equipment, land, space, capital, or labor or as a provider of goods or services to buyers (individuals, businesses, or households) whether or not the firm is profitable.

This conceptualization is consistent with identifying a sample of new firms from the Dun & Bradstreet (D&B) credit rating files, which is a listing of business entities, designed to provide assessment of those creditworthy as customers of other businesses. Profitability is not a criterion for inclusion in the D&B data files, nor is it provided as part of the D&B case records. Hence, inclusion in the KFS cohort, drawn from the D&B credit rating files, is unrelated to firm profitability. In fact, 17% of the KFS cases report no income or revenue in calendar year 2004, the year in which the cohort was selected.[1]

Fortunately, a substantial amount of data is assembled in both projects, which facilitates the potential for harmonized comparisons of the cases. For this assessment, it is convenient to consider several stages of the business creation process, summarized in Table 14.1 and identified as (1) no presence (not included in any major business registry) and no revenue, (2) presence (listed in

Table 14.1 PSED and KFS case comparisons

Start-up stage	Criteria	PSED II	Kauffman firm survey
		n = 854	N = 4,928
1. No presence, no revenue	No listing in registries, no revenue	24.6 %	Not available
2. Presence, no revenue	Multiple listings in registries, no revenue	13.9 %	17.3 %
3. No presence, revenue	No listing in registries, revenue but not profitable	14.4 %	Not available
4. Presence, some revenue	Listings in registries, revenue but not profitable	35.0 %	48.9 %
5. Presence, profitable during initial year	Listings in registries, revenue exceeds expenses, initial period (first year)	12.1 %	33.7 %

Weighted to represent the population from which sample was drawn.

one or more registries) but no revenue, (3) no listings and some revenue but not profitable, (4) presence and some revenue but not profitable, and (5) presence and profitable in the initial period.[2] It is possible to compare the nature of the samples from the two projects for three of these stages. There is no data from the KFS project from entities in two categories. First, none can be included prior to their inclusion in the D&B file including those with no revenue (stage1). Second, those that may have revenue and not included in the D&B listing will also not be included (stage 3).

The focus of this analysis will be on the initial stages and the first year of KFS data collection. Data on operating firms after the first full year of operation are available for the KFS sample after the first follow-up interviews. For the PSED II cohort a full year of operational data are available only after the second follow-up interviews are completed; these data are not available at this time.

The major features of the two projects are presented in the next section. A precise comparison of the different types of nascent and new firms requires allocation of cases in both projects. The third section provides a discussion of the selection and allocation of cases from PSED II to the different start-up categories. The fourth section discusses the allocation of the KFS cases. The fifth section provides a preliminary comparison of these cases from the two projects on the nature of the respondents and the nascent or new business entities. The final section considers the optimal strategy for future comparisons and the benefit of such analyses.

14.2 Overview of Major Project Features

The two projects followed a similar strategy to develop a representative sample of eligible cases for a cohort to be tracked in subsequent years. The major features are summarized in Table 14.2. The PSED II procedure started with

Table 14.2 Major features: PSED II and KFS

	PSED II	KFS
Source of sample	Adults identified as active nascent entrepreneurs in a random sample of households	New entries in the D&B market identified files reporting *initial* registration in one or more of five registries in 2004.
Screening sample stratification	Gender	Gender
Oversample	None	Medium, high-tech
Initial screening	31,845	32,469
Eligible cases identified	1,571	6,030
Eligible case response rate	77.3%	81.7%
Total completed interviews	1,214	4,928
Oversample (medium, high-tech)	None	2,034
Initial interview administration	Phone	Phone (77%), Internet (23%)
Incentive payments	$25	$50
Initial interview length (average phone)	60 min	36 min
Screening interview variable count	53	Not relevant
Initial interview variable count	847	659
Time to first follow-up	12 months	12 months
First follow-up sample	972	3,998
First follow-up administration	Phone	Phone (41%), Internet (59%)
First follow-up length (average phone)	26 min	28 min
First follow-up response rate	81%	81%
First follow-up variable count	1,477	946
Total variables: all data collection	2,377	1,405

screening items included in 31,845 phone interviews with adults identified in a random sample of US households; these were conducted as part of omnibus surveys completed by the Opinion Research Corporation (Princeton, NJ). These screening items took an average of 2 min in these phone interviews. The screening sample was stratified by gender to achieve an equal number of men and women in the initial interview; a total of 53 variables were obtained from the nascent entrepreneur and socio-demographic modules.

The names and phone numbers of eligible cases were then relayed to the University of Michigan Survey Research Center and initial contact was attempted in less than a week after the screening interview. Of the 1,571 cases initially identified as eligible, detailed phone interviews were completed with 1,214; while this was 77% of the cases initially identified as eligible, some could not be located or were later determined to be ineligible. Respondents received a cash payment of $25 for participating in a detailed phone interview that averaged 60 min in length; the range was from 30 to 90 min. A total of 847 variables were included in the data set from the Wave A interviews.

Exactly 52 weeks after the completion of the initial interview, the first call to complete the initial follow-up interview as made. These 26 minutes phone interviews were completed with 972 or 81% of those completing the first detailed interview; they received an additional $25 for participation. Because there were different interview schedules for the different dispositions at the first follow-up interview, Wave B, a total of 1,477 variables were added to the data set.

Weights were computed for the entire screening sample by the University of Michigan Survey Research Center to provide adjustments to match the sample with the U.S. population on gender, age, ethnicity, and household income. The screening sample can be considered to represent the adult population of the United States at the time the screening was conducted. These screening sample weights are the basis for all case weights for each wave of detailed data collection.

The KFS procedure started with the complete file of new entries in the D&B Market Identifier File of firms started in 2004, in June 2005, and in November 2005—a total of 251,282 potential respondents. This pool was stratified using data on the gender of the principal to ensure that the percentage of women-owned businesses equaled that in full D&B population frame. In addition, an oversample of new entries in the sectors considered to have a medium or high technology emphasis was identified.[3] A final screening sample of 32,469 was the basis for locating a suitable cohort. Letters were sent to each potential respondent informing them of the study, the offer of $50 for participation, and providing instructions on completing the web-based schedule on the Internet. The initial questions excluded those cases that are branches or subsidiaries of existing businesses or a business inherited from someone else. The sample focuses on independent start-ups, a business purchased from someone or another business, or establishment of a franchise.

A critical part of the screening process was identifying those new firms that had entered in one or more of five registries for the first time in 2004. Of the 32,469 that were approached, eligibility was not determined for almost half (47%), and of the remainder, 6,030 were considered to be eligible. Detailed initial interviews were completed with 82% of this group, a total of 4,928 KFS new firms. Of these, 77% completed a phone interview that averaged 36 min and 23% completed the web-based schedule on the Internet.

About 81%, 3,998, completed the first follow-up interview completed 1 year after the initial detailed interview, receiving another $50 for their participation.

Case weights were developed for the cohort, with adjustments for differential response rates, location, sales volume, population size, legal status, employee count, gender of owner, industry sector, and business size to provide a sample with characteristics matching the initial population of D&B new businesses. The relationship of the new D&B listings to new listings in other censuses of U.S. businesses developed by the Bureau of Labor Statistics or the U.S. Census has not, at this time, been determined.

The PSED is designed to identify those active in the firm creation process and follow them until they launch a new firm or disengage from the process.

Information is obtained on a wide range of activities associated with implementing a new firm. When the respondent, reporting for the nascent enterprise, reports that the effort has developed a revenue stream or income that exceeds all expenses, salaries, and wages for more than 6 months, the initiative is assumed to have completed the transition from a nascent enterprise to a new firm. To provide the capacity to determine when the new venture would be included in standard listings or registries of operating businesses, a number of questions regarding incorporation into these registries are employed, including legal registration, obtaining a phone or Internet listing, filing for a fictitious or "doing business as" [DBA] name, obtaining an EIN number, initial state unemployment insurance payments, initial federal social security payments, initial filing of a federal tax return, or listing in the D&B credit rating files.

The selection process for the KFS cohort began with a sample taken from the D&B files as having started operations in 2004; they were interviewed from July 2005 to July 2006. This D&B "start date" relies on self-reports of the firm's principals and the respondent defines this event. In the KFS they were then asked about incorporation in five registries, obtaining an EIN number, legal registration, filing initial state unemployment insurance, federal social security, or initial federal tax returns. Only if they reported that none of these five had occurred before 2004 and at least one had occurred for the first time in 2004 were they included in the cohort.

For PSED II data on all six registrations relied on interview responses. For the KFS sample listing in the D&B files is a precondition for inclusion; information about five activities affecting inclusion are based on interview responses. The wording of these items, summarized in Table 14.3, is very similar in both projects and for most the month and year the activity first occurred is obtained. There is a slight difference with regard to federal tax returns; this information is obtained for any nascent enterprise in PSED II, only for those reported as sole proprietorships in the KFS.

There is a considerable difference between projects with regard to the information on listing in the D&B credit rating files. The KFS was taken from these files so that all cases, by default, can be assumed to have a D&B listing. In the PSED II project, the respondent was asked if they knew if they were listed in these files. The procedures employed by D&B to capture new listings for their database poses something of a problem. All other registration listings reflect some active effort on the part of the firm owners; D&B has developed procedures to identify and include new firms without the knowledge of the principles. Many of the D&B procedures are based on new customers of businesses supplying goods and services to businesses, such as Radio Shack or Federal Express; others are based on adding new listings of any corporate registrations taken from the records of the individual states (Dun & Bradstreet, 2002).

These D&B procedures have two consequences. First, many of the PSED II nascent enterprises may be listed with Dun & Bradstreet without the knowledge of the start-up team. Second, many of the new listings in the D&B files may not

Table 14.3 Identification of firm registration events

	PSED II	KFS
Listing in Dun & Bradstreet	E36: To the best of your knowledge, has this new business been listed with Dun & Bradstreet, the credit rating agency? (Month/Year)	Source of sample, assumed for all cases
Legal form registration	C1: What is the current legal form of this new business—would you say it is a sole proprietorship, a general partnership, a limited partnership, a limited liability corporation or LLC, a sub-chapter S with no more than 20 shareholders, a general corporation, or has the legal form not been determined yet? (Month/Year)	B2a: I am going to read you a list of some different forms of legal status a business can have. As of December 31, 2004, which form of legal status did (NAME BUSINESS) have? (Six forms listed.)
Federal EIN number	E26: Has an application for a federal EIN or employer identification number be made for this business, will an application be made in the future, or is it not relevant for this business? (Month/Year)	B3: Does (NAME OF BUSINESS) have an employer's identification number, which is also known as an EIN? (Month/Year)
State unemployment insurance	E29: For this new business, have any payments been made to a state unemployment insurance fund? (Month/Year)	B7: Did (NAME BUSINESS) pay any state unemployment insurance taxes for calendar year 2004? (Month/Year)
Federal social security, FICA	E32: For this new business, have any payments been made to the federal social security system, also known as FICA? (Month/Year)	B10: Did (NAME BUSINESS) pay any federal social security taxes, which are also know as FICA payments, for calendar year 2004? (Month/Year)
Federal tax return	E34: Has a federal income tax return ever been filed for this new business, whether or not it reported a profit and tax payment, such as a Schedule C or C-EZ for a sole proprietorship, Form 1065 for a partnership, or one of the corporate Form 1120s? (Month/Year)	Sole proprietorships only: B5: As part of your 2004 income tax return, did you submit a Schedule C or Schedule C-EZ to report income or loss from (NAME BUSINESS)?

have generated any revenue or reached the point of being a profitable operating business, with revenue greater than expenses. Indeed, 17% of the KFS firms report no revenue at all at the time of the first interview and 49% report revenue but no profits; 34% report both revenue and profits.[4]

In fact, none of these registry listings in either project are contingent on a profitable operation. Some do not require any economic activity, such as registering a legal form or acquiring an EIN number or obtaining a D&B listing; two only require that the firm have paid employees, state unemployment insurance payments, and federal social security payments, and federal income tax returns require only economic activity where either a profit or loss may be reported.

This is the primary rationale for development of different subgroups associated with the transition from a start-up firm or nascent enterprise to a profitable new venture that would be included in standard registries. While most profitable and established businesses, particularly those with employees, will appear in a variety of registries, there is no invariant sequence of registration activity and developing positive monthly cash flow. More details in the processing of the different cohorts to identify those cases in the different stages are provided below.

14.3 Identifying PSED II Cases by Start-Up Stage

The PSED procedure is unique in identification of participation in the start-up process from conception, considered to be that time when the nascent entrepreneur begins to make a serious effort to implement a new firm. Those considered to have an operational firm are excluded from the initial data collection, Wave A. Information on nascent enterprises that have made the transition to operational new firms is first available from the Wave B sample. As a result, this comparison starts with the 972 cases where data are available from both Wave A and Wave B interviews. Analysis of the start-up process begins by defining a time-line that is unique for each case; the time-line begins with identifying conception, or entry into the start-up process.

Conception is defined, in operational terms, for those nascent enterprises that have not had 6 or more months of revenue exceeding expenses prior to the initial detailed interview.[5] Among these cases, those reporting only 2 start-up activities, from a total of 34 activities, are not considered committed to the process and are excluded from the sample. Among the rest, if they have reported 2 or more start-ups activities within a 12-month period, the conception date is that month when the earliest activity was reported. This excludes those where start-up activities are so infrequent that no 2 activities occur within a 12-month period. The date of conception occurs prior to the initial detailed interview [Wave A] for almost all cases; for some it is as much as a decade before. This adjustment to retain the most serious of the start-up efforts further reduces the sample to a total of 854 cases.

The timing of the transitions, from conception to a change in status for the PSED II cohort is presented in Fig. 14.1.[6] This is presented through the first quarter of the fifth year following conception. The white area at the bottom of the bars represents those actively engaged in the start-up process, assumed to be all cases as they enter the process. The black portion in the middle represents those that report profitable monthly cash flow for more than 3 months. The

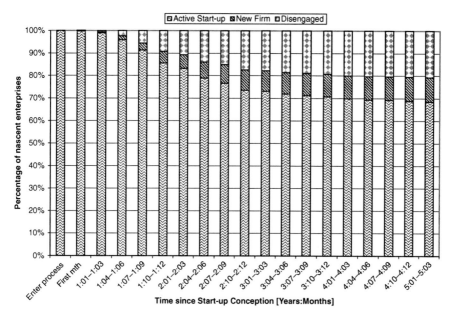

Fig. 14.1 PSED nascent enterprises transitions, time since conception

grey portion at the top represents those that report disengagement from the start-up initiative. The pattern stabilizes at the beginning of the 4th year [4:01–4:03], where 70% are still active in the start-up process, 20% have disengaged, and 10% have reported new firms.[7]

Concurrent with many other activities, nascent teams pursue activities that will lead to incorporation of the new firm in a variety of registers. Using the six that were emphasized in the KFS allows counts of the number of nascent enterprises with one or more listings during the start-up process. This pattern is presented in Fig. 14.2. It is to be noted that 15% report at least one listing in the very first month and those with at least one listing increase to about 58% after 3 years. On the other hand, 2 in 5 do not report any listings 5 years after beginning the start-up process, although some may be included in the D&B files without their knowledge.

The percentage reporting each type of listing for each quarter following entry into the process is presented in Table 14.4. The most common form of listing activity is registration of a legal form [41% at the end of 3 years]; followed by an initial federal tax return [33%], obtaining an EIN number [27%], initial federal social security payment [19%], initial state unemployment insurance payment [10%], and knowledge they are listed in the D&B files [5%]. As an EIN number is not required to file a Schedule C with the annual household federal tax return, an EIN number is not mandatory for all tax filings. Further, FICA payments may be associated with filing a Schedule C with a household return, which may account for the higher prevalence of FICA initial payments than state unemployment insurance payments. Finally, it is clear that a very small proportion, about 1 in 20, are aware of any listing in the D&B databases.

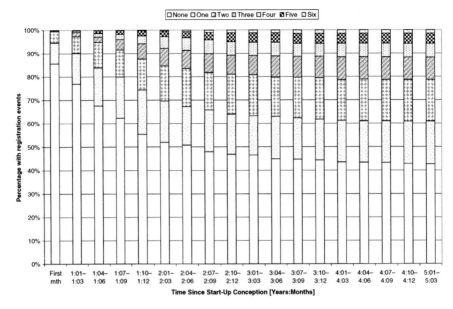

Fig. 14.2 Number of timing of registration events during the start-up process

Table 14.4 Prevalence of registration listings during start-up

Year: Month	None (%)	Legal form (%)	Tax return (%)	EIN No (%)	FICA (%)	Unemployment insurance (%)	Dun & Bradstreet listing (%)
First month	85.6	9.7	2.0	6.3	1.4	0.0	0.4
1:01–1:03	76.1	17.9	3.5	11.3	3.3	1.8	0.4
1:04–1:06	67.7	24.9	6.2	15.5	6.1	3.9	1.2
1:07–1:09	62.2	28.2	10.2	18.3	8.4	5.2	2.1
1:10–1:12	55.4	32.5	16.9	21.3	11.5	6.4	2.9
2:01–2:03	51.9	34.6	22.1	23.3	14.6	7.3	3.1
2:04–2:06	50.6	35.5	24.9	24.3	15.5	7.8	3.7
2:07–2:09	47.9	37.2	27.8	25.9	16.7	8.1	4.5
2:10–2:12	46.9	37.9	29.7	26.1	17.8	8.8	4.8
3:01–3:03	46.5	38.0	30.8	26.3	18.1	8.9	4.9
3:04–3:06	44.8	39.1	32.1	26.3	18.4	9.1	5.1
3:07–3:09	44.7	39.2	32.9	26.8	18.6	9.2	5.1
3:10–3:12	44.3	40.1	33.1	26.8	18.7	9.2	5.2
4:01–4:03	43.5	40.6	33.3	27.2	19.4	9.6	5.2
4:04–4:06	43.3	40.8	33.5	27.3	19.4	9.6	5.2
4:07–4:09	43.2	40.9	33.6	27.3	19.4	9.6	5.2
4:10–4:12	42.8	41.2	33.7	27.4	19.5	9.6	5.2
5:01–5:03	42.6	41.3	33.9	27.5	19.5	9.6	5.2

14 PSED II and the Kauffman Firm Survey

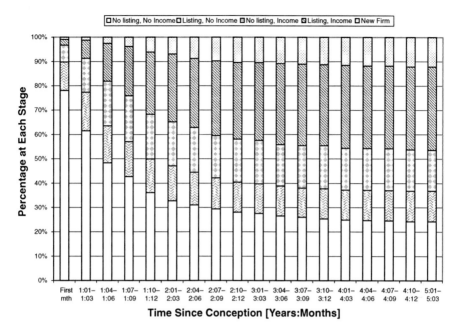

Fig. 14.3 PSED II: case allocation into start-up categories over time

It would be of considerable value to know which of these new PSED II firms have been included in the D&B files without their knowledge—and when this occurred. This would provide a potential for further calibrating the comparison between the PSED II cases and the KFS cases.

The number of cases, over time, that would fall into the five start-up stages presented in Table 14.1 is presented in Fig. 14.3. As these classifications reflect the activity as an economic factor and incorporation into different registries, the proportion in each category grows over time. Stability in the proportion in each category, based on the Wave A and Wave B data, appears to occur during the third year. For this reason, the case allocation for the comparisons is based on allocation during the first quarter of the fourth year [4:01–4:03].

The counts, unweighted, of allocations to the five categories, are provided in Table 14.5. These categories will be the basis for the comparisons with the KFS

Table 14.5 PSED II case allocations during 1st quarter, fourth year of start-up

Start-up stage: criteria	Count	Percent
1. No listing in registries, no revenue	211	24.7
2. Multiple listings in registries, no revenue	106	12.4
3. No listing in registries, revenue but not profitable	147	17.2
4. Listings in registries, revenue but not profitable	289	33.8
5. Listings in registries, revenue exceed expenses in 1st year	101	11.8
Total	854	100.0

14.4 Identifying KFS Cases by Start-Up Stage

Identifying cases from the KFS cohort for comparing the start-up stages is somewhat less complex. The KFS study was designed to capture a sample of new firms in the very early stages of business activity and follow them in the early years as active firms. As they were taken from the D&B files of listed businesses and screened to ensure they were included in at least one other registry, none could be considered as "unlisted entities." As a result, none could be considered for two of five categories associated with the PSED II sample.

Classifying the KFS cases into the different start-up stages is based on reports of income and profitability. There are two sources of information in the first wave interview schedule related to the issues of funds.

1. [F15] In calendar year 2004, did [NAME BUSINESS] receive any revenue (money) from the sales of goods, services, or intellectual property? [YES or NO]
2. [F23] Profit is the business' income after all expenses and taxes have been deducted. What was [NAME BUSINESS]'s total profit or loss for the calendar year 2004? [PROFIT or LOSS]

In all three cases—profit, revenue, or loss—questions about the amounts were provided to the respondent. Of the 35% that reported no revenue in 2004, 31% reported on a later question that the firm had made a profit; this was 15% of the sample. While reporting a loss when no revenue was received would not cause a problem, it is difficult to resolve the inconsistency between reports of no revenue and reports of profits. As a consequence, classification into the three categories based on revenue and profits were based on the reports of amounts. Only those that did not provide any amount for revenue or profits were considered to have no revenue or no profits.

The classification of all KFS cases is presented in Table 14.6. Once the cases selected for the representative sample were identified, the final weight after application of the nonresponse model [WGT_FINAL] was adjusted such that

Table 14.6 KFS case classifications

Start-up stage: criteria	Count	Percent
1. No listing in registries, no revenue	–	–
2. Multiple listings in registries, no revenue	855	17.3
3. No listing in registries, revenue but not profitable	–	–
4. Listings in registries, revenue but not profitable	2,411	48.9
5. Listings in registries, revenue exceed expenses in 1st year	1,663	33.7
Total	4,928	100.0

the sum of the weights for each of the three categories equaled the number of cases. In other words, the average value of the weighs for each start-up stage equaled 1.0.

14.5 Stages in the Start-Up Process: PSED, KFS Comparisons

The issue for resolution is the extent to which the PSED II and KFS samples appear to be drawn from the same population. The strategy for resolution is to identify cases that appear to be in the same stage of the start-up process and compare these sub-samples on a range of basic features.

If there is a match between sub-samples, it would appear they may be drawn from the same population. In that case, the PSED II data may be considered a description of the start-up or gestation process prior to inclusion in the KFS cohort; the KFS data may be considered a description of the business life course after completion of the start-up or gestation process. If there is no match between these sub-samples, these two cohorts may have been drawn from different populations; this would reduce confidence that the two data sets reflect experiences in the business life course of the same population of business ventures.

Comparisons will consider the nature of the primary respondents and the features of the business entities.

14.5.1 Respondent

Primary respondent characteristics are presented in Tables 14.7 and 14.8. For these presentations, data from the PSED II project are presented for five start-up categories and the KFS project for the three categories where cases have been allocated. The column to the far right provides comparisons based on the entire samples.

It is clear there are differences. The KFS cohort has a larger proportion of men, almost 70%, compared to 60% for the PSED II cohort. These differences are statistically significant for start-up stages 4 and 5 and the total sample. More dramatic is the difference in the ages of the primary respondents, which tends to be somewhat older for the KFS cohort. This is statistically significant for all three stages where comparisons are possible. Most striking is the very low proportion of those under 25, at about 2%, compared to 10% for the PSED II cohort. The difference is also found among those 55 years and older. It would appear that the new ventures of older men are more likely to be included in the D&B listings.

The bottom of Table 14.7 present comparisons based on the ethnic classification of the primary respondent.[8] While the majority for both projects report that they are White, the PSED II project seems to have a larger proportion of respondents in other ethnic categories except for start-up stage five, where the two samples are similar.

Table 14.7 Respondent characteristics by start-up stage: PSED II, KFS (1/2)

Category	1	2	3	4	5	All
Business registration status	None	Listings	None	Listings	Listings	
Revenue, profits	None	None	Income	Income	Profits	
Respondent gender						
PSED II						
Men	62.9%	61.3%	56.1%	57.5%	61.2%	59.6%
Women	37.1%	38.7%	43.9%	42.5%	38.6%	40.4%
KFS						
Men		68.4%		65.7%	73.0%	68.7%
Women		31.6%		34.3%	27.0%	31.3%
Statistical significance (χ^2)		(0.122)		(0.005)	(0.009)	(0.000)
Respondent age						
PSED II						
18–24 yrs old	13.5%	5.1%	12.2%	7.4%	11.8%	9.8%
25–34 yrs old	27.3%	21.2%	32.5%	29.0%	17.6%	25.6%
35–44 yrs old	27.1%	25.4%	26.0%	26.6%	41.2%	28.2%
45–54 yrs old	23.7%	35.6%	19.5%	21.9%	16.7%	23.3%
55–64 yrs old	9.2%	11.0%	7.3%	11.8%	7.8%	10.0%
65–74 yrs old	1.9%	1.7%	1.6%	2.7%	3.9%	2.5%
75–up yrs old	1.0%	0.0%	0.8%	0.7%	1.0%	0.7%
KFS						
18–24 yrs old		1.2%		2.7%	2.2%	2.3%
25–34 yrs old		20.3%		19.7%	19.9%	19.9%
35–44 yrs old		30.8%		35.5%	33.5%	34.0%
45–54 yrs old		28.5%		26.2%	27.1%	26.9%
55–64 yrs old		15.0%		13.7%	14.4%	14.1%
65–74 yrs old		3.5%		2.0%	2.4%	2.4%
75–up yrs old		0.6%		0.3%	0.5%	0.4%
Statistical significance (χ^2)		(0.022)		(0.000)	(0.000)	(0.000)
Respondent ethnicity						
PSED II						
White	73.2%	73.7%	62.0%	78.6%	78.4%	74.1%
Black	12.2%	13.6%	14.9%	8.5%	6.9%	10.8%
Hispanic	3.4%	0.0%	9.1%	3.7%	9.8%	4.8%
Mixed/other	11.2%	12.7%	14.0%	9.2%	4.9%	10.3%
KFS						
White		79.5%		77.4%	81.9%	79.2%
Black		9.3%		9.9%	6.3%	8.6%
Hispanic		6.3%		6.6%	6.6%	6.5%
Mixed/other		4.9%		6.2%	5.3%	5.7%
Statistical significance (χ^2)		(0.000)		(0.060)	(0.633)	(0.000)

The presence of those born outside the United States is presented at the top of Table 14.8; the PSED II samples have a slightly higher proportion of U.S. born respondents, although there is no statistically significant difference for any of the three start-up stages.

Table 14.8 Respondent characteristics by start-up stage: PSED II, KFS (2/2)

Category	1	2	3	4	5	All
Business registration status	None	Listings	None	Listings	Listings	
Revenue, profits	None	None	Income	Income	Profits	
Respondent nativity						
PSED II						
Born in the United States	92.9%	94.1%	95.9%	92.3%	95.1%	95.1%
Born outside the United States	7.1%	5.9%	4.1%	7.7%	4.9%	4.9%
KFS						
Born in the United States		88.3%		89.2%	89.1%	89.0%
Born outside the United States		11.7%		10.8%	10.9%	11.0%
Statistical significance (χ^2)		(0.058)		(0.093)	(0.053)	(0.000)
Respondent education						
PSED II						
Up to HS degree	26.7%	23.3%	30.3%	15.8%	18.4%	21.8%
Post-HS, no BA degree	41.4%	32.5%	44.3%	39.6%	38.8%	39.7%
College degree	20.5%	24.2%	17.2%	28.2%	27.2%	24.0%
Graduate experience, degree	11.4%	20.0%	8.2%	16.4%	15.5%	14.5%
KFS						
Up to HS degree		16.5%		12.4%	16.2%	14.4%
Post-HS, no BA degree		35.6%		38.8%	37.5%	37.8%
College degree		24.3%		23.2%	25.0%	24.0%
Graduate experience, degree		23.6%		25.6%	21.2%	23.8%
Statistical significance (χ^2)		(0.296)		(0.003)	(0.566)	(0.000)

In a similar fashion, the proportion with different levels of education, shown at the bottom of Table 14.8, are quite similar. For the two comparisons there is no statistically significant difference; for start-up stage 4 and all case comparisons there are more KFS cases with graduate experience.

14.5.2 Business Venture

The samples from the two projects are compared on six business aspects in Tables 14.9–14.13. Again, the different start-up stages and full cohorts are the basis for comparison.

The nature of the start-up venture is presented at the top of Table 14.9; there are statistically significant differences for all comparisons. This is mainly due to the absence of multi-level marketing and business sponsored new ventures in the KFS sample. Multi-level marketing, such as those promoting Amway products to their friends, work colleagues, and neighbors, are a small but

Table 14.9 Venture characteristics by start-up stage: PSED II, KFS [1/3]

Category	1	2	3	4	5	All
Business registration status	None	Listings	None	Listings	Listings	
Revenue, profits	None	None	Income	Income	Profits	
Nature of start-up venture						
PSED II						
Independent start-up	90.9%	77.5%	85.6%	73.2%	77.7%	80.6%
Existing business purchase or takeover	3.3%	2.5%	1.6%	4.4%	7.8%	3.7%
Franchise	1.4%	5.8%	2.4%	3.7%	1.0%	2.9%
Multi-level marketing	1.9%	5.0%	4.0%	10.4%	4.9%	5.9%
Sponsored by an existing business	2.4%	9.2%	6.4%	8.4%	8.7%	6.9%
KFS						
Independent start-up		94.0%		91.4%	92.8%	92.3%
Existing business purchase or takeover		4.8%		5.2%	5.0%	5.1%
Franchise		1.2%		3.4%	2.2%	2.6%
Multi-level marketing		0.0%		0.0%	0.0%	0.0%
Sponsored by an existing business		0.0%		0.0%	0.0%	0.0%
Statistical significance (χ^2)		(0.000)		(0.000)	(0.000)	(0.000)
Current legal form						
PSED II						
Sole proprietorship	31.9%	30.7%	39.3%	45.9%	44.4%	39.0%
General partnership	4.3%	4.4%	9.8%	5.5%	11.1%	6.4%
Limited partnership	2.9%	2.6%	0.8%	2.7%	1.0%	2.3%
Corporation, LLC	5.2%	17.5%	3.3%	17.5%	12.1%	11.7%
Corporation, sub-chapter S	1.9%	8.8%	0.0%	6.8%	10.1%	5.2%
Corporation, general (C-corp)	0.5%	4.4%	1.6%	2.1%	1.0%	1.9%
Not yet determined	53.3%	31.6%	45.1%	19.5%	20.2%	33.5%
KFS						
Sole proprietorship		31.5%		33.6%	41.5%	35.9%
General partnership		4.5%		4.0%	3.4%	3.9%
Limited partnership		2.8%		1.4%	1.3%	1.6%
Corporation, LLC		30.4%		32.3%	28.8%	30.5%
Corporation, sub-chapter S		20.9%		20.0%	20.1%	20.2%
Corporation, general (C-corp)		10.0%		8.7%	5.8%	7.9%
Not yet determined		0.0%		0.0%	0.0%	0.0%
Statistical significance (χ^2)		(0.000)		(0.000)	(0.000)	(0.000)

significant category among PSED II cases. They may not, however, have a D&B listing separate from the corporation they represent. In all cases where a PSED II case is sponsored by an existing business, the majority of the ownership is held by natural persons, the business or institutional ownership is less

Table 14.10 Venture characteristics by start-up stage: PSED II, KFS (2/3)

Category	1	2	3	4	5	All
Business registration status	None	Listings	None	Listings	Listings	
Revenue, profits	None	None	Income	Income	Profits	
Nature of location						
PSED II						
Personal residence	36.2%	43.7%	52.5%	56.2%	46.6%	48.1%
Existing business site (customer related, other)	3.9%	5.0%	4.9%	7.7%	13.6%	6.6%
Business specific	3.4%	10.1%	4.1%	13.0%	16.5%	9.4%
Not needed yet	56.5%	40.3%	37.7%	20.7%	20.4%	34.6%
Other/mixed	0.0%	0.8%	0.8%	2.3%	2.9%	1.3%
KFS						
Personal residence		47.7%		46.4%	54.2%	49.3%
Existing business site (customer related, other)		3.8%		3.2%	4.9%	3.9%
Business specific		46.0%		49.4%	39.8%	45.6%
Not needed yet		0.0%		0.0%	0.0%	0.0%
Other/mixed		2.6%		1.0%	1.1%	1.3%
Statistical significance (χ^2)		(0.000)		(0.000)	(0.000)	(0.000)

than a majority. Not only are these cases excluded in the initial KFS survey screening for eligibility, many may not have independent D&B listings in the early stage of development. A precise comparison of cases from the two cohorts might require that multi-level marketing and business sponsored cases be dropped from the PSED II sample.

The bottom half of Table 14.9 presents the legal form reported at the time of the interview. As shown in Table 14.3, a different form of the question was used in the two projects. The option of "not determined yet" was part of the PSED II interview schedule; no such option was explicitly provided in the KFS interview. Perhaps as a consequence, all the KFS cases are assigned to a legal form, while 20–50% of the PSED II cases have no legal form. The much larger proportion of KFS cases in a corporate form (LLC, subchapter S, C-corp) may reflect the systematic addition of new incorporation filings from state records into the D&B registries. As these D&B registries are the source of the KFS sample, it may account for the lower proportion of sole proprietorships.

The location of the nascent, new business ventures is presented in Table 14.10. Again there is a difference in the way questionnaire items were presented, the option of "not needed yet" was part of the PSED II item, but not the KFS item. The major difference, consistent for all three start-up stages, is the larger proportion of a business-specific site reported for the KFS cohort. The proportion at a personal residence is about the same for both projects.

The top of Table 14.11 reports on the size of the start-up team. For the KFS interview data is only obtained on natural humans; the PSED II schedules allows for responses—based on expected ownership of the nascent venture—that

Table 14.11 Venture characteristics by start-up stage: PSED II, KFS (3/3)

Category	1	2	3	4	5	All
Business registration status	None	Listings	None	Listings	Listings	
Revenue, profits	None	None	Income	Income	Profits	
Size of start-up team						
PSED II						
One owner-manager	51.9%	52.1%	61.0%	49.3%	54.9%	52.7%
Two owner-managers	31.9%	31.1%	31.7%	42.3%	36.3%	35.8%
Three owner-managers	10.5%	7.6%	4.1%	5.0%	4.9%	6.4%
Four owner-managers	5.2%	8.4%	3.3%	3.0%	2.9%	4.4%
Five or more owner managers	0.5%	0.8%	0.0%	0.3%	1.0%	0.6%
KFS						
One owner-manager		66.0%		68.7%	72.2%	69.5%
Two owner-managers		27.5%		25.1%	22.6%	24.7%
Three owner-managers		4.3%		4.6%	3.1%	4.1%
Four owner-managers		1.5%		1.3%	1.3%	1.4%
Five or more owner managers		0.7%		0.3%	0.4%	0.4%
Statistical significance (χ^2)		(0.000)		(0.000)	(0.003)	(0.000)
Number of employees						
PSED II						
No paid employees	99.5%	97.5%	93.5%	88.3%	84.3%	92.7%
1–5 paid employees	0.5%	1.7%	4.8%	7.7%	13.7%	5.4%
6–10 paid employees	0.0%	0.0%	1.6%	2.0%	1.0%	1.1%
11–20 paid employees	0.0%	0.0%	0.0%	1.3%	1.0%	0.6%
21 and more paid employees	0.0%	0.8%	0.0%	0.7%	0.0%	0.2%
KFS						
No paid employees		68.1%		56.1%	59.1%	59.2%
1–5 paid employees		25.2%		36.0%	33.5%	33.3%
6–10 paid employees		3.5%		4.3%	3.5%	3.9%
11–20 paid employees		1.9%		2.2%	2.7%	2.3%
21 and more paid employees		1.3%		1.3%	1.2%	1.3%
Statistical significance (χ^2)		(0.000)		(0.000)	(0.000)	(0.000)]

include other businesses or institutions. These juristic owners, which occur in about 10% of the PSED II cases, have been excluded for this comparison.

Nonetheless, the differences are quite dramatic, as the KFS samples have a somewhat larger proportion of one owner-manager ventures than the PSED II samples. Across the three sub-groups, the proportion of one-person start-ups for PSED II is 52%, compared to 69% for the KFS samples; the KFS samples are 30% higher. The KFS samples have an average of 1.9% with four or more owners, compared to 5.5% for the PSED II sample. For a sole person that is developing their own business, a letter offering $50 for completing a

14 PSED II and the Kauffman Firm Survey

Table 14.12 Venture industry sector: PSED II compared to KFS

NASIC 2-digit	Category Number of cases	PSED II 847	KFS 4,928
11	Agriculture, forestry, fishing	4.3%	1.2%
21	Mining	0.1%	0.1%
22	Utilities	0.0%	0.1%
23	Construction	9.1%	11.0%
31	Manufacturing	6.3%	6.4%
42	Wholesale	4.1%	5.9%
44	Retail	19.4%	14.2%
48	Transportation, warehousing	1.9%	2.7%
51	Information	3.9%	3.1%
52	Finance and insurance	3.3%	4.5%
53	Real estate, property rental, leasing	5.0%	5.2%
54	Professional, scientific, technical services	12.3%	16.1%
55	Management of companies, enterprises	0.0%	0.3%
56	Administration, waste management, remediation services	6.6%	11.1%
61	Educational services	2.1%	0.5%
62	Health, social services	4.1%	3.5%
71	Arts, entertainment, recreation	4.1%	2.6%
72	Accommodations, food, beverages	5.1%	2.4%
81	Consumer service, other	8.4%	9.1%
	Total	100.0%	100.0%

Table 14.13 Venture industry sector by start-up stage: PSED II, KFS

Category	1	2	3	4	5	All
Business registration status	None	Listings	None	Listings	Listings	
Revenue, profits	None	None	Income	Income	Profits	
Primary economic sector						
PSED II						
Extractive	3.4%	6.0%	3.3%	5.4%	2.9%	4.4%
Transform, distribution	24.0%	32.8%	20.3%	23.4%	30.4%	25.2%
Business services	27.4%	21.6%	28.5%	29.8%	24.5%	27.1%
Consumer services	45.2%	39.7%	48.0%	41.5%	42.2%	43.3%
KFS						
Extractive		1.2%		1.5%	1.1%	1.3%
Transform, distribution		28.7%		27.5%	31.7%	29.1%
Business services		36.6%		34.3%	42.0%	37.3%
Consumer services		33.6%		36.8%	25.1%	32.3%
Statistical significance (χ^2)		(0.000)		(0.000)	(0.000)	(0.000)

self-administered questionnaire over the internet or responding to a phone interview may have been an attractive option. This may have resulted in KFS samples with a larger proportion of one-person ventures.

In contrast, the size of the ventures in terms of the number of employees, presented at the bottom of Table 14.11, show the opposite pattern. The average number of cases across the three start-up stages with no employees in the PSED sample is 90%; it is 61% for the KFS sample. Again, this may reflect how D&B identifies their new listings. Those with employees may be more likely to be included in the many sources used by D&B to compile listings of new business, which are, in turn, the source of the KFS sample.

The economic sector of the business ventures were classified based on the North American Standard Industry Classification [NASIC]. A comparison based on the full samples and 20 different sectors is presented in Table 14.12. There appears to be a slightly higher proportion of retail and agriculture, forestry, and fishing nascent ventures in the PSED II cohort; the KFS cohort seems to have a slightly higher proportion of professional, scientific, and technical services as well as administration, waste management, and remediation services new ventures.

Because of the small size of the PSED II sample, these 20 sectors were collapsed into four categories for a comparison by start-up stage. This is presented in Table 14.13. The biggest differences are associated with more business service ventures associated with the KFS cohort and more consumer service and extractive nascent enterprises in the PSED II cohort. These differences are statistically significant for all four comparisons.

There are then, small but significant differences in the industry sectors represented by the KFS and PSED II cohorts.

14.6 Overview

What, then, are the major differences between the PSED and KFS samples? A summary of comparisons based on the three stages where the presence of listings and reports of revenue and profits are harmonized is presented in Table 14.14.

Differences in the characteristics of the respondent—either a sole proprietor or a key member of a start-up team—are not major. The KFS cohort has a slightly higher proportion of men and whites and a smaller proportion of younger persons.

Differences in the character of the business venture, either a nascent enterprise or a venture reporting revenue and profits, are more substantial. The KFS sample has—compared with the PSED II sample—more independent start-ups, twice as many established in a corporate form, and twice as many with specific sites for the venture activity. In the KFS sample 7 in 10 are one-person operations, compared with 5 in 10 in the PSED II sample. Only 10% of the PSED sample report employees at the time of the interview, compared with 40% for the KFS sample. There are small differences in the economic sectors represented by the two cohorts; the KFS sample seems to have a larger proportion of new ventures in more sophisticated sectors.

14 PSED II and the Kauffman Firm Survey

Table 14.14 Cohort comparison overview: PSED II, KFS

Dimension	PSED II	KFS
Gender	60% men	68% men
Age	More under 34 years old	More over 45 years old
Ethnicity	77% white	80 % white
Native born	94 % U.S. born	89 % U.S. born
Education	No difference	No difference
Nature of start-up	76% independent, More multi-level marketing, business sponsored	92% independent
Legal form	40% sole proprietorships, 27% corporate form, 24% not determined,	37% sole proprietorships, 57% corporate form
Locations	49% personal residence, 27% not needed yet	47% personal residence, 47% specific site
Size of start-up team	52% one person 5% four or more	69% one person 2% four or more
Number of employees	90% none	61% none
Economic sector	Slightly more in agriculture, retail	Slightly more in professional, scientific, technical services; administrative, waste management, remediation services

In sum, it would appear that the business ventures represented by the KFS sample are somewhat different from those in the PSED II sample; they represent different populations. One advantage of the PSED II sample is that the population represented by the sample is known; the KFS sample is based on new D&B listings. Other than the fact that they are D&B listings, little is known about the population represented by the D&B new registrations. While they may approximate new firms in the United States, it seems to be a listing of convenience, not a systematic effort to assemble a precise census of entities with known characteristics.

These differences may reflect the commercial objectives of Dun & Bradstreet. Their major clients seek information on the credit worthiness of potential customers or potential clients for marketing campaigns. A dormant listing in their file is not a major problem. Few will inquire about the credit rating of an inactive firm and an undelivered mailing or unanswered phone call is a low-cost error. In contrast, not having an active firm in the file can be a major problem. In short, the bias is to include and keep all listings with the slightest potential for commercial activity, there is less incentive to delete the inactive. The high proportion of ineligible cases in the D&B sample, eligibility could not be determined for 47% of the 32,459 cases selected for the sample, is consistent with this orientation (DesRoches et al., 2007). Similar problems have been reported in other efforts to utilize the D&B files to generate samples of new firms (Reynolds, West, & Finch, 1985).

14.7 Commentary

There is considerable value and interest in developing a portrayal of the life course of U.S. businesses, both the typical firms implemented by millions of individuals as well as that small proportion, some with a technological focus, with growth potential. Firms that realize their growth potential are known to provide disproportionate contributions to job growth and wealth creation. But it takes many years for business creation to take place, and a systematic study of the life course is accelerated if two different projects can track different parts of the firm creation and establishment process.

But the value of such efforts is maximized when the samples selected for analysis represent a known population. This not only increases confidence in the extent to which patterns found in the sample represent the greater population, it also provides for the capacity to extrapolate from the sample to estimate values for the broader population. The PSED II screening procedure, based on a representative sample of households, facilitates estimates of the number of U.S. nascent entrepreneurs at about 12 million (Reynolds & Curtin, 2008). For this reason, it is possible to use the PSED II cohort to estimate the number of persons, and nascent enterprises, that move through the start-up process to create new firms as well as the resources they absorb, both formally and informally, in the firm creation process.

The KFS cohort is based on new listings in the Dun and Bradstreet credit rating files. The comparisons with the PSED II cohort was based on identifying different stages of the start-up process based on the presence of income and profits and listing of the new ventures in a variety of business registries. This excluded about 42% of the PSED II cohort for which there would be no direct match with KFS cases; these are nascent enterprises that have not been incorporated into any existing business registry.

The results indicated that the nature of the individuals reporting on the ventures, nascent entrepreneurs, or new firm owner-managers, was broadly similar, with slightly more men and older respondents in the KFS cohort. But the nature of the business ventures themselves—the proportion of independent start-ups, corporate forms, one-person start-up teams, and the presence of employees was quite different. It appeared that the business ventures represented two different populations, albeit populations with some overlap.

What is to be done? This depends on the objectives and the desired level of precision.

If there is no interest in developing analysis of new firms in the early years, then analysis of the KFS cohort can proceed with no adjustment. Considerable care would be required in any analysis that used the PSED II cohort and the KFS cohort to provide a description of *all* early stages of the business life course. Extrapolation to the total population of new firms would be facilitated by a calibration of the D&B new firm census with other censuses of new firms. Both the Bureau of Labor Statistics (BLS) and the U.S. Census develop counts of new employer firms; the BLS on a quarterly basis, the U.S. Census on an annual basis (National Research Council, 2007). However, these government archives are based on mandatory tax filings and access to the identity of the individual firms would be difficult and operationally very complex. It is unlikely to be a viable option.

If more precision is desired for the early stages of business creation, it would be possible to enhance the PSED II cohort to provide more precision regarding the relation of these nascent enterprises to the D&B lists. What is required is information on incorporation of the PSED II cases into the D&B business registries; preferably both the mechanism by which inclusion takes place as well as the date of inclusion would be obtained. This may be done by providing D&B with a list of the business enterprises, nascent and established, maintained for the PSED II follow-ups. Once the D&B listing details for each PSED II case is known, it would then be possible to develop a PSED II sub-sample that would match the new incorporations into the D&B registries.

This information could the be used to (1) assess the nature of the business creation stages—prior to incorporation into the D&B listings—and (2) create an estimate of the early stage activity that is missed by the D&B procedures. There is wide agreement that D&B coverage of established businesses is relatively complete, but there is considerable ambiguity about coverage of emerging enterprises and at what stage in the start-up process a D&B listing first occurs.

There is growing evidence that the business creation process is relatively stable in the United States, with little change in human participation rates or firm birth rates over the past several decades (Reynolds, in press). A calibration of the procedures used by D&B to identify and incorporate new ventures into their database would do much to clarify the population represented by the KFS sample. It would provide a useful asset for exploring a basic feature of the U.S. economy, the business creation activity that is critical for adaptation and growth.

Notes

1. Weighted frequencies based on reports of dollar amounts of revenue, profits, and losses provided by the respondent.
2. Data on enterprises that become present and profitable after the initial PSED II interview is available, but for periods of less than 1 year.
3. High- and medium-tech industry sectors were based on the percentage of research and development employment in the industry in the late 1980s (Hadlock, Hecker, & Gannon, 1991). There were no items in the KFS interview schedule to provide a firm specific assessment of an emphasis on technology.

4. Based on reports of dollar amounts of revenue and profits.
5. These criteria and their application are discussed in more detail in Reynolds (2007) and Reynolds and Curtin (2008).
6. This analysis included all details on the occurrence and timing of start-up activities from PSED II Waves A and B data collection and, as a result, is somewhat more complete than the preliminary analysis presented in Reynolds and Curtin (2008). It accounts for a larger number of cases in the current analysis, as the additional information identified more cases that had completed 3 or more behaviors and 2 within a 12-month period. Additional changes can be expected as additional follow-up interviews are completed.
7. This outcome, 10% as new firms, is somewhat less than the 33% found in the PSED I analysis after 5 years (Reynolds, 2007). This reflects a longer time frame, three rather than one follow-up interview, and the use of a more precise definition of "firm birth" in the PSED II data set. In PSED I, firm birth reflected the respondent's interpretation of the transition, rather than being based on reports of positive monthly cash flow for 6 or more months.
8. In attempts to harmonize ethnic classification of the primary respondent in both projects, those that reported several ethnic categories are placed in the mixed/other category. Those responding yes to the Hispanic item are classified as Hispanic, even if they later indicate another category on a separate item.

References

DesRoches, D., Barton, T., Ballou, J., Potter, F., Zhao, Z., Santos, B., et al. (2007). *Kauffman firm survey (KFS) baseline methodology report: Final report* (Reference No. 6091-180). Princeton, NJ: Mathematica Policy Research, Inc.

Dun & Bradstreet. (2002, October). *Increase your profitability by fueling sales and marketing with D&B quality information.* PowerPoint sales presentation.

Hadlock, P., Hecker, D., & Gannon, J. (1991, July). High technology employment: Another view. *Monthly Labor Review, 114*(7), 26–30.

National Research Council. (2007). Understanding business dynamics: An integrated data system for America's future. In J. Haltiwanger, L. M. Lynch, & C. Mackie (Eds.), *Panel on measuring business formation, dynamics, and performance.* Committee on National Statistics, Division of Behavior and Social Science and Education. Washington, DC: National Academies Press.

Reynolds, P. D. (2007). New firm creation in the United States: A PSED I overview. *Foundations and Trends in Entrepreneurship, 3*(1), 1–150.

Reynolds, P. D. (in press). Screening item effects in estimating the prevalence of nascent entrepreneurs. *Small Business Economics.*

Reynolds, P. D., & Curtin, R. T. (2008). Business creation in the United States: Panel Study of Entrepreneurial Dynamics II initial assessment. *Foundations and Trends in Entrepreneurship, 4*(3), 155–307.

Reynolds, P. D., West, S., & Finch, M. (1985). Estimating new firms and new jobs: Considerations in using the Dun and Bradstreet Files. In J. A. Hornaday et al. (Eds.), *Frontiers of entrepreneurship research* (pp. 383–399). Wellesley, MA: Babson College.

University of Michigan Survey Research Center. (2007). *PSED 2 poststratification weights.* Available at: www.psed.isr.umich.edu.

Chapter 15
Future Opportunities

Paul D. Reynolds and Richard T. Curtin

The business creation process is the lifeblood of the economy. It is the continuous flow of new businesses that is the most fundamental determinant of a vibrant economy. The Panel Study of Entrepreneurial Dynamics focuses on the conditions that prompt people to start a new business and the factors that are associated with success or failure of those efforts. The research project aimed to provide a valid and reliable description of the business creation process for a nationally representative sample, to facilitate empirical tests of existing theories from several disciplines, and contribute to the development of more robust theories of entrepreneurship. The contributions to the book demonstrate the success of the project in all three areas.

The chapters presented in this volume are related to one of these three objectives. Eight chapters emphasize detailed analysis of distinctive aspects of the business creation process. Chapter 2 focused on the distinctive psychological and cognitive processes of nascent entrepreneurs, Chapter 3 on the relationship between contextual motivations and growth aspirations, Chapter 4 on how family background might affect participation in firm creation. Chapters 5, 6, and 7 emphasized different aspects of team formation and supportive social networks. Chapters 8 and 9 focused, respectively, on business planning as part of the start-up process and the roles of human and social capital or technological expertise.

Five chapters emphasize the development of descriptions of the firm creation process. Chapter 10 reviewed the types of financing developed by new firms. Chapter 11 attended to conceptual issues in defining the conception, or entry into the business creation process or firm births while Chapter 12 explored the use of start-up activities to define major characteristics of an operating business. Chapter 13 focuses on cross-national descriptions of business creation and Chapter 14 on the relationship between two panel studies, each emphasizing a different stage of the business life course.

P.D. Reynolds (✉)
George Mason University, Fairfax, VA, USA
e-mail: pauldavidsonreynolds@gmail.com

15.1 Future Research Opportunities

While many of these assessments were comprehensive and detailed, most of the research terrain is still unexplored. There are three major directions for additional analysis.

The first set of opportunities would take advantage of additional data on the future developments of these nascent enterprises. The chapters in this volume were based on the initial detailed interview (Wave A) and the first follow-up (Wave B) in the PSED II cohort; the majority of the nascent enterprises are still in the start-up mode 12 months after the first interview. Data from the 24-month follow-up (Wave C) was just being made available as this work was being prepared for publication in late 2008. At the same time interviews to complete the 36-month follow-up (Wave D) were just being implemented. A consolidated, four-wave PSED II data set should be available late in 2009; such a data set is already available for PSED I.

Once the consolidated data set that incorporates this additional information is prepared, there will be information on the outcome status of a much greater proportion of the PSED II cohort, summarized in Table 15.1. The actual results from the Wave C interviews are included in the fourth column. Projections for Wave D in the sixth column are based on preliminary data for Wave D. While the response rates for the Wave B and Wave C follow-ups have been 80%, Wave C results include data from some interviews with respondents missed in the Wave B follow-up. This level of success is included in the Wave D projections.

Table 15.1 Cumulative status of PSED II start-up efforts by survey wave: actual and projected

Status	Wave A	Wave B	Wave C	Wave D (preliminary)
New firm established (initial profits)		128	182	196
Quit all efforts		231	406	507
Total final outcome		359	586	703
Start-up phase	1,214	613	472	382
Unknown status		242	156	129
Total cases	1,214	1,214	1,214	1,214
		29.6	48.3	57.9

Data on the transition to a new firm or disengagement (quits) are available for 48% of the cases when Wave C data are combined; it is expected to be available for 58% of the cases when Wave D is completed.

Therefore, when the PSED II four-wave consolidated data set is available, it will be possible to pursue detailed assessments of the impact of a wide range of variables and processes on the outcome of these efforts to create a new firm. It will be possible to determine the differences between those that developed a new firm reporting initial profits, those that disengaged or quit, and those that continue to contribute to the start-up process.

The second type of opportunity is for the data collection period to be extended beyond Wave D for which funding has been obtained. It has been found that 58% of the cases has either started a firm or quit all start-up efforts by Wave D. While it is likely that a small proportion of the cases will remain in the start-up phase for years to come, it is essential for the overall research to allocate those still remaining in the start-up phase between the more or less "permanent" start-ups from more serious efforts. While the screener questionnaire attempted to exclude those whose efforts were more of a hobbyist, it may be that some have all but given up efforts to establish a new business, but have not abandoned the plan. Given than 31.5% of the initial sample was still in the start-up phase at the end Wave D, additional follow-up interviews would significantly reduce the proportion with unknown outcomes.

The third type of opportunity for further analysis is related to the wide range of individual, contextual, or procedural characteristics that have not, as yet, been explored with the PSED II data set. In other words, the majority of the factors and processes that are part of the business creation process have yet to be explored in detail, in relationship to each other, or in comparison to outcomes (new firm or quits) after the Wave C or Wave D interviews. There are, as well, other measures of new firm contributions, such as job creation, sales, or impact on the markets. Many of the assessments of factors affecting firm creation have been summarized in Davidsson (2006), but this would include the effects or influences related to:

- Age, gender, and ethnic background;
- Nature and diversity of educational background;
- Influence of personal traits and dispositions;
- Household income or net worth;
- The community and economic context, perceived and reflected in objective measures;
- Variations in competitive strategy;
- Variations across economic sectors;
- The nature or combination of various start-up activities;
- Measures of business experience and background.

Of particular importance would be potential interactions between combinations of different factors, such as sector of emphasis related to the economic structure where the new firm is launched or interaction between household financial status, motivation, and personality traits. When these various independent variables are taken in combination, the opportunities for analysis are almost infinite.

The perspective of the PSED project is unique in the field of entrepreneurial research. This project focused on the conditions that surround the first emergence of an idea for a new business and the process that brings that idea to fruition. In contrast, the more typical study in this field focuses on business startups that are more advanced, and are more concerned about the success of the fledging business in its first several years of operation. These analyses are complimentary, emphasizing different stages of the firm creation process. The PSED panel begins with the germination of the business idea through a profitable launch; the more typical study begins at the launch and follows the business through its adolescent years.

Predicting which start-up will be eventually successful is a daunting task. To be sure, the disengagement (quit) rates are highest in the early phases of the business start-up process; it might seem reasonable to limit the study's focus to only those who have passed that first hurdle. Nonetheless, it is the germination of that new business idea, the conception of a firm in gestation that critically determines the number of potential start-up enterprises. Moreover, while the exceptional innovation may garner most headlines, it may be that an even greater share of economic progress is due to the many small improvements contributed by more ordinary new business ventures. Quite apart from these assessments of economic impact, the decision to focus on the initial phases of a business start-up was driven by a theoretical interest in determining which of the many factors played a key role in the birth of a new firm.

Business creation has a central role in economic growth and adaptation; it is a very popular career option for many, and a vigorous, effective entrepreneurial sector is critical for the United States to maintain a global competitive advantage. Understanding the many issues affecting business creation is both a fascinating experience and can make a contribution to the national well-being.

Reference

Davidsson, P. (2006). Nascent entrepreneurship: Empirical studies and developments. *Foundations and Trends in Entrepreneurship*, 2 (1), 1–76.

Appendix A
Panel Study of Entrepreneurial Dynamics II: Research Design

A.1 Research Goals

The primary objective of the research design for the Panel Study of Entrepreneurial Dynamics (PSED) was to collect valid and reliable data on the basic features of the business start-up process based on nationally representative samples of the adult population in the United States. The business start-up process was defined as beginning when entrepreneurs took their first steps toward the establishment of a new firm and as ending when the new firm became profitable. The research program had two primary goals: to determine the economic and demographic characteristics of people who attempted to start new businesses and to determine which personal, economic, or market factors helped to facilitate or interfered with the establishment of new firms. Representative samples of the U.S. population would insure that the survey estimates could be generalized to the entire population of people or start-up firms.

These ambitious research goals required that every adult in the United States be eligible for the survey and that the collected data for nascent entrepreneurs be comprehensive with follow-up interviews extending over the subsequent years. As a matter of science, such a design is straightforward; as a matter of cost, it can be prohibitively expensive. Two decisions about the research design were made to significantly reduce costs. First, since nascent entrepreneurs are relatively rare in the population, accounting for less than one-in-twenty adults, the procedures used to identify nascent entrepreneurs were separated from the process that collected the detailed panel data. Second, the window of eligibility was broadened to include all people in any phase of the business start-up process, from those who had just begun the process to those who had made substantial progress but had yet to establish an ongoing and profitable business. While both decisions had significant cost advantages, neither decision had significant disadvantages with regard to the overall research objectives.

A.2 Identification of Nascent Entrepreneurs

The identification of a representative sample of nascent entrepreneurs was a distinct challenge. The research design required that nascent entrepreneurs be identified at the very beginning of the business start-up process. As a result, it was necessary to identify potential start-up initiatives before they were included in any business registries, such as Dun & Bradstreet. The research design required screening all adults in the population to determine whether they qualified as nascent entrepreneurs. Given the low prevalence rate, this meant screening about 20 adults to find each person in the business start-up process. To reduce the cost of screening, a national omnibus survey was located that provided large ongoing national samples, which could identify potential candidates at costs much closer to marginal costs of the added questions than the very high fixed costs of conducting a short screening survey.

Opinion Research Corporation (ORC) of Princeton, New Jersey, was commissioned to conduct the screening survey. ORC conducted two representative samples each week of 1,000 adults living in the contiguous 48 states and the District of Columbia. The interviews were conducted by telephone, and the sample was based on random digit dial (RDD) techniques to create representative samples of U.S. households. Once a household was contacted, an individual aged 18 or older was selected as the respondent, with quotas enforced so that half the respondents were men and half, women. A total of 31 national samples were screened. Each sample included at least 1,000 interviews and was completed over a 4-day period; about half of the interviews were started on Thursday and completed on Sunday, and the other half were started on Friday and completed on Monday. The survey used a three-call design (initial call plus two callbacks), although 4% required four or more calls to complete.

The identification of nascent entrepreneurs was based on answers to a series of questions designed to elicit information on the key selection criteria. First, respondents were asked three questions about whether they were involved in any business start-up on their own behalf or for an employer, or if they currently owned a business. The wording of the questions about whether any of these conditions applied to the respondent were:

a. Are you, alone or with others, currently trying to start a new business, including any self-employment or selling any goods or services to others?
b. Are you, alone or with others, currently trying to start a new business or new venture for your employer, an effort that is part of your normal work?
c. Are you alone or with others, currently the owner of a business you help manage, including self-employment or selling any goods or services to others?

Table A.1 shows the distribution of responses to each of these questions. Overall, 22.1% of all respondents said one or more of the above statements

Appendix A

Table A.1 Determination of eligibility in screening interview

Total sample size	31,845	100%
Met general criteria:		
a. Currently trying to start a new business on own behalf?	3,393	10.7%
b. Currently trying to start a new business for your employer?	1,830	5.8%
c. Currently the owner of a business you help manage?	4,573	14.4%
Total met for any general criteria	7,043	22.1%
Met behavioral criteria		
d. Took actions to help start new business in the past 12 months?	3,427	10.8%
Met ownership criteria		
e. Will own this new business?	3,029	9.5%
Met profit criteria		
f. Revenues less than expenses for more than six of the past 12 months?	2,393	7.5%
Consented to detailed interview		
g. Granted permission for University of Michigan to contact them?	1,671	5.3%
h. University of Michigan confirmed accuracy of information provided?	1,587	5.0%

was true for them. The most common report was that they were a current business owner, followed by starting a business on their own behalf, and lastly engaged in a new business venture for their employer. Multiple activities were common, as 40% reported being involved in two or more of the activities, with 12% who reported all three activities.

This was the most general criteria. Respondents were then asked in progressive order other qualification questions. The next criterion was behavioral, and respondents were asked if they took any action in the past 12 months to further the new business venture:

d. Over the past 12 months have you done anything to help start a new business, such as looking for equipment or a location, organizing a start-up team, working on a business plan, beginning to save money, or any other activity that would help launch a business?

Unless they took some specific action in the last 12 months they were eliminated as candidate entrepreneurs. This criterion had a large impact on the selection process, reducing the number of candidate entrepreneurs by half, with active entrepreneurs falling to 10.8% of the total sample (see Table A.1). Whether someone should be considered as trying to start a new business who has not undertaken any recent actions in that regard is of course debatable; for the purposes of this research, only currently active entrepreneurs were considered.

The next criterion involved whether they expected to own all or part of the new firm. Without an ownership stake, the person is acting as an employee not an owner or entrepreneur:

e. Will you personally own all, part, or none of this new business?

This question had only a small additional impact, reducing the number of candidate nascent entrepreneurs from 10.8% to 9.5% of the original sample.

This small additional impact was no doubt due the widely understood "ownership" in the prior questions.

Given that the study focused on the business start-up process, a definition of the start as well as the end of the process was required. Just as taking some specific actions during the past 12 months was used as a marker of the start of the process, the end of the start-up process was defined as the establishment of an ongoing profitable business. The critical issue was to provide a definition of when the firm was "born" and when the start-up process was complete, not whether the firm survived the initial years following its establishment. A standard definition of what it means for a new business to be "profitable" was difficult to devise, especially what costs were included and the length of time over which the calculation was made. The research design viewed businesses as still being part of the start-up process if revenues did not cover all operating costs, including salaries of all managing owners, for more than six of the prior 12 months. The questions were

f. Has this business received any money, income, or fees for more than six of the past 12 months? (IF YES): Has monthly revenue been more than monthly expenses for more than six of the past 12 months? (IF YES): Did the monthly expenses include salaries or wages for the owners active in managing the business for more than six of the past 12 months?

These questions reduced the number of candidates who were still in the start-up process to 7.5% of the total sample. It should be noted that this is an unweighted estimate, provided to illustrate the attrition of cases in the interview process. Substantive analyses should utilize the case weights developed to ensure the sample values represents the true population values; the developments of these weights is discussed below.

The final step was to ask whether those who qualified for the detailed interview would give their consent for ORC to provide their first names, phone number, and demographic information to the University of Michigan for a follow-up study. The questions were

g. A national study of the work in career patterns of all Americans, including those not currently working, is being conducted by the University of Michigan. They would like your permission to allow them to contact you for the study. We would provide the University of Michigan your telephone number and demographic information. This is completely voluntary, and all the information will remain confidential. Those who participate will receive a payment of $25. May they contact you? (IF NO): Of course your participation in this study is voluntary, but it is an interview that many people find very interesting. Can the University of Michigan researchers contact you and tell you what is involved? You can change your mind at any time.

The second question was a probe for those who initially refused permission. Of the total 1,671 who agreed, 93% agreed in response to the first question.

Appendix A

As part of their initial contact with the 1,671 respondents obtained by the University of Michigan, 84 cases could not be verified because of incorrect or disconnected phone lines or respondents who admitted that they were not involved in a new business start-up. As a result, the base sample was reduced to 1,587, or 5.0% of the original sample.

A.3 Completion of Detailed Interviews with Nascent Entrepreneurs

Each week that the screening survey was conducted, the sample of respondents who were eligible and consented were transferred from ORC to the University of Michigan. The cases were then immediately contacted by the Survey Research Center (SRC) to conduct the first detailed interviews. The first screening interview was conducted on September 22, 2005 and the last on January 29, 2006. In turn, the first detailed interview was conducted on September 29, 2005 and the last on March 1, 2006. Of the total 1,587 sample cases, interviews were conducted with 1,214, or 76.5% of the eligible cases. The phone interview took 60 minutes to complete. Each respondent was sent a check for $25 at the completion of the interview.

The second interview was scheduled one year later in the same week that the initial interview took place. For a variety of reasons, some respondents were not immediately available during the scheduled week. Most of the short delays were caused by finding an agreeable time when the respondent could do the interview, the repeated calls required to convince some respondents to complete the follow-up interviews, and the time required to find respondents who had moved. This resulted in an extension of the overall interviewing period for the second interview. The second interviews were conducted from October 3, 2006 to March 24, 2007. Of the total 1,214 eligible cases, interviews were conducted with 972, or 80.1% of the eligible cases (see Table A.2). There were five respondents who had died by the time of the second interview; they were included in the base used to determine completion rates. The dates on which each interview was actually conducted are included as part of the data record so that analysts can use that timing information to align responses between waves.

The average number of calls required to complete the first detailed interview was 6.3, and the median was 4.0. To complete the second interview required substantially more effort at contacting respondents, as the average number of calls to complete the second interview increased by 50% to 9.6 from 6.3. Most of the increase was accounted for by respondents who were most difficult to contact: whereas the median number of calls increased from 4 to 5, the most intensive efforts—cases in the 90th percentile or higher—took at least 15 calls to complete the initial interview and 23 calls to complete the second interview (see Table A.2). The number of calls needed to complete the interview is also included in the data file so that analysts could determine if respondents who were particularly hard to interview provided different responses from those who

Table A.2 Detailed interviews: success, effort, understanding, and interest

	Wave A	Wave B
Sample disposition		
Business start-up activities still in process	1,214	613
Established business		128
Quit all efforts to start business		231
No contact		242
Total cases	1,214	1,214
Completion rate	76.5%	80.1%
Dates interviews completed		
Start date	September 29, 2005	October 3, 2006
End date	March 1, 2006	March 24, 2007
Number of calls to complete interview		
33rd percentile	2	3
50th percentile (median)	4	5
66th percentile	6	8
90th percentile	15	23
Mean	6.3	9.6
Understanding of questions		
(Interviewer ratings)		
Excellent	58%	63%
Good	31	29
Fair	9	7
Poor	2	1
Total	100%	100%
Interest in interview		
(Interviewer rating)		
Friendly and interested	81%	86%
Cooperative but not particularly interested	17	12
Impatient	2	2
Hostile	0	0
Total	100%	100%
Interview's impact on interest in new business		
(Respondent rating)		
More interested	58%	NA
No effect	40	
Less interested	2	
Total	100%	

more readily cooperated with the interview request. For example, those more reluctant to cooperate may have reported less success in their endeavors; this would have implications for the potential bias arising from those who refused to do the follow-up interview on estimates of success or failure for overall start-up efforts.

It was of some interest to determine if the language and concepts used in the detailed interview were understood by the respondents. Needless to say, the questions needed to be worded in a way that respondents could provide detailed information about specific features on the new venture, including various aspects of their business plans, ownership structure, legal status, financial investments and liabilities, and so forth, as well as detailed financial information about the nascent entrepreneur. Significant efforts were made to insure that respondents would understand each question. While it is impossible to provide a robust assessment of whether each respondent understood all of the questions, the interviewer's assessment of the respondent's understanding of the questions is a useful indicator. This assessment is based on the feedback given by respondents to the interviewer as each question was asked. In the initial interview, interviewers thought that 89% had an "excellent" or "good" understanding of the questions; in the second interview, interviewers judged that 92% had the same level of comprehension of the questions (see Table A.2).

The overall quality of the data not only depends on the respondents understanding of the questions, but also on their motivation to make the effort to carefully considers their answer and their willingness to provide detailed answers. One measure of the motivation of respondents is whether they were interested in the topic and were cooperative during the interview. Interviewers thought that 81% of all respondents were "friendly and interested" (see Table A.2). Just 17% were judged by the interviewers to be "friendly but not particularly interested," and a scant 2% were thought to be "impatient" or "hostile."

Rather than subjective assessments on the part of the interviewer, respondents were directly asked about whether the interview had an impact on their own interest in starting a business. It is a well-known finding in all sciences from quantum physics to sociology that observation affects reality. It is of course impossible to determine what impact the initial interview may have had on the ultimate outcome of the business venture. Nonetheless, the respondents report of whether the interview increased or decreased their interest in starting a new business can be taken as an indicator of their interest in the interview and their willingness to cooperate in subsequent interviews. When asked at the end of the initial interview whether the interview had made them more or less interested in starting the new business, 58% reported that they were more interested compared with just 2% who reported that they were less interested (see Table A.2).

A.4 Data Editing and Cleaning

The detailed interviews were conducted using a computer-assisted program that automatically guided the interviewer and respondent to the proper question sequence. The program not only led the interviewer to ask the next appropriate question depending on the respondent's answers to previous questions, it also checked for consistency in the respondent's answers. Of course, the program did not allow the interviewer to enter an invalid code; the real benefit is that the program identifies potential or actual inconsistencies across a broad range of circumstances. When the program detected a potential error, it automatically presented the interviewer an appropriate probe to clarify the respondent's answer.

The consistency checks ranged from very simple cross-checks based on the last response to more complex consistency checks based on the responses to a number of questions or the responses to questions asked in the previous interview. For example, one of the most straightforward checks was on frequencies or dollar amounts, where the answer entered was outside of the range expected. In this case, the computer automatically displayed a follow-up question for the interviewer that asked the respondents to verify and, if necessary, correct their response. In most cases this revealed an easily correctable misstatement by the respondent or an incorrect recording by the interviewer. To be sure, there were some cases where the respondents did confirm that their response, however unexpected, was actually correct. Answers considered outside of the expected range were defined as simply uncommon, but not unreasonable; in effect this meant that all particularly large or small responses were probed for their accuracy.

More complex consistency checks involved, for example, all the component questions to insure that they added to the correct total; if an error was detected, the program would ask for clarification by the respondent, typically repeating the appropriate questions. In some cases the program insisted on a correction (that the components add to 100%, for example, or that some component or the total was changed to be consistent), while in other cases, if the respondent repeatedly verified that the answer was indeed correct, it was accepted.

A good deal of effort was put into creating a comprehensive set of consistency checks because the best time and the best source to correct any errors are during the actual interviews with the corrections made by the respondent. Respondents can be called again at a later date (and some were), but this approach is much more expensive and provides less reliable data. More importantly, this consistency-check approach meant that inconsistent or missing data would not need to be imputed by researchers. Importantly, it is not claimed that the data are all accurate, but that any unexpected answers were verified by the respondent. Clearly, respondents can be wrong. Nonetheless, even though some apparent inconsistencies remained, they were not deleted from the data set. The process of business creation is fraught with the unexpected, and some actual facts about the business may well have been well outside of the normal range of expected values. The purpose of the data collection was to accurately reflect the reports of the respondents.

A.5 Missing Data Rates

It is difficult to verify whether the respondent provided complete and accurate reports of the information requested in the survey. One indicator of the quality of the collected data is the amount of "missing data" due to the respondents' confusion about the meaning of the question or their refusal to provide an answer. The cognitive abilities of the respondents as well as their willingness to provide the effort to understand and answer questions are critical to obtaining completed and accurate responses. The questions were carefully designed so that they could be easily understood by every respondent, a challenging task given the desired details on the ownership structure and finances of new businesses. The success of this effort was confirmed by the high interviewer ratings of the respondents' understanding of the questions mentioned earlier. In addition, the willingness of respondents to undergo the effort to provide the detailed answers was aided by the respondents' perception that the interview was interesting.

Missing data rates are one indicator of whether people understood the questions and were willing to provide answers. A summary of the average missing data rates for different questionnaire groups is included in Table A.3. The groups differ in terms of how much information is required from the respondent and the sensitivity of that information. The groups differed in the number of questions included (see the table for the exact question numbers), with the questions selected generally asked about the entire sample in the initial Wave A interview. The first group contained relatively straightforward questions about attitudes, motivations, and preferences; these questions were not intrusive and demanded the least cognitive effort to answer. Nearly all respondents provided an answer to these questions, with an average missing data rate

Table A.3 Average missing data rates for selected Wave A questions

	Average missing data rates (%)
Motivations, attitudes, and preferences (36 Questions: AF1-AF10, AP1-AP12, AW1-AW14)	0.3
Descriptions of start-up activities (30 questions: AB8, AC1, AC2, AC4, AD1, AD2, AD6, AD9, AD11, AD13, AD16, AC18, AD20, AD22, AD24, AD26, AD28, AE1 AE5 AE11, AE18, AD20, AE24, AE26, AE28 AE30, AE32, AE34, AG1, AG3)	1.1
Dollar values for start-up funding (15 questions: AR6-AR20)	2.6
Respondent demographics (30 questions: AH1, AH2, AH3 AH5, AH6, AH10, AH15, HA16, AX1-AX9, AZ0-AZ13, AZ28, AZ30	0.3
Dollar values for household income, assets, and debts (6 questions: AZ15b, AZ29, AZ32, AZ33, AZ34, AZ37b)	5.0

of less than one-third of 1% (0.3%). The questions on which behaviors the respondent had completed as part of the business start-up process were somewhat more demanding, and a few of the questions could be considered as asking about proprietary topics. Just 1.1% of all respondents, however, did not provide an answer. The most challenging questions were about the dollar amounts invested or borrowed to support the start-up, with separate questions covering various amounts. These questions entailed a higher cognitive burden, presuming a willingness to provide what would otherwise be confidential data. As anticipated, the missing data rate was higher, but it still averaged a relatively low 2.6%. Questions about the demographic characteristics of the respondent and their families were reported by nearly all respondents, with an average missing data rate of just 0.3%. Finally, questions that asked for dollar amounts on the household's financial situation presented greater cognitive and privacy challenges, but nonetheless an average of just 5.0% of all respondents refused to provide the information.

Overall, these missing data rates are far below the average for surveys of a similar type—or even any other surveys. For example, the missing data rate on income for the screener questionnaire conducted by ORC was 22.4% compared with just 6.1% for the detailed questionnaire conducted by the University of Michigan. This low level of missing data will boost case counts in all analyses and greatly reduce the need for imputation of missing data.

A.6 Online Project Documentation

All project documentation, including questionnaires, data files, and codebooks are available on the project website: www.psed.isr.umich.edu. The website always includes the latest version of the data sets and documentation. The best way to review the questions asked is by reading the questionnaires—a special version that was designed for easy reading, indicating the flow of questions and which respondents were asked what question. The actual questionnaire was programmed in a computer-assisted telephone interviewing program, commonly called a CATI application. All of the data and documentation are freely available to any interested researcher. A bibliography of books, journal articles, and working papers is also available on the website.

A.7 Questionnaires and Codebook

The goal of the panel survey was to follow all nascent entrepreneurs to the completion of the start-up process. Some questions were repeated in each panel wave, whereas some were asked only once. In general, questions about the enduring characteristics of the nascent entrepreneur or firm were asked only once, such as the age of the respondent. Questions were repeated about

Appendix A

changing characteristics of the respondent and of the fledging firm (such as the income of the entrepreneur or the finances of the nascent firm). A summary of the modules included in each interview schedule is provided in Table 1.2.

There is one codebook for all waves of the detailed interview data that is available on the PSED project website. A second codebook exists for the screener data. For any case that completed the detailed interview, their answers to the screener questionnaire are included in the codebook and data files for the detailed interviews. This division was desirable given that the screener data file includes 31,845 cases, which would greatly expand the size of the data set for the 1,214 cases in the detailed interview file. Researchers can of course merge both files if they choose.

Given the length of the questionnaire, the main codebook for the detailed interview is more than 500 pages. The codebook can be viewed electronically, and any page or group of pages can be easily printed since it is in Adobe PDF format. An index at the back of the codebook lists the question numbers from the questionnaire and the relevant page number to find the associated codebook entry.

The codebook contains the definition of all numeric codes in the data file. The codebook entry for each question lists the wording of the question, the definition of the codes, the frequency of responses, any variations in the wording of the question, and the variable names for each wave that the question was asked. The variable names are typically the question numbers given in the questionnaire, with "A" added as a leading digit for Wave A questions and a "B" for Wave B questions. Thus, question E18 for Wave A has the variable name AE18 and for Wave B the identical question is named BE18. No frequencies are listed for open-ended questions, such as dollar amounts. The sum of the frequencies equals the total number of cases that were eligible to be asked the question. Eligibility depends on a number of factors, including the respondent's answers to prior questions or answers in a prior panel interview. All respondents who were ineligible to be asked a question were coded with the SAS or SPSS system missing data value.

A.8 Format of Data Files

The data sets are available on the PSED website in SAS and SPSS formats. Both files are stored as self-extracting zip files that can be downloaded; simply double-click on the file and select a directory location for the file. Readily available translation programs can be used to create other types of file formats, such as STATA.

There are two versions of the data file. The first version includes all the data for all 31,845 respondents contained in the screening interviews. The second version includes all the data for the 1,214 cases that completed the first detailed interview, including the data from the screening interview. The first data file is required for analysis of the prevalence of entrepreneurs in the total population. The second data file is for the analysis of the detailed interviews of the nascent entrepreneurs.

The data files are organized with cases as rows and variables as columns. The responses to each panel wave are included as separate variables. In most cases, the later variable simply provides updated information on some action or dollar figure. There were some entirely new questions in Wave B, especially questions regarding any discontinued efforts to start a business as well as special questions on any new business established.

A.9 Survey Weights

Survey weights were developed to address the potential biases in the collected data due to non-coverage and non-response. Coverage biases may result when some potential respondents were excluded from the initial sample, and response biases may result when some selected respondents could not be located or would not complete the initial or second interview. The survey weights included in the data file were designed to provide unbiased estimates based on either the screener or the detailed interview data.

Coverage bias may have resulted from the sample selection procedure used in the screener survey conducted by ORC. The ORC's sample was drawn as an RDD sample of the U.S. (the contiguous 48 states and the District of Columbia) landline telephone household population. ORC provided weights for each weekly sample based on the probability of selection, non-response, and post-stratification adjustments. These weights served as the base weight that underwent additional adjustments by SRC. Perhaps the most important additional step was to base a second round of weight adjustments on the combined outcome of all of the 31 samples; ORC weighted each of the 31 samples separately. The final combined screener weights were more reliable and introduced less variation in the data due to the weights.

Potential non-response bias may affect the results of ORC's screener survey as well as the results of the detailed interviews. Not all cases could be contacted, and if contacted, not all cases agreed to be interviewed. Potential biases due to differential non-response were corrected separately for the screener, the initial interview and the second interview. Based on data from the Current Population Survey (CPS) conducted by the U.S. Census, the screener and detailed interview data were post-stratified so that the observed distributions were consistent with known totals from an independent and reliable source.

Every analysis done using either the screener data or the detailed data files should use the weights provided. Estimates that ignore the weights may risk bias. In addition, special software that can accommodate survey weights is recommended for variance estimation (Proc Survey Means in SAS, for example). At minimum, for any analysis the sum of the weights should be adjusted to

Appendix A

equal the sum of the cases included in the analysis to help insure accurate estimates of variance and statistical tests. The three weight variables are:

Screening weight: WT_Scrn
Wave A weight: WT_WaveA
Wave B weight: WT_WaveB

Whenever an analysis is based on any data from Wave B, the second interview wave, the appropriate weight variable is WT_WaveB, even if some of the variables included in the analysis were part of the Wave A questionnaire.

A.10 Calculation of Screening Weights

The revised post-stratification weights for ORC's screener sample were based on the combined 31 weeks of independent samples, using ORC's weight as a base. The ORC weight included adjustments for differences in the probabilities of selection as well as initial post-stratification adjustments. Additional post-stratification adjustments were based on income, sex, age, and the race of the respondent. These variables were selected because they were important predictors of entrepreneurial status. Imputations of missing information on race, age, and especially income were done using standard estimation techniques (there was no missing data on sex). Imputations were needed for 2% of all cases for age, for 2.8% of cases for race, and for 22.4% of cases for income. The data for the imputed cases, observed cases, and the combined totals are shown in Table A.4.

The combined imputed and observed screener data were then distributed into the cross-classification of the four variables—sex, age, income, and race. Counts of the interviews in each of the 80 cells (2 sex * 4 age * 5 income * 2 races = 80 cells) were then calculated from the screener data; in four instances, the cell sizes were smaller than 20 and these cells were combined with adjacent cells to yield a total of 76 adjustment cells. The control totals for these cells were taken from the Current Population Survey of March 2005. The base ORC weight was then used along with the imputations to develop survey estimates for each of these cells. The adjustment factor was then calculated for each cell as

$$W_{Scrn\_PostStrat} = \frac{\hat{\pi}_{CPS,i}}{\hat{\pi}_{ORC,i}}$$

where i indexes all 76 adjustment cells created by the cross-classification of sex, age, income and race; $\hat{\pi}_{CPS,i}$ is the estimate of the population proportion in cell i derived from CPS; and $\hat{\pi}_{ORC,i}$ is the estimate of the population proportion in cell i derived from the ORC screening interview. The final screener weight based on the combined ORC weight and the new SRC post-stratification weight was calculated as

Table A.4 Observed and imputed post-stratification variables for screening interview

	Observed values		Imputed values		Combined values	
	Frequency	Percent	Frequency	Percent	Frequency	Percent
Age						
18–29	4,302	14	59	9	4,361	14
30–44	7,281	23	126	20	7,407	23
45–64	12,563	40	399	63	12,962	41
65 or older	7,063	23	52	8	7,115	22
Total	31,209	100	636	100	31,845	100
Missing as % sample				2.0%		
Race						
African American	2,102	7	45	5	2,147	7
White/other	28,867	93	831	95	29,698	93
Total	30,969	100	876	100	31,845	100
Missing as % sample				2.8%		
Income						
< $25,000	5,309	21	214	3	5,523	17
$25,000–40,000	4,850	20	1,073	15	5,923	19
$40,000–60,000	5,592	23	3,199	45	8,791	28
$60,000–100,000	5,441	22	1,381	19	6,822	21
$100,000 or more	3,524	14	1,261	18	4,786	15
Total	24,716	100%	7,128	100	31,845	100
Missing as % sample				22.4%		

$$WT_{Scrn} = W_{ORC} * W_{Scrn\_PostStrat}$$

The final step was to trim some extreme weights at the 2nd and 98th percentiles. The resulting weights were then centered such that the sum of the weights equals the total number of cases. In the screener data set, this weight is called WT_SCRN.

Table A.5 shows the unweighted percentages of subgroups for the demographic variables compared to percentages that are weighted using the newly developed weight, and the percentages as estimated by the Current Population Survey conducted in March 2005.

A.11 Weights for Detailed Panel Interviews

The weights for the detailed interviews were devised to correct for non-response on the part of the nascent entrepreneurs who were identified in the screening interview. Some of those identified as in the process of starting a business did not agree to be contacted by the University of Michigan, others, who initially agreed to be interviewed, could not be located for the detailed interview, and finally some who were contacted refused to do the detailed interview. As a

Appendix A

Table A.5 Distributions for CPS, unweighted and weighted screener survey

	CPS March 2005	PSED screener survey Unweighted	PSED screener survey Weighted
Sex			
Male	48	50	48
Female	52	50	52
Total	100%	100%	100%
Age			
18–29	22	14	22
30–44	29	23	29
45–64	33	40	33
65 or older	16	23	16
Total	100%	100%	100%
Race			
White/other	88	93	88
African American	12	7	12
Total	100%	100%	100%
Income			
< $25,000	21	21	21
$25,000–40,000	16	20	16
$40,000–60,000	18	23	18
$60,000–100,000	25	22	25
$100,000 or more	20	14	20
Total	100%	100%	100%

result, the nascent entrepreneurs who were identified in the screening interview differed from the set of people who completed the detailed interviews.

The weighted results from the screening interview were used to determine the demographic characteristics of nascent entrepreneurs. These estimates were then used as control totals for the development of post-stratification weights for the detailed interviews. The variables selected were income, age, race, and ethnicity. Given that the total number of cells in the cross-classification of these four variables was quite large, many of the individual cells had fewer than ten cases. The total number of cells was reduced by collapsing cells that were closest in terms of a dozen key survey variables. The result was the creation of 29 distinct cells for the four variables. The weight was then defined as

$$W_{WA\_PostStrat} = \frac{\hat{\pi}_{SCRN,i}}{\hat{\pi}_{WA,i}}$$

where i indexes all 29 adjustment cells; $\hat{\pi}_{SCRN,i}$ is the estimate of the entrepreneurial population proportion in cell i derived from the screening interview; and $\hat{\pi}_{WA,i}$ is the estimate of the population proportion in cell i derived from the initial Wave A interviews.

The final step was to combine the post-stratification weight for the detailed interviews with the original ORC weight

$$WT_{WaveA} = W_{ORC} * W_{WA\_PostStrat}$$

Given that there were some extreme weight values, an analysis of the impact of trimming the weights was conducted for a dozen key survey variables. The differences between the estimates based on the untrimmed weights and estimates based on trimmed weights are a measure of the "bias" assuming that the estimates based on the untrimmed weights are unbiased. The goal was to find the trimmed weight with the lowest "bias" as well as the lowest standard error of the estimate. The more the weights are trimmed, the greater the potential for bias and the less inflation of variance due to weighting. The criterion used was the mean squared error (MSE), which is the combination of the impact on "bias" and standard errors. The best choice for trimming occurred at the 3rd and 97th percentiles of the distribution. The trimmed weights were spread across the other cases in the cells. The resulting weights were then centered such that the sum of the weights equaled the total number of cases.

The weights for the second Wave B interview were calculated in a similar fashion. The Wave B weights accounted for non-response in Wave B, so that the final Wave B weight accounted for non-coverage in the screener interview and non-response to the screener interview as well as the first and second interviews. The same cross-classification of income, age, race, and ethnicity were used to define the post-stratification cells. Since there were somewhat fewer interviews completed in Wave B than in Wave A, three additional cells were collapsed with the nearest cell, yielding a total of 26 post-stratification cells.

The first step was to calculate the post-stratification weight as

$$W_{WB\_PostStrat} = \frac{\hat{\pi}_{SCRN,i}}{\hat{\pi}_{WB,i}}$$

where i indexes all 26 adjustment cells; $\hat{\pi}_{SCRN,i}$ is the estimate of the entrepreneurial population proportion in cell i derived from the weighted screening interview; and $\hat{\pi}_{WB,i}$ is the estimate of the population proportion in cell i derived from the Wave B interview using the Wave A weights. The same procedure was used to trim extreme weights at the 3rd and 97th percentiles. The final Wave B weight was defined as the combination of the Wave A weight and the new Wave B weight as

$$WT_{WaveB} = WT_{WaveA} * W_{WB\_PostStrat}$$

The impact of the weights for variables that were common in the screener and the detailed panel Waves A and B are shown in Table A.6. Although the calculation of the weights were based on imputation of missing data, the distributions included in the table match the data contained in the public use

Table A.6 Comparison of unweighted and weighted distributions for samples of respondents eligible for detailed interviews

	Eligible cases in screening survey		Cases that completed detailed interview			
			Wave A		Wave B	
	UnWt	Wt	UnWt	Wt	UnWt	Wt
Region						
West	26	25	25	23	27	23
North Central	21	21	21	21	21	22
Northeast	17	17	17	18	17	17
South	36	37	37	38	35	38
	100%	100%	100%	100%	100%	100%
Sex						
Male	65	63	63	63	61	59
Female	35	37	37	37	39	41
	100%	100%	100%	100%	100%	100%
Age						
18–29	22	31	18	29	15	24
30–44	34	37	33	39	32	40
45–64	40	29	45	30	49	33
65 or older	4	3	4	2	4	3
	100%	100%	100%	100%	100%	100%
Income						
Under $25,000	17	19	18	19	18	22
$25,000–39,999	18	16	20	20	18	20
$40,000–59,999	23	17	24	19	24	24
$60,000–99,999	25	28	23	25	23	21
$100,000 or more	17	20	15	17	17	13
	100%	100%	100%	100%	100%	100%
Education						
Grade school	8	8	7	8	5	7
High school	24	23	22	22	20	22
Some college	31	33	33	35	33	34
College degree	37	36	38	35	42	37
	100%	100%	100%	100%	100%	100%
Marital status						
Married	58	55	57	53	59	55
Divorced	14	12	16	13	16	14
Widowed	3	3	3	2	3	2
Never married	25	30	24	32	22	29
	100%	100%	100%	100%	100%	100%

data files. It should be noted that most of the variables included in this table (region, sex, education, and marital status) were not included in the calculation of the weights; age and income were included in the estimation of the weights.

The differences between the unweighted and weighted estimates for the screener survey reflect the impact of differences in selection probabilities, non-coverage, and non-response. In general, all of the differences were generally very small, with the notable exception of age. The weighted screener distributions represent what would be expected if a complete representative sample of nascent entrepreneurs were interviewed.

Differences between the unweighted and weighted results for Wave A and Wave B interviews mainly reflect non-response and panel attrition. Comparisons of the results for each wave indicate the expected close correspondence, with the weighted results for Wave A and Wave B shifting toward the target represented by the weighted screener distribution.

About the Contributors

Howard E. Aldrich is Kenan Professor of Sociology at the University of North Carolina, Chapel Hill, where he won the Carlyle Sitterson Award for Outstanding Teaching in 2002. He is Chair of the Department of Sociology and Adjunct Professor of Management as well as Adjunct Professor of Strategy and Entrepreneurship in the Kenan Flagler Business School. In 2000, he received two honors: the Swedish Foundation of Small Business Research named him the Entrepreneurship Researcher of the Year and the Organization and Management Division of the Academy of Management presented him with an award for a Distinguished Career of Scholarly Achievement. His book, *Organizations Evolving*, won the Academy of Management George Terry Award as the best management book published in 1998–1999, and was co-winner of the Max Weber Award from the American Sociological Association's Section on Organizations, Occupations, and Work. Undergraduate work was completed at Bowling Green State (BA, 1965) and graduate work at the University of Michigan (MA, 1966; PhD, 1969).

John C. Alexander is a Professor of Finance at Clemson University, where he holds the Breazeale Professorship of Investments. A tenured teacher of graduate and undergraduate investments and corporate finance, he is actively involved in research and has been published in several prestigious periodicals including the *Financial Analysis Journal, The CFA Digest, Journal of Finance, Journal of Banking and Finance* and the *Financial Review*. He has also been a frequent speaker at professional meetings and a guest lecturer at other colleges and universities within the country and abroad. Dr. Alexander completed his BBA in Finance at Stetson University in 1984, and received his MBA the following year. In 1991 he earned his Ph.D. in Finance from Florida State University. His research interests include investments and entrepreneurial finance. In addition to his University responsibilities, he has continued to consult with corporations, particularly in the area of portfolio management and business valuation.

Phillip C. Anderson is a Ph.D. student in the Technological Innovation and Entrepreneurship group at the MIT Sloan School of Management. Using the Panel Study of Entrepreneurial Dynamics II (PSED II) data, his research explores how the characteristics and contributions of founding teams affect nascent venture outcomes. In a separate study, his research explores the evolution of complementary capabilities in high-tech firms. He earned degrees at the University of California Los Angeles (M.B.A.), Illinois Institute of Technology (M.S.E.E.), and Purdue University (B.S.E.E.).

Bart Bonikowski is a Ph.D. candidate in sociology at Princeton University. His research interests include the effects of social networks on the population distribution of tastes and attitudes, the relationship between access to cultural resources and social inequality, and cross-national differences in popular attitudes. His past work has examined the generation of risk-based social classification schemata by state surveillance practices, ecological niche competition among musical genres, and the impact of trade networks on cross-national attitudinal similarity. He is currently conducting a comparative study of collective representations of the nation in thirty countries.

Candida G. Brush is Professor of Entrepreneurship, holder of the Paul T. Babson Chair in Entrepreneurship, and Chair of the Entrepreneurship Division at Babson College. She is a visiting Adjunct Professor to the Norwegian School of Engineering and Technology in Trondheim, Norway. Dr. Brush is a founding member of *the Diana Project International*, and received the 2007 Swedish International Award for Entrepreneurship and Small Business Research. Her research investigates women's growth businesses and resource acquisition strategies of in emerging ventures. She is the author of 100 refereed journal articles, books and other publications. She is an Editor for *Entrepreneurship Theory and Practice*, and serves on several editorial boards. Dr. Brush is an active angel investor and board member of several emerging ventures and nonprofit organizations.

M. Diane Burton is an Associate Professor at the School of Industrial and Labor Relations (ILR) at Cornell University. Prior to joining the ILR school, she was on the faculty at the MIT Sloan School of Management and the Harvard Business School. She earned her Ph.D. in sociology at Stanford University and served as a lecturer and researcher in Organizational Behavior and Human Resources Management at the Stanford Graduate School of Business. Burton studies employment relations and organizational change in entrepreneurial companies. Her primary research is a major study of high-technology start-ups in Silicon Valley including the study of entrepreneurial teams and executive careers. Most recently, she had been studying R&D teams in a high-technology company. Her work has been published in the *American Sociological Review, American Journal of Sociology*, and *Organization Science*. In addition to her scholarly publications, she is the author of several best-selling HBS cases. Burton serves on the editorial boards of *Administrative Science Quarterly*, the *Journal of Business Venturing*, and *Organization Science*. She earned her undergraduate degree at Carnegie Mellon University, and an M.Ed. from the Harvard University Graduate School of Education.

Nancy M. Carter leads Catalyst in developing groundbreaking research on issues related to women's advancement in business and the professions. Prior to joining Catalyst, she was Leverhulme Visiting Professor at the London Business School and held the Richard M. Schulze Chair in Entrepreneurship at the University of St. Thomas, Minneapolis. She has worked professionally in advertising and marketing research and works closely with government and private sector initiatives in promoting women's advancement. She has published widely on gender, organizations, strategy, and entrepreneurship. Her book, *Clearing the Hurdles*, documents women's challenges in accessing resources for building their businesses. In 2007 she was honored with the prestigious *International Award for Entrepreneurship and Small Business Research* for her work on the *Diana Project*, a research initiative on women entrepreneurs and the venture capital industry. Her research on women and minority entrepreneurs has been funded by the National Science Foundation, the U.S. Small Business Administration, the National Business Women's Council, and the Ewing Marion Kauffman Foundation. Dr. Carter received her Ph.D. in Business Administration from the University of Nebraska, an M.A. in Mass Communications from California State University, and a B.A. in Journalism from the University of Nebraska. She is married and the mother of two adult sons.

Richard T. Curtin is a Research Professor and Director of the Survey of Consumers at the University of Michigan. As Co-Principal Investigator of the PSED research program he supervises all data collection and the website that provides open access to all material. He completed his graduate degree at the University of Michigan (Ph.D., 1975). Since becoming director of the University of Michigan's survey of consumer confidence in the early 1970s he has completed over 1,000 reports on trends in consumer expectations and consults widely with harmonized projects in other countries. He has published widely on survey methodology and analysis and has co-authored a number of chapters and monographs on the PSED research program.

Per Davidsson earned his Ph.D. at the Department of Economic Psychology at the Stockholm School of Economics, Sweden. He is currently Professor in Entrepreneurship and Assistant Dean of Research at the Faculty of Business, Queensland University of Technology, Australia. He has additional affiliations with the Jönköping International Business School, Sweden, Zhejiang University, China, and University of Louisville, United States. He is also an elected officer of the Entrepreneurship Division of the Academy of Management. Professor Davidsson has led and/or participated in multiple international-collaborative research projects addressing a broad array of entrepreneurship issues at the individual, team, organizational, regional, and national levels. This includes involvement on executive/advisory boards for the PSED I and PSED II studies in the United States and being one of the chief investigators for Swedish and Australian counterpart studies. His primary areas of expertise being new venture creation, small firm growth, and research methods; he is author of more than 100 published works on entrepreneurship topics including some of the best-cited works in the leading niche journals in this field. Further, he is associate editor of *Small Business Economics*, former manuscript editor of *Entrepreneurship Theory & Practice*,and serves on the editorial boards of several other leading journals.

Amy E. Davis is an Assistant Professor of Entrepreneurship and Small Business at the College of Charleston. Her research in entrepreneurship focuses on social networks, start-up teams, and gender. She received a dissertation fellowship from the Ewing Marion Kauffman Foundation for her dissertation "More (or less) than the sums of their parts? Status, teams and entrepreneurial outcomes." She has a Masters of Arts and Ph.D. in Sociology from the University of North Carolina at Chapel Hill and a Bachelor of Arts in Sociology from the University of Georgia. Her research has been published in *Frontiers of Entrepreneurship Research* and *Work and Occupations*.

Linda F. Edelman is an Associate Professor of Strategic Management at Bentley University. Before coming to Bentley she was a research fellow at the Warwick Business School. She received her MBA and her DBA from Boston University. Linda is the author of 14 book chapters and 30 peer-reviewed articles. In addition she has made over 50 scholarly and professional presentations. Her work has appeared in journals such as *Journal of Business Venturing,Journal of Small Business Management,Entrepreneurship Theory and Practice,Academy of Management Learning and Education,Organization Studies*, and *British Journal of Management*. She is on the editorial board of three peer-reviewed journals. Her current research examines the resource profiles and strategies of new ventures with a particular focus on nascent entrepreneurs.

Casey J. Frid is a doctoral student studying entrepreneurship and public policy at Clemson University. His research interests include emerging firm financing, nascent entrepreneurship, and public policy. His dissertation investigates nascent entrepreneur financing and its effects on firm emergence and performance. He holds an M.B.A. from Clemson University and a postgraduate degree in entrepreneurship from the Federal University of Juiz de Fora, Brazil. Prior to his doctoral studies, he worked as a consultant developing export and marketing strategies for start-ups in both Brazil and the Southeastern United States.

William B. Gartner is the Arthur M. Spiro Professor of Entrepreneurial Leadership at Clemson University. Before coming to Clemson University he was at the University of Virginia, Georgetown University, San Francisco State University, and the University of Southern California. All his degrees are from the University of Washington in Seattle: BA (1975) Accounting, MBA (1977) Business Policy, and Ph.D. (1982) Business Policy. He is one of the co-founders of the Entrepreneurship Research Consortium, which initiated and developed the Panel Study of Entrepreneurial Dynamics I (PSED I). He was the lead editor of *The Handbook of Entrepreneurial Dynamics*, which provides an overview of the PSED I research project. His research has been funded by the Small Business Administration, Kauffman Foundation, Coleman Foundation, U.S. Department of Education, Small Business Foundation of America, the Corporate Design Foundation and the National Endowment for the Arts. His research on nascent entrepreneurs explores their actions to launch new ventures. He also collects and analyzes the stories entrepreneurs tell about their experiences through the support of grants from the Hollingsworth Foundation and IDEA (International Danish Entrepreneurship Academy). He is the 2005 winner of the FSF-NUTEK Award for outstanding contributions to entrepreneurship and small business research.

Diana M. Hechavarria is doctoral student in Management at the University of Cincinnati's Lindner College of Business. Her research interests include nascent entrepreneurship, and topics in organizational theory. In particular, Diana explores the various dynamics confronted in the different stages of launching a new firm. Her teaching interests address new venture planning, entrepreneurship, and family business. Diana's research experience includes participation in various conferences and symposiums, such as the Academy of Management, the Panel Study of Entrepreneurial Dynamics Symposium, the George Mason Entrepreneurship Conference, Bancaja Young Entrepreneurs Conference, and the International Council for Small Business. Additionally, she has been involved in the coordination of the Panel Study of Entrepreneurial Dynamics II (PSED II) and the documentation of the Global Entrepreneurship Monitor (GEM) research initiative. Diana received her B.A. degree in Sociology with a minor in Women's Studies from the University of Florida (2004), and an M.A. in Liberal Studies with a concentration in Entrepreneurship from Florida International University (2007).

Benson Honig (Ph.D., Stanford University) is the Betty and Peter Sims Professor of Entrepreneurship, Wilfrid Laurier University, Canada, and Director, the Centre for the Study of Nascent Entrepreneurship and the eXploitation of Technology (NeXt). Studying entrepreneurship worldwide, his research interests include business planning, nascent entrepreneurship, transnational entrepreneurship, social entrepreneurship, social capital, and entrepreneurship in environments of transition. He has published over 25 peer-reviewed articles, including those in the *Academy of Management Learning and Education*, *Journal of Business Venturing*, *Journal of Management*, *Entrepreneurship, Theory and Practice*, *Entrepreneurship and Regional Development*, the ILO, and others. He serves on five editorial boards, including JBV and ET&P. He lives in Dundas, Ontario, Canada with his wife Dena and two children, Alon and Shanee. He states: "I love what I do; I must be one of the luckiest people on earth!"

Phillip H. Kim is an Assistant Professor of Management and Human Resources at the University of Wisconsin-Madison School of Business. He is also a faculty member of the Weinert Center for Entrepreneurship at the Wisconsin School of Business. His research interests include entrepreneurial teams and social networks, cross-national differences in technology entrepreneurship, institutional accounts of industry emergence, and entrepreneurship in regulated industries. He earned his M.A. and Ph.D. in Sociology at the University of North Carolina at Chapel Hill and his B.S. and B.A.S. at the University of Pennsylvania.

Jianwen (Jon) Liao is an Associate Professor of Entrepreneurship and Strategy at the Stuart School of Business, Illinois Institute of Technology. He has held visiting appointments at DePaul University, Hong Kong University of Science and Technology (HKUST), Cheung Kong Graduate School of Business (CKGSB), Peking University, and China European International Business School (CEIBS). Dr. Liao's research focuses on venture creation process, entrepreneurial growth strategies, and management of technological innovation as well. His research has appeared in academic journals such as *Small Business Economics, Entrepreneurship Theory and Practice, Journal of Small Business Management, Family Business Review, Journal of High Tech Management Research, Frontier of Entrepreneurship Research*, and *Journal of Management Inquiry*, among others. He received his Ph.D. in Management from Southern Illinois University at Carbondale.

Kyle C. Longest is an Assistant Professor of Sociology at Furman University. His research interests focus on social psychology and adolescence, with special attention to education, substance use, and identity. His work has appeared in journals such as the Journal of Marriage and Family and the Journal of Drug Issues. He completed his Ph.D. in the Department of Sociology at the University of North Carolina, Chapel Hill. He earned his BA in both Sociology and History at Indiana University, Bloomington.

Tatiana S. Manolova (D.B.A., Boston University) is an Assistant Professor of Management at Bentley University. She completed undergraduate work in international economic relations at the Higher School of Economics, Sofia, Bulgaria and has an MBA from the University of Tampa, Tampa, FL. Research and teaching interests include strategic management (competitive strategies for new and small companies, in particular), international entrepreneurship, and management in transitional economies. Tatiana is the author of over 25 peer-reviewed scholarly articles and book chapters. Recent publications appear in the *Journal of Business Venturing, Entrepreneurship Theory and Practice*, and *The Academy of Management Learning and Education*. She is currently affiliated with the *Panel Study of Entrepreneurial Dynamics*, which investigates the new firm creation process; and with *Diana International*, which explores growth strategies of women business-owners worldwide. In May, 2006, she served as a panelist at *The First Global Symposium on Growth Strategy and Growth Financing for Women Entrepreneurs*, organized by the Swedish Entrepreneurship and Small Business Research Institute (ESBRI). A native of Bulgaria, Tatiana worked for a state-owned cosmetics manufacturer and was a founding partner in two entrepreneurial ventures prior to coming to the United States to pursue her doctoral studies in strategy and business policy.

Charles H. Matthews is Distinguished Professor of Entrepreneurship and Strategic Management and Founder and Executive Director, Center for Entrepreneurship Education & Research College of Business, University of Cincinnati. Dr. Matthews is an internationally recognized scholar and innovative teacher in the field of entrepreneurship. His teaching and research interests include small, entrepreneurial, and family-owned ventures, decision-making, and leadership succession. He was a charter member of the ERC PSED I and served on the advisory board for PSED II. His research has been published in the *Journal of Small Business Management*, the *Journal of Small Business Strategy*, *Entrepreneurship & Regional Development, Frontiers of Entrepreneurship Research, Family Business Review, The International Journal of Operations & Production Management, The Center for the Quality of Management Journal, Quality Management Journal*, and *Industry & Higher Education*. He founded the UC Center for Entrepreneurship Education & Research in 1997, is a past President of the Fellow of the United States Association for Small Business and Entrepreneurship, and served as President of the International Council for Small Business in 2008–2009.

Alicia Robb is a Senior Fellow with the Kauffman Foundation and their Principal Investigator on the Kauffman Firm Survey, a longitudinal study of firm start-ups in the United States. She is also a Research Associate at the University of California, Santa Cruz and a Senior Economist with Beacon Economics. She specializes in minority entrepreneurship, women's entrepreneurship, entrepreneurial finance, small business dynamics, lending discrimination, government procurement, and economic development. She is also the Founder and President of the Foundation for Sustainable Development, an international development organization working with local nonprofit organizations in six countries throughout Latin America, East Africa, and South Asia. She received her Ph.D. in Economics from the University of North Carolina at Chapel Hill, specializing in economic development and econometrics. She has worked as a staff economist for the economic consulting firm Christensen Associates and as an economist for the Office of Economic Research in the Small Business Administration and for the Division of Research and Statistics at the Federal Reserve Board of Governors. She has taught economics courses in universities in the Washington, DC, and San Francisco Bay areas, as well as abroad.

Paul D. Reynolds is a Distinguished Visiting Professor in the School of Public Policy at George Mason University. Previous faculty appointments included the University of California, Riverside, University of Minnesota, Marquette University Babson College, London Business School, and Florida International University and visiting and research appointments at the University of Michigan, University of Pennsylvania Wharton School, INSEAD in France, and Nanyang Technical University in Singapore. He completed undergraduate work in engineering at the University of Kansas (B.S., 1960); all graduate work was completed at Stanford University, with degrees earned in business (1964, M.B.A.), psychology (1966, M.A.), and sociology (1969, Ph.D.). Over the past 20 years he was the coordinating principal investigator of two longitudinal studies of U.S. business creation (Panel Studies of Entrepreneurial Dynamics, I and II) and the founding principal investigator of a 40-nation comparison of entrepreneurial activity (Global Entrepreneurship Monitor). Reynolds currently serves as co-principal investigator of the second U.S. Panel Study of

Entrepreneurial Dynamics. He is the author or co-author of 5 books, 6 edited collections, 42 research reports and monographs, 85 peer-reviewed journal articles and book chapters, 7 data sets in the ICPSR archives, and over 200 presentations to professional and policy audiences. In 2004 Reynolds received the annual Swedish International Award for Entrepreneurship and Small Business Research.

Martin Ruef is Professor of Sociology at Princeton University, following previous faculty appointments at the Stanford Graduate School of Business and the University of North Carolina, Chapel Hill. His research considers the social context of entrepreneurship from both a contemporary and a historical perspective. Drawing on the PSED I and II surveys, he has examined team formation, innovation, exchange processes, and boundary maintenance among nascent entrepreneurs. Professor Ruef has also written on the institutional evolution of the U.S. healthcare field, as well as the agricultural and industrial transformation of the American South following the Civil War. His books include *Institutional Change and Healthcare Organizations* (with W. Richard Scott and colleagues), *Organizations Evolving* (with Howard Aldrich), and *The Sociology of Entrepreneurship* (co-edited with Michael Lounsbury). In addition, Professor Ruef's work on entrepreneurship has appeared in the *American Sociological Review*, the *American Journal of Sociology*, *Industrial and Corporate Change*, *Advances in Strategic Management*, and *Research in the Sociology of Work*. He is currently working on a monograph on entrepreneurial groups, which considers the interplay of social networks, identities, and collective action.

Mark T. Schenkel is an Assistant Professor of Entrepreneurship at Belmont University. He completed his Ph.D. in Strategy and Entrepreneurship at the University of Cincinnati, where he also served as Assistant Director of the University of Cincinnati Center for Entrepreneurship Education & Research. His primary research interests include opportunity recognition, entrepreneurial cognition, strategic decision-making, and corporate entrepreneurship. His work is published or forthcoming in *Entrepreneurship & Regional Development*, *Frontiers of Entrepreneurship*, *Journal of Small Business Management*, *New England Journal of Entrepreneurship*, *British Journal of Management*, *Academy of Management Review*, and *Management Research News*.

Claudia B. Schoonhoven is Professor of Organization and Strategy, Merage School of Business, University of California, Irvine, and Director of the Don Beall Center for Entrepreneurship and Innovation. She earned degrees at Stanford University (Ph.D., M.A.), University of Illinois Champaign-Urbana (B.A.), and Dartmouth College (M.A.). Professor Schoonhoven's prior positions were at the Tuck School, Dartmouth College, (1993–1998), Stanford University (1976–1977), San Jose State University (1977–1993), and she was a Visiting Scholar at the Graduate School of Business, Stanford University (1984–1985 and 1991–1992). Schoonhoven's research focuses on the evolutionary dynamics of technology-based firms, innovation, and entrepreneurship. She is co-author of *The Innovation Marathon: Lessons from High Technology Firms* and *The Entrepreneurship Dynamic in Industry Evolution*. Her research has been published in the *Administrative Science Quarterly, the Academy of Management Journal, Organization Science, Journal of Applied Behavioral Science*, the *Strategic Management Journal*, and other journals and books. The past Editor-in-Chief of *Organization Science*, Schoonhoven was elected a Fellow of the Academy of Management, to the Academy's Board of Governors, Chair of the Organization and Management Theory Division of the Academy, and President of the Western Academy of Management.

Kelly G. Shaver is Professor of Entrepreneurial Studies and Chair of the Department of Management and Entrepreneurship in the College of Charleston School of Business and Economics. He completed his education at the University of Washington in Seattle (B.A., 1963; M.S., 1965) and Duke University (Ph.D., 1969). Shaver was with the College of William and Mary Department of Psychology from 1968 to 2005, moving from Assistant to Full Professor; he was on leave from 1977 to 1979 to serve with the National Science Foundation as director of the Social and Developmental Psychology Program. He has been the author and co-author of 10 books, 4 chapters, and 69 peer-reviewed journal articles emphasizing psychology. His emphasis on entrepreneurship developed in the late 1980s resulting in participation in the creation of 4 books, 5 chapters, and 39 peer-reviewed journal articles related to entrepreneurship. He has been an editor of *Entrepreneurship Theory and Practice* (1994–1999) and Chair of the Academy of Management Entrepreneurship Division (2003–2004). He served as an elected member of the PSED I executive committee and was active as the team leader of the personality dimension modules for both PSED I and PSED II interview schedules.

Index

Note: The notations 'f', 't', and 'n' along with the locators represent 'figure', 'table' and 'note' present in the respective page.

A

Abandoned, 74, 96, 129–131, 279, 305
Absorptive capacity, 158
Academic entrepreneurship, 223
Active entrepreneurs, 309
Active nascent entrepreneurs, 7, 13 n3, 38, 222, 225, 229, 231, 235, 244, 265
Activities, 239–256
Advice, 118t, 119, 125–126
Advisory committee, PSED II, 10
Affiliate-workers, 128
Age, 98, 99t, 101t, 103t, 105, 106t, 108t, 109, 294t, 301t
Alertness to entrepreneurial opportunity, 157
All affiliates, 126, 127t–128t, 130
Archival record, 221
Argentina, 9, 13 n6, 264
Australia, 10, 263–278
Autonomy, 11, 41–42, 43, 44–45, 59, 97, 168, 173t, 178t

B

Background characteristics, 47, 160, 166
Banks, 100, 186–187, 188, 211t
Boundary, 243–244, 248–249, 252t, 254t
Bricolage, 208, 267
Build a business kids can inherit, 22t, 54t, 60
Business conception, 279–302
Business conception date, 284, 286–287
Business creation, 1–4, 9–12, 15
Business creation process, 303–306
Business dynamics, 1–2, 331
Businesses, 1–13
Business failure, 232
Business (firm) life course, 1–2, 4f, 38–39, 221, 279, 291, 301, 303
Business growth aspirations, 35–47
Business idea, 42, 222, 272, 275, 306
Business location, 285, 297–298, 297t, 299
Business opportunity, 8, 37–38, 40, 97, 139, 246, 248
Business planning, 137–153, 303, 305, 309, 313
Business profitability criteria, 228–229
Business purchased, 283
Business registration, 294t, 295t, 296t, 297t, 298t, 299t
Business registry, 7, 223, 232–233, 280–281, 300, 301, 308
Business sponsored new ventures, 293–294
Business start-up, 303–306
Business start-up process, 307–324

C

Calls to complete interviews, 314t
Canada, 9, 51, 264
Candidate entrepreneurs, 309
Capital Structure, 186
Career choice, 3, 160, 166, 276
Career reasons, 22t, 23, 28–30
Case weights, 283t, 283–284, 290, 310
Case weights, KFS sample, 283t, 291–298
Chapter teams, 10, 12–13
China, 10
Closely held, 51
Codebook, 316–317
Coercive isomorphism, 150
Cognitive, 303
Cognitive capability, 160–162

335

Index

Cognitive capital, 160, 168, 172t, 173t, 178t, 180–181
Comparison group, 267, 268t
Comprehensive Australian Study of Entrepreneurial Emergence (CAUSEE), 10, 263–278
Compute Assisted Telephone Interview (CATI), 316
Conception, 219–236, 303, 306
Conflict, 97–98, 131, 189
Context-aspiration typology, 10–11, 36, 39–46, 46t
Context for entrepreneurship, 35–47
Contextual motivation, 35–47, 303
Contribution, 71–92, 115, 116, 116–117, 123, 126, 129, 131
Corporation (limited company), 272
Corridors of knowledge, 157, 158
Costs of acquiring additional information, 158
Co-workers, 95–96, 102–103, 104, 111
Cox proportional hazard estimates, 245, 251
Creative destruction, 2
Cronbach alpha, 24, 26, 28, 29t, 30–31
Cross-national descriptions, 303
Cross-study, 12
Cultural support, 276
Current Population Survey (CPS), 9, 141, 320, 321–322, 323t

D

De alio entrants, 225–256
Debt, 186, 188, 189, 192, 196
Demographic characteristics, 20–21, 73, 96, 98, 100, 116, 117, 130–132, 247, 307, 316, 321
Demographic composition, 100, 102, 103–104, 105, 107
Demographic diversity, 122–123, 129, 131
Demography, 95–113
De novo entrants, 225–226
Differentiation, 73–75, 86, 89
Disengagement, 4, 194, 287, 304, 306
Dun and Bradstreet (D&B), 256, 300
Duration (of team formation), 109–111

E

Early stage activity index, 268
Ecological, 226
Economic activity, 227, 228–229, 231
Economic adaptation, 2
Economic sector, 275, 278–279, 300, 301t, 305

Economic transaction, 226, 232–233, 235–236
Education (attainment), 245–246, 271
Effectuation, 267
EIN number, 286, 287t, 286, 287
Embeddedness, 52–53, 97, 128, 163
Emergence, 129–130, 131
Emergence of new industries, 1, 221, 234
Emerging organizations, 239–240, 242–243, 245–246, 247, 248, 253–254, 255–256
Employee size, 277, 285, 288, 298t, 300, 301t, 300, 309
Employer firms, 1, 228, 301
Employment, 118t, 126, 130, 132
Employment status, 126, 130–131, 221, 226–227
Entrepreneur, 2, 3–4, 5, 7, 8t, 9, 10, 12, 13 n3
Entrepreneurial behavior, 30, 35–36, 51, 53, 223
Entrepreneurial business venture, 37, 38–39, 40–43, 44, 45, 46t
Entrepreneurial career choices, 276
Entrepreneurial climate, 4
Entrepreneurial education, 139, 140, 142, 144t, 145, 150, 151, 153
Entrepreneurial networks, 163
Entrepreneurial personality, 3
Entrepreneurial process, 1, 2, 10, 227, 229, 235–236
Entrepreneurial researchers, 220
Entrepreneurial ventures, 38–39, 51, 158, 220, 221, 248, 330
Entrepreneurship, 1, 2–3, 6–7, 9–10
Entrepreneurship Research Consortium, 328–329
Entry into business creation, 271
Equality, 71, 72, 73, 74, 75, 81t, 82t, 84, 85, 89, 92, 356
Equity, 71–92, 186, 188, 189, 192, 193t, 210t, 211t, 214t
Ethnic background, 107–108, 111, 141, 305
Ethnic composition, 103t, 104, 106t, 110t, 120t, 123t, 231t, 233t
Ethnicity, 96, 98, 99t, 100, 101t, 102, 103t, 105, 106t, 107, 108t, 110t, 112, 113 n4, 120–121t, 123t, 125t, 128t
Event history analysis, 246, 248–249
Ewing Marion Kauffman Foundation, 12, 327, 328
Exchange, 241, 242, 244–245, 246, 247, 249, 250, 251t, 252t, 253, 254–255, 280, 332
Executive Committee, PSED I, 333
Existing/sponsored business, 55

Index

Expectancy, 10–11, 19, 21, 22t, 23, 27–28, 31t
Expectations, 7, 8t, 37, 38, 188, 191–192, 195–196, 197, 199–201, 206–207, 327
Expected job growth, 52, 62, 66
Expected sales growth, 54, 62
Explicit knowledge, 161, 165, 167, 169, 170–173, 175t, 176t, 181

F

Factor analysis, 28, 29, 47 n5
Failure, 247, 250–251, 252t, 251, 303, 312
Family background, 51–66, 271, 303
Family based motivations, 52
Family business, 51, 52–53, 59, 60t, 61, 62, 65–66, 329, 330, 331
Family business background, 51, 65–66
Family/entrepreneurial role models, 52–53
Family financial support, 53, 54t, 56
Family history and role models, 54t
Family influence, 51–66
Family legacy, 52, 58t, 60t
Family life, 22t, 41–42, 52, 53, 54t, 59, 66
Family owned, 51, 52, 62, 331
Family team, 54, 55t, 56t, 57, 61–62, 63, 64f, 65, 195
Family teams investment, 63–65
Family tradition, 22t, 28, 29t, 42, 54t, 58t, 59, 60, 66
Federal social security, 226, 249, 286, 287t, 286, 287
Federal tax form Schedule C, 286, 287t, 287
Federal tax returns, 286, 287t, 287
Finance, 185–186, 187, 192t, 194–195, 196, 199
Financial institutions (capital), 4, 53, 76t, 98, 100, 116, 117t, 139, 147, 150, 153, 189, 193t, 195, 209t, 213t
Financial resources, 116, 150, 186, 187, 207–208
Financing, 53, 57, 143, 185–215, 220, 242, 267, 303, 328, 330
Firm birth, 1, 4f, 5, 12, 35, 219–220, 221, 223, 225, 226, 228–229, 231, 233, 234, 235–236, 281, 303, 304 n7, 303
Firm conception, 219–236
Firm creation, 219, 220, 225–226, 229, 234–235, 263–264, 269, 272, 275–276, 279, 283–284, 300, 303, 305, 306, 330
Firm death, 232, 233
Firm gestation process, 221, 232, 235, 279
Firm growth, 10–11, 37, 43–44, 200–201t, 204–205t, 232, 233, 327–328

Firm profitability, 280
Firm size, 199, 200t, 202t, 204t
Firm survival rates, 234
Follow-up interviews, 5, 7, 9, 11, 61, 62, 130, 140, 174, 211t, 220, 222, 227, 229, 246, 247, 248, 267, 283, 285, 304 n6, 307, 311
Formal education, 145, 150, 151, 159, 161, 169
Formal education level, 145, 165, 170–173t, 176t
Formal planning, 151
Founder, 115–132
Founder, definition of, 115–116, 126, 129–131
Founding, 35, 36–37, 39, 46–47
Founding team, 115, 123, 126, 266–267
Founding team configuration, 129
Founding team, definition of, 115, 117, 126, 129
Founding team, size of, 128–129, 130t, 131
Four-wave consolidated data set, 304
Franchise, 55t, 221, 285, 296t
Friends, 95–96, 99t, 103, 105, 106t, 110t, 111
Friends and Family, 122, 187, 194, 210t
Full-time, 75–76, 78, 82t, 86, 87t, 92
Functional diversification, 96–98, 105, 109, 111
Funding, 52, 55–56, 57, 65, 185–186, 187–191, 194–197, 199, 200–201t, 202–203t, 204–205t, 206–207, 210t, 213t, 214t, 226, 307, 317t

G

Gender, 58t, 60t, 75, 77–78, 96, 98, 99t, 100, 101, 102, 103t, 104–105, 106t, 107, 108t, 110t, 120t, 121t, 122, 123t, 124t, 125t, 127t
Gestation window, 219–236
Global competitive advantage, 306
Global Entrepreneurship Monitor (GEM), 6–7, 9–10, 37, 38, 263, 264, 268, 329, 331–332
Government administrative data, 236
Government registries, 234
Government support programs, 147
Greater flexibility in life, 54t, 58t, 59, 60, 65–66
Greece, 9–10
Groups, *see* Teams
Growth, 189, 194, 199, 200t, 202t, 203, 204t
Growth aspirations, 35–47, 203, 303
Growth orientation, 142, 144t, 145t, 146t, 148t, 149t, 151

H

Helper(s), 115–132
Helping, 7, 131–132, 166, 267
High-tech context, 170–173t, 174
Homeowners, 272t, 271, 274, 275
Homophily, 96, 98, 107, 112, 122, 123t, 127t, 129
Household federal tax return, 287
Human capital, 95–113, 126, 131, 142, 143

I

Immigrants, 271, 274, 275, 276
Impression formation, 25
Impression management, 24–25, 32 n4
Independent start-up, 54–55, 285, 296t, 298, 300
Industrial organization, 220, 221, 226, 233, 235–236
Industry competitiveness, 247
Industry directories, 226, 234
Industry experience, 142–143, 145, 147, 152, 189, 190–191, 194, 201, 203t, 205t
Industry tenure, 97, 99, 101t, 103t, 104, 106t, 108t, 228t, 230t, 231t, 232t
Informal planning, 138
Information, 95–96, 97, 98, 99–100, 116, 117, 122, 132
Information access, 159
Informed consent, 31t, 310, 311
In-group bias, 97–98, 104–105, 110–111, 112
Initial behavior, 229, 230
Initial thought, 229, 233, 232
Innovation, 2–3, 28, 29, 30, 225, 306, 325–326, 330, 332–333
Innovative entrepreneurship, 2
Institute for Social Research (U of Mich), 7, 267, 268t
Institutional isomorphism, 137–153
Institutional owners, 98–99, 109, 110t, 233t, 294–295
Institutional theory, 138–139, 140, 142
Intellectual property protection, 11
Intentionality, 241–242, 243, 245, 247–248, 250, 251t, 252t, 254t, 255t, 255
International, 10–11, 37, 38, 243
International customers, 276t, 275, 277
Interview consistency checks, 314
Interview data file, 311–312, 317–318
Intrapreneurs, 3, 4
Intrinsic motivation, 11, 41–42, 43, 44, 45f

K

Katz and Gartner framework, 2
Kauffman Firm Survey (KFS), 279–302, 331
Key non-owner, 8t, 120t, 121t, 125t, 171t
Kinship, 11, 51, 59, 71, 97, 102–103, 104, 111
Knowledge of self (self efficacy), 166, 170t, 175t
Knowledge stocks, 158, 159, 160

L

Labor market, 12, 97–98, 102, 140, 220, 221, 226, 227, 228–229, 235–236
Labor productivity, 1, 9
Latvia (L-PSED), 10
Legal entity, 8t, 55–56, 75, 76t, 82–83, 85, 98–99, 106t, 118, 196, 230t, 231t, 232
Legal form, 8t, 194, 200t, 202t, 204t, 244, 258 n3, 274, 277–278, 287t, 288, 289, 296t, 301t
Legal registration, 191, 196, 213t, 214t, 226, 284
Legitimacy, 57, 138, 150, 151, 152, 239, 246f
Liability of adolescence, 233
Liability of newness, 105, 138, 151
Life context, 159–160, 166–167
Loans, 186, 187, 189, 192, 194, 207, 211t, 213t, 214t
Logistic regression, 129–130, 143
Longitudinal project, 5, 277, 279–280
Loss (of owners), 72, 105, 107, 246–247, 287t, 286, 290
Low-tech context, 174

M

Managerial, supervisory, or administrative experience, 117t, 122, 142–143, 165–166, 170t, 175t
Market Identifier File (D&B), 12, 283
Market participation, 5, 226, 227, 228
Markets, 1, 2–3, 4, 5, 12
Marriage/spouses, 11, 51, 86, 100, 129, 330
Material resources, 126, 131
Maximize growth, 273t
Methodological limitations, 77–84, 104, 113 n7, 194–195, 197
Mimetic isomorphism, 139, 147, 153
Minority, 10–11, 53, 83, 91, 97–98, 190, 200t, 202t, 204t, 205, 272, 327, 331
Missing, 77–83, 141
Missing data imputation, 80, 314, 319, 322–323

Index

Missing data rates, 315–316
Modules, interviews, 7, 8t, 9, 13 n4, 19, 112, 267, 282, 317, 333
Multidimensionality, 157–158
Multi-level marketing, 55, 295, 296t, 297, 301t

N

Nascent business, 103, 112, 116, 222, 226–227, 248
Nascent enterprises, 5, 9, 11, 12, 54, 56t, 100–101, 220, 222, 226, 229, 269, 274, 275t, 276, 277, 279, 281–282, 288, 289f, 298, 300, 301, 304
Nascent entrepreneur, 5, 7, 8t, 9, 10, 12, 13 n3, 32 n2, 35–47, 61t, 150, 153, 158, 168, 174, 205–206, 225, 227, 229, 232, 235, 245, 247, 255, 256
Nascent entrepreneurial process, 35, 52
Nascent firms, 37, 128, 200t, 202t, 204t, 220, 227, 232, 236, 236 n10, 244, 277, 317
Nascent teams, 287
Nascent ventures, 37, 38, 39–40, 41, 45–46, 53, 57, 116, 117, 121–122, 123, 124, 125–126, 128, 129, 130t, 131, 132, 138, 157–181, 196, 229, 242, 244, 245, 246
National context, 263, 276, 277
National differences, 263, 276
Nationally representative samples, 83, 98, 223, 303, 307
National Science Foundation (NSF), 327, 333
Native born, 272t, 301t
Nature of opportunity, 162
Necessity-entrepreneurial business ventures, 41–42, 43, 44–45, 46
Necessity entrepreneurs, 37–38, 41, 47 n3
Necessity-small business ventures, 41, 42–43, 44, 45, 46t
Negative age dependent mortality, 233
Netherlands, 9–10, 13 n6, 264
Network, 7, 47, 74
Network constraint, 96, 97–98, 105, 111
Net worth, 190
New business, 219, 221–222, 223, 225, 226, 232, 234, 246–247, 265–266, 269, 274, 283, 285, 287t, 295, 298, 303, 305–306
New firm, 1, 2, 3–4, 5, 7–8, 279–280, 281, 283, 284, 286, 287, 289, 290, 299, 300, 301, 303, 304, 305, 306, 307, 309, 329, 330
New firm birth, 219–220, 221, 223, 226, 227, 229, 231–232, 233, 235–236

New firm characteristics, 239–256
New firm creation, 2–3, 4, 5, 35, 37, 220, 226, 229, 263, 269, 275–276, 279, 330
New firm emergence, 129–130, 131
New firm owner, 268, 269, 300
New operational firm, 129–130, 220
New organizational entry, 226
New venture creation, 221–222, 225–328, 255, 264
Nonbirth outcomes, 235
Non-family team, 130t
Non-owning founders, 11
Non-response bias, 318
Non-white ethnic groups, 101, 130t, 271
Normative forces, 139, 142, 143, 147, 153
Normative isomorphism, 142
North American Standard Industry Classification (NASIC), 298
Norway, 9–10, 13 n6, 264, 326

O

Occupation, 99t, 100, 101t, 102, 103t, 104, 106t, 110t, 113
Odds-ratios, 130
Omnibus telephone survey, 5–6
Operating business, 7, 12, 215, 227, 245, 279, 280, 284, 285–286, 303
Operating new firm, 263
Opinion Research Corporation (ORC), 7, 267, 268t, 282, 308
Opportunity, 206–207, 221, 235
Opportunity development, 3–4, 38, 46, 52, 160, 161, 163
Opportunity-entrepreneurial business ventures, 43
Opportunity entrepreneurs, 2, 186, 187, 188, 189, 225, 226, 241, 272, 275, 309
Opportunity entrepreneurship, 37, 38, 41
Opportunity exploitation, 161, 329
Opportunity recognition, 2–3, 161, 332
Opportunity-small business ventures, 42
Organizational birth, 219, 233, 235
Organizational conception, 219
Organizational ecology, 220, 233, 235
Organizational formation, 214
Organizational gestation, 219
Organizational populations, 221, 233
Outcome status, 46t, 61, 62, 304
Owner, 95–113, 115–132
Ownership, 11, 20, 52–53, 55, 56, 61, 63, 116, 117, 121–122, 123, 126, 128, 130, 132

Ownership structure/start-up team ownership, 55t, 61, 313, 315
Owner-workers, 128, 130t
Owning, 24, 73, 91, 131–132

P

Panel attrition, 324
Panel studies, 303
Panel Study of Entrepreneurial Dynamics (PSED), 2, 5, 35, 52, 101t, 103t, 106t, 108t, 110t, 140, 185, 186, 191, 219–220, 228t, 233t, 235, 244, 264, 279–280, 303, 307–324
Parents, 54t, 57, 58t, 59–60, 61, 66, 142, 144t
Partnership, 274, 275t, 287t, 296t
Passive investors, 126, 132
Performance, 126, 129, 131
Personal background, 158, 159–160, 166–167
Personal characteristics, 19, 35, 263, 270
Personal orientation toward entrepreneurship, 57
Planning, modification, 141, 142, 143, 144t, 145t, 149t, 152–153
Positive monthly cash flow, 5, 6–7, 141, 222, 246, 269, 288, 304 n7
Post-stratification case weights, 141, 319–320, 321–322
Pre-birth activities, 223
Prevalence rates, 10, 264, 267–275, 276, 308
Privately held, 51, 159–160
Process loss, 72
Profitability, 5, 227, 228–289, 231, 233, 234, 235–236, 280, 290
Project website, 223, 236 n7, 316, 317
Propensity to plan, 143–144, 145
Properties of emerging organizations, 239–240, 242–243, 245–246, 253–254, 255–256
Property completeness, 249, 251t, 252t, 255t, 256t, 255
Proprietary technology, 169
PSED, 319, 323t, 327, 328–329, 331, 332, 333
PSED I, 5, 6, 7, 9, 10, 11, 13, 283–313
PSED II, 2, 4–5, 6t, 7–8, 9, 10, 11, 12, 13, 19–32, 279–302
Psychological, 19, 20, 47, 76, 96, 131, 303
Public website, 10
Purchase/take-over, 55

Q

Quits, 306t, 307, 308, 314t

R

Random Digit Dial (RDD), 140, 264–265, 308
Random mixing, 104
Reactivated businesses, 222
Recent active nascent entrepreneur, 225, 244
Recent confirmed active nascent entrepreneur, 225
Reciprocity, 163
Recruitment (of owners), 96, 98, 107, 109, 111, 112 n1, n2
Registry, 221, 223, 224, 232–233, 234–235, 280–281, 286, 290, 300
Relational capital, 164, 168, 172t, 177t, 180, 181
Relatives started a new business, 60
Representative sample, 2, 5, 9, 20, 36, 83, 98, 112, 220, 221, 222, 223, 225, 264–265, 276, 280, 281–282, 290–291, 300, 303, 307, 308, 324
Reshape, 75
Resource advantages, 267
Resource(s), 71–73, 75–76, 84, 85, 86–87, 90–91t, 92, 241–242, 243, 244–245, 246, 248, 250, 251t, 252t, 254t, 255t, 254–256
Respect, 38–39, 40, 41–43, 44f, 45, 52
Respondent motivation for the interview, 8, 78, 122, 291–293, 323
Respondent reaction to interview, 80, 87, 90, 112, 125, 195, 222, 314, 315, 317
Respondent understanding of the interview, 308–309, 310, 311–312, 313–314, 315, 316, 318
Response rates, 9, 170t, 171t, 172t, 173t, 258 n3, 284t, 283, 304
Reverse-scoring, 22t, 23, 26–27, 179
Right censoring, 111
Risk, 2, 3, 174, 248, 251, 318–319
Role, 71, 73, 75, 76t, 82t, 85–86, 89t, 90, 91, 92

S

Sample attrition, 105–106, 107, 109, 231t
SAS file format, 80, 317, 318–319, 331–332
Screener data file, 317
Screening criteria, 222
Screening items, 7, 141, 265, 267, 282
Screening procedure, 7, 9–10, 222, 265, 267, 300
Sectoral analysis, 226
Self-efficacy, 27, 166, 170t, 175t, 179
Self-employment, 3, 6, 58–59, 86, 140–141, 160, 221, 308
Self-realization, 28, 29, 30
Skills, 22t, 26, 28, 71–72, 76t, 96–98, 102, 126, 166, 170t, 180, 206–208

Index

Small business venture, 37, 38–39, 41, 42–43, 44, 45, 46t, 52
Social capital, 11, 24, 72–73, 132, 142, 157–181, 303, 329
Social cost, 263
Social entrepreneurs, 3, 131, 329
Socialization, 150
Social networks, 95–113, 263, 267, 303, 326, 328, 329, 332
Social norms and culture of the community, 168, 172t, 173t, 178t, 180
Social perception, 25
Social relation or social tie, 99–100, 139, 157, 158, 162, 164, 241–242
Social security, 209t, 226, 249, 251t, 252t, 255t, 257, 286, 287t, 286, 287
Social skills, 9–10, 19, 21, 22t, 23, 24–26, 30–32
Social ties, 96, 98, 132, 163
Sole proprietorship, 55t, 56t, 61, 274, 275t, 277, 286, 287t, 296t, 297, 301t
Solo entrepreneur, 80, 83–84, 90, 91, 97–98, 116, 124, 127t, 128, 131, 137–153
Spell time, 251
Spousal pair, 54, 55, 56t, 57, 61, 62, 63, 64f, 65f, 116, 122, 123
SPSS, 75, 317
SPSS file format, 32 n1, 317
Standard deviation, 21, 24, 25, 26, 28, 29
Start-up activities, 7, 8t, 21, 220, 221, 222–225, 234, 239–256, 269, 288, 304 n6, 305, 307, 314t, 317t
Start-up categories, 281, 289
Start-up experience, 122, 127t, 129, 130t, 169, 170–172t, 174, 175t, 176t, 180, 205t
Start-up process, 4f, 5, 11, 12, 35, 36, 37, 117t, 122, 174
Start-up stage, 274, 283t, 288–292, 293, 294t, 295t, 296t, 297t, 298t, 299t, 298
Start-up status, 245, 256
Start-up team, 7, 8, 11, 55, 56t, 57, 61, 62, 63f, 64f, 76t, 117, 122, 193t, 222, 234, 269, 274t, 278–279, 286–287, 297–298, 300, 301t, 300, 328
Start-up team affiliates, 117–120, 121
Start-up type, 51, 52, 53, 54, 55–56, 57, 61, 62, 63, 64f, 65f
Start-up ventures, 61, 264, 293–294
STATA, 75, 251
STATA file format, 317
State corporation registries, 286, 287t, 289, 291, 296t, 295, 301

State unemployment insurance, 209t, 212t, 226, 286, 287t, 286, 287
Status, 7–8, 11, 37, 41–42, 43, 44f, 46t, 61–62, 85, 98–99
Strangers, 83, 95, 99t, 103, 117t, 121t, 122, 125t, 223t
Strong tie, 53, 98, 105, 111, 129, 163, 168
Structural capital, 167–168, 172t, 177t, 180
Sub-samples, 291, 301
Support, 105, 117, 125t, 126, 142, 144t, 146t, 147, 152, 162, 168, 180, 192, 203, 208, 226, 233
Survey weights, 318–319
Survival, 4, 12, 102, 186, 205–206, 207, 208, 232, 233, 234, 236, 239, 240, 241, 243, 244, 251, 256, 277
Sweden, 9–10, 13 n6, 51, 150, 264, 327

T
Tacit knowledge, 161–162, 163, 165–166, 167, 169–170, 171t, 174, 175t, 176t, 179
Taylor Nelson Sofres of Australia, 265
Team formation, 31–32, 96–105, 111, 303, 332
Team planning, 137–153
Teams, 74–75, 77–78, 90–92, 96–112, 115–116, 120–121t, 124–125t
Team size, 65, 75–76, 77–78, 80t, 84, 85, 86, 90, 91, 105, 126, 127t, 128, 130t, 131, 194, 274t, 275
Team startups, 143, 145t, 146t, 147, 148t, 149t, 151, 152
Technological expertise, 303
Technology, 157–181, 274–275, 277, 279, 282, 285, 303 n3
Total Entrepreneurial Activity (TEA) index, 268
Transition to a new firm, 227, 232, 304
Transition points, 4
Turnover, 105, 107, 109, 112 n2

U
Uncertainty, 2, 139
University of Michigan, 309, 310, 311, 316, 320–321
University of Michigan Institute for Social Research, 7, 266
University of Michigan Survey Research Center, 282, 283
University of Wisconsin Survey Research Laboratory, 7

U.S. Bureau of Labor Statistics, 283, 301
U.S. Census, 1, 141, 283, 301, 318
U.S. Small Business Administration, 1, 139

V
Varstocases, 75
Venture capital, 2–3, 100, 130, 139, 150, 186, 187, 193t, 194, 327
Venture idea, 267

W
Weak tie, 97, 162
Wealth creation, 43, 44–45, 300
Web-based interview, 283
Weighting variables, 322
Worked for parents, 58t
Work experience, 142–143, 165–166, 167, 170t, 171t, 175t, 176t, 179
Working full-time, 86–87, 115, 122, 128, 131, 246, 271